History of Universities

VOLUME IX

1990

History of Universities

VOLUME IX

1990

Oxford University Press

1990

History of Universities is published annually as a single volume.

Editor:
Laurence Brockliss (Magdalen College, Oxford)

Assistant Editor:
Mark Curthoys (Christ Church, Oxford)

Bibliography Editor:
John Fletcher (University of Aston in Birmingham)

Editorial Board:
P. Denley (Westfield College, London)
W. Frijhoff (Erasmus Universiteit, Rotterdam)
N. Hammerstein (University of Frankfurt)
D. Julia (Institut Universitaire Européen, Florence)
J. K. McConica (St Michael's College, Toronto University)
N. G. Siraisi (Hunter College, New York)

Papers for publication in History of Universities as well as
books for review should be sent to the editor, Dr. L. W. B. Brockliss,
Magdalen College, Oxford, OX1 4AU, United Kingdom.

A leaflet 'Notes to OUP Authors' is available on request from the editor.

Details of subscription rates and terms are available from
Oxford Journals Subscription Department, Walton Street,
Oxford, OX2 6DP, United Kingdom.

Typeset by Latimer Trend & Company Ltd, Plymouth
Printed in Great Britain by
Biddles Ltd, Guildford and King's-Lynn.

Contents

Essay Review

Book Reviews

Contents

Bibliography

Universities, Scholasticism, and the Origins of the German Reformation

R. Emmet McLaughlin

In what must be seen as a welcome development, recent studies of the German Reformation have moved away from the traditional focus upon the individual Reformers and their theologies to a concern for the 'common man' and the political, economic, and social forces of the age.[1] While this new social history has undoubtedly both expanded the scope of Reformation historiography and deepened understanding of the volatile elements fuelling change in the era, certain aspects of human experience and certain sectors of German society have suffered relative neglect. Specifically, religion *per se* and the educated elites have not yet been integrated into the new regnant vision of the German Reformation. That religion should have become marginal to the understanding of the Reformation might appear paradoxical, but it is in fact quite logical since it is the marxist analysis of society in which economic distinctions are constitutive of social and political reality that informs most of the current scholarship. This is an approach which is ideologically and methodologically 'colour blind' to religion as an autonomous sphere of human experience and action. There have been recent exceptions, primarily the work of Robert Scribner, that suggest that the study of the Reformation may be entering a new phase in this regard.[2] Scribner has made good use of the findings of anthropologists to recapture a sense of pre-modern religion, particularly with regard to its ritual dimension. It will be intriguing to see whether these insights can be successfully accommodated by the earlier social historical scholarship.

The anthropological approach, while invaluable for understanding the religious life of the mass of the population, does little to illumine the religious motives and actions of the educated elite, at least in those areas in which their education caused them to be

different from the rest of the population. And the concentration on
the 'common man' that is a hallmark of the new Reformation
historiography has, in general, limited interest in the various elites
that ruled early modern Germany.[3] None the less, such groups
exercised a power and influence disproportionate to their numbers,
as their social inferiors could unhappily attest. In the fragmented
religious world of the later Middle Ages the educated elite played a
role unprecedented in the history of Christianity. They paved the
way for both the magisterial Reformers and the Catholic Counter-
Reformation. My focus here will be upon the way in which
university scholasticism reshaped the role, practice, and religious
world-view of the late medieval German clergy. No monocausal
explanation for the changes ushered in by the Reformers, their
supporters, and their allies will be offered. The focus will be upon the
intellectual and the religious, but as will be seen, the universities and
scholasticism were fully integrated into the fabric of their society.
They were moulded by forces beyond the classroom and the
scholar's study. In turn, they played a role on the greater stage of
late medieval history. Interpenetration of *studium* and *saeculum* was
complete. We should no more segregate the schools than we would
the courts, counting-houses, ateliers, and manors.[4]

   Students of the Reformation have long been interested in the
medieval background of Luther's Reformation breakthrough. Most
recently the works of Steven Ozment, Heiko Oberman and the
Institut für Spätmittelalter und Reformation (Tübingen) have contributed to a clearer understanding of the 'continuity and discontinuity' between late medieval scholastic speculation and Protestant
theology.[5] Few of the issues which would exercise the Reformers had
not been hotly debated in the centuries preceding Luther.[6] If some of
the Protestant answers were novel, the questions themselves were
long-established: Scripture versus tradition, justification and predes-
tination, the shape of the Church, and the nature of the eucharist.
Protestant theology marks a departure, not creation *ex nihilo*. In
both the content of their theology and their self-perception as
theologians, Protestant divines often had more in common with
their medieval predecessors than with their non-theologian contemporaries.[7]

   Oberman has also called attention to the vitality and impact of the
university as an institution at the beginning of the sixteenth century.[8]
This is an important shift of perspective, for it allows us to begin to

gauge the true importance of scholasticism for the High and Later Middle Ages, and by implication for the Reformation. To quote Lewis Spitz, 'the magisterial Reformation was a university movement in its inception and early development.'[9] The bond uniting the content of scholastic theology and the institutions which developed it, the medieval universities, was the scholastic method. The requirements of its form both moulded the practices and organization of the universities, and determined to a large extent the focus and products of scholastic speculation.[10] For our purposes the method can be defined as a way of discovering and illuminating philosophical and theological truths by the critical and speculative examination of authoritative texts (both christian and classical).[11] It was marked by a deep concern for language, both in its analysis of grammar and its emphasis on definition and signification. It proceeded on the basis of an Aristotelian-based dialectic which became ever more sophisticated. It was characterized by a love of distinctions, divisions, classifications, and formal oppositions, which powerfully reinforced a drive to impersonal abstraction, rationalization, and order. It was fuelled by the clash of individuals and ideas, often taking the shape of *problemae dialecticae*, the *pro forma* speculative question, and the staged academic *disputatio*. Its written products were most typically the commentary, the gloss, the *quaestio*, the collections of *sententiae* and *exempla*, the encyclopedic *Speculum*, and the manuals of instruction for students. With regard specifically to the theological, programme, captured in the phrase *credo ut intellegam*, its 'employment of the human reason in penetrating and explaining the truths of revelation, the supernatural truths of religion',[12] tended to strip the objects of its study of their mystery. In this it stands in contrast to the monastic meditative approach, as described by Jean Leclercq, which sought to achieve 'a certain appreciation, of savoring and clinging to the truth . . .'.[13] The latter sought 'wisdom' (*sapientia*), a personal appropriation of divine truths which transforms the individual. The scholastics, on the other hand, sought 'knowledge' (*scientia*), an 'objective' intellectual understanding of those same truths.[14] The two could certainly be combined (and were by a number of the great scholastics, e.g. Bonaventure), though they need not be. The scholastic approach, however, made possible not only a sophisticated speculative creativity at one end of the intellectual spectrum, but also mass education at the other end.[15] This approach included not only the speculative research side of the scholastic endeavour, but also the teaching function of the schools which was served by the compilations of *sententia* and *exempla*. Bible commentaries, and the production of introductory textbooks (e.g. Alexander de Villa Dei's *Doctrinale* or Aquinas' *De principis naturae*). Overall the impact of instructional aids was to bring order where a certain laissez-faire attitude had prevailed, by '*divisiones*', or '*distinctiones*', or concordances, or rules of sermon making. Even the *summae*, beginning with Abelard's *Sic et non*, were primarily designed as 'compendious collections of instances', which provided order and a way through the 'mass of words' confronting the student.[16] Scholasticism created not only the *quaestio* and the *summa*, but also the reference book.[17]

But ideas, methods, and institutions are not hypostatized entities existing apart from the human beings who create, employ and are moulded by them. Scholasticism and the universities were embodied by the masters, students, and 'graduates' who were both the makers and the bearers of the university culture, of scholastic culture. It is of course legitimate to distinguish people from the ideas, the method from the institution, and to acknowledge that the method preceded the institutions which in turn would create an educated elite, but in the concrete reality of the later Middle Ages they form a seamless whole. For the purposes of this essay, therefore, 'scholasticism' will be used as the shorthand term to refer not only to the ideas and arguments produced by the universities, but the institutions themselves, and the cadres of teachers and students who passed through them.[18]

Having established the object of our investigation, we will also have to delimit it chronologically. While not denying the importance of short-term developments, or even events, many of the most significant changes wrought by scholasticism and the universities can only be appreciated when viewed from a longer perspective, if not the *longue durée*, then at least the *durée moyenne*. Only by contrasting scholastic Europe (post 1100) with that of the early Middle Ages is it possible to evaluate the role of scholasticism in preparing the way for the Reformation.

New parameters often require new or revised questions, and new distinctions. Most scholars who have dealt with the scholastic origins of the Reformation have concentrated on what one might call Luther-production, that is, the way in which scholasticism influenced Luther's 'breakthrough' and later theological formulations. Less often asked is how scholasticism prepared the ground for the Luther-reception.[19] In what way did the universities and scholasticism create an audience for Luther's message? To pose that question is to help build bridges between the intellectual history of Reformation origins and its broader historical roots—political, social, religious, and economic. The historical significance of Reformation theology lay primarily not in the quality of the insights that propelled it, but in its ability to move large numbers of people in important, even violent ways.[20] It is a question of how the ideas of a few influenced the actions of the many.

A similar distinction must be applied to the universities themselves. These exercised five functions that have a bearing on our question. 1. They were centres of creative scholarship, reflection, and speculation. This is true in our period, even if it was more characteristic of the universities in their earlier phases of development (i.e. before ca. 1350). 2. They were authoritative consultative bodies possessing specialized knowledge of theology and law. This achieved greater importance in the fourteenth and fifteenth centuries than it had been earlier. 3. They were teaching institutions that transmitted received wisdom. This assumed a predominant role in the life of fifteenth-century universities, often to the exclusion of creative scholarship. 4. They were institutions which moulded character, outlook, and expectations, both religious and secular. Then as now the universities served as important agents of socialization. The university experience produced the university man. 5. Finally, they were centres of a communication network that covered the whole of Western Christendom.[21]

I will focus my attention on Germany and Switzerland, in part in order to make the study more manageable, but also because only in Germany and Switzerland was the Protestant Reformation aboriginal. Much, however, of what holds true of those two regions will apply as well *mutatis mutandis* to the rest of Europe.

The study of medieval and early modern universities is in the midst of a renaissance.[22] New journals, collaborative projects, monographs, and conferences reveal the breadth and strength of the renewed scholarly interest in pre-modern institutions of higher education. Building upon older studies that focused for the most part on individual universities, scholars, and traditions, recent scholarship has been intrigued by the function and impact of the universities within society as a whole.[23] It is clear that from their very inception the universities owed their strength and attractiveness to their ability to prepare individuals for careers in law, medicine, Church and State.[24] Even where no specific or directly applicable professional education was involved, the prestige that learning conveyed sufficed to give individuals an advantage in the pursuit of place and power.[25] And while the early period of university development managed to maintain the heady mix of speculative daring and vocational training, the passage of time brought an ever greater emphasis on the latter. This development was matched by an increasing dependence on and domination by secular governments. Even the once-independent University of Paris was reduced to the status of a national university by the late fifteenth century, although it still maintained some of its international status as *primus inter pares.*

The German universities were late in coming and never experienced that early phase of freedom and creativity. Beginning with the foundation of Prague (1348) by Charles IV and ending with Frankfurt-an-der-Oder (1506), all of the universities were created by government fiat—imperial, princely, ecclesiastical, or municipal. And all were firmly incorporated into the power structures of both Church and State. They have never impressed by their scholarly output.[26] But to equate lack of creativity with lack of impact or influence would be to gravely misjudge the system. The German universities found their *raison d'être* precisely as educational institutions in which skills were inculcated and decoctions of received knowledge (in most cases the products of twelfth and thirteenth-century speculation) were imparted. The products of late medieval German universities were less often newly-coined ideas than repackaged practical wisdom and newly-minted 'graduates' (about a quarter of a million between 1348 and 1517).[27] In a seeming paradox, it was during this intellectually fallow period that the universities—not only of Germany, but also of the rest of Europe—had both their most public and most pervasive impact.

Certainly the decisive role of the universities, especially Paris, in the conciliar movement has few if any equals in the history of those institutions for the highly visible influence that they exercised upon the political life of the time. Individual professors (either as independent actors or as agents for the contending rulers) and universities as corporations took centre stage with the players of the age—popes, emperors, kings, and prelates. Even aside from their involvement in the councils, universities were increasingly viewed as authoritative institutions which were expected to provide expert judgments on issues of sacred and profane learning. Alongside the Church's hierarchy (*sacerdotium*) and secular government (*regnum-imperium*), the university (*studium*) became recognized as a pillar of the medieval social order.[28]

Less visibly but of longer duration and of greater lasting significance were the ways in which the universities helped to adjust certain key parameters of medieval society and religious life. Perhaps the broadest-based and most enduring contribution to Western Society came in the area of literacy.[29] Most obviously they created the need for more schools on the lower levels of instruction to prepare young men for university. They also provided the trained personnel to staff those schools. In this way they both created the demand and supplied it. And this was true in an even broader sense. Just why educated men were suddenly so much in demand beginning in the twelfth century remains something of a mystery. To be sure, the economic expansion which had begun already at the end of the tenth century might be expected to require increasing levels of literacy as commerce, its legal instruments, and banking functions became more complex. But it is hard to believe that 'educated' men were needed where a bare professional literacy would suffice.[30]

Again, the growth in the scope and complexity of both secular and ecclesiastical administrations would seem to demand educated bureaucrats, counsellors, and governors. But perhaps we are confusing chicken and egg here.[31] There is perhaps a tendency to assume that the building of ever larger (geographically defined) states out of the patchwork of feudal entities of itself required a more numerous, more educated administrative apparatus. But one could imagine an entirely different relationship in which the existence of such an inchoate apparatus provided the impetus for the establishment of larger units in the first place. Perhaps, and this is an intriguing possibility, there is no necessary connection between the two. The Carolingians were able to establish and then rule an empire larger than any later medieval state with an administrative staff that was tiny by comparison.[32] And it was in the ninth century when levels of literacy and the supplies of educated civil servants must be presumed to have risen as a result of educational reforms that the governance of the empire decayed. The presence of a literate bureaucracy seems to have played only a marginal role. Even during the twelfth and thirteenth centuries the relationship between the use of writing and effective governance is not always clear. As Clanchy has remarked about the development of chancery and judicial rolls in the thirteenth century: '. . . making of such records is an indicator of the efficiency of the government rather than its cause. They are a notable step in the transition from memory to written record because documents make more documents in their own image, not because they made for more effective government in themselves'.[33] Even given such documents, there was no *a priori* need for highly educated or cultured individuals to produce or use them. In fact, Hubert Walter, Archbishop of Canterbury, was educated at Exchequer, not in the schools,[34] even though it was he who is credited with initiating reforms at the beginning of the thirteenth century that would produce the royal administrative apparatus and record-keeping system familiar to all students of late medieval England. To look further afield, there have been large states of surprising complexity and durability in Africa and South America—one thinks of the Inca—who managed rather well administratively without any writing at all. What needs to be explained is why attitudes towards the function and significance of written documents in that period should change, and change in a way that required larger literate bureaucracies.

Another suggestion to explain the demand for educated men would revolve around the Gregorian Reform and the Investiture Crisis. These clashes called forth a flood of polemic, legal argumentation, and political-theological speculation, which in turn required educated advocates.[35] As with state-building activities of the same period, perhaps we should see both the Reform and the Crisis as in some measure the effects, rather than the causes, of the presence of educated clerics in both the Imperial and Papal courts. In any event, it is hard to believe that the demand for controversialists would be so large as to explain the size and number of schools in the period.

The approach offered recently by Alexander Murray is more promising.[36] In the wake of the Gregorian attacks on simony, new criteria by which to choose among aspirants for church positions came to the fore. Education seems to have taken the place of wealth. But this explanation to a great extent begs the question. Just why should education and not nobility of descent, personal piety, or political influence be accorded such a singular status? In point of fact all these factors (simony too) would continue to play a role in clerical promotion. But of all of them education is the least obvious. It was also an innovation. Neither education, nor quite often even literacy, had been essential to clerical office-holding. Learning was an ornament, not a prerequisite. This attitude reached back to the ancient Church. Given the composition of the Church in the Roman Empire, it was not unlikely that clergy were often illiterate. Estimates suggest that only 25 per cent of the Empire's population was literate.[37] Since Christianity drew heavily from the middle and lower classes, one must assume that the literacy rate for christians would not be any higher than that for the empire as a whole. Widespread illiteracy was compounded by the mistrust felt by the early christians toward education, whether pagan learning or even christian learning.[38] Even the bishops were intellectually limited and decidedly conservative and non-speculative, often in conscious contrast to their more daring and creative 'heretical' opponents.[39] The *Didascalia Apostolorum* (third century), and the *Apostolic Constitutions* (fourth century) which were in large part derived from the *Didascalia*, both assume the possibility of illiterate bishops.[40] To be sure, Augustine did write *De doctrina christiana*. The first three books (AD 396) on the interpretation of Scripture were directed not at the clergy, however, but to learned christians generally.[41] Augustine's defensive tone is also evidence for the continuing strong distrust of pagan learning and learning generally. The fourth book on christian oratory was only added at a much later stage (AD 427)—though it seems to have been part of the original plan—when Augustine issued a revised and completed work. The likely audience for this latter book was the clergy, specifically the bishops, but Augustine nowhere explicitly addresses the clergy as such. He also undercuts the value of the fourth book by saying that not all whom 'we wish to educate for the utility of the church' need study it.[42] He also claimed that anyone who read Scripture and christian authors carefully, and listened to good orators, could simply imitate them.[43]

Whatever Augustine's actual commitment to a programme of study for christian clergy, it was not shared by the rest of the hierarchy. During the fourth and fifth centuries the major councils made no mention of any education requirement for entry into the priesthood. Only towards the end of the fifth century do we find papal rescripts decrying illiterate clerics. The *Statuta Antiqua Ecclesiae* from the same period tried to apply some restrictions, at least on bishops, but this was isolated.[44] Distrust of pagan learning continued and certainly contributed to the low expectations placed upon the clergy.[45] Though attempts were made in the Carolingian period to raise the educational level of the clergy, here too literacy was not required. It is even doubtful whether better education would have contributed much to an improvement in the life of the Church. Piety, not learning, was what was needed, and what the Church required of its clergy.[46] The fact that many serfs were pressed into the clerical ranks by their masters would also argue for little or no literacy.[47] Interestingly, it was not the possible lack of learning which made the Church loathe to allow serf-priests, but merely the degradation of the office. But we do not have to look to the serf-priests to find an acceptance of clerical illiteracy. The eleventh century saw illiterate bishops.[48] There is a reference to an illiterate archbishop as late as the fourteenth century in Germany, and it was not rare to find illiterate cathedral canons.[49]

Eventually, however, the prestige accorded to an impractical learning among high ecclesiastics at the German imperial court in the tenth century became a counter in the high-stakes game of high-born clerics competing for positions of power and wealth.[50] But the emphasis on education also opened the way for parvenus who had mastered the arts, but lacked the pedigree. Rulers and patrons of all stripes would often prefer the less nobly born because of the newcomers' personal dependence on their lord. Having made their way into both secular and ecclesiastical systems, the educated proceeded to restructure the functioning and in many cases the purpose of the apparatus to which they belonged. They remade both Church and State in their own likeness and image.[51] Not surprisingly the new forms of state and church organization required the services of the educated. The written word became central to the processes of government and religion in ways which could not have been imagined in the early Middle Ages.

Once started, the process fed itself. An increasingly educated elite required ever more graduates to meet the new needs of Church and State. The universities inherited this self-perpetuating system. The network of the university-trained in churches and at courts served to float the rising social value placed on university education.[52] Inevitably this led to competition between the nobility and university men in both secular and ecclesiastical spheres. It also introduced a new divisiveness within the ranks of clergy which had a profound influence upon the shape of christian belief and practice in the closing centuries of the Middle Ages.[53]

The later Middle Ages and the Renaissance have been viewed as an age in which clerical domination of religious life suffered irretrievable losses.[54] This, however, misunderstands the nature and extent of clerical influence both in that period and in the early Middle Ages with which it is implicitly compared. Put baldly, in the later period increasing numbers of the laity were no longer satisfied merely with being administered to by the priests or prayed for by the monks. Instead, they sought, often at the suggestion of the clergy itself,[55] to imitate them by personal conversion to a more 'religious' life (e.g. *Devotio Moderna*) or by acquiring 'parts of the priestly or sacred culture, whether it be abbreviated books of hours for noble women, set prayers for confraternities and tertiaries, chantry priests for guilds and patricians who could afford them, windows and burial sites in churches, or even stolen hosts and oils as charms.'[56] Also in imitation, some desired a deeper understanding of the sacred mysteries once reserved to the clergy.

Although each of these appropriations might promote a certain lay autonomy, they did so by accepting and interiorizing the clerical values as their own. This in large measure explains a growing lay dissatisfaction with larger numbers of the clergy who did not in fact measure up to the now shared standard. And even then it was more likely that the formulation of that dissatisfaction and the leadership for reform or revolution would be provided (at least initially) by discontented clerics.

The role of the clergy in establishing religious values for the period was to be expected. It was the clergy, even the bad ones, who had a personal professional interest in the doctrine and praxis of Christianity. They were also more likely to have the opportunity and wherewithal to pursue this interest. Furthermore, those in the general populace who were more religiously inclined tended to become clerics, either willingly or unwillingly. The clergy regularly co-opted new movements and absorbed new impulses.[57] Even those groups that broke away from the Church almost inevitably reconstituted a 'clerical' order within their ranks.[58] The organizational imperative—the need for order, continuity, and identity—demanded leadership and guaranteed that that leadership, however constituted, would exert a dominating influence on the life and faith of each group.

The later Middle Ages and the era of Reformation, therefore, saw a continuing clerical dominance of religious values.[59] This is not to deny a 'secularization' in the same period.[60] There were sectors of political and economic life which were increasingly self-conscious and articulate of an autonomy which they had in fact always enjoyed in practice. Even here, however, the role of the clergy, particularly the mendicants, is striking.[61] As for the de-sacralization which characterizes so much of Reformation and post-Reformation religious and secular life, its roots lay anchored in the late medieval clergy itself.[62] As the new Protestant ministry demonstrated, clericalism and sacralism are not necessarily co-inherent. The wedge which divided the two also caused fissures within the clergy, and played the decisive role in creating the clerical religious values which found popular Christianity increasingly distasteful.[63]

The wedge was education, university-based and scholastic in content. As we have seen, the new ranks of the educated found throughout Church and State heightened the value of their own education and created the need for yet more of their fellows by revising both the purpose and praxis of their respective institutions. This is clearest for the Church. By the fifteenth century reformers were demanding that all levels of the pastoral hierarchy, beginning with the parish priest, be university educated. This was new and unprecedented. As we have seen, education had never been an essential precondition for clerical office or pastoral authority. In the ancient Church education was viewed with suspicion. In the early medieval Church, education was valued as a rare and elevating possession of the few. It was certainly neither necessary, nor even particularly useful, for the daily life of the Church. In most instances simple literacy would suffice. And even that was not absolutely essential. Generally, parish priests learned their craft as apprentices to older more experienced pastors.[64] In the tripartite vision of society that was common among the educated clergy in the eleventh and twelfth centuries there were the lower classes who laboured, the nobility who fought and the clergy who prayed.[65] Berthold of Regensburg in the thirteenth century, however, and Heinrich of Langenstein in the fourteenth would qualify the peculiar office of the clergy as study and the pursuit of knowledge.[66] In the later Middle Ages it was increasingly felt, particularly by 'progressive' clerics, that a measure of university education was desirable even at the parish level.[67] This implies that what was going on at that level had changed dramatically from the earlier Middle Ages, and that the new tasks required new skills.

I will focus on three shifts in religious understanding and expectation which determined the shape of late medieval Christianity: preaching, the sacrament of Penance, and the eucharist. A new concern for each was already evident in the first major Church council guided in some large measure by reform circles at the University of Paris, Fourth Lateran (1215).[68] In *Omnis utriusque sexus* the Council ordered that all christians confess at least once a year to their own priest and receive the eucharist each year at Easter. Bishops were ordered to provide themselves with qualified assistants for preaching and hearing confessions. In order to assure that the responsible clergy would be capable of meeting the needs of their flocks in these three areas, further decrees were issued seeking to restrict entry into the pastoral ranks to those with sufficient education.[69] To elevate educational standards, the Council reconfirmed the 18th canon of Lateran III (1179), which had ordered each cathedral to provide a benefice for a master to teach *gratis* clerics and the poor. Going a step further Lateran IV also ordered that alongside of the master who would be responsible for 'the art of grammar and other branches of knowledge,' each metropolitan church enlist 'a theologian who shall instruct the priests and others in Sacred Scripture and in those things especially that pertain to the *cura animarum.*'[70] Though these efforts were probably not particularly effective, the intention was realized through other means. In any event, the universities had begun both to determine the praxis and the content of pastoral care.

Surely one of the most striking aspects of late medieval church life was the prominence and profusion of preachers and preaching.[71] There was no difficulty in finding the Word preached. If anything the late medieval church was concerned to control both its content and exercise.[72] This fervour for preaching in season and out was unprecedented, certainly in the medieval church, but also in the primitive and ancient church.[73] Deriving impetus from both the penitential prophetic impulse of the wandering preachers of the late eleventh and twelfth centuries and the exegetic edificatory (both moral and dogmatic) programme of the schools, late medieval preaching was dominated by the expectations and prescriptions of the universities.[74] The universities served as training centres for young preachers, especially from the mendicant orders.[75] Though there was no instruction in preaching *per se*, students attended the sermons of their seniors, often collecting transcriptions of these and other examples. The students would then try their hand at first at the university and then to wider audiences. The collection of Fra Nicola da Milano from the late thirteenth century provides an example of this progression from student *reportata* of Bolognese professorial sermons, to Fra Nicola's own academic sermons at Milan and a minor *studium* in Lombardy, and finally the more popular *collationes* for the Confraternity of the Virgin at Milan and Imola.[76] The personal experience of students at the universities was reinforced by *Artes praedicandi*, scholastic manuals on how to compose a sermon, over 300 of which survive.[77] The earliest seem to be those of Alan de Lille (*Summa de arte praedicatoria* before 1203)[78] and Thomas of Chobham (*Summa de arte praedicandi* before 1221–1222).[79] Alan was one of the dominant masters at Paris in the late twelfth century and Thomas was one of the students in the reform circle of Peter the Chanter. Around 1230–1231 the 'thematic' sermon made its appearance at Paris and this form would dominate the later *Artes Praedicandi* attributed to Bonaventure, Aquinas and Henry of Hesse.[80] Other manuals from the universities were produced by William of Auvergne, John of Wales, Thomas of Waleys, and Richard of Basevorn.[81] More immediately useful than the *artes* were the sermon collections that poured forth from the universities. By a conservative estimate six out of thirteen of the most popular mendicant collections in the thirteenth century came from Paris alone.[82] Perhaps the most important impact that the universities had was to insist upon the importance, the centrality, of preaching as such.[83]

The parish clergy, pressed as they were by the competition of the Mendicant orders and later by the endowed preacherships, saw the sermon take on a larger profile within the life of the parish and in their own duties.[84] In Germany, for instance, we have evidence that the homily was being reintroduced into the liturgy of the Mass on a regular basis. For example, a weekly sermon was required of the pastor of Gressweiler in Alsace.[85] And the episcopal statutes issued in Basel in 1503 made the same demand for all its parishes.[86] For the first time there were even occasional examinations of preaching proficiency during visitations.[87] At the beginning of the sixteenth century the *Manuale curatorum* of Ulrich Surgant, a handbook for practising parish priests would open with an extended treatment of preaching before proceeding to the sacramental activities which had previously been the major and in many cases sole subject of such treatises.[88]

But the sacraments themselves experienced a new valuation even within the more limited (because no longer exclusive) field allowed them in the life of the Church. It has long been recognized that Penance underwent a major reformulation at the hands of scholastic theologians and canon lawyers.[89] The inner disposition of the penitent (be it contrition or attrition) just as the gravity and the very sinfulness of an act came to be dependent upon the intention of the individual rather than merely upon the objective act itself. As a result an examination of both the circumstances of the original fault and the spiritual state of the confessing penitent became the real focus of the priest's role in the sacrament. Diagnosis of sin, exhortation to repentance, and the prescription of a regimen of penances became the real contribution of the confessor. A close connection between preaching and the exercise of this sacrament resulted. The purpose and effect of priestly absolution on the other hand became increasingly unclear.

The disagreement concerning the very wording of the formula of absolution reflected a growing awareness that the sacraments, not just Penance, but the eucharist and Holy Orders as well, were gradually being undermined. The switch from the deprecative 'May God forgive you' to the indicative 'I absolve you' was promoted by university theologians, not least Thomas Aquinas, in order to counteract that tendency. Against the background of an increasing focus on interior states (attrition, contrition) and the role of the conscience, an effort was made to preserve the objectivity of religious action by emphasizing formal external actions.[90] Dennis Martin has analysed this development in the works of two fifteenth-century writers:

[Johann von] Paltz's [d. 1511] answer, too, was aimed at a world which maintained trust in external institutions as channels of grace. It was an answer that presumed a world view which had been eroding steadily in the thirteenth and fourteenth centuries. Karl F. Morrison has helped illuminate the shifts in understanding of mediation and sacrament that forced the exteriorizing, institutional approach, like that of Paltz, and the sacramental mystical theology of [Nicholas] Kempf [ca. 1416–1497] and pre-thirteenth century contemplative monastics to give way to interiorizing, pietistic spiritualities of the Reformation and modern eras ... The ... rug was being pulled out from under both Paltz and Kempf even as they wrote.[91]

It is interesting that the vernacular version of Johannes of Freiburg's *Summa confessorum* prepared by his successor at Freiburg, Berthold, in the years 1294–1296, consciously reworked the text to emphasize the older contritionist point of view.[92] The employment of *opus operatum*, the acceptance of transubstantiation, and the fabrication of an indelible sacramental character for the clergy[93] were all efforts to provide a mechanical surrogate for the naive sacrality of the early Middle Ages. By their very appearance they betrayed the extent to which the universities had sapped the foundations of sacramental realism.

The explication of the new vision of Penance was effected by the doctors of canon law and theology, and was embodied in the numerous *Summae confessorum* which were ubiquitous from the thirteenth century on.[94] The model was provided by the Dominican Doctor of Canon Law Raymond de Penaforte with his *Summa de casibus conscientiae* (between 1220–1245), which was reworked by Johannes, *lector* at the Dominican *studium* at Freiburg, at the end of the thirteenth century in his *Summa confessorum*. These formed the basis of the two most influential compilations of the later Middle Ages, the *Sylvestrina* of the Dominican Sylvester Prierias and the *Angelica* of the Franciscan Angelus de Clavasio.[95] The sacrament had become complex and sophisticated. Its successful application required deft and highly trained practitioners. Thirteenth-century theologians (e.g. Albertus Magnus, Aquinas, and Bonaventure) could still assure confessors of the ease of distinguishing sins according to their severity, while authors of fourteenth- and fifteenth-century manuals came to emphasize the complexity and difficulty, advising simple confessors to consult the more learned and experienced.[96]

Through their speculation, teaching, and publications the universities strove to meet the need which they had in large measure created. In the process, however, they had also made the sacrament a potentially oppressive factor in late medieval religiosity. By the careful analysis of the numberless forms which sin could assume, the scholastics made sin a pervasive and perhaps unavoidable reality for many christians. Even more insidious was the emphasis upon intentionality. One of the hallmarks of theological speculation from the twelfth century on, it involved an ever increasing concern for the interior spiritual state of the believer. This was most normally addressed in moral and sacramental theology by discussion of the *intentio* of the actor. Abelard's focus upon intention as constitutive of moral acts was often attacked, but after some refinement became part of the Church's teaching. In the more purely theological realm, intention determined both the fact and the degree of sin and merit. In the eucharist both the intention of the officiant and of the recipient were determinative for its objective reality and effectiveness. The cult of 'devotion' in the later Middle Ages, and the development of a mystical tradition are also part of this trend. The role of contrition in Penance serves much the same function. The impact of this entire approach was to devalue external actions, and to see interior spiritual states as necessary and perhaps even sufficient in and of themselves in worship and christian living.[97] Carried to a logical and extreme end the yardstick of intentionality with its tendency to second-guess one's own motives would establish a standard, as Luther would clearly show, against which no concerned and perceptive christian could hope to measure.

The last of the three institutions which suffered major re-valuation at the hands of university scholasticism was the eucharist.[98] Interestingly the formulation and expression of the new understanding of the eucharist was achieved by a number of distinct but complementary lines of approach. The first was the fourfold exposition of the text, at first, of the mass as a whole, but eventually of only the canon of the mass.[99] The western tradition of allegorizing the mass went back to the Carolingian explication of the mass, but it really only became an important influence during the twelfth century at the hands of Honorius Augustodunensis, Jean Beleth, and others. The results were absorbed into scholasticism by Pseudo-Hugh of St Victor, Stephan of Autun, Ricard of Cremona, and Lothar Segni (Innocent III). From them it entered the mainstream of scholastic literature, finding its way into pastoral manuals of all sorts. In the later Middle Ages the allegorical interpretation of the canon was quite common, found either as part of larger manuals, or as free-standing treatises, e.g. *Quadruplex missalis expositio*, Basel 1509 and 1512; *Canon sacratissime Misse una cum expositione*, thirteenth German editions 1497–1520; Hugo of Saint Cher, *Expositio misse*, five German editions 1495–1515.[100] The exercise was in its very nature inimical to the 'reality' of the eucharist since, as Brian Stock has noted, '. . . allegory, which initially gave rise to new understanding, also spawned alienation, that is, the feeling that the more one interpreted, the further one got from actualities. . . .'[101] This approach viewed the words of the mass not so much as constitutive of the real presence of Christ and the recapitulation, in some way, of his sacrifice, but rather as merely evocative of other moral, anagogical, or historical lessons. From being an event in its own right, the eucharist came to be, in this genre, simply the occasion for contemplation of general truths and memorializing in every detail the life and death of Christ.[102] The canon, and the mass as a whole, became obscured, buried beneath layers of allegorical speculation, and leeched of the immediate physical presence of Christ. Though in the detail of his arguments in the massive *Canonis misse expositio* Gabriel Biel (d. 1495) of the University of Tübingen might defend transubstantiation and reject both a spiritualization of the sacrament and the reduction of the mass to a mere memorial, the impact of those tomes and the scores of lesser expositions could not help but undermine in practice the very positions he sought to uphold.[103]

If the genre of the *Expositio* tended to shift the centre of gravity within the understanding of the eucharist, the content of much scholastic speculation served to reinforce that movement. The issues which reached a wider clerical audience through pastoral manuals concerned the modes of reception of the eucharist and the requirements for worthy reception. They were complementary in their effects. On the one hand it was argued that a pious disposition and intention to participate in the fruits of the mass either by those present but not receiving the bread and wine or by those absent from the liturgical congregation but pausing to assume the same devotional attitude at the moment of consecration, could for all intents and purposes receive in full measure the grace and merits of the mass and partake of the body and blood of Christ in a spiritual manner. This was the essential part of the transaction. Where this inner disposition was lacking reception of the elements was fruitless. Where it was present communion with Christ was perfect. Actual reception of the bread and wine were encouraged for those who had already achieved this inner participation, but it remained unclear what if any advantage was gained.[104]

If worthy reception was praised, unworthy participation was painted in the most forbidding tones derived from the Apostle Paul.

Whoever, therefore, eats the bread or drinks the cup of the Lord in an unworthy manner will be guilty of profaning the body and blood of the Lord. Let a man examine himself, and so eat of the bread and drink of the cup. For any one who eats and drinks without discerning the body eats and drinks judgement upon himself. That is why so many of you are weak and ill, and some have died. (I Cor. 11:27–30)

Fear of unworthy reception combined with the knowledge that spiritual reception (whose standards were considerably less rigorous) provided the benefits without the risks may have played an important role in the decision of many to avoid actual reception of the elements.[105] This in turn reinforced the tendency to literally 'view' the eucharist as a memorial occasion for the cultivation of spiritual dispositions and devotions.[106]

There was one group for whom the option of non-communication was not available—the officiating priests. They were strictly enjoined by canon law to receive the elements at their required daily mass. Scrupulosity with regard to the celebration of mass, and especially of a new priest's first mass, was a widely recognized phenomenon in the professional literature.[107] Luther's difficulty at his first mass was far from atypical. This points up a conclusion which also has a bearing on the impact of the new theories of Penance. In so far as the scholastic reformulation of received belief and practice imposed new burdens and produced 'oppressed consciences', it was first and foremost the educated and committed cleric who was to feel the full impact.[108] As the conduits by which scholastic teaching was to reach a larger audience, and as the practitioners of the scholastically conceived ministries, the clergy, particularly of the middle ranks where full pastoral responsibilities were usually exercised, had of necessity to assimilate the scholastic revisions first and most fully. In so far as the offer of Luther and the other early reformers to console 'oppressed consciences' was understood and welcomed, it would have been among the educated clergy that the strongest initial response was found. But, of course, it was from this same class of people that the Reformers themselves were drawn.

And by the sixteenth century educated clerics were common in Germany. If by no means a majority, they constituted a significant minority of the pastoral corps, both in numbers and in the importance of the positions which they held. This was simply an outgrowth of the spate of university foundations in Germany. At the time of the thirteenth and final pre-Reformation university foundation (1506) there were approximately 3–4,000 students attending German universities with another 2,000 German students studying abroad.[109] Measured against the population as a whole, the student population had achieved a level which would remain fairly constant until the second half of the nineteenth century.[110] In other words, the universities were already supplying society with sufficient numbers of trained individuals to meet the needs of the early modern state and church, and this at a time before the full elaboration of both these entities. In a sense, as Rainer Schwinges has argued, supply may well have outstripped demand.[111] Measuring the participation of the clergy in these developments has always presented problems. Matriculation lists are notoriously inconsistent and unreliable. Identifying clerics can often be impossible both because the status of students was often not given, and because when status was indicated, often the very vague *clericus* was employed.[112] None the less, even by a conservative count, matriculated clergy maintained a fairly constant absolute numerical presence at the universities during the fifteenth century: an average of 75 new matriculants each year.[113] As the total enrolment grew, therefore, the proportion of ordained clergy to the laity and quasi-lay *clerici* steadily declined from 13.1 per cent in the period 1401–1405 to 2.7 per cent in the period 1501–1505. Though there was a healthy increase in the next 15 years (3.6 per cent for 1506–1510, 4.3 per cent for 1511–1515, and 3.4 per cent for 1516–1520) the pattern remained fairly stable. The constancy of these numbers might be explained in part by the limited number of benefices available to support clerical students. Within the body of clerics at school, however, the proportion of regular to secular showed a significant shift in the second half of the fifteenth century. Members of orders came to represent two-thirds of the total. This meant that there was actually a decline in absolute terms of ordained secular clergy matriculated at the universities. And yet our admittedly imperfect figures concerning actual parish clergy reveals unexpectedly high levels of education. Detailed regional studies have produced figures for university-educated clergy in Germany ranging from 19 per cent to 60 per cent with an average of 40 per cent.[114] This is an astonishingly high figure when one compares it not with the educational expectations of the modern world, but with those of the ancient and medieval Church. How can the apparent inconsistency of declining secular clerical enrolments at universities and impressive levels of education out in the field be explained? The very value of education caused the apparent decline. In the competitive benefice market education was increasingly seen as an advantage in the procuring of a post, rather than as something to be pursued once one had already received an appointment.[115] Thus among the numbers of lay students were concealed many future pastors.

To be sure, most priests never received a degree. But that was not expected of the average student in any event. Presence at the university itself was perhaps the most important aspect of the cleric's education there.[116] The religious life of the late medieval university embodied visibly the shifts already outlined. Generations of schoolmasters and reformers strove to inculcate the lessons of piety and discipline alongside the more purely academic pursuits. This was of course not limited to the universities. The flood of students that they pumped out made of each city or village school, as well as the simple *studia* of the mendicants, an outpost of the new religious culture since religious instruction was part and parcel of primary and secondary education.[117] The Fifth Lateran Council (1512–1517) would merely codify long-standing practice:

Since youth like every age is prone to evil and requires painstaking labour to habituate it to the good, we decree that masters and teachers instruct their pupils not only in grammar, rhetoric, and other subjects of this kind, but impart to them also religious instruction, dealing especially with the commandments, the articles of faith, hymns, psalms, and the lives of the saints. On festival days their instruction ought to be limited to matters pertaining to religion and good morals, urging them to go to Church, to attend Mass, vespers, and the divine offices, and to listen attentively to the sermons and instructions.[118]

At the university level, alongside the mendicant *studia generalia*, the task fell to the residential colleges, which were designed to watch over the education, morals, and piety of their charges. By 1500, 145 had been founded in university towns throughout Europe.[119] Particular weight was placed upon frequent confession: the Spanish College of Bologna stipulated two annual confessions, the College of Dormans-Beauvais in Paris and the Collegium Sapientiae in Freiburg required four, and Ave Maria College in Paris urged weekly confessions for all of its charges.[120] The colleges also played a major role in promoting the use of the books of hours for private prayer and mediation for a larger lay public through the creation of abbreviated offices for the use of the students.[121] Perhaps most striking was the way in which preaching was integrated into the life of the college, thus creating a taste for preaching in a way that complemented the university's role in training and motivating the preachers who would meet the resulting demand. The daily mass at both the College of Boissy and that of Master Gervais in Paris were carefully scheduled not to interfere with the university sermons on

Sundays and feast days, at which all students were to be present.[122] The College of Saint-Benoît in Montpellier made provisions for sermons on all Sundays and feast days, plus a monthly sermon by one of the city's friars.[123] The *lector theologorum* at the College of Master Gervais was also required to 'report' on the university sermons or to provide his own *collatio* (evening sermon) at the major meal later in the day.[124] Theology students at that college were required to preach two or three *collationes* a year in the college, and they were to be ready to preach in the city by the end of their seventh year.[125] The College of the Sorbonne also required that theology students be preaching 'public sermons in the parishes' by their seventh year.[126] Merton College expected its fellows to preach often ('saepius') in the parish churches which the college owned, while Lincoln College specified Lent as the time for such labours in its appropriated churches.[127] At the Spanish College theology students who had completed at least four years of study took turns preaching every Sunday and feast day at an early hour in the morning.[128] Perhaps the most famous example of efforts to inculcate piety at the university was that of the College of Montaigu in Paris reformed by Jean Standonck, an adherent of the *Devotio Moderna*.[129] Desiderius Erasmus, Jean Calvin, and Ignatius Loyola would be its three most famous alumni.

But the colleges and mendicant convents were not the only factories of university religiosity. Secular clerics who were professors often filled the benefices of university towns. One thinks of Jean Gerson who held Saint-Jean-en-Grève, but who also preached regularly in the other churches of Paris.[130] Or Ulrich Surgant, who was professor of Law and pastor of St Theodor in Basel.[131] Preaching, Penance, and the eucharist were thus presented *verbo et exemplo*. This is not to suggest that the universities were peopled by more pious or more devout christians. At least as regards the students this was manifestly not the case. It was not that university education necessarily produced a deeper piety;[132] rather it produced a different piety.

Alongside the experience of university Christianity there would also have been some opportunity for academic instruction in the art of pastoral care. Theology was not much studied, but since it had little practical value for the parish priest this was unimportant.[133] canon law on the other hand was popular among clerical students. And it was by canon law that the life of a pastor was prescribed, his duties enumerated, the methods of administering his flock detailed.[134]

Most students, however, never progressed to the higher faculties of either theology or canon law.[135] For them the general education afforded by the Arts faculty had to suffice. And by and large it did. Having been initiated into the scholastic mysteries they were prepared to make good use of the guides, manuals and *summae* which presented the content and method of pastoral care in no-nonsense dry-as-dust scholastic fashion.[136] Lacking any literary merit, they were all that the humanists hated most in scholasticism. They had all the charm of an auto-repair manual—and they were just as practical. They are an excellent example of the uninspired utilitarian seriousness of much late medieval scholasticism.[137] In the hands of one able to decode its contents, these books could serve as the basis of self-instruction and/or the training of less educated subordinates and colleagues out in the field.[138] For this reason bishops ordered their purchase by their clergy,[139] and a good many pastors seem to have obeyed.[140]

Written at first almost exclusively by mendicants, then often by parish clergy for parish clergy, the manuals entered the mainstream of clerical life through the manuscript and book trade centred on the universities. They were in effect trade books and one of the mainstays of early printing, as an examination of any good collection of incunabula and early books will make clear.[141] Their presence and use throughout the Church reinforced the Word-ordered tendencies in late medieval religion, and helped generate the further shift to the bookish religiosity of the Reformation and modern eras.

The manuals were textbooks with all their implicit claims to unquestioned accuracy and authority. For the most part issues were not argued out, but rather questions concerning law, doctrine, or practice were answered simply on the basis of received consensus or the authority of one doctor or another. In fact, the reader of such manuals could not have avoided the impression that it was not the pope or hierarchy who established the norms of christian belief and behaviour, but rather the learned doctors, whose examination, criticism and explication of scripture, conciliar legislation, and papal decrees determined the Church's teaching. The manuals thus not only reinforced the widespread conception of the universities as corporate religious authorities, they also gave a higher profile to individual doctors as arbiters of faith and morals. This would help lay the groundwork for Dr Luther's successful rejection of both papal and university authority. And the network of printers, colporteurs, and customers that had been organized around the distribution of manuals would serve just as well to spread the message of the Reformers.

While the humanist network undoubtedly played a crucial role in the initial phases of Luther's protest by providing temporary support and refuge for the dissenter's views among an important elite,[142] the task of reaching a mass audience required different paths. Popular pamphlets, broadsides, and songs appealed to a wider illiterate and semi-literate audience.[143] An engaging lay literature was produced for those in lay society who could appreciate it.[144] The clergy no doubt were avid readers of much of this. But for them there was also the mass of theological controversial literature, most in Latin, most beyond the grasp of the mass of the laity (and not a few of the clergy). The universities, their graduates, and their books had created an audience for the theological strains of the protest, strains which would make a Reformation out of a reform and a revolution out of a revolt. This audience, the pastoral corps for the most part, were more likely to feel oppressed by the penitential system, and to share a vision of Christianity that was more verbal and less sacramental than the mass of the population (including many clerics). And it was the capture of large segments of the pastoral clergy with the pulpits and parishes that they controlled that made possible the widescale evangelization of the population and provided the movement with an institutional continuity not dependent on the vagaries of popular enthusiasm. Scholasticism thus provided a vital link between the inspiration of the few and the aspirations of the many.

The Christianity produced in the universities, purveyed by the manuals, and imbibed by generations of late medieval clerics (and through them wider and wider circles of lay people), was not proto-Protestant if Protestant is defined by *sola fide* justification, exclusive scriptural authority, and the priesthood of all believers. But then again, it was not Catholic in the way that the Early Middle Ages and most traditional late medieval christians would have conceived of it. It looked forward to the Reformation (and the Counter-Reformation), narrowing the gap that new Protestants would have to bridge in order to join the new faith and creating some of the dissatisfaction that would drive them there. This university Christianity was not the product of any one school (*via antiqua, via moderna*), but rather of the scholastic enterprise as a whole. The drive to understand traditional Christianity (*fides quaerens intellectum*) of necessity made the sacraments less mysterious and thus less sacred. By its very nature scholasticism placed a premium on the written text and the spoken word. In the eucharist, it introduced a reflective moment into what had been an unmediated experience of the divine. It injected theology into the mainstream of christian consciousness in an unprecedented manner, thus making possible the theological revolution that was to follow.

Villanova University
Villanova, PA 19085
USA

REFERENCES

1. The first indication of this shift was Bernd Moeller, *Reichstadt und Reformation* (Gütersloh, 1962); *idem*, 'Probleme der Reformationsgeschichtsforschung', *Zeitschrift für Kirchengeschichte*, 76 (1965), 246–57. Two of the more influential representative monographs are Thomas A. Brady, *Ruling Class, Regime, and Reformation at Strassburg, 1520–1555* (Leiden, 1978); Peter Blickle, *Die Revolution von 1525* (2nd rev. edn., Munich, 1981). For more extensive bibliography see R. Po-chia Hsia, *The German People and the Reformation* (Ithaca, N.Y., 1988), 285–94.
2. Robert W. Scribner, 'Ritual and Popular Religion in Catholic Germany at the Time of the Reformation', *Journal of Ecclesiastical History*, 35 (1984), 47-77; *idem*, 'Cosmic Order and Daily Life: Sacred and Secular in Pre-Industrial German Society', in Kaspar von Geyerz (ed.), *Religion and Society in Early Modern Europe, 1500–1800* (London, 1984), 17–32; *idem*, 'Ritual and Reformation', *The German People and the Reformation*, 122–44. See also John Bossy, *Christianity in the West* (Oxford, 1985). Another exception for a slightly later period, R. Po-chia Hsia, *Society and Religion in Münster, 1535–1618* (New Haven, 1984).
3. The one exception is the economic elites of the cities, as in Brady, *Ruling Class, Regime and Reformation*.
4. Recent research on the medieval and early modern universities has in fact emphasized the larger context in which the university arose and functioned. For a broad overview see J. M. Fletcher and Julian Deahl, 'European Universities, 1300–1700: The development of Research,

1969–1981, and a summary bibliography', in James M. Kittelson and Pamela J. Transue (eds.), *Rebirth, Reform, Resilience: Universities in Transition 1300–1700* (Columbus, 1984), 324–57. For a forceful presentation of this approach see Rainer Christoph Schwinges, *Deutsche Universitätsbesucher im 14. und 15. Jahrhundert* (Stuttgart, 1986), 1–10.

5. Ozment's early work was particularly directed at this issue: *Homo Spiritualis: A Comparative Study of the Anthropology of Johannes Tauler, Jean Gerson and Martin Luther (1506–1516)* (Leiden, 1969); *idem, Mysticism and Dissent: Religious Ideology and Social Protest in the Sixteenth Century* (New Haven, 1973); *idem*, 'Homo Viator: Luther and Late Medieval Theology', in Ozment (ed.), *The Reformation in Medieval Perspective* (Chicago, 1971), 142–54; *idem*, 'Humanism, Scholasticism, and the Intellectual Origins of the Reformation', in F. Forrester Church and Timothy George (eds.), *Continuity and Discontinuity in Church History: Essays presented to George Huntston Williams on the occasion of his 65th Birthday* (Leiden, 1979), 139–48; *idem*, 'Luther and the Late Middle Ages: The Formation of Reformation Thought', in Robert M. Kingdon (ed.), *Transition and Revolution: Problems and Issues of European Renaissance and Reformation History* (Minneapolis, 1974), 109–52. See also *idem, Age of Reform: 1250–1550* (New Haven, 1980). Oberman's *Harvest of Medieval Theology* (Cambridge, Mass., 1963) marked out the programme for the *Studies in Medieval and Reformation Thought* published by Brill in Leiden. But see also the more recent work by Oberman, *Luther: Mensch zwischen Gott und Teufel* (Berlin, 1982).

6. Heiko Oberman, *Forerunners of the Reformation: The Shape of Late Medieval Thought* (Philadelphia, 1981).

7. This is the thrust of Ozment's 'Humanism, Scholasticism and the Intellectual Origins of the Reformation', 146–7.

8. *Werden und Wertung der Reformation: Vom Wegenstreit zum Glaubenskampf* (Tübingen, 1977).

9. 'The Importance of the Reformation for the Universities: Culture and Confessions in the Critical Years', *Rebirth, Reform, Resilience*, 46. Cf. Gerhard Ritter, 'Romantic and Revolutionary Elements in German Theology on the Eve of the Reformation', in *The Reformation in Medieval Perspective*, 18: 'The Lutheran Reformation grew from the soil of late medieval scholastic theology.'

10. On the ways in which the scholastic method shaped the life and practice of the universities see P. Glorieux, 'L'enseignement au moyen âge: Techniques et méthodes en usage à la faculté de théologie de Paris au xiiie siècle', *Archives d'histoire doctrinale et littéraire du moyen âge*, 35 (1968), 65–186. The three major forms of instruction were the *lectio, disputatio*, and *predicatio*. All involved the critical examination of authoritative texts, the attempt to overcome apparent inconsistencies, and the desire to construct overarching synthetic systems.

11. This definition is based upon M.-D. Chenu, *Toward Understanding*

Saint Thomas, trans. A.-M. Landry and D. Hughes (Chicago, 1964), 58–9, and David Knowles, *The Evolution of Medieval Thought* (New York, 1962). The most extensive examination of the method is Martin Grabmann, *Die Geschichte der scholastischen Methode* (Freiburg, 1911).

12. Knowles, *The Evolution of Medieval Thought*, 88.
13. Jean Leclercq, *The Love of Learning and the Desire for God: A Study of Monastic Culture* (New York, 1974), 6.
14. Friedrich W. Oediger, *Über die Bildung der Geistlichen im späten Mittelalter* (Leiden, 1953), 1–21, draws this comparison nicely.
15. The definition of scholastic method that I use here is broader than that employed by D. L. D'Avray, *The Preaching of the Friars: Sermons diffused from Paris before 1300* (Oxford, 1985), 163–80.
16. M. T. Clanchy, *From Memory to Written Record, England, 1066–1307* (Cambridge, MA, 1979), 84–5, lists the main elements of the summa as 'compiled for instruction, . . . a selection of authoritative statements, . . . organized systematically.'
17. But even the *quaestio* began to show up in sermons during the 15th century, D'Avray, *Preaching of the Friars*, 256.
18. Given the restricted focus of my topic this essay can only make a small contribution toward the task of fully combining the three 'Blickwinkeln' of university research indicated by Schwinges, *Deutsche Universitätsbesucher*, 6–7, i.e. the institutional, scholarly, and social.
19. Although some have been careful to distinguish Luther from the larger phenomenon of the Reformation, Heiko Oberman, 'Headwaters of the Reformation: Initia Lutheri—Initia Reformationis', in Heiko Oberman (ed.), *Luther and the Dawn of the Modern Era* (Leiden, 1974).
20. Ramsay MacMullen has described this distinction nicely: 'My object is history. It might be, but isn't, theology. Accordingly, my view focuses naturally upon significance, the quality of weight that distinguishes historical phenomena from the (sometimes much more engrossing or at least more diverting) items of merely human interest. . . . Significance, in its turn, indicates the degrees to which many people, not just a few, are made to live their lives differently in respects that much engage their thoughts, not in respects they do not think about very carefully. . . . Significance must be compounded of both "many" and "much," in a sort of multiplicand of the two elements.' *Christianizing the Roman Empire (A.D. 100–400)* (New Haven, 1984), 1.
21. This was true even before the introduction of printing. See R. H. Rouse and M. A. Rouse, *Preachers, Florilegia and Sermons: Studies on the Manipulus Forum of Thomas of Ireland* (Toronto, 1979) on the *pecia* system of manuscript production.
22. See note 4.
23. See the comments by James H. Overfield, 'Nobles and paupers at German universities to 1600', *Societas*, 4 (1974), 175–6. With regard to the older literature, Gerhard Ritter's *Die Heidelberger Universität: Ein*

28 History of Universities

Stück deutschen Geschichte: Erster Band: Das Mittelalter (1386–1508)
(Heidelberg, 1936) is the best of its kind and remains quite valuable.
Still to be replaced as an overview is Hastings Rashdall, *The Universities of Europe in the Middle Ages*, F. M. Powicke and A. B. Emden
(eds.) (Oxford, 1936). But see also, J. Verger, *Les Universités au moyen
âge* (Paris, 1973).

24. The motive force behind the rise of the universities is still much
debated. The 'careerist' position has most recently been defended by
Alexander Murray, *Reason and Society in the Middle Ages* (Oxford,
1986), 218–27, chapter 9.2, 'University Careerism: the "lucrative
sciences"'. Cf. Peter Clasen, 'Die Hohen Schulen und die Gesellschaft
im 12. Jahrhundert', in his *Studium und Gesellschaft im Mittelalter*,
Johannes Fried (ed.) (Stuttgart, 1983), 1–26. Clasen also undertook an
intriguing examination of the penetration of those trained in Roman
Law into the law courts of Italy, 'Richerstand und Rechtswissenschaft
in italienischen Kommunen des 12. Jahrhunderts', ibid., 27–126.
Herbert Grundmann, 'Vom Ursprung der Universität im Mittelalter',
Ausgewählte Aufsätze (Stuttgart, 1983), vol. 3, 292–342, presented the
case for disinterested joy in learning. Most recently, Stephen C.
Ferruolo, *The Origins of the University: The Schools of Paris and their
Critics, 1100–1215* (Stanford, 1985) has also argued against the
'careerist' position.

25. Although as D. Zanetti, 'A l'université de Pavie au xve siècle: Les
salaires des professeurs', *Annales* 17 (1962), 433, remarked 'L'université donnait le prestige, non la fortune' (cited by Schwinges, *Deutsche
Universitätsbesucher*, 5). The prestige of education often needed to be
combined with other social factors to be fully effective.

26. Despite Heiko Oberman's *Harvest of Medieval Theology*, Gerhard
Ritter's *Die Heidelberger Universität* (esp. 418–21) still argues elo-
quently for the intellectual poverty in both quantitative and qualitative
terms of the last generations of scholastic speculation.

27. Schwinges, *Deutsche Universitätsbesucher*, 29. This figure refers only to
students listed on the matricula. Schwinges makes no attempt to
estimate the full number of students. He finds such efforts 'fragwür-
dig'. By 'graduates' I do not mean students who received degrees (these
were relatively rare), but rather students who had in fact studied at the
university for however long.

28. Guy Fitch Lytle, 'Universities as Religious Authorities in the Later
Middle 1517. Ages and Reformation', in *Reform and Authority in the
Medieval and Reformation Church*, Guy Fitch Lytle (ed.) (Washington,
DC, 1981), 69–97; Herbert Grundmann, 'Sacerdotium-Regnum-
Studium: Zur Wertung der Wissenschaft im 13. Jahrhundert', *Archiv
für Kulturgeschichte* 34 (1952), 5–21.

29. The literature on literacy is immense, but for the medieval and early
modern periods consult: M. T. Clanchy, *From Memory to Written
Record*; J. W. Adamson, 'The Extent of Literacy in England in the

Fifteenth and Sixteenth Centuries: Notes and Conjectures', *The Library* 10 (1929), 163–93; Franz H. Bäuml, 'Varieties and Consequences of Medieval Literacy and Illiteracy', *Speculum* 55 (1980), 237–65; Jane Coleman, *Medieval Readers and Writers, 1350–1400* (New York, 1981); Herbert Grundmann, 'Litteratus-illitteratus: Der Wandel einer Bildungsnorm vom Altertum zum Mittelalter', *Ausgewählte Aufsätze* (Stuttgart, 1978), vol. 3, 1–66; Jo Ann Hoeppner Moran, *The Growth of English Schooling, 1340–1548: Learning, Literacy and Laicization in Pre-Reformation York Diocese* (Princeton, 1984); M. B. Parkes, 'The Literacy of the Laity', in *The Medieval World*, David Daiches and Anthony Thorlby (eds.) (London, 1973), 555–76; Brian Stock, *The Implications of Literacy: Written Language and Models of Interpretation in the Eleventh and Twelfth Centuries* (Princeton, 1983); *idem*, 'Medieval Literacy, Linguistic Theory, and Social Organization', *New Literary History* 16 (1984), 13–29; James Westfall Thompson, *The Literacy of the Laity in the Middle Ages* (Berkeley, 1939); Richard Gawthrop and Gerald Strauss, 'Protestantism and Literacy in Early Modern Germany', *Past and Present* 104 (August 1984), 31–55.

30. As early as the 6th century we have evidence of successful, but illiterate, merchants employing scribes to do their written work, Grundmann, 'Litteratus-illitteratus', 23, and Pierre Riché, *Education and Culture in the Barbarian West from the Sixth through the Eighth Century*, trans. John J. Contreni (Columbia, S.C., 1976), 22. Simple accounting, basic writing skills, and the businessman's equivalent of the *Ars dictatoris* or *dictaminis* should have sufficed for the needs of even the more complex commercial arrangements. University education would hardly have been useful, and certainly not necessary. Even the use of mathematics was advanced by the growing governmental bureaucracies rather than the merchants, Murray, *Reason and Society*, 189–203.

31. Schwinges, *Deutsche Universitätsbesucher*, 6, 328–9, has noted that a flood of the university-trained *preceded* the elaboration of secular administration in 15th-century Germany.

32. See F. L. Ganshof, 'Charlemagne et l'usage de l'écrit en matière administrative', *Le Moyen Age* 57 (1951), 1–25. Ganshof makes clear the rudimentary nature of the Carolingian administrative bureaucracy, which itself represented a short-lived advance over the administrative vacuum under the Merovingians. Though Charlemagne and his immediate successors fostered the use of writing, there was no imperial chancery as such. At the local level the counts were often without the services of full-time scribes. And the written remains of both local and imperial origin often reveal a low level of literacy and conceptual inability to construct clear and effective arguments. Written administrative documents remained occasional substitutes and complements to the spoken word in the conduct of government. Cf. A. Dumas, 'La parole et l'écriture dans les capitulaires carolingiens', *Mélanges Louis*

Halphen (Paris, 1951), 208–16. It would also seem that Anglo-Saxon government was not 'governed by a bureaucracy using documents in its routine procedures before 1066', Clanchy, *From Memory to Written Record*, 17. As late as the Angevin Henry II (1154–89), noted for his innovations in law and administration, royal statutes were promulgated orally and only haphazardly recorded by chroniclers, ibid., 252.

33. *From Memory to Written Record*, 50.
34. Or so Gerald of Wales complained, Clanchy, *From Memory to Written Record*, 53–4.
35. See *Monumenta Germaniae Historica: Libelli de lite imperatorum et pontificum saec. xi et xii conscripti* (Hannover, 1891–97), 3 vols.; D. Carl Mirbt, *Die Publizistik im Zeitalter Gregors VII* (Leipzig, 1894). More generally on the controversies, Norman Cantor, *Church, Kingship and Lay Investiture in England, 1089–1135* (Princeton, 1958); Augustin Fliche, *La réforme grégorienne* (3 vols., Louvain, 1924–37); Giovanni Miccoli, *Chiesa gregoriana: Richerche sulla riforma del secolo xi* (Florence, 1966); Gerd Tellenbach, *Church, State and Christian Society at the Time of the Investiture Contest*, trans. R. C. Bennet (Oxford, 1940). The most recent overview is Uta-Renate Blumenthal, *The Investiture Controversy: Church and Monarchy from the Ninth to the Twelfth Century* (Philadelphia, 1988).
36. *Reason and Society*, 215.
37. MacMullen, *Christianizing the Roman Empire*, 21.
38. See Gunnar af Hällström, *Fides simpliciorum according to Origen of Alexandria* (Helsinki, 1984); H. J. Carpenter, 'Popular Christianity and the Theologians in the Early Centuries', *The Journal of Theological Studies*, new series 14, 294–310.
39. L. William Countryman, 'The Intellectual Role of the Early Catholic Episcopate', *Church History* 48 (1979), 261–8.
40. Richard H. Connolly (ed.), *Didascalia Apostolorum: The Syriac Version Translated and Accompanied by the Verona Latin Fragments* (Oxford, 1929), 30; F. X. Funk (ed.), *Didascalia et Constitutiones Apostolorum* (Paderborn, 1905), vol. I, 31–3.
41. Peter Brown, *Augustine of Hippo* (Berkeley, 1969), 259–69.
42. *De doctrina christiana*, IV, 3, *Corpus Christianorum Series Latina XXXII* (Turnholt, 1962) 118, lines 13–16.
43. Ibid., IV, 1–5, pp. 161–21.
44. Paul Henri Lafontaine, *Les conditions positives de l'accession aux ordres dans la première législation ecclésiastique (300–492)* (Ottawa, 1963), 226–7. Bede accepted the presence of an illiterate clergy, Grundmann, 'Litteratus-illiteratus', 6, n. 19.
45. See Georg Hörle, *Frühmittelalterliche Mönchs- und Klerikerbildung in Italien* (Freiburg i. B., 1914). Richard Stachnik, *Die Bildung des Weltklerus im Frankenreiche von Karl Martell bis auf Ludwig den Frommen* (Paderborn, 1926), contrasts this Roman Gregorian tradition with an Anglo-Saxon Augustinian ideal of a liberal education

based on the classics. But his belief in a Carolingian masterplan to construct a hierarchy of schools based on the seven liberal arts and culminating in centres for theological study, strains the evidence, as does his optimistic evaluation of its successful implementation.
46. H. Fichtenau, *The Carolingian Empire*, trans. Peter Munz (Toronto, 1978), 170.
47. Ibid., 157–9. See also Ulrich Stutz, 'The Proprietary Church as an Element of Medieval Germanic Ecclesiastical Law', in Geoffrey Barraclough (ed. and trans.), *Medieval Germany* (Oxford, 1948), vol. II, 52.
48. Grundmann, 'Litteratus-illiteratus', 7, n. 22.
49. Oediger, *Über die Bildung der Geistlichen*, 135–6.
50. C. Stephen Jaeger, 'The Courtier Bishop in *Vitae* from the Tenth to the Twelfth Century', *Speculum* 58 (1983), 291–325. Cf. his *The Origins of Courtliness: Civilizing Trends and the Formation of Courtly Ideals, 923–1210* (Philadelphia, 1985). On the learned culture of the 10th century see Pierre Riché, 'La "Renaissance" intellectuelle du Xe siècle en occident', *Cahiers d'histoire* xxi (Lyon, 1976), 27–42. One can see an interesting case of the allure and prestige of education in the autobiography of Guibert de Nogent, John F. Benton (ed.), *Self and Society in Medieval France: The Memoirs of Abbot Guibert de Nogent (1064?–c.1125)* (New York, 1970), 90–2. What we see here is the effect of prestige or 'social honour', which, according to Max Weber, is typical of societies organized upon the basis of *Stand* or social class, not economic class, *Max Weber on Charisma and Institution Building*, S. N. Eisenstadt (ed.) (Chicago, 1968), 170, 177.
51. R. I. Moore, *The Formation of a Persecuting Society: Power and Deviance in Western Europe, 950–1250* (Oxford, 1987), esp. chap. 4, 'Power and Reason', has argued that the rise of bureaucracy and a new literate elite produced an intolerance not found in the early Middle Ages. Certainly the Inquisition could not have operated, nor perhaps even have been conceived, without the tools and outlook provided by the schools, see James Given, 'The Inquisitors of Languedoc and the Medieval Technology of Power', *American Historical Review* 94 (1989), 336–59. As will be obvious, I share Moore's preference (pp. 106–9) for Max Weber's emphasis upon learned elites in this instance over Emil Durkheim's vision of an undifferentiated society as a whole putting forth this new vision of Church and State.
52. Laetitia Boehm, 'Libertas scholastica und Negotium scholare: Entstehung und Sozialprestiges des akademischen Standes im Mittelalter', in Hellmuth Rössler und Günther Franz (eds.), *Universität und Gelehrtenstand 1400–1800: Büdinger Vorträge 1966* (Limburg/Lahn, 1970), 15–61. An interesting example of this were the efforts of the Councils of Constance (Concordat of 1418) and Basel (Decree of 31st Session) to require that preference be given university graduates for collegial canonries and parishes. Oediger, *Über die Bildung der Geistlichen*, 65,

points out that the moving force behind these efforts were academics seeking to improve their own chances.

53. The reliance upon writing as opposed to oral communication was resisted in the Church in the 11th and 12th centuries, Clanchy, *From Memory to Written Record*, 209–14.

54. In his sections on religion, Jacob Burckhardt, *Civilization of the Renaissance in Italy*, trans. S. G. C. Middlemore, ed. Irene Gordon (New York, 1960), 321–55, 378–85, certainly gave that impression. The most massive formulation of this viewpoint is Georges de Lagarde, *La Naissance de l'esprit laïque au déclin du Moyen Age* (5 vols., Paris, 1956–70).

55. As just one example, the *Devotio Moderna* was introduced and promoted by four bishops/archbishops of Prague, see Manfred Gerwing, *Malogranatum oder der dreifache Weg sur Vollkommenheit: Ein Beitrag zur Spiritualität des Spätmittelalters* (Munich, 1986).

56. John Van Engen, 'The Christian Middle Ages as an Historiographical Problem', *American Historical Review* 91 (1986), 547. For a good overview of late medieval piety, see Francis Oakley, *The Western Church in the Later Middle Ages* (Ithaca, N.Y., 1979), and Francis Rapp, *L'Eglise et la vie religieuse en occident à la fin du moyen âge* (Paris, 1971).

57. The classic high medieval example was the Franciscan Order, Laurentio Landini, *The Causes of the Clericalization of the Order of Friars Minor, 1206–1260, in the Light of Early Franciscan Sources* (Chicago, 1968). More generally on the Franciscans, John R. H. Moorman, *A History of the Franciscan Order: From its Origins to the Year 1517* (Oxford, 1968).

58. On the Cathars, Waldensiens, Lollards, and Hussites, see Edward Peters, *Heresy and Authority in Medieval Europe* (Philadelphia, 1980), and Malcolm Lambert, *Medieval Heresy* (New York, 1977).

59. Recent scholarship has emphasized the role of anticlericalism in the Reformation, e.g. Henry J. Cohn, 'Anticlericalism in the German Peasants War', *Past and Present* 83 (1979), 3–31; Hans-Joachim Goertz, 'Aufstand gegen den Priester: Anticlericalismus und reformatorische Bewegung', in Peter Blickle (ed.), *Bauer, Reich, und Reformation* (Stuttgart, 1982), 182–209. This is a part of the effort to recover the history of the non-elite. None the less, anticlericalism in itself did not preclude clerical leadership. Late medieval clergy were often the most forceful exponents of anticlericalism. Nor did mere anticlericalism provide a positive programme for reforming the Church. If one were to look for a form of lay piety that threatened to escape the dominance of the clergy it would be the rural ritual life. The existence of a powerful and widespread anticlericalism prior to the Reformation has been denied in the case of England, C. Haigh, 'Anticlericalism and the English Reformation', *History* 68 (1983), 391–407. For a response see A. G. Dickens, 'The Shape of Anti-clericalism and the English

Reformation', in E. I. Kouri and Tom Scott (eds.), *Politics and Society in Reformation Europe. Essays for Sir Geoffrey Elton on his Sixty-Fifth Birthday* (New York, 1987), 379–410.

60. Here we rely on the definition provided by Peter Berger, *The Sacred Canopy. Elements of a Sociological Theory of Religion* (New York, 1969), 107: '... the process by which sectors of society and culture are removed from the domination of religious institutions and symbols. When we speak of society and institutions in modern Western history, of course, secularization manifests itself in the evacuation of the Christian churches of areas previously under their control or influence—as in the separation of church and state, or in the expropriation of church lands, or in the emancipation of education from ecclesiastical authority. When we speak of culture and symbols, however, we imply that secularization is more than a social structural process. It affects the totality of cultural life and of ideation, and may be observed in the decline of religious contents in the arts, in philosophy, in literature, and most important of all, in the rise of science as an autonomous, thoroughly secular perspective on the world. Moreover, it is implied here that the process of secularization has a subjective side as well. As there is a secularization of society and culture, so there is a secularization of consciousness.' Needless to say the process had not advanced far at the time with which we are concerned.

61. Lester K. Little, *Religious Poverty and the Profit Economy in Medieval Europe* (Ithaca, 1978), argues that the mendicants provided the theological 'space' for christians to pursue profits in the commercial world of the later Middle Ages. It should be borne in mind that the Church's attempts to intervene in the economic life of Europe dates only from the second half of the Middle Ages. For example, it was only in the 12th century that the Church directed its attention to lay usurers, John W. Baldwin, *Masters, Princes and Merchants: The Social Views of Peter the Chanter and His Circle* (Princeton, 1970), vol. 1, 296. See also John T. Noonan, *The Scholastic Analysis of Usury* (Cambridge, MA, 1957), and J. Gilchrist, *The Church and Economic Activity in the Middle Ages* (New York, 1969).

62. By 'desacralization' is meant a shift in perspective which draws a sharp distinction between physical universe and an increasingly limited sphere of the sacred. A 'desacralized' nature robs the judicial ordeal of its cogency. A 'desacralized' monarchy becomes a secular government. In religion *per se* 'desacralization' entailed at first a limitation of the sacred to specific people (e.g. priests), places (e.g. churches), and objects (e.g. sacraments). An emphasis upon interior devotion in the later Middle Ages would begin to deprive these externals of objective sacrality. Protestantism (with the Reformed being more thorough-going) would effectively exclude the truly sacred from the earthly plane. On the entire complex of ideas see Rudolf Otto, *The Idea of the*

Holy, trans. John W. Harvey (Oxford, 1958); Mircea Eliade, *The Sacred and the Profane: The Nature of Religion*, trans. Willard R. Trask (New York, 1959); and Peter Berger, *The Sacred Canopy*. Yves Congar, 'The Sacralization of Western Society in the Middle Ages', in *Sacralization and Secularization*, Roger Aubert (ed.) (New York, 1969), 61–3, places the beginning of the process during the Investiture Crisis with the desacralization of kingship. M. D. Chenu, *La théologie au xiie siècle* (Paris, 1957), 19–20, saw a nascent desacralization of nature in the 12th century.

63. Brian Stock, *The Implications of Literacy*, argues that beginning in the 11th century a new relationship between oral and literate modes of thought and communication began to separate out a literate clerical religious outlook and place it in contrast to the oral popular one, the latter being viewed both with disdain and suspicion.

64. Oediger, *Über die Bildung der Geistlichen*, 76–8.

65. On this see Georges Duby, *The Three Orders: Feudal Society Imagined*, trans. Arthur Goldhammer (Chicago, 1980).

66. Oediger, *Über die Bildung der Geistlichen*, 1.

67. The *Reformatio Sigismundi* (ca. 1438): 'No bishop should assign a priest to a parish church unless the priest has brought a diploma from a university testifying to his learning. This diploma, and nothing else, should qualify him. The parish priest must be, at the very least, a *baccalarius* . . .', in Gerald Strauss, *Manifestations of Discontent in Germany on the Eve of the Reformation* (Bloomington, 1971), 12. The *Reformatio* reflected the views of the educated secular clergy. The hierarchy and the laity in 15th-century Germany did not necessarily share this concern for clerical education, James H. Overfield, 'University Studies and the Clergy in Pre-Reformation Germany', *Rebirth, Reform, Resilience*, 257, 273 n. 11.

68. For an examination of the impact of the Parisian masters on some issues before the Council, see John W. Baldwin, *Masters, Princes and Merchants* (Princeton, 1970), vol. 1, 315–43. It is well to remember that Innocent III was himself a university product. Also see Leonard E. Boyle, 'The Fourth Lateran Council and Manuals of Popular Theology', *The Popular Literature of Medieval England* (Tennessee Studies in Literature, vol. 28) (Knoxville, 1985), 30–43.

69. See canon 27 where bishops are ordered to provide suitable instruction for priests, and to exclude 'ignorant and unformed men', H. J. Schroeder (ed.), *Disciplinary Decrees of the General Councils* (St Louis, 1937), 267. Care was also taken to assure that priests in charge of parochial churches be provided with a sufficient living to attract and support clerics 'with more than a very limited knowledge of letters', canon 32, ibid., 269.

70. Lateran III, canon 18, ibid., 229. Lateran IV, canon 11, ibid., 252.

71. On the later medieval Church in general, Francis Rapp, *L'Eglise et la*

vie religieuse en occident à la fin du Moyen Age (Paris, 1971); Francis
Oakley, *The Western Church in the Later Middle Ages* (Ithaca, N.Y.,
1979). As D. L. D'Avray, *The Preaching of the Friars*, 1, has pointed
out, J. B. Schneyer's *Repertorium der lateinischen Sermones des Mittelalters für die Zeit von 1150–1350* (Münster, 1969–), which lists only
the incipit, explicit, and manuscript locations of sermons for the
period, runs to 9 volumes and 7,300 pages.

72. For a general overview of medieval preaching, F. R. Albert, *Die
Geschichte der Predigt in Deutschland bis Luther* (Gütersloh, 1892–6);
R. Cruel, *Geschichte der Predigt im Mittelalter* (Detmold, 1879);
Anton Linsenmayer, *Geschichte der Predigt in Deutschland von Karl
dem Grossen bis zum Ausgang des 14. Jahrhunderts* (Munich, 1886);
Jean Longère, *La prédication médiéval* (Paris, 1983). Johann Baptist
Schneyer, *Geschichte der katholischen Predigt* (Freiburg, 1969). Specifi-
cally on late medieval preaching, see J. W. Blench, *Preaching in
England in the late 15th and 16th centuries: A study in English Sermons
1450–1600* (Oxford, 1964); Gerald Robert Owst, *Literature and Pulpit
in Medieval England* (Cambridge, 1938); idem, *Preaching in Medieval
England: An Introduction to Sermon Manuscripts of the Period 1350–
1450* (Cambridge, 1926). On the limitations placed on preaching,
England was especially rigorous, a result of its experience with the
Lollards, Owst, *Preaching in Medieval England*, 72–93. In Germany,
however, as a result of complaints by laity and clergy alike, in 1508 the
Bishop of Breslau ordered a limitation on the number of sermons
preached in the city, A. O. Meyer, *Studien zur Vorgeschichte der
Reformation aus schlesischen Quellen* (Munich, 1903), 81–3. The *Direc-
torium Sacerdotale* of Joannes Pfeffer (Basel 1483?) contains a warning
against too frequent preaching, Pars 4, paragraph 69.

73. Early medieval preaching was a subject of controversy in the nineteenth century, cf. Cruel, Linsenmeyer, and Albert. For a particularly
negative picture, M. Rieger, 'Die altdeutsche Predigt', in Wilhelm
Wackernagel, *Altdeutsche Predigten und Gebete aus Handschriften*
(Basel, 1876), 291–445. But no one has ever doubted that late medieval
preaching far outshone, at least in quantity, the preceding age, cf.
Réginald Grégoire, *Homéliaires liturgiques médiévaux. Analyse des
manuscrits* (Spoleto, 1980); Henri Barré, *Les Homéliaires carolingiens
de l'école d'Auxerre* (Vatican, 1962); Milton McCormick Gatch,
Preaching and Theology in Anglo-Saxon England: Aelfric and Wulfstan
(Toronto, 1977). As for the ancient Church, the pre-Constantinian
legal position of the Church did not encourage extra-liturgical preaching. After the Edict of Milan, it is true, there was an explosion of
preaching, but the bishops tended to keep a monopoly. Even so,
preaching was rare in Rome already by the middle of the fifth century,
L. Duchesne, *Christian Worship, its Origin and Evolution: A Study of
the Latin Liturgy up to the time of Charlemagne* (London, 1927), 161–

180, 197. On the question of preaching before the 12th century see my forthcoming, 'The Word Eclipsed?' Preaching in the Early Middle Ages'.

74. Albert Lecoy de la Marche, *La Chaire française au moyen age, spécialement au xiiie siècle d'après les manuscrits contemporains* (Paris, 1868); L. Bourgain, *La Chaire française au xiie siècle d'après les manuscrits* (Paris, 1879); Carlo Delcorno, *La predicazione nell'età comunale* (Florence, 1974); Homer Pfander, *The Popular Sermon of the Medieval Friar in England* (New York, 1937); M. M. Davy (ed.), *Sermons universitaires parisiens du 1230–1231* (Paris, 1931). D. L. D'Avray, *The Preaching of the Friars*, 6, argues that it is difficult, if not impossible, to distinguish 'spontaneous, itinerant preaching, on the one hand, and a different, academic type of preaching, represented by the sermon collections that have come down to us'.

75. On the whole topic see D'Avray, *The Preaching of the Friars*.

76. G. G. Meersseman, *Ordo Fraternitatis: Confraterniti e pieta dei laici nel medioevo* (Rome, 1977), 1121–43 (esp. 1127–30).

77. James J. Murphy, *A Select Bibliography of Medieval Rhetoric* (Toronto, 1971), 71.

78. P. L. 210, 110–98.

79. Corpus Christianorum Continuatio Medievalis, 82 (Turnholt, 1988).

80. See Harry Caplan, *Of Eloquence. Studies in Ancient and Mediaeval Rhetoric* (Ithaca, N.Y., 1970) (Aquinas) 51–78; (Henry of Hesse) 135–60. *S. Bonaventurae Opera omnia* 9 (Quaracchi, 1882–1902), 8–21.

81. On these see James J. Murphy, *Rhetoric in the Middle Ages* (Berkeley, 1974), 310–55.

82. D'Avray, *The Preaching of the Friars*, 159.

83. D'Avray, *The Preaching of the Friars*, 184–6, argues that university masters provided an 'ideology' for preaching.

84. On the endowed preacherships, Julius Rauscher, *Die Prädikaturen in Württemberg vor der Reformation* (Stuttgart, 1909); Florenz Landmann, *Das Predigtwesen in Westfalen in den letzten Zeiten des Mittelalters* (Münster i. W., 1900). Note that most South German endowed preacherships required a university-educated incumbent, Rauscher, *Prädikaturen*, vol. 2, 161.

85. Oediger, *Über die Bildung der Geistlichen*, 116.

86. C. 4, Hartzheim-Schannat, *Concilia Germaniae* (Cologne, 1765), vol. 6, p. 8.

87. Oediger, *Über die Bildung der Geistlichen*, 101.

88. On Surgant, see Dorothea Roth, *Die Mittelalterliche Predigttheorie und das Manuale Curatorum des Johann Ulrich Surgant* (Basel, 1956), and Rudolf Hirsch, 'Surgant's List of Recommended Books for Preachers (1502–03)', *Renaissance Quarterly*, 18 (1965), 199–210. It was only with the Council of Trent that weekly Sunday sermons were imposed as a universal rule on parish priests, Session 5, Decree

Concerning Reform, chapter 2, *The Canons and Decrees of the Council of Trent*, trans. and intro. by H. J. Schroeder, O. P. (Rockford, Illinois, 1978), 24–6. A theological reflection of the new importance of preaching were the discussions of the relative worth of the Mass and the sermon, see for example the piece by Sylvester Prierias in Heiko Oberman, *Forerunners of the Reformation*, 265–7.

89. Karl Müller, 'Der Umschwung in der Lehre von der Busse während des 12. Jahrhundert', *Theologische Abhandlungen. Carl von Weizsäcker zu seinem siebzigsten Geburtstage 11. December 1892. gewidmet* (Freiburg i. B., 1892), 287–320. Paul Anciaux, *La théologie du sacrement de penance au xiie siècle* (Louvain, 1949). The best recent treatment is Thomas N. Tentler, *Sin and Confession on the Eve of the Reformation* (Princeton, 1977).

90. See Karl F. Morrison, *The Mimetic Tradition of Reform in the West* (Princeton, 1982), esp. 222–40.

91. 'Popular and Monastic Pastoral Issues in the Later Middle Ages', *Church History*, 56 (1987), 351.

92. Rudolf Stanka, *Die Summa des Berthold von Freiburg. Eine rechtsgeschichtliche Untersuchung* (Vienna, 1937), 28, 32–3. On the importance of conscience beginning in the twelfth century, M. D. Chenu, *L'Eveil de la conscience dans la civilisation médiévale* (Montreal, 1969).

93. See J. Galot, *La Nature du caractère sacramental* (Paris, 1968). Cf. Cyrille Vogel, 'Laica commune contentus. La retour du presbytre au rang des laïcs (éléments du dossier)', *Revue des sciences religieuses*, 47 (1973), 56–122.

94. See Tentler, *Sin and Confession*. Cf. Leonard E. Boyle, 'The Summa for Confessors as a Genre, and Its Religious Intent', *Pursuit of Holiness in Late Medieval and Renaissance Religion*, Charles Trinkaus and Heiko Oberman (eds.) (Leiden, 1974), 126–30; Pierre Michaud-Quantin, *Sommes de casuistique et manuels de confession au moyen âge (xii–xvi siècles)* (Louvain, 1962).

95. Thomas N. Tentler, *Sin and Confession on the Eve of the Reformation* (Princeton, 1977), 31–9. It should be noted that before Raymond of Penaforte, Thomas of Chobham had already produced a *summa* entitled, 'Cum miserationes', F. Broomfield (ed.), *Thomae de Chobham. Summa Confessorum* (Louvain, 1968).

96. Oediger, *Über die Bildung der Geistlichen*, 103–4.

97. On the role of 'intention' see Heinz-Joachim Fischer, 'Intention', *Dictionnaire de spiritualité* (Paris, 1937–), vol, 7/2, cols. 1838–1858; A. Thouvenin, 'Intention', *Dictionnaire de théologie catholique* (Paris 1930–1967), vol. 7, cols. 2267–2280; R. Naz, 'Intention', *Dictionnaire de droit canonique* (Paris, 1935–1965), vol. 5, cols. 1462–1464; O. Lottin, *Psychologie et morale au xiie et xiiie siècles* (Paris, 1954), vol. 4/1, 309–486.

98. The best introduction to this is Gary Macy, *The Theologies of the*

Eucharist in the Early Scholastic Period. A Study of the Salvific Function of the Sacrament according to the Theologians c. 1080–c. 1220 (Oxford, 1984). Macy is extending his research into later periods, *idem*, 'Reception of the Eucharist according to some early Dominican Theologians of the 13th and 14th centuries', a paper given at the 22nd International Congress on Medieval Studies, Kalamazoo, Michigan, May 7, 1987. Cf. David Burr, *Eucharistic Presence and Conversion in Late Thirteenth-Century Franciscan Thought* (Philadelphia, 1984).

99. Cf. Mary Martina Schaefer, 'Twelfth Century Latin Commentaries on the Mass: Christological and Ecclesiological Dimensions' (Ph.D. Diss., Notre Dame, 1983).

100. For a survey of the allegorical interpretation of the mass, beginning with Theodore of Mopsuestia, see Nathan Mitchell, *Cult and Controversy: The Worship of the Eucharist outside the Mass* (New York, 1982).

101. 'Medieval Literacy, Linguistic Theory, and Social Organization', *New Literary History* 16 (1984), 13–29.

102. 'Misse officium tam provida reperitur ordinatione dispositum, ut que per Christum ex quo descendit de celo humanam sibi assumans naturam. usque dum in celum ascendit gesta sunt magna ex parte continent. et ea tam verbis quam signis admirabili quadam specie representat. Nam tota vita Christi in hoc seculo celebrata quasi una solennissima fuit missa. ideo totum misse officium ad Christi vita passionemque representandam ordinatur', *Speculum offici misse expositorium* (Heidelberg, 1495), fol. bV verso.

103. Gabriel Biel, *Canonis Misse Expositio*, Heiko Oberman and William J. Courtney (eds.) (Wiesbaden, 1963–67), 4 vols. Biel was himself concerned that scholastic speculation not subvert the sacrament, see Heiko Oberman, *The Harvest of Medieval Theology. Gabriel Biel and Late Medieval Nominalism* (Grand Rapids, Michigan, 1967), 272, note 86.

104. Macy's Kalamazoo paper (see note 98) working from the theological literature found much the same thing as is contained in the pastoral manuals. See e.g., Johannes Altensteig, *Lexicon Theologicum* [originally published Hagenau 1517] (Cologne 1619), 161; Guido de Monte Rocherii, *Manipulus curatorum* (Cologne ca. 1480), 29–30; Joannes de Burgo, *Pupilla oculi* (Paris 1507), fol. XX verso, paragraphs S and Y, fol. xxi paragraphs ag and ay. Cf. Enrico Cattaneo, *Il Culto Cristiano in Occidente. Note Storiche* (Rome, 1978), 306.

105. See Jacques Toussaert, *La Sentiment religieux en Flandre à la fin du Moyen Age* (Paris, 1963), 116–21. For an overview of the entire medieval period, Peter Browe, 'Die öftere Kommunion der Laien im Mittelalter', *Bonner Zeitschrift für Theologie und Seelsorge* 6 (1929), 1–28.

106. Historians of liturgy have decried the enervation of late medieval worship, its tendency to overemphasize the interior and the visual to

the detriment of the communal and participatory, Cattaneo, *Il Culto Cristiano*, 285–7; Gregory Dix, *The Shape of the Liturgy* (London, 1945), 598–600; Josef A. Jungmann, 'Lo stato della vita liturgica alla vigilia della Riforma', *Eredità liturgica e attualità pastorale* (Rome, 1962).

107. There were treatments of the problem in all the confessional manuals. But there was a genre devoted exclusively to it, the most important example of which is Johann Heynlin, *Resolutorium dubiorum circa celebrationem missarum*, 13 editions 1492–1506.

108. Lawrence G. Duggan, 'Fear and Confession on the Eve of the Reformation', *Archiv für Reformationsgeschichte*, 75 (1984), 153–75, argues against accepting a widespread *Angst* oppressing the christian population of late medieval Europe. But if there was an exception it would be among those clergy who had the manuals at hand.

109. Herman Mitgau, 'Soziale Herkunft der Deutschen Studenten bis 1900', *Universität und Gelehrtenstand 1440–800. Büdingen Vorträge, 1966*, Hellmuth Rössler and Günther Franz (eds.) (Limburg/Lahn, 1970), 255. Mitgau and Overfield (see below) base their calculations on Franz Eulenberg, *Die Frequenz der deutschen Universitäten* (Leipzig, 1904).

110. Mitgau, 'Soziale Herkunft', 235, 237.

111. *Deutsche Universitätsbesucher*, 30–4.

112. In fifteenth-century Germany the term did refer to someone in holy orders, perhaps only in minor orders, but not merely a literate person as seems to have been the case earlier in England, Clanchy, *From Memory to Written Record*, 177–201.

113. For these and following figures, James H. Overfield, 'University Studies and the Clergy in Pre-Reformation Germany', *Rebirth, Reform, Resilience*, 254–92. Overfield excluded those individuals who were only identified as *clerici* without further confirming information.

114. Overfield, 'University Studies and the Clergy', 260; Oediger, *Über die Bildung der Geistlichen*, 66–7 n. 3. In addition to the studies cited by Overfield, see Reinhold Kiermayr, 'On the Education of the Pre-Reformation Clergy', *Church History* 53 (1984), 7–16, who suggests that the variation among localities may in part have to do with the propinquity of a university. Schwinges, *Deutsche Universitätsbesucher*, 401, found that parochial clergy attending the University of Cologne were drawn overwhelmingly from the bishoprics immediately surrounding the city. Kiermayr (p. 15) found that 37% of the clergy in the central German town of Duderstadt had attended university, and that in 1517 the figure had reached 53%. Such levels of education mark a shift from the preceding two centuries. As late as the fourteenth century the German cleric's lack of education, and often of literacy, was proverbial, Gerhard Ritter, *Die Heidelberg Universität*, 21.

115. As Schwinges, *Deutsche Universitätsbesucher*, 410–11, has argued, fewer and fewer ordained benefice holders were listed on the matricula

because the benefices were increasingly given to people who had already completed their studies. For England, an analysis of early fourteenth-century licences to study at University while drawing benefice revenues by John R. Shinners, Jr., 'University Study Licences and Clerical Education in the Diocese of Norwich, 1325–35', *History of Education Quarterly* 28 (1988), 400, found that approximately 20% of new rectors applying for licences already held a masters degree. One must assume that there were others who had studied at University but had not proceeded to take a degree.

116. A point made already by Ritter, *Die Heidelberger Universität*, 402, 406.
117. On religious education at the lower level see Oediger, *Über die Bildung der Geistlichen*, 72–3. By the fifteenth century every city and many of the smaller towns and larger villages in Germany had a school, ibid., 68; Schwinges, *Deutsche Universitätsbesucher*, 36, 374.
118. H. J. Schroeder (ed. and trans.), *Disciplinary Decrees of the General Councils* (St Louis, 1937), 495.
119. A. L. Gabriel, *The College System in the Fourteenth Century* (Baltimore, n.d.), 5.
120. Berthe M. Marti, *The Spanish College in the Fourteenth Century* (Philadelphia 1966), 272; M. D. Chapotin, *Le College de Dormans-Beauvais* (Paris, 1870), 76; *Die Urkunden über die Universität Freiburg. i. B.* (Freiburg, i. B., 1875), 7–8; Astrik L. Gabriel, *Student Life in Ave Maria College, Medieval Paris: History and Chartulary of the College* (Notre Dame, 1955), 332.
121. Gabriel, *College System*, 12.
122. P. Feret, *La faculté de théologie de Paris: Moyen Age* (Paris, 1896), vol. 3, 614, 644, 652.
123. L. Guiroud (ed.), *Le College de Saint-Benoît* (Montpellier, 1890), 197–8. The Statutes were issued around 1365.
124. Feret, *La faculté de théologie*, 646.
125. Ibid., 646.
126. P. Glorieux, *Aux origines de la Sorbonne: I: Robert de Sorbonne* (Paris, 1966), 195.
127. *Statutes of the Colleges of Oxford* (Oxford, 1853), Vol. I (Merton 1270), 14 (Lincoln 15th century), 29–30.
128. Marti, *The Spanish College*, 270–2. The statutes were issued in 1375.
129. Augustin Renaudet, 'Jean Standonck, un Réformateur Catholique avant la Reforme', *Bulletin de la Société préhistorique française* 14 (1908), 1–81; Marcel Godet, 'La congrégation de Montaigu 1490–1580', *Bibliothèque de l'Ecole des Hautes Etudes*, no. 198 (Paris, 1912).
130. D. Catherine Brown, *Pastor and Laity in the Theology of Jean Gerson* (Cambridge, 1987), 7.
131. Dorothea Roth, *Die Mittelalterliche Predigttheorie und das Manuale Curatorum des Johann Ulrich Surgant* (Basel, 1956), 12–13.
132. Although it must be pointed out that in the early fourteenth century sanctity and education were closely associated, A. Vauchez, 'Culture et

sainteté d'après les procès de canonisation', in *Le scuole degli ordini mendicanti (secoli xiii–xiv)*, 165.

133. Overfield, 'University Studies and the Clergy', 269–70. At Cologne between 1395 and 1495 the matriculated students were divided among the faculties as follows: Medicine (0.4%), Theology (2.6%), Canon and Roman Law (13.6%) and Arts (approx. 80%), Schwinges, *Deutsche Universitätsbesucher*, 468. However, it should be noted that of those who did study theology, members of the religious orders and lower parish clergy (pastors, *plebani*, presbyters etc.) constituted the overwhelming majority, ibid., 480. See Ritter, *Die Heidelberger Universität*, 331–2, for a good characterization of the theology produced at the German universities. On the other hand some secular clergy attended mendicant convents for the theological lessons, which were specifically left open to the public. Oediger, *Über die Bildung der Geistlichen*, 62–3, is in error when he claims that the mendicant schools were closed to outsiders. See I. Frank, *Hausstudium und Universitätsstudium der Wiener Dominikaner bis 1500* (Vienna, 1968), 54–8; C. Douais, *Essai sur l'organisation des études dans l'ordre der Frères Prècheurs au trezième et au quartorzième siècle* (1216–1342) (Paris-Toulouse, 1884), 76. The theological instruction in simple *studia* far from university towns was offered publicly. Mendicant *studia* provided theological instruction at universities where the papacy at first refused to allow a theological faculty. These convents usually formed the basis of the later theological faculties, see P. Mandonnet, 'La crise scholaire au début du xiiie siècle et la fondation de l'ordre des frères prècheurs', *Revue d'histoire ecclésiastique* 15 (1914), 34–49; Hans Jürgen Brandt, 'Excepta facultate theologica: Zum Ringen um die Einheit von "imperium", "sacerdotium", und "studium" im Spätmittelalter', in R. Bäumer (ed.), *Reformatio ecclesiae: Beiträge zu kirchlichen Reformbewegungen von der Alten Kirche bis zur Neuzeit: Festgabe für E. Iserloh* (Paderborn, 1980), 201–14. In general on the mendicant schools, *Le Scuole degli Ordini Mendicanti (secoli xiii–xiv)* [Convegni del Centro di Studi sulla Spiritualità Medievalé] (Todi, 1978).

134. This can especially be seen in the *pastoralia*, the manuals of guidance for the clergy, which were almost exclusively collections based on Canon Law. The one exception was the impact of Aquinas' moral theology on the confessional literature, Leonard E. Boyle, 'The Quodlibets of St. Thomas and Pastoral Care', *The Thomist* 38 (1974), 252–3.

135. See note 133.

136. Leonard E. Boyle has done much to call our attention to them, see the collection of his articles, *Pastoral Care, Clerical Education and Canon Law, 1200–1400* (London, 1981). Recently he has also attempted to provide a systematic categorization by *genre*, see his 'The Fourth Lateran Council and Manuals of Popular Theology', 38–43. Tentler's *Sin and Confession on the Eve of the Reformation* is the most impressive

use of them to date. See also, Cyrille Vogel, Les *'libri paenitentiales'* (Typologie des sources du moyen age occidental 27) (Turnhout, 1978). For preaching, Harry Caplan, *Mediaeval Artes Praedicandi: A Hand-List* (Ithaca, N.Y., 1934); *idem, Mediaeval Artes Praedicandi: A Supplementary Hand-List* (Ithaca, N.Y., 1936); Harry Caplan and W. H. King, 'Latin Tractates on Preaching: A Book-List', *Harvard Theological Review*, 42 (1949), 185–206. Th. M. Charland, *Artes Praedicandi, Contribution à l'Histoire de la Rhétorique au Moyen Age* (Paris/Ottawa, 1936). For an evaluation of the wider range of preaching aids see D. L. D'Avray, *The Preaching of the Friars*, 64–90. For liturgical guides, see Jean-Michel Hanssens (ed.), *Amalarii episcopi opera liturgica omnia*, 3 vols. (Rome, 1948–50); Cyrille Vogel, *Medieval Liturgy: An Introduction to the Sources* (Washington, D.C., 1986). For very interesting glimpses of their use, Florenz Landmann, 'Drei Predigt- und Seelsorsbücher von Konrad Dreuben, einem elsässischen Landpfarrer aus der Mitte des 15. Jahrhunderts', *Archiv für elsässischen Kirchengeschichte*, 7 (1933), 209–40; *idem*, 'Predigten und Predigtwerke in den Händen der Weltgeistlichkeit des 15. Jahrhunderts nach alten Bücherlisten des Bistums Konstanz', *Kirche und Kanzel* 6 (1923), 130–6, 203–11, 277–84; 7 (1924), 53–60, 119–25, 207–14; Oediger, *Über die Bildung der Geistlichen*, 117. On the usefulness of university education in using these preaching aids, D'Avray, *The Preaching of the Friars*, 182–3, 191–3.

137. What Ritter, *Die Heidelberger Universität*, 421, referred to as 'Die praktische-seelsorgerliche Richtung'. This is one of the reasons why Humanism found a welcome among some theologians.

138. John R. Shinners, 'University Study Licenses and Clerical Education', 404–5. Cf. Robert M. Ball, 'The Education of the English Parish Clergy in the Later Middle Ages with Particular Reference to the Manuals of Instruction' (Ph.D. Diss., Cambridge, 1976).

139. E.g., Louis Binz, *Vie religieuse et réforme ecclésiastique dans le diocèse de Genève pendant le grand schisme et la crise conciliare (1378–1450)* (Geneva, 1973), Vol. I, 169–71; Oediger, *Über die Bildung der Geistlichen*, 122–5.

140. Oediger, *Über die Bildung der Geistlichen*, 131.

141. On the university book trade, see for example, Graham Pollard, 'The University and the Book Trade in Medieval Oxford', in Paul Wilpert (ed.), *Beiträge zum Berufsbewusstein des mittelalterlichen Menschen* (Berlin, 1964), 336–44. On the impact of printing in general, Elizabeth L. Eisenstein, *The Printing Press as an Agent of Change* (Cambridge, 1979). On the crucial role that the Church played in supporting early printing, and the importance of clerically oriented books, M. Besson, *L'Eglise et l'imprimerie dans les anciens diocèses de Lausanne et de Genève jusqu'en 1525* (2 vols., Geneva, 1937–38); Hanns Bohatta, *Liturgische Drucke und liturgische Drucker* (Regensburg, 1926); Franz Falk, *Die Druckkunst im Dienst der Kirche zunächst in Deutschland bis*

zum Jahre 1520 (Cologne, 1879). And more recently see the discussion in Miriam Usher Chrisman, *Lay Culture, Learned Culture. Books and Social Change in Strasbourg 1480–1599* (New Haven, 1982), 81–102.

142. Bernd Moeller, 'The German Humanists and the Beginnings of the Reformation', in his *Imperial Cities and the Reformation. Three Essays*, H. C. Erik Midelfort and Mark U. Edwards, Jr. (eds. and trans.) (Philadelphia, 1972), 19–38.

143. On this see Hans-Joachim Köhler (ed.), *Flugschriften als Massenmedium der Reformationszeit* (Stuttgart, 1981); Robert Scribner, *For the Sake of Simple Folk: Popular Propaganda for the German Reformation* (Cambridge, 1981); Paul A. Russel, *Lay Theology in the Reformation. Popular Pamphleteers in Southwest Germany, 1521–1525* (Cambridge, 1986).

144. See especially, Steven Ozment, *Reformation in the Cities. The Appeal of Protestantism to Sixteenth-Century Germany and Switzerland* (New Haven, 1975).

The Relationship Between the University and the City of Louvain in the Fifteenth Century

Edward De Maesschalck

Medieval universities were founded and developed in existing cities. They relied on safety within the city walls, could use the infrastructure of streets and buildings, and profit from the material advantages brought by trade and industry. For the rest, they wished to lead their own lives, organize their own jurisdiction, be exempt from all kinds of duties and taxes and in general retain clerical privileges and acquire new ones. Inevitably, this led to conflicts which usually were settled to the advantage of the universities. In their opposition to local authorities the universities often had powerful friends at their disposal: the pope, the bishop, the king, parliament, etc. The ultimate sanction for forcing a city to its knees was *secessio* which frequently signified the starting signal for the founding of a new university in another town. This constant tension and occasional bloody struggle between city and university finally produced a *modus vivendi* which differed from area to area. In the English universities of Oxford and Cambridge the town in the long run was completely dominated by the university, to such an extent that 'the burghers lived henceforth in their own town almost as the helots or subjects of a conquering people'. It never came to such a pass in Louvain.[1]

By the late Middle Ages local city governments had become better aware of the financial and legal implications of a university. Councillors had often been students themselves and were in possession of a university degree. The experience of centuries of bickering had by then been moulded into ready-made models and acceptable customs. When it came to new foundations the municipality was definitely better prepared. When a city itself took the initiative, by budgeting for the recruitment and payment of professors it was immediately in a stronger position from which it could exercise some

control over its university. This scenario pertained in the foundation
inter alia of Perugia (1308), Cologne (1388), Rostock (1419), Poitiers
(1431), Greifswald (1456) and Basle (1459).[2] It also pertained in the
foundation of Louvain where the magistracy emulated the example
of Cologne in particular. The Louvain City Council would actually
consult their Cologne counterparts as late as the sixteenth century to
help solve difficulties with its university.[3]

1. Foundation of the university

The University of Louvain was founded in 1425 by Pope Martin V.
According to the papal bull of foundation, the university was
instituted at the request of the Duke of Brabant, the chapter of St
Peter's Louvain (to which the 'scholastic' belonged who was responsible for schools in Louvain) and finally the city of Louvain itself.[4]
The order in which the bull ranked the three instigators of the
foundation reflected their reciprocal relationship in the contemporary hierarchy of authority: king, church and local council. Historians have been led astray by this official ranking. They have looked
specifically for an initiative from some grand lords in Brabant and
the Duke's counsellors. The 'scholastic', in their eyes, had merely led
the negotiations in Rome while the city of Louvain had done little
but gratefully accept the offer of a university in the hope of
improving the city's economy.[5] In other words the city of Louvain
acted simply from a kind of shopkeeper's mentality, chiefly interested in material advantage and financial gain. Such motives did
indeed play their part in the founding of a few universities, especially
from the turn of the sixteenth century, but they were not commonplace in the Middle Ages.[6]

Indeed, when we look at the sources we soon form a quite
different picture.[7] The city of Louvain spent a fortune on messengers, gifts, dinners, bribes and ambassadors to get influential
people to favour the idea of founding a university and to be able to
complete the business quickly. Nothing was left to chance. The city
for instance provided the necessary buildings: for the arts faculty a
house in New Street (the so-called *vicus*); for the law and medical
faculties a house in Mint Street, later (to be more precise, after the
theology faculty was set up in 1431) replaced by part of Cloth Hall in
Namur Street; finally a prison. Furthermore, the city bore the

expenditure for attracting and paying the professors, letting the outside world know about the opening of the university, and so on. In short, the city spent enormous sums and this is reported explicitly in the minute book of the local council.[8] The city even surrendered certain privileges and taxes[9] and did not ask for a *quid pro quo*, at least not in the short term. There must, then, have been motives above and beyond material advantage and financial gain for setting up such an enterprise. Recent studies have placed the foundation in quite a different perspective. Firstly and most importantly, at the beginning of the fifteenth century the St Peter's chapter-school was, with the city's help, evolving towards the status of an academic institution. From 1418 one can find an annual item in the city accounts for a payment to the rural dean 'as an aid to the Louvain school, because he had invited two great masters to lead the school which had attracted many students from outside the city'.[10] We are clearly dealing here with a pre-university situation. We can see that Louvain University had not suddenly dropped from the sky. Besides, the city was at that period in not quite such financial straits as has previously been alleged. There had been a distinct recovery which can be demonstrated by the city's large-scale building policy (which included the town hall and St Peter's Church). Cloth manufacturing, admittedly, was no longer flourishing but other manufactures were: linen weaving, tapestry weaving, feathers and leather processing, breweries, etc.[11] Finally, the city was living in a kind of political euphoria. The large cities dominated the 'states' (the representative institution of the province) and they in their turn had some power over the king. After the democratic unrest in Brussels in 1421 Louvain even considered tempting the duke back to Louvain and thus once again becoming the first city in Brabant. When that failed they thought of some other means of increasing the city's power and prestige and that was by founding a university.[12] A desire for prestige is probably the key to explaining why a university was founded in Louvain.

The papal bull also listed a specific reason: the bishoprics of Liège, Cambrai, Utrecht, Thérouanne and Tournai were rich in cities, people, and goods but there was not a single university within their boundaries. This hindered scholarship and forced prospective students to travel far afield.[13] But this reason applied to all the cities in the Netherlands and therefore hardly explains the siting of a university at Louvain. As an additional reason, the bull also noted

that the city was an appropriate location for an academic community because of its wealth, its mild climate (a commonplace) and
an abundance of space and housing.[14] There certainly was enough
room in Louvain, particularly between the first and second city
walls, although as we shall see later that did not prove to be the place
where the academics would prefer to settle.

2. The payment of professors

We now know that the university was not forced on Louvain but
that Louvain truly wanted the university and that it spared no
expense. Until 1440 payment of the professors alone cost the city
purse 11 per cent of its total expenditure. However, the city's annual
accounts mostly stayed in the black, at least for a period.[15]

Initially the city also paid the arts professors but that came to an
end as early as 1428. The arts faculty had a flood of students and
unlike the higher faculties it demanded tuition fees. Besides, a
number of professors had another source of income at their disposal. They provided board and lodging to young grammar students in
boarding schools or *pedagogia*. These professors, the so-called
'regents', soon belonged to the richest group of academics. During
the following years the arts teaching gradually moved from the
central *vicus* to the *pedagogia*, so that the young lodgers stayed there
to the end of their arts studies. Initially the number of *pedagogia*
oscillated between three and seven, but eventually in 1439 it was
stabilized at four: Pig, Falcon, Lily and Castle. The regents never
received an actual salary from the city but were indirectly subsidized
by incentive premiums and exemption from excise duties especially
on the purchase of beer.[16]

The city of Louvain therefore only needed to pay the professors in
the higher faculties. On average the professors received 144 guilders
a head per annum. These salaries were not over-generous because a
master bricklayer earned, on average, 50 guilders a year in the
fifteenth century.[17] And remember that this was an average salary:
some professors earned up to twenty times more than their less
fortunate colleagues which meant that some princely salaries were
being paid but also some real starvation wages.[18]

From the beginning the city understood that it was paying too little. It therefore lived in the fear that many professors, invariably the best, would be looking for another employer. Thus the city tried as quickly as possible to couple the chairs to secure benefices which had no residential obligation. As early as 1428 the duke reserved, at the express request of the city, no fewer than fifteen canon's prebends for the professors, this as a supplement over and above their salary.[19] In 1443 at the initiative of the city a second chapter was founded in St Peter's Church for a further fifteen prebendaries: the incomes partly stemmed from the old chapter (in the case of the canonries) and also from ten parish cures from a wide area round Louvain.[20] To convince the pope and all concerned the city again spent a fortune on messengers, gifts, backhanders as well as compensation to priests who had to forgo their income.[21] From that moment, however, most professors could manage with the income from their benefices and the city at most had to pay out supplements.[22] The city tried a few more times to attract benefices to its university. For instance, during the fifteenth century negotiations were held with various chapters, including those of Hoksem and Fosse, for a transfer of a portion of their income to Louvain but without success.[23]

Not only theologians and canonists could be considered for these benefices but also civil lawyers and arts students and professors. The pope issued special admission rights to benefices as well as a dispensation from the need to be ordained as a deacon or priest.[24] Moreover, most of the students in the higher faculties received their income from a benefice of some kind, always without any residential obligation. In 1483 the university received an astonishing privilege from the pope by which all important collators in the hereditary domains of Burgundy would regularly have to appoint a member of the university to benefices in their gift.[25] In the course of the sixteenth century the arts faculty received yet more privileges.[26] Joint appointments at a fixed income became institutionalized; thus the Louvain professor, Adrianus Florentii the later Pope Hadrian VI, always had at least four benefices.[27] In the best arrangement a 'less educated' locum was appointed to be resident and he had to live on a starvation wage. From an official list of benefices from the end of the fifteenth century we know that in the rural deaneries of Louvain, Geldenaken and Zoutleeuw alone 102 benefices were occupied by members of the university who were resident in Louvain:

71 chaplaincies, 22 parish cures and 9 sextonships.[28] In the field of pastoral care Brabant and especially the area around Louvain became a desert but the city council did not see that as its main concern.

3. The appointment of professors

Louvain's city government appointed the professors, not only those to whom it paid their salary directly but as a rule also those who were paid via a benefice. The benefices allotted in 1428 were handed out by the town clerk jointly with the University Council, but in those cases it was a question of a supplement only. The more important benefices, incorporated in 1443, were exclusively given out by the city itself, more precisely by the two burgomasters.[29] Naturally, some appointments were contested by the university or by certain faculties, but as a rule the city always won its case. We have examples of this from various faculties, even examples of professors who were dismissed because they did not come up to expectation. A number of examples from the medical faculty show that the city when appointing or dismissing professors also took note of the students' opinion.[30] The only occasion when the city had to climb down was over a plan of 1447. Until then the incomes from the prebends of the second chapter had been distributed equally. From then on they were to depend on the ability and merit of the professors. A violent protest arose against this plan from altogether 63 *magistri*. There was the danger in their eyes that henceforth 'the city could appoint or dismiss as it pleased and make the professors unequal according to its own whim'.[31]

Today one can hardly imagine that a city council would have such rights over the appointment of professors but it was quite usual in the Middle Ages. It was the same in many other university towns, especially in the German-speaking regions.[32] It must be said, however, that Louvain's town clerk and other functionaries were in no way illiterates. Between 1430 and 1580 an average of 31 per cent of the Louvain aldermen and 36 per cent of the Louvain burgomasters were in possession of a university diploma. This percentage was even higher among the town's officials and reached 100 per cent during the sixteenth century.[33] But in those same years the city gradually lost its monopoly over appointments, particularly because new chairs were being founded, paid for by the Emperor Charles V, his son Philip II or the States of Brabant. Besides, from the seventeenth century the town clerk had to ask advice beforehand from the relevant faculties for every appointment in its power.[34]

4. Fiscal immunity

Most of the difficulties between city and university arose as a consequence of the university's fiscal immunity. When the university was founded the Duke of Brabant awarded the academics the right to move about freely to and from Louvain without payment of tolls, taxes or admission dues, and this right was also awarded to members of their families and applied equally to their clothing, their luggage and above all their books.[35] In turn the city promised in vague terms that it would exempt the university from all possible taxes, but in practice nothing much had come of this. Most city taxes had to be paid by the academics directly or indirectly. These were chiefly the excise taxes on the consumption, production, and transport of goods such as grain, fish, meat, salt, wool, and cloth. Then, too, there were exceptional imposts levied on freight traffic, shipping, the slaughter-house, on wheat and rye, etc. These were raised in times of hardship such as floods, threat of war or major financial difficulties, so that the university easily accepted their implementation. But later these duties were often not abolished.[36]

In fact fiscal immunity was in practice mostly limited to immunity from the excise duty on the consumption of drink (beer and wine): for the academics a most important item. In Louvain this immunity was also enjoyed by the clerics and a few important gentlemen. The exemption from the excise duty on drink was very precious to the university for as early as 1432 it had threatened *secessio* if it did not obtain satisfaction on that point. A compromise was then worked out, the first of many because accommodating the different interested parties was very difficult.[37]

If beer was brewed in the city excise duty was levied on the brewer who naturally covered this in the price of his beer. Beer brewed outside the city carried no excise but when imported a toll would normally be demanded. According to the agreement of 1432 students and professors of the university did not have to pay this toll. The same applied to the import of wine. Naturally the university mostly stored up with beer from outside Louvain. As a result the city lost considerable income from a numerous clientele. It therefore gave permission to the largest institutions, viz. the *pedagogia*, to buy beer from Louvain brewers at a reduced cost so that in reality they only had to pay half the excise; the city then paid compensation to the brewers for their loss. Thereby the price of Louvain beer was the same as that of imported beer because no transport costs had to be paid. The city from its side preferred half the excise to no excise at all. Thus everyone was satisfied. But immediately other members of the university also wished to benefit from this regulation and this was granted in 1441 after lengthy negotiations. At that moment the greatest difficulties arose.[38]

Firstly, an enormous administration developed with checks on beer deliveries inside as well as outside the city, checks being made on freight papers, the loads, even the city labourers loading the cellars who were placed under oath.

Secondly, checks were urgently needed on those entitled to university membership. For who in fact had managed to become a member? Everyone who was enrolled by the rector, which included not only the professors, the graduates and the students, but the maids and servants, the widows of university members, and a whole array of officers such as public notaries, beadles, messengers, and booksellers (as long as they did not start up a profit-making business outside the university). Then there were the religious institutions which were gradually being incorporated into the university: the mendicant orders (Dominicans, Franciscans and Augustinians) from 1447, the Carmelites in 1461, the Carthusians in 1521. After that there was an escalation of incorporation. And what about a student who never came to the lessons or who was studying at a private school; or a student who did attend the courses but who was not signed up so that he could evade the expenses? The result was a bureaucracy with checks on testimonials, attendance notes, etc. All those lists and notes regularly turn up in the city accounts where in fact they provide an interesting source for a better knowledge of the university environment.[39]

Thirdly, checks were needed on the consumption of the liquor itself. Beer and wine purchased free of tax were in principle for private consumption, but an exemption was only given if the drinks were bought wholesale, in measures of one or half an *ame* (respectively 130 or 65 litres). Such a quantity was, however, beyond both the pocket as well as the drinking capacity of most students for the beer did not keep very well. So the students started selling the untaxed beer to their fellow students, their landlord, the neighbours . . ., and they inevitably tried to make a little profit on the transaction. Such further sales were finally regulated in 1488.[40] Two to four university publicans, to be appointed by the university, were to be given permission to keep a cellar open for retail sales, especially to poor students. In principle no profit was allowed to be made. But the publicans would get compensation for spills, leaks, use of candlelight, etc. Not surprisingly, the compensation was jacked up by the cellarers: wrong measures were used; the wine was adulterated. The result was a network of spies, tittle-tattle, disputes and lawsuits which were contested as high up as the Brabant Council and the ducal court. This battle continued without interruption until the end of the Ancien Régime.

It is of some interest to know that the city of Louvain occasionally asked advice from the town council of Cologne about all such matters. In 1481 it asked advice on the problems surrounding the import of beer, brewing undertaken by members of the university, all kinds of excise duties, whether university members could start a small business (the answer was 'no'), whether Cologne had complete freedom of appointment (yes), finally whether persons in debt could hide behind university jurisdiction (no).[41] And here we reach the area of jurisdiction.

5. Jurisdiction

As we know a medieval university was a world apart and it enjoyed the *privilegium fori*: its own judicial powers in all sorts of areas. Incidentally, this was one of the conditions laid down by the pope at the foundation of the University of Louvain. A number of authorities had had to part with their rights: the city and the chapter had done so spontaneously and loyally—they had of course taken the initiative. Things were already more awkward with the duke of Brabant and became very difficult indeed with the ordinary, i.e. the bishop of Liège. Both wanted above all to safeguard their rights to try very serious crimes committed by the laity and the clergy respectively. However, in practice the university won its case.[42] The rector in fact got full legal power over civil as well as criminal affairs in cases which only concerned the members of the university. In mixed affairs when non-university people were also involved, jurisdiction was in the hands of the *conservator privilegiorum* or guardian of the university's privileges. In practice this was the abbot of Saint Gertrude of Louvain. The members of the university could not be summoned for any offence or dispute by a law court outside Louvain (*jus de non evocando*, 1427), whilst in turn the *conservator* could summon everyone to his lawcourt (*jus tractus*, 1469).[43] These were privileges usually enjoyed by medieval universities and were given in order that the students could devote themselves undisturbed to their studies without paying through the nose or travelling all over the country for all sorts of lawsuits.

Were the members of the University of Louvain noticeably ill-disciplined? The young student population naturally brought much noise and commotion to the town. For the fifteenth century we have at our disposal the statutes of the university and some of its faculties, as well as material about a few specific cases which all point in the same direction.[44]

One of the biggest problems came about through games of chance. Everything was fair 'game' to gamble on: dice, cards, ballgames. Students pawned their clothes and sold their books. In 1457 the duke himself had to interfere and withdraw a licence he had given to various citizens of Louvain for using a house for games of chance. This happened as the result of a joint request from the city and the university.[45] A little later the duke intervened against the Louvain pawnbrokers and book wholesalers.[46] In 1465 the university went as far as a general ruling which made financial transactions between citizens and students under twenty-five years old illegal unless there had been permission from a higher authority.[47] Some Louvain citizens must have made quite a lot of money from the students. For example, in 1485 a big row erupted between the head of the Lily *pedagogium*, Carolus Viruli, and a Louvain married couple who had enticed students into their house by chatting them up, lending them money, serving them warm meals and even putting them up for the night, only to send a bill to the astonished parents later.[48]

The second big problem, after the students' wish to squander their money, was violence. The statutes are full of it: carrying weapons, lawlessness, vandalism, night revels, starting up quarrels, intimidation, frightening people, etc. There was a special functionary within the university, the *promotor*, who acted as a police commissioner, investigative judge, public prosecutor and prison warder.[49] The prison had been given by the city and was situated in the Mechlin inner city gate. The *promotor* virtually had sole responsibility—from the sixteenth century he was aided by permanent officers—and he was supposed to work by day and patrol the city at night. An additional handicap arose because he never got permission from the city government to enter a citizen's house or an inn. Thus he could at most besiege the house while the student would escape by the back door or a window on the roof.[50] In short he caught few students but the city police caught all the more. The following day the city police had to hand the student over to the *promotor*. Duke Charles the Bold tried in 1477 to restrict the night riots and established a curfew. If anyone was caught four times after the curfew by the city police he automatically lost his status as a member of the university.[51]

The last major problem which crops up in the statutes—even among the arts students (between fourteen and eighteen years old)— was their special interest in the fair sex: visits to brothels and bathhouses, participating in dance parties and masked carnival celebrations, violations of honour and actual rapes. A persistent tradition has it that Brussels had refused the offer of a university because the students 'would rape the daughters of the citizens'.[52] But the pattern of student lasciviousness was exaggerated. Figures are only available from the seventeenth century admittedly, but these show that while more than 50 per cent of the offences concerned violence only 2.6 per cent concerned visits to brothels. Rape did not occur at all, at least not according to the statutes. It is also worth noting that theft occurred very rarely or at least rarely led to conviction.[53]

In general the punishments handed out by the university were very lenient and this often offended the population. Torture was not used to obtain confessions. Most often a student was fined—even for murder and manslaughter. Then there was corporal punishment (flogging), especially for younger students, sometimes incarceration for a long spell (mostly in monasteries), banishment, and—characteristic of the fifteenth century—penitential pilgrimages. The worst punishment consisted of the loss of university privileges for then a student would come within the much more severe jurisdiction of the city or the duke. But on the whole the situation was not too bad in Louvain. According to a survey from the seventeenth century there were only five convictions per annum among what were then *c.*1,400 students.[54]

As regards the conservatorial lawcourt one abuse should be mentioned which was frequent in the fifteenth century and of which the Louvain citizens shamelessly took advantage. Many students in Louvain obtained their income from a benefice or hereditary rent. In this way they had a fixed income and were not always begging for money from home. Now it often happened that a parent had a debenture bond or debt which had not been paid off and which he then transferred to his son/student. The son then arranged for the case to be brought before the powerful conservatorial lawcourt. Here families would mostly be assured of a good outcome because this court had all kinds of repressive means available to enforce its decisions, including excommunication and interdiction. Not surprisingly, in the long run the ordinary citizens of Louvain capitalized on the existence of this court and sold their own promissory notes at a cheap price to students. In 1456 such methods were forbidden unless the transaction concerned members of the same family. The students who won their lawsuit also had to prove that for at least two years they had spent the proceeds on their studies. This regulation was later confirmed by successive kings.[55]

6. Housing

It is natural that accommodation played an important part in the relationship between city and university and between citizens and members of the university. The statutes of the university merely demanded that 'a member of the university must reside in an honourable and suitable place in Louvain or nearby', in other words not in a brothel or an inn.[56] For the rest students did as they pleased. The arts faculty did not like to see its students move in with citizens and preferred them to stay in a *pedagogium*. Financial profit may well have been one motive but educational reasons were the decisive factor. In a *pedagogium* students took part in disputes and received revision lessons, and here they were also obliged to speak Latin, whilst with a landlord 'the man is only bothered about his work and the woman never stops talking about her linen, chickens and eggs'. This denigratory, but apt pronouncement is to be found in a fifteenth-century model letter by the *pedagogium* teacher, Carolus Viruli.[57]

We can learn from a census of 1526 exactly where the students lived.[58] The total university population came to 1,821, excluding the inhabitants of the incorporated monasteries.[59] As the population of Louvain was *c.*19,000 at this date, students made up 10 per cent of the inhabitants. As a proportion of the population the University of Louvain was one of the largest if not *the* largest university in Europe. Students in Paris amounted to only 5 per cent of the population in the late Middle Ages; in Leyden in the seventeenth century they formed 3 to 5 per cent. In absolute figures Louvain was altogether the largest university of the Holy Roman Empire.[60]

Table: *Members of the University of Louvain in 1526*

No. in boarding establishments:		*No. living within the inner city*
—in *pedagogia*	313 (17.1%)	313
—in colleges	212 (11.6%)	212
—in religious institutions	42 (2.3%)	8
SUB-TOTAL	567 (31.1%)	533
No. lodging with private individuals:		
—'commensals' with university members	347 (19.0%)	282
—those who only hired a room with university members	85 (1.6%)	64
—'commensals' with citizens	65 (3.5%)	52
—those who only hired a room with citizens	455 (24.9%)	332
SUB-TOTAL	952 (52.2%)	730
No. in own (rented) house:	302 (16.5%)	183
TOTAL	1821 (100%)	1446

The table above reveals that in 1526 students boarding in public institutions formed 31 per cent of the total, those boarding with private individuals 52 per cent, while those who lived in their own house comprised 16.5 per cent. There is a further distinction to be made between 'commensals' who had board and lodging and the 'camerists' who only rented a room and therefore had to provide their own food. It was also possible to lodge either with members of the university, generally older students or professors who exercised a little supervision, or with citizens. Those who had lodged with citizens were the students who really lived out and they formed the largest group. In the fifteenth century that group was probably larger still. More than half the living-out students were 'camerists' lodging with single women or widows, which shows that the phenomenon of the student landlady already then was commonplace. Nearly 60 per cent of the 'camerists' were students of law, c.30 per cent were arts students, and the other 10 per cent studied theology.[61]

As usual in medieval universities the law students especially abused their freedom and regularly ran riot in Louvain. This hindered their studies and was the cause of enormous irritation to the university and city authorities. In 1477 Duke Charles the Bold intervened, compelling all law students to take up lodgings in boarding establishments, the *tutelae*, until their bachelor's degree. Fortunately for the future lawyers the duke was killed in a battle near Nancy, three days after the proclamation of this draconian measure. The reform remained a dead letter[62] and discipline problems continued. In the seventeenth century 80 per cent of offences at the university were still being committed by law students and the worst rioters were still the 'camerists'.[63]

On the basis of the census the concentration of members of the university can be calculated per block of houses. From the plan (Fig. 1) one can see that the university community much preferred to live in the centre of the city: nearly 80 per cent lived within the inner city wall. To be more precise, the majority of university members were to be found near the heart of the university, the halls, *vicus* and *pedagogia*. The area close to the inner city wall formed a secondary point of attraction because of its peaceful and agreeable surroundings, an area of large vegetable plots, orchards and even vineyards. Conversely, one can observe how students and professors carefully avoided the busy commercial centre round the Old Market, Brussels Street and Shipstreet. The few colleges which were established there were ensconced within blocks of houses so that noise from the city would hardly be audible. A typical example of this was the location of the *Collegium Trilingue* or Busleyden's College (Fig. 2).[64]

Most colleges and *pedagogia* began on a small scale with the purchase of a house but they expanded in the course of time until they had virtually taken over a whole block of houses. The develop-

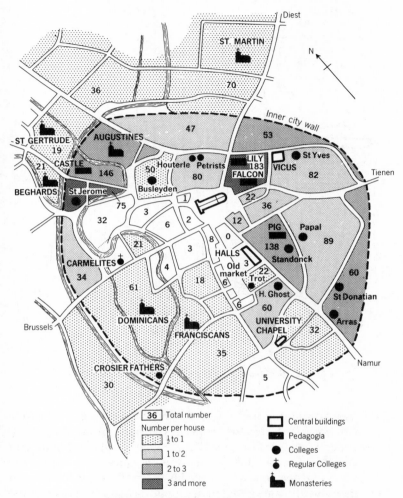

Fig. 1: *Concentration of university members at Louvain in 1526*

ment of Lily *pedagogium* (Fig. 3)[65] and of Holy Ghost College
(Fig. 4)[66] were typical. Holy Ghost College was the first college to
be established in Louvain. It was mostly intended for poor theology
students and was situated close to the halls in Prooststreet (now
Namur Street). The institution then spread from the old brewery
chamber 'Hollant' (A) in a westerly and southerly direction (B and

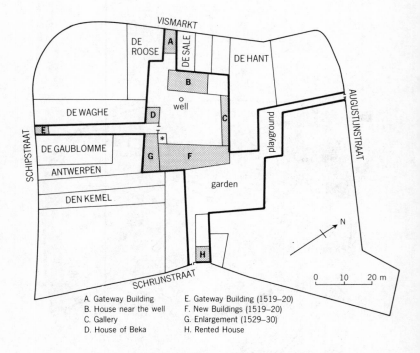

Fig. 2: *Busleyden's College (Trilingue) about 1530*

C). It is worth noting that this first college was almost exclusively built with donations from the people of Louvain. From 1411 to 1450 the founder, known as Louis the Rich, regularly had a seat in the city government and for a while he also was the ducal land agent. The foundation and the endowment of this first college for the poor in 1445 undoubtedly came about in the euphoria and enthusiasm of the pioneering years when the city tried to provide 'its' university with all it needed. A considerable expansion of the college took place in 1513 through Catharina Pynnock, the sister of the well-known Louvain bailiff Lodewijk Pynnock. She too lived during the early years of the university.[67]

The institutions of Louvain University gradually spread out over the area of the city, if initially the development was hardly spectacular (Fig. 5). At first members of these university institutions were

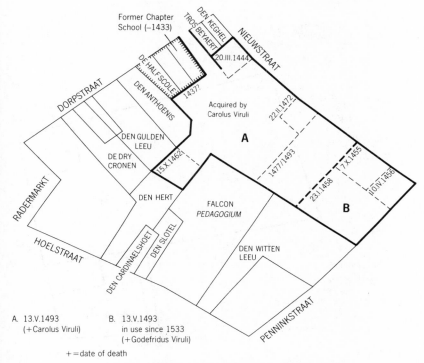

Fig. 3: *Property of Viruli College (Lily* pedagogium*)*

satisfied with a housing complex with sometimes a vegetable plot, orchard or recreation ground outside the centre. From the sixteenth century changes came about. As a consequence of a devaluation of the coinage and inflation the academics increasingly bought property which had proved to be a safer investment than the traditional hereditary rents. Eventually goods in mortmain of which the city government was very wary became a problem. When the Papal College was founded in 1523 by Adrian VI, the town council raised the alarm for the first time in the history of the university. It refused to grant permission for the purchase of any estate and gave as its reason the *Joyeuse Entrée* of the Archduke Charles (a constitutional law promulgated in 1515). The town council maintained this stand for four years in spite of pressure from the Emperor, the High Court at Mechlin and the Governess of the Netherlands. In the end the city

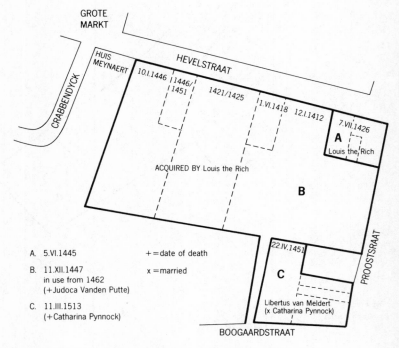

Fig. 4: *Property of Holy Ghost College*

backed down but on condition that apart from young men from Utrecht, birthplace of the founder Adrianus Florentii, young men from Louvain too would have preference in obtaining scholarships at the Papal College. This is a neat example of good diplomacy.[68]

7. The Louvain students

Apart from endowments attached to Holy Ghost and the Papal Colleges few scholarships were established in Louvain by or for its people. This was understandable because Louvain's native students already studied at less cost than others. At the turn of the sixteenth century more students came from Louvain itself than from Antwerp and Brussels, although Antwerp numbered three times as many inhabitants and Brussels had double the population.[69] Louvain

University recruited 80 per cent of its students from the Low Countries. Of the students from the Netherlands 35 per cent came from Brabant, 19 per cent from Flanders, 14.8 per cent from Holland, 8.6 per cent from Hainault, 6.5 per cent from Zeeland and 4.9 per cent from Liège. The other regions each represented less than 1.5 per cent of the intake. In all only 19 per cent of the students came from French-speaking regions.[70] On the other hand, many students travelled from the Netherlands to foreign universities, in the first place to Cologne,[71] and in the case of law students mainly to Orléans. The natives of Louvain were, however, disinclined to undertake long journeys for their studies. During the period 1430–1600 only 8 per cent of Louvain aldermen with a university degree possessed a diploma from a foreign university, this in contrast with 31 per cent of Antwerp aldermen, 34 per cent of the aldermen of Ukkel, and no fewer than 51 per cent of the councillors in the Brabant Council.[72] The presence of a university in Louvain itself must be the most significant explanation for this.

8. Conclusion

Let us finally draw up a balance of the advantages and disadvantages of having a university in Louvain.

Advantages
The university provided an important stimulus for the Louvain citizenry to study at a university. Of all towns in the Netherlands Louvain provided the majority of the students. The city government too was well educated.

In the fifteenth century the city managed to keep its hold over the university through a monopoly in appointments.

From the beginning of the sixteenth century the university flourished whilst the economy of Louvain was going downhill. The university developed into one of the most significant reasons for Louvain's existence and it represented an increasingly important clientele for Louvain traders.[73] In the footsteps of the university Louvain also became one of the most important bookprinting centres in the Netherlands. In the fifteenth century 269 publications came out in Louvain printed and published by nine printers, a record only broken by Antwerp where eleven printers produced 392 publications.[74]

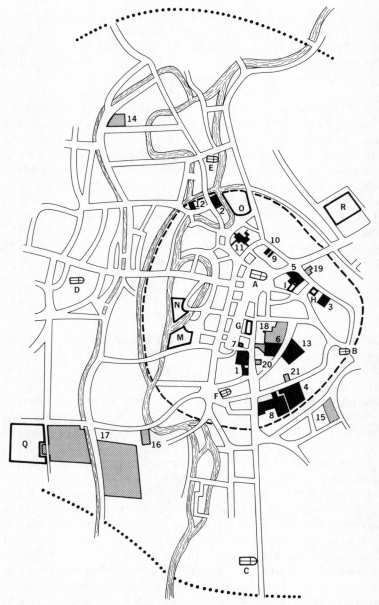

Fig. 5: *The Colleges of Louvain and their Property in 1530*

COLLEGES (location)
1. H. Ghost
2. Gomple
3. St Yves
4. St Donatian
5. Viruli
6. Standonck
7. Trot
8. Arras
9. Petrists
10. Houterle
11. Busleyden
12. St Jerome
13. Papal

PROPERTY (belonging to the Colleges)
Gardens, meadows, farms
14. Gompel College
15. Viruli College
16. Standonck College
17. Arras College
other
18. Standonck College (Pig *Pedagogium*)
19. Standonck College (rented houses)
20. Arras College (rented houses)
21. Papal College

PARISH CHURCHES
A. St Peter
B. St Michael
C. St Quentin
D. St Jacob
E. St Gertrude

UNIVERSITY BUILDINGS
F. Chapel
G. Halls
H. *Vicus*
I. Falcon *Pedagogium*
J. Castle *Pedagogium* (see 2)
K. Lily *Pedagogium* (see 5)
L. Pig *Pedagogium* (see 18)

INCORPORATED INSTITUTIONS
M. Franciscans
N. Dominicans
O. Augustinians
P. Carmelites
Q. Carthusians
R. St Martin

Disadvantages

Continual friction between members of the university and the inhabitants regularly disturbed the city's tranquil atmosphere.[75] Especially indiscipline and evasion of excise duties roused hostility among the citizens. In general, however, this friction did not permanently harm the fundamental understanding between city and university.

The danger of an increase in goods in mortmain was great. We must also remember that the university attracted a large number of monks and nuns. If you number these with the members of the university it amounts to 16 per cent of the city population in 1526. Louvain was thus a true enclave of popery.

Apart from being trade customers the practical advantage of a university in one's own city was rather slight. The presence of lawyers probably brought more lawsuits than peace. The presence of medical doctors was no guarantee of better health. Certainly in the fifteenth century the medical course was almost totally theoretical. The only measure taken with regard to the population was the following: a medical doctor who was called to a dying man had to ensure that he first confessed. If he did not the doctor had to leave him to his fate.[76] Finally, the presence of theologians caused more intolerance than devotion. And do not forget in this connection the unbridled benefice system whereby pastoral care was being systematically neglected. On the other hand, the Louvain colleges would, from the sixteenth century, take care of the training of a new kind of priest who had to re-Christianize the countryside and throw up a dam against Lutheranism and Calvinism. Louvain thus acted as the breeding ground of the Catholic seminaries in the Netherlands.[77]

To conclude: the university was neither a blessing nor a curse. The city of Louvain had ventured on an enterprise of which it could not possibly have foreseen all the consequences. But Louvain did gain an image and influence which far exceeded the borders of the Netherlands. And that was the reason why it had all started, viz. the prestige and honour of the city. In that sense the city ultimately succeeded in its goal.

Weidestraat 13
3031 Oud-Heverlee
Belgium

REFERENCES

The following works or sources will be referred to in an abbreviated form in the notes: *Doc.* = *Documents relatifs à l'histoire de l'université de Louvain*, ed. E. Reusens (5 vols.; Louvain, 1881–1903); *Leuvense stedelijke archiefbronnen* = L. Van Buyten, 'Leuvense stedelijke archiefbronnen betreffende de Oude Universiteit Leuven', *Arca Lovaniensis*, III (Louvain, 1974), 103–33; *Rectorale rechtbank* = C. Vandenghoer, *De rectorale rechtbank van de oude Leuvense universiteit* (Brussels, 1987); *Salaires* = J. Paquet, *Salaires et prébendes des professeurs de l'université de Louvain au XVe siècle* (Léopoldville, 1958); *Stadsfinanciën* = R. Van Uytven, *Stadsfinanciën en stadsekonomie te Leuven van de XIIe tot het einde der XVIe eeuw* (Brussels, 1961); *Statuts Université* = 'Statuts de l'université de Louvain antérieurs à l'année 1459', ed. A. Van Hove, in *Bulletin de la Commission royale d'histoire*, LXXVI (1907), 597–662; *Universities* = J. IJsewijn and J. Paquet, *The Universities in the Late Middle Ages* (Louvain, 1978).

1. H. Rashdall, F. M. Powicke and A. B. Emden, *The Universities of Europe in the Middle Ages* (vol. III; Oxford, 1969), p. 106. A similar conclusion in A. B. Cobban, *The Medieval English Universities, Oxford and Cambridge to c.1500* (Berkeley, Los Angeles, 1988), pp. 257–74.
2. J. Paquet, 'Bourgeois et universitaires à la fin du Moyen-Age. A propos du cas de Louvain', *Le Moyen Age*, LXVII (1961), 334–9.
3. A. G. Weiler, 'Les relations entre l'université de Louvain et l'université de Cologne au XVe siècle', in *Universities*, pp. 49–81.
4. Bull 9 Dec. 1425 by Pope Martin V, published in *Doc.*, i. 6.
5. E. J. M. Van Eijl, 'The Foundation of the University of Louvain', in *Universities*, pp. 29–41.
6. W. T. M. Frijhoff, 'Hoger onderwijs als inzet van stedelijke naijver in de vroegmoderne tijd', in P. B. M. Blaas and J. Van Herwaarden, *Stedelijke naijver* (The Hague, 1986), pp. 82–127.
7. City Accounts, Louvain 1425–1430, published in *Doc.*, i. 3–4, 19–23, 74–6, 104–11.
8. '... ende de stat daer omme groten cost gedaen ende geleden heeft ...' Act of 20 June 1426 by the city of Louvain, published in *Leuvense stedelijke archiefbronnen*, p. 118.
9. See below in the text under the headings 'Fiscal immunity' and 'Jurisdiction'.
10. '... vander scolen van Loven te hulpen, omme dat hij II grote meesters hadde ontboden de scole te regeren, der vele gesellen van buten toe quamen'. City accounts Louvain 2 Dec. 1418. Cited by L. Van Buyten, 'De oorsprong en de stichting van de Leuvense universiteit', in *550 jaar Universiteit Leuven. Catalogus* (Louvain, 1976), pp. 26–7.
11. *Stadsfinanciën*, pp. 645–6.
12. Van Buyten, pp. 23–5.
13. Bull 9 Dec. 1425 by Pope Martin V, published in *Doc.*, i. 6.

68   *History of Universities*

14. 'Verum opidum prefatum ... adeo rerum copia, aeris temperie, multitu-
    dinis capacitate atque domorum et aliarum rerum necessariarum com-
    moditate per Dei graciam est repertum, quod ad huiusmodi receptan-
    dum refovendumque studium aptum plurimum et ydoneum existere
    perhibetur': ibid.
15. Between 1428 and 1441 the city spent an average of 1,456 guilders per
    financial year. See *Salaires*, p. 9, and compare *Stadsfinanciën*, p. 243.
16. More about the *pedagogia*, see E. De Maesschalck, 'De strijd om de
    Leuvense pedagogieën (1426–1569). Eigendomsrecht en macht in de
    faculteit van de artes', *De Brabantse folklore*, 243 (Sept. 1984), 163–201.
17. 3,000 *plak* (= a type of coin) or 50 guilders. See *Stadsfinanciën*, p. 561.
18. *Salaires*, pp. 7–12.
19. Act 9 Oct. 1428 by Duke Philip of Saint-Pol, published in *Doc.*, i. 81–90.
    Also, see *Salaires*, pp. 17–19. The benefices were: 7 St Peter's Louvain,
    2 St Goedele's Brussels, 2 St Gommarus' Lier, 1 St Peter's Anderlecht,
    1 St Peter's Hilvarenbeek, 1 St John's 's Hertogenbosch, 1 St Oeden-
    rode.
20. Bull 23 May 1443 by Pope Eugenius IV, published in *Doc.*, i. 133–42.
    Also, see *Salaires*, pp. 20–3. The benefices came from: St Peter's
    Louvain, Hakendover, Holsbeek, Korbeek-Lo, Neerlinter, Knegsel,
    Burcht, Schelle, Boom and Erps.
21. City accounts, Louvain 1442–1445, published in *Doc.*, i. 180–208.
22. In 1446 the city share in the paying of salaries fell to 635 guilders. It
    gradually increased again but in the fifteenth century it would rarely
    exceed 1,000 guilders per annum. See *Salaires*, p. 9.
23. *Salaires*, p. 19.
24. Bull 9 December 1425 by Pope Martin V, published in *Doc.*, i. 15–18.
25. Bull 28 April 1483 by Pope Sixtus IV, published in *Doc.*, i. 227–34.
26. See A. Fierens, 'Les ambitions de la faculté des arts de Louvain au
    début du XVIe siècle', in *Mélanges d'histoire offerts à Moëller* (vol. II;
    Louvain and Paris, 1914), pp. 56–68; also J. Roegiers, 'Benoemings-
    recht', in *550 jaar universiteit Leuven. Catalogus* (Louvain, 1976), pp.
    46 ff.
27. R. R. Post, 'Studiën over paus Adriaan VI', *Archief voor de geschiedenis
    van de katholieke kerk in Nederland*, III (1961), 341–50.
28. C. Buve, 'Lijst van eenige pastoors en beneficianten, die de lessen der
    Hoogeschool volgden in de 16de eeuw', in *Bijdragen tot de geschiedenis,
    bijzonderlijk van het aloude Hertogdom Brabant*, I (1902), 282–9.
29. *Salaires*, pp. 23–9.
30. K. Bafort, 'Bijdrage tot de vroegste geschiedenis van de Faculteit der
    geneeskunde aan de universiteit te Leuven', licentiate dissertation
    (Louvain, 1958), pp. 145ff.
31. '... dat de stad alle jaeren sal mogen haere doctoren veranderen, op
    ende af setten na haren genuchten ende boven den selven doctoren ...
    maken inequal, na dat hen des redelyc dunken sal'. See *Salaires*, pp. 26–
    8.

32. Paquet, 'Bourgeois et universitaires à la fin du Moyen-Age', 334 ff.
33. H. De Ridder-Symoens, 'De universitaire vorming van de Brabantse stadsmagistraat en stadsfunktionarissen. Leuven en Antwerpen (1430–1580)', in *Verslagboek vijfde colloquium De Brabantse Stad* ('s Hertogenbosch, 1978), pp. 22–126. It may be that the level of education of the well-off in Louvain was higher than might appear from the figures relating to the aldermen. We know that many citizens refused to serve in the city government because they would then lose their university privileges. This was so general that according to a complaint of 1495 'the families of Louvain are destined to disappear'. See *Stadsfinanciën*, p. 122.
34. F. Claeys Bouuaert, *L'ancienne université de Louvain. Etudes et documents* (Louvain, 1956), pp. 122–6.
35. Act 7 November 1426 by Duke John IV, published in *Doc.*, i. 39.
36. *Stadsfinanciën*, pp. 83–94; F. Claeys Bouuaert, pp. 38–41.
37. Report University Council 18 July–10 August 1432, published in *Actes ou procès-verbaux des séances tenues par le conseil de l'université de Louvain*, ed. E. Reusens (vol. I; Brussels, 1903); act 10 August 1432 by the city of Louvain, published in *Doc.*, i. 209–12.
38. Review of the problems in *Stadsfinanciën*, pp. 84–92.
39. E. De Maesschalck, 'Cameristen of kotstudenten te Leuven in 1531–32', *Lias* VII:1 (1980), 61–92. This study was done on the basis of such documents in the city accounts.
40. Act 1 February 1488, published in *Leuvense stedelijke archiefbronnen*, pp. 128–33.
41. Weiler, 'Les relations entre l'université de Louvain et l'université de Cologne', pp. 70–2.
42. With regard to the Duke of Brabant, see *Rectorale rechtbank*, pp. 26–7. With regard to the bishop of Liège, see *Rectorale rechtbank*, pp. 33–37 as well as *Doc.*, i. 26–50, and M. Bruwier, 'Les conflits juridictionnels et bénéfiaux entre l'université de Louvain et l'évêque de Liège de 1425 à 1560', *Revue d'histoire ecclésiastique* XLIV (1949), 569–82.
43. Bull 9 Sept. 1427 by Pope Martin V, published in *Doc.*, i. 57–9; bull 7 May 1469 by Pope Paul II, published in *Doc.*, i. 220–3. Also, see *Rectorale rechtbank*, pp. 202–8. The pope nominated a number of dignitaries as possible *conservatores* and left the actual choice to the university. These included: the abbot of Saint-Gertrude, the abbot of Parc Abbey near Louvain, the bishop of Utrecht, the dean of St Gudule's in Brussels, the dean of St Peter's Louvain, and the dean of St Jacob's Louvain. In practice the abbot of St Gertrude held the post.
44. *Statuts Université*, pp. 597–662; 'Statuts primitifs de la faculté des arts de Louvain', ed. E. Reusens, *Bulletin de la Commission royale d'histoire* 3 IX (1867), 147–206. For a survey, see E. De Maesschalck, 'Tuchtproblemen met rechtsstudenten in het 15de eeuwse Leuven. Pogingen tot oplossing', in *Liber amicorum Dr. J. Scheerder* (Louvain, 1987), pp. 189–201.

45. Act 6 June 1457 by Duke Philip the Good (Louvain, *Stadsarchief*, no. 1369).
46. Act 28 September 1466 by Duke Philip the Good, published in *Doc.*, i. 217–20.
47. *Statuts Université*, supplement VII/2 (=28 May 1465).
48. Report, Council of the Faculty of the Arts, 2 June 1485 (Brussels, Algemeen Rijksarchief, Fonds Universiteit Leuven, No. 712, fo. 29 r).
49. *Doc.*, i. 331–56; *Rectorale rechtbank*, pp. 117–27; C. Vandenghoer, 'Criminaliteit en ordehandhaving binnen de Leuvense Civitas Academica', in *Liber amicorum Dr. J. Scheerder*, pp. 203–8. The *promotor* has an affinity with the proctors of Oxford and Cambridge.
50. *Rectorale rechtbank*, p. 32.
51. Act 3 January 1477 by Duke Charles the Bold, published in *Doc.*, i. 693.
52. '... violeren souden der liede kindere': according to the author who continued the *Brabantsche Geesten*. See E. J. M. Van Eijl, 'The Foundation of the University of Louvain', p. 30.
53. Vandenghoer, 'Criminaliteit', p. 216.
54. Ibid., pp. 213–14. Admittedly in the seventeenth century it is generally assumed students all over Europe were better behaved.
55. *Statuts Université*, supplement IV (=26 April 1456); act 3 January 1457 by Council of Brabant, published in *Leuvense stedelijke archiefbronnen*, pp. 125–7.
56. 'Inprimis statuimus et ordinamus quod quilibet doctor, magister, licentiatus, baccalarius et scolaris in loco honesto et decenti in opido Iovaniensi vel ejus suburbiis moretur, si presens voluerit reputari': *Statuts Université*, XIV/1.
57. J. IJsewijn, 'The "Declamatio Lovaniensis de tutelae severitate". Students against Academic Authority at Louvain in 1481', *Lias* III: 1 (1976), 9.
58. J. Cuvelier, *Les Dénombrements de foyers en Brabant (XIVe–XVIe siècle)* (Brussels, 1912), pp. 304–27.
59. The number of those actually studying can be estimated at c.1450; the number of members of the university and regular and secular clergy taken together comprised 2,750 or c. 16 per cent of the population. See E. De Maesschalck, 'Scholarship Grants and Colleges established at the University of Louvain up to 1530', in *Universities*, p. 485; *Stadsfinanciën*, p. 484.
60. Frijhoff, 'Hoger onderwijs als inzet van stedelijke naijver in de vroegmoderne tijd', p. 87.
61. De Maesschalck, 'Cameristen of kotstudenten', 62–3.
62. De Maesschalck, 'Tuchtproblemen met rechtsstudenten', pp. 189–201.
63. *Rectorale rechtbank*, pp. 93–4.
64. The plan was first published by E. De Maesschalck, 'De gebouwen van het Busleydenkollege in Erasmus' tijd', in J. IJsewijn and J. Roegiers, *Charisterium H. De Vocht* (Louvain, 1979), pp. 64–73. It is a corrected version of the plan by H. De Vocht, *History of the Foundation and the*

Rise of the Collegium Trilingue Lovaniense (Vol. II; Louvain, 1953), p. 46.

65. E. De Maesschalck, 'Kollegesstichtingen aan de Universiteit te Leuven (1425–1530)', Ph.D. thesis (Louvain, 1977), pp. 392–401, and appendix 48.
66. Ibid., pp. 288–94, and appendix 46.
67. Ibid., pp. 146–60, and 208–210; also *Doc.*, iii. 10–13.
68. De Maesschalck, 'Scholarship Grants and Colleges', pp. 489–90; Id., 'Kollegestichtingen aan de Universiteit te Leuven', pp. 1047–50.
69. Between 1485 and 1527 765 students from the town of Louvain were registered at the university or 4% of the students from the Netherlands, this against 3.9% from Antwerp, 2.9% from Brussels, 2.9% from Mechlin, 2% from Lille, 1.9% from Ghent, 1.8% from Amsterdam, 1.5% from 's Hertogenbosch, 1.5% from Bruges, 1.5% from Mons, 1.3% from Haarlem, 1.3% from Delft, 1.3% from Diest, 1.1% from Zierikzee, 1.1% from Dordrecht. See H. De Prins, 'De inschrijvingsfrequentie van de Leuvense universiteit (1485–1527)', licentiate thesis (Louvain 1967), pp. 101–2.
70. Ibid., pp. 90–1.
71. 28% of the students in Cologne in the period 1485–1527 came from the Netherlands. See Ibid., pp. 185–190.
72. H. De Ridder-Symoens, 'Milieu social, études universitaires et carrière des conseillers au Conseil de Brabant (1430–1600)', in *Liber amicorum J. Buntinx* (Louvain, 1981), p. 294.
73. This is shown e.g. in texts from the years 1535 and 1538. See *Stadsfinanciën*, pp. 484–5.
74. See J. Dauwe, 'Het Leuvense boekbedrijf', in *Geschiedenis van het stadsgewest Leuven tot omstreeks 1600* (Louvain, 1980), pp. 263–71.
75. Already quite early on the city saw itself forced to punish every abuse committed by its citizens against the university's members or institutions by organizing a penitential pilgrimage to Saint-Josse-sur-Mer. See act of the City Council, 12 June 1429, published in *Leuvense stedelijke archiefbronnen*, p. 122.
76. This measure was taken by the University Council in 1469. See J. Molanus, *Historiae Lovaniensium libri* XIV (Brussels, 1861), p. 572.
77. E. De Maesschalck, 'De invloed van de Leuvense universiteitscolleges op het ontstaan en de uitbouw van de seminaries in de Nederlanden', in *Verslagboek zesde colloquium 'De Brabantse stad'* (Antwerp, 1981), pp. 7–13.

Ovidius Methodizatus: the *Metamorphoses* of Ovid in a Sixteenth-Century Paris College

Ann Blair

I

In the first issue of this journal Anthony Grafton introduced a novel approach to the study of humanist education by analysing the manuscript annotations entered in the margins of a *Sammelband* of schooltexts used in the final form of a late-sixteenth-century Paris college.[1] He found that the notes taken by one Gerald de Mayres on Horace's *Odes* among other texts at the lectures of Claude Mignault, although conventional in offering short moral lessons and information on ancient *realia* of different kinds, distinctively avoided parallels with Greek literature, readily available from the great commentaries of Lambin, and instead focused on the formal structure of the poems and on the different types of arguments used by Horace. But Claude Mignault was not just any obscure teacher of the 'first class' at the Collège de Reims in 1572–3. In addition to a commentary on Alciato's emblem-book, he published in 1577 a commentary on Omer Talon's *Rhetoric* and argued in support of its Ramist theses. Mignault even drew material for his lectures at Reims from Ramus's own commentary on the *Odes*: Mignault can thus be identified as a fairly explicit follower of Ramus's 'single method' in his years at the Collège de Reims and this commitment alone might account for his predominant concern with the argumentative structure of all the texts that he assigned. It is with especially good reason then that Grafton wonders whether Mignault was a 'typical regent master'.[2]

A second case study based on student annotations taken under remarkably similar circumstances is made possible by the recent acquisition by Princeton University of another *Sammelband* of schooltexts.[3] Although such sources are rarely extant given the constant use to which they were subjected and the inexpensive nature of the pamphlet editions they contained, this volume is a model of its genre due to the clarity and diligence with which its student owner maintained it. This unique and hitherto unstudied source offers as direct a view as possible of the largely oral instruction that took place in the college classroom. School regulations, humanist pedagogical manuals and textbooks or printed commentaries on the texts assigned in class can all help to reconstruct different aspects of a secondary education in the Renaissance;[4] but only the notes of an actual schoolboy can reveal what exactly a master succeeded in passing on to his pupil. Student notes such as those gathered in Princeton's *Sammelband* effectively reveal, for a specific time and place, both the tacit assumptions and skills and the explicit knowledge imparted to a young member of the educated élite as he was taught to read selected texts from the classical canon.

The *Sammelband* in question, with its painstakingly neat and abundant notes, was the property of a Pierre Guyon in the 'third class' at the Parisian Collège de Lisieux in 1570–1. Subscriptions identify the lecturer as regent master Louis Godebert from Picardy, about whom nothing more is known. While Mignault's Reims and Godebert's Lisieux were both minor colleges which have not been studied individually, they were evidently comparable to better known colleges which delineated successive *ordines* to cover the equivalent of a secondary education in approximately six classes.[5] Students might enter in the middle of the curriculum or move rapidly from one class to the next, but the third class would have been less advanced than the first. Positioned between the lower forms which studied Latin grammar and the last form which focused on rhetoric, the crowning discipline in a system designed to develop Latin eloquence,[6] the third class at the Jesuits' Paris college (the Collège de Clermont) was devoted to the 'perfection of grammar',[7] and at the Protestant gymnasium of Strasburg it also included an introduction to the 'theory of rhetoric'.[8]

Although the two reading lists overlap in one place, Cicero's *De optimo genere oratorum*, the texts assigned in Pierre Guyon's third class are less numerous and generally simpler than those which Mignault covered with his top form; they also include fewer Greek texts.[9] Furthermore, just as Mignault included a manual not of rhetoric but of dialectic to give his students a taste of studies to come if they went on to the arts faculty, thus Godebert, in his lower form,

assigned handbooks not of grammar but of rhetoric, foreshadowing
a discipline in principle reserved for a later class. Both masters were
aware of their position within a system that promoted students
successively from grammar to rhetoric to dialectic and looked
beyond the topics specifically assigned to their level.

Guyon's *Sammelband* comprises fourteen separate works pub-
lished in Paris between 1551 and 1570,[10] predominantly by Denys du
Pré and Thomas Brumen, who specialized in school editions:[11]
Ringelberg, *Rhetorica*; a compendium of Quintilian's *Institutiones
oratoriae* II, III and V; Cicero, *De optimo genere oratorum*, *Pro M.
Marcello oratio*, *In M. Antonium Philippica nona*, *Pro lege Manilia*,
Pro O. Ligario and *Post reditum in Senatu oratio*; Ovid, *Metamorphoses* I, and selected elegies from *De ponto*; Virgil, *Aeneid* II; L.
Florus, *De gestis Romanorum*; Pliny the Younger, *De viris illustribus*[12] and Suetonius, *De claris grammaticis et rhetoribus*; a compendium of Jean Despautère's *De syllaborum quantitate*;[13] and finally,
on the last two pages, the 'Golden Verses of Pythagoras' in Greek
only, added without title page or colophon.[14] All but Cicero's *Pro
Marcello* and the Suetonius are annotated—some sparsely, others
abundantly—in the margins and on additional interleaved folios,
usually in an Italic cursive hand, adorned with pen flourishes and
carefully planned tapering.[15] The volume is bound in French calf
personalized with a gilt engraving of Guyon's name and two
favourite mottoes: 'in labore quies' and 'virescit vulnere virtus';[16] it
opens to a manuscript frontispiece complete with self-portrait and
quatrain.[17] We can assume that Guyon, like most students in
Parisian colleges, came from a well-to-do family,[18] but can conclude
little else from his display of adolescent exuberance.

The edition of Ovid selected by Godebert is similar to Mignault's
choice for the *Odes* of Horace.[19] While the odes constitute natural
units which were preceded in Mignault's edition by introductory
summaries, in Godebert's edition Ovid's continuous text is broken
into sections, each beginning with a 'most learned argument' attributed, probably spuriously, to Lactantius. As in Mignault's *Odes*
the text is supplied with brief running notes, in this case by Gilbertus
Longolius.[20] Longolius's annotations, first published in Cologne in
1534,[21] offer no textual variants,[22] but point in one or two words to
the topic covered, the figures of speech, types of arguments and
poetic metre used. Longolius is more expansive when offering
sources for Ovid's stories, often Greek texts from which he quotes in

the original. Although Guyon's annotations never allude to the printed notes, they cover roughly the same range of material, excepting Longolius's erudite quotes from Greek authors and interest in scansion. Despite the presence of Despautère's manual on scansion in the *Sammelband*, questions of metre do not appear in the manuscript commentary; Despautère's *De quantitate* itself is lightly annotated and, as we shall see, Godebert remains thoroughly uninterested in the poetic aspects of the *Metamorphoses*.

School editions of Ovid such as the one Godebert selected represent a particular phase in the history of Ovid commentary, characteristic of France in the period 1530–80.[23] Editions designed for schoolboys offered publishers a delightfully stable market and the widespread use of the *Metamorphoses*, particularly books I and XV, as an introduction to poetry helps to explain the enormous popularity of editions of Ovid, which numbered nearly three hundred in the sixteenth century, as compared with the one hundred editions of Virgil and ninety of Horace published in the same period.[24] Until the 1530s most editions of the *Metamorphoses* included a printed commentary which dwarfed the text to a small section at the centre of the page. Re-editions of Bersuire's *Ovidius moralizatus* and the allegorical and typological commentaries by the Lyonnais Dominican Peter Lavinius coexisted alongside editions influenced by the humanist movement, notably with the commentaries of Raphael Regius, a distinguished professor of rhetoric and Latin grammar at the University of Padua (1482–6 and 1503–9).[25] Many editions sported the annotations of both Lavinius and Regius, as publishers welcomed the accumulation of different commentaries, however disparate in approach, in one edition. By the 1530s, however, the fairly plain school edition prevailed. Although some of Ovid's less known works were still the object of printed commentary, no editions of the *Metamorphoses* with full commentary were published in France after 1528.[26] By the 1580s the editions of the *Metamorphoses*, still designed for schoolboys, had evolved again, to include specially expurgated editions of Ovid favoured by Jesuit teachers, and 'rhetorical' editions which emphasized variant readings and figures of speech.[27] With the editions from the intermediate period, such as those used by Mignault or Godebert, the bulk of the commentary was transmitted by the master in oral lessons; consequently the texts were supplied with wide margins and interleaved folios,[28] on which Guyon neatly marked out in red ink the space reserved for annotations.

Not only did Godebert use the same type of edition as Mignault, but he also proceeded to instruct his students in many of the same ways. Like Geraldus de Mayres, Pierre Guyon took down in haste and in a minuscule hand an interlinear paraphrase, presumably under dictation from his master.[29] What little French appears in Guyon's notes occurs in translations of mottoes or proverbs added without relevance around the text.[30] French was generally forbidden in all aspects of college life and Latin was taught primarily in Latin.[31] The paraphrase was thus no doubt in part designed to insure that the pupils understood the text word by word, although some terms would also be explained in more detail in the margin. But the exercise provided synonyms not only for difficult but also for simple words. In offering unusual words to 'explain' obvious ones, the paraphrase can be understood as training for the students' writing skills, teaching them to vary their vocabulary and to serve as their own thesauri. It was not an exercise reserved for poetry, nor even for classical works, since all the texts in the collection, including Ringelberg's *Rhetorica*, are paraphrased in the same way. The paraphrase evidently constituted the first part of the analysis of each passage, running ahead of the commentary, at least in the sessions that can be delineated by Guyon's use of inks of different colours.[32] In Guyon's notes the paraphrase continues some sixty lines beyond the end of the commentary;[33] when it stops, about one hundred lines short of the end of Ovid's Book I, it does not end abruptly, but rather with spotty coverage of the last nine lines, with no discernible grammatical or linguistic logic to the words selected for treatment.[34] It seems clear none the less that the paraphrase was taken down in class rather than as a student exercise. Haste apparently forced Guyon to abandon his careful italic hand for a French cursive, less elegant and less legible to us, which he otherwise used primarily at moments of relaxed attention, for example when adding a subscription, motto or proverb, particularly in the vernacular.[35]

The commentary was the focus of the lesson, and was probably dictated as well.[36] Godebert draws on a number of sources to provide the wide-ranging comments characteristic of the *modus parisiensis*. Although he could have found much of his material in any number of works, similarities of expression and specific combinations of comments suggest that Calepinus's *Dictionarium octo linguarum* and its counterpart for proper names, Gesner's *Onomasticon propriorum nominum*, were among Godebert's usual works of reference.[37] Caelius Rhodiginus's *Lectiones antiquae* and Polydore Vergil's *De inventoribus rerum*, in addition to other, as yet unidentified, compendia, probably suggested cross-references to other ancient works. Above all, Godebert consulted existing commentaries on the *Metamorphoses*. He clearly aligns himself with the humanist approach of Regius and Micyllus, a later commentator, as opposed to the moralizing and allegorizing school of Lavinius.[38] Despite differences on specific points, Godebert provides grammatical or interpretive commentary cast in basically the same mould as Regius's; in his rhetorical analysis Godebert expands on, but does not significantly diverge from Regius. But in the low-level dialectical analysis that Godebert provides throughout the text, he differs from earlier commentators and gives an overall emphasis to his reading that clearly locates it amid contemporary concerns for modes of argument and persuasion.[39]

If Mignault had unusual reasons, given his commitment to Ramism, for treating Horace's *Odes* as a series of arguments to be analysed for their formal structure, there is no indication that Godebert was anything other than an obscure regent master drawing his lecture material not from original inspiration nor from any particular 'system' but from a basic array of reference works and, when he added to these, from the interests of his colleagues and students. Godebert was not a committed Ramist, for the controversy that raged in the 1560s and 1570s over the Ramist method elicited published responses from those who took sides. But evidently there was no need to be a Ramist in the late sixteenth century to be simply concerned with methods of argumentation. Ramus served as a lightning rod for debate on the nature of dialectic and rhetoric precisely because the interest of contemporaries for these issues had already been aroused and continued to be fed. It would not be surprising if that interest were first developed in the colleges where the cultured élite received the basic education that enabled them to appreciate the controversy even if they did not participate in it. If we can take Godebert to be an undistinguished grammar master of his time—and the evidence, or rather the lack thereof, suggests that we can—at the level of ordinary secondary school instruction it appears to have been perfectly normal and uncontroversial to teach schoolboys to classify arguments just as when younger they had learned to parse sentences.

Godebert does not go as far as Mignault toward reducing his texts to strictly reasoned and technically labelled arguments. He does not venture for example into the syllogistic analysis characteristic of the dialectic practised in an arts faculty; nor does he make bold methodological claims about the all-encompassing nature of dialectic characteristic of the Ramist method. Indeed by introducing technical terms found in Melanchthon's *Erotemata dialectices* into his analysis, Godebert expands rather than restricts the purview of rhetoric. Although he is clearly no Ramist, Godebert still shares with Mignault a deep and persistent interest in methods of argumentation and presentation. Beneath the differences, often loudly proclaimed, between the methodological schools, this fascination with dialectic in its various forms stands out as highly characteristic of late sixteenth-century French thought. While the theoretical aspects of this interest in rhetoric and dialectic have already been analysed at some length, what Guyon's abundant lecture notes can give us is a detailed picture of how a presumably ordinary grammar master like Godebert actually implemented these approaches in the classroom, in the most unlikely context of lectures on Ovid's *Metamorphoses* to young adolescents.[40]

II

Godebert's first and most important task is to provide a grammatical analysis designed to establish the meaning of the text. By comparison with Mignault teaching Horace, Godebert spends more time on tasks of this kind; in addition to the less advanced level of his pupils, the more unusual vocabulary found in Ovid's *Metamorphoses* and the less partisan nature of Godebert's concern for dialectic may account for this difference in emphasis. The 'grammar' of interest to Godebert is not, however, what the modern reader might at first expect, since he never discusses the form of a word. While it is true that by the third class there was no need to rehearse the basics of the Latin language, even Regius, whose commentary derived from lectures delivered at the University of Padua, has a few comments concerning purely linguistic problems, both grammatical and philological.

Regius points out for example the patronymic forms in 'Coricidas nymphas' (1. 320) and 'Cephisidas undas' (1. 369),[41] while Godebert who also comments on these two phrases does not. Furthermore Regius alone mentions that aspect of Latin grammar that first comes to the mind of the modern student, when he explains for line 379 that 'Themi' is the Greek vocative form.[42] Regius also discusses variant readings.[43] He asserts for example that 'Amphitrite' should not be spelled 'Amphitrites',[44] while Godebert's comment on the term only explains its meaning, both in mythological and etymological terms.[45] And Regius calls for an emendation in line 462: '*iritare* [the text in his edition reads *irritare*]: to provoke, to stimulate. But it is written with one "r". For with two "r" 's it means to make void and without effect',[46] Unlike Regius, Godebert does not discuss words from a formal rather than a semantic or etymological point of view; his 'grammatical' task is to interpret the meaning of the text, while rhetoric and dialectic discuss its form. There is no place in Godebert's lessons for philological or any formal analysis of an individual word.

Godebert's most basic 'grammatical' duty is to define new words: nectar 'is said to be the beverage of the gods, as ambrosia is their food'; *muscus* 'is a low grass with small leaves which usually grows in humid and watery places and has a heavy odor'; *murex* (purple-fish) 'is a fish of the shellfish variety from whose blood purple is made'; *iugerum* (acre) 'is that amount of field which one pair of cattle can plough in one day'; *pellex* [or *paelex*] is a woman 'who has slept with a married man'.[47] When, on rare occasions concentrated near the beginning of the text,[48] Godebert offers an etymology, it is in an effort to provide a deeper understanding of the meaning of the word. 'That region of the world which rises above the four elements is called *caelum* either because it is embossed (*celata*) with heavenly bodies and stars as if with gems, or because it is concave, for the Greeks call what is concave κοῖλον, or because it hides (*celet*) and contains all these things here below.'[49] Or *lucus* 'properly means an impenetrable forest which, because the sun shines very little through it, is called *lucus* by antiphrasis'.[50] More straightforward etymologies serve directly to explain the meaning of a new word. *Zephyrus* 'or *Zoiphoros*, that is life-bearing, blows from the West at the equinox and the Latins call it *favonius*'.[51] Or 'the sceptre of Neptune is called [trident] because it has three teeth and points'.[52] In addition to defining new words Godebert glosses terms that he finds characteristic of Ovid's usage. 'By the name *fera* [Ovid] understands all kinds of brute animals which live on the earth, which are called thus because they move with all their force.'[53] And when Godebert finds Ovid's usage contradictory, he at least makes it explicit: 'by the term "ether" [Ovid] means sometimes "sky" and sometimes "fire", because of the very small weight of which it consists'.[54]

Above all, however, Godebert explains difficult passages. Sometimes this means dispelling an ambiguity. When the poet says that 'the maker of the world did not permit the winds to hold the air *passim*', Godebert specifies: 'the poet does not mean by these words that some part of the region of air is lacking in winds [i.e. *passim* understood in the sense of "everywhere"] but he says rather that one and the same wind cannot wander throughout the air and that each is assigned a certain and definite place [i.e. *passim* in the sense of "at random"]'.[55] Godebert often explains the meaning of an expression in its particular context. When Ovid says that Pyrrha and Deucalion saved from the flood knelt down 'to kiss the icy stone', Guyon's notes explain: 'he means the stone of which the altar was made, and he calls it icy because there was no fire, since it had been put out by the waters of the flood'.[56] Godebert also dispels any confusion due to a literal interpretation of Deucalion's calling his wife Pirrha 'sister': 'here he calls Pirrha his sister not because she was really his sister, since she was the daughter of his uncle Epimetheus but because he loved her specially, like a sister'.[57]

Godebert's task of interpretation sometimes extends beyond simple explication of the poet's intent, to the resolution of difficulties posed by a conflict between the text and what Godebert believes to be true. When Ovid claims that air is as much lighter than water and earth as it is heavier than fire, Guyon writes: 'If air were not [negation probably added by mistake] lighter than earth by as much as it is heavier than fire, it seems that it would not have to be more distant from the earth than from fire, which nonetheless is less in accordance with truth if one looks at the natural site and location of each element, but Ovid says this because earth with water are believed to form a kind of single body for the convenience of some animals and to occupy the same place'.[58] Despite the confusing double negative, possibly due to Guyon's error, Godebert evidently objects to Ovid's statement because according to the Aristotelian hierarchy of the elements earth is in fourth position, separated from air by water, and thus more distant from air than air is from fire.

Godebert reconciles Ovid's statement with Aristotelian philosophy
by explaining that for the purposes of his description Ovid considers
water and earth as a single unit. The same problem is at issue a few
lines above when Ovid describes the creation of water 'in last place',
surrounding the earth. Godebert's resolution here is less satisfactory: 'At first view Ovid could seem here to assign the third place
among the elements to earth, which however occupies the last place
because it is the heaviest element, but if the matter is examined
closely, it will easily appear from Ovid's own words that the third
place is given to water, which he says touches the earth on all points
of its surface.'[59]

Both passages were known to be contentious. Of the first Regius
notes: 'these verses racked many people for a long time and gave
many occasion to criticize Ovid as little aware of the nature of the
elements',[60] while Guyon flagged the second with a special pointing
finger in the margin. Godebert does not consider, however, the
possibility that Ovid might be modifying intentionally the positions
traditionally assigned to water and earth; he prefers to explain away
the contradiction with Aristotelian philosophy and his own convictions as only apparent.[61] Godebert is evidently unwilling to let Ovid
hold a view contradictory to Aristotle's, and leaves unchallenged his
many assumptions, that ancient philosophy was of one piece on such
fundamental issues, that Ovid was a reliable philosopher, and that
the Aristotelian hierarchy of the elements corresponds to the truth in
natural philosophy.

If Godebert's task of interpretation involves saving the consist-
ency of his pupils' picture of natural philosophy, it preserves all the
more vehemently the truths of Christianity. Although Ovid had
already become such a familiar figure for Christian commentators
that, like many, Godebert rarely struggles with the strangeness of his
paganism,[62] on the creation of man he can brook no compromise. Of
the two accounts given by Ovid for the creation of man Godebert
comments that the one according to which man 'comes from God on
high the author of all things ... is directly in accordance with the
truth ... which the holy scriptures prove and confirm', while the
other account which attributes the creation of man to Prometheus
who fashioned man in the image of God from earth sprinkled with
river water and then gave him a soul from the fire in the sky, 'is a
fable and full of error'.[63] Less explicitly Godebert also Christianizes
Ovid's account by introducing the notion of divine providence,

which is not present in the *Metamorphoses*, to explain the creation of the elements and the animals out of chaos.[64] Similarly when Ovid remarks that it is a wonder that the winds which are so powerful do not tear the world apart, Godebert interprets Ovid's rather fearful statements as a praise of God's providence: 'the poet praises divine providence thanks to whose arrangement the winds are constituted in different and opposite parts of the air, so that they will not by chance come together and with most powerful gusts overturn each part of the world'.[65] Finally, when Ovid praises the golden age as a time when man was satisfied with what grew naturally, Godebert expands this virtue into three well-known Christian qualities: '[Ovid] praises the golden age from the continence, sobriety and abstinence of those who lived then, who required no other food to eat than what the untilled earth supplied for them'.[66] Although a far cry from Lavinius's constant parallels between the Biblical and Ovidian stories of the creation and the flood, Godebert's interpretation involves a gentle Christian shading of the pagan text, which no doubt helped make an ancient world more familiar. Divine providence and Christian virtues could still be recognized amid the complex pagan mythology and its sometimes confusing morality.

In most cases Godebert had little choice but to confront the world of ancient mythology and geography: interpretation also involved the explanation of ancient *realia*, in particular the numerous proper names in Ovid. Godebert makes them seem familiar by dint of repetition and by creating connections between new names and well-known ones. Each story in Ovid's text is repeated in the marginal notes, in addition to being summarized in the printed text. Furthermore summaries of the stories of Daphne and Io appear in Guyon's marginal annotations to Ringelberg's *Rhetorica*.[67] Clearly Godebert would seize every opportunity to reinforce this knowledge. New names are attached to stories, even when these do not help directly in understanding the *Metamorphoses*. Thus each of the three mountains of Arcadia—Maenala, Cyllene and Lichaeus—comes with its connection to other figures in the ancient world. For example 'Cylene or Cylenus is the name of a mountain in Arcadia where Maia forced by Jupiter gave birth to Mercury, who for that reason is called Cylenus although some believe that that name is given to him because he was educated by the nymph Cylene'.[68] Godebert thus lays the foundations for later readings, just as in other texts like Ringelberg's he would repeat the stories in Ovid whenever possible.

Furthermore Godebert cross-references his own comments. Referring to the phrase 'fatidicamque Themim' of line 321, the teacher notes: 'the daughter of Heaven and Earth; when she fled marriage with Jupiter, she was forced by him in Macedonia. She presided over the oracles before Apollo and is therefore called prophetic here'.[69] Then some fifty lines later he returns to the same point: 'Cepisis or Cepifis is a river in Beotia not far from the foot of mount Parnassus near which the goddess Themis gave her oracles; that is why its waters are called prophetic by the poets'.[70] In fact the reference to Themis in the second case is unnecessary since in this passage Ovid does *not* call the river prophetic. But the constant cross-referencing of a geographical area and a cast of mythological characters is an excellent pedagogical strategy to familiarize the pupils with a world necessarily alien to their northern European and sixteenth-century sensibilities.

Although Godebert generally displays little sense of historical distance from the ancient world of Ovid, as Grafton found was the case with Mignault,[71] on a few occasions he does choose to emphasize the difference rather than ignore it. He explains with unusual detachment that 'it was customary for the ancients, before sacrificing to the gods, to wash themselves with water by which they believed all their vices and crimes would be laid bare and washed away'.[72] Similarly he notes with a sense of distance that 'the ancients believed that some divinity resided in the rivers and therefore worshipped them piously'.[73] Finally, Godebert attributes to ancient custom the use of torches at weddings.[74] In an isolated instance Godebert even reveals a historical sense about linguistic usage: when Jupiter is called *tyrannus*, he comments, following Regius: 'this name was honorable among the ancients and meant the same thing then as the term "king" does to us, but since those who were called by that name abused their power for the ruin of their people, thus it happened that *tyrannus* is appropriated to designate a cruel man'.[75]

These instances of distance created by Godebert's reference to the 'customs of the ancients' are part of Godebert's effort to make sense of the text; at some points the peculiarities of 'ancient custom' simply have to be recognized. Godebert is not interested in the historical context of the *Metamorphoses* in any deep sense. When the opportunity presents itself, as Ovid invokes his ruler Augustus and describes the outrage at the murder of Caesar by way of analogy with the indignation of the gods at the crime of Lycaon, Godebert emphasizes the rhetorical device of *captatio benevolentiae* as much as the historical context of Ovid's invocation: 'the poet seeks the favor of Augustus by recalling the murder of his uncle Julius Caesar which was committed in a miserable way by those who had sworn allegiance to him in the Roman senate where he was stabbed with twenty-three blows, as Suetonius Tranquillius writes in his life of Caesar'.[76] Regius by contrast gives a long description of the event, listing for example the names of the conspirators.[77]

Godebert appears to be more interested, however, in what can be learned from Ovid about ancient natural philosophy. In his introductory comments Godebert notes: 'Especially in this first book, Ovid acts not only as a poet, but also as a philosopher who treats accurately what the ancient philosophers reported in their writings about the first origin of the world, the distinction of the elements, the division of the ages and the arrangement of the whole world by its creator'.[78] The *Metamorphoses* had been read since antiquity for their descriptions of nature and causal accounts of change. Medieval encyclopedias often borrowed heavily from Ovid, while more specialized works of natural history and natural philosophy have also been shown to quote from him.[79] But Godebert's interest in Ovid as a philosopher remains interpretive: he rarely discusses any of Ovid's positions, but simply explains them. Like Mignault, Godebert does not indulge in digressions of a purely encyclopedic nature.[80]

Godebert's comments about the natural world thus usually serve directly to gloss the text. On two occasions Godebert reminds his students that *vena* refers 'not only to the vein of the animal body in which blood is contained but also to the vein of the earth in which there are passages containing metals'.[81] Godebert also explains naturalistically how the earth could have trembled and spewed forth water on Jupiter's order: 'under the earth in various channels many vapors and waters are hidden, which, when they seek to exit from them, rush forth and shake the earth with such force that it is seen not only to move but very often to gape open'.[82] Similarly when Ovid describes the formation of creatures from humidity and heat in the Nile delta as on earth after the flood, Godebert ensures that the pupils take it as a credible naturalistic account rather than a poet's fable: '[Ovid] explains the causes of the generation of such animals, that is moisture and heat, from the proper mixture of which the philosophers write that all things are born'.[83]

Even when Godebert expands on Ovid's description of the creation of the five climatic zones on the earth, he is content to repeat the ancient belief that the world is divided into two frigid zones, two temperate zones and a 'middle zone which because of the excessive heat of the sun cannot be inhabited by men and for that reason is called torrid'.[84] The inhabitability of the torrid zone had in fact already been discussed in the Middle Ages and maintained by a number of Islamic authors, but all doubts were in any case dispelled by the discovery of men in the New World some eighty years prior to Godebert's lectures.[85] The grammar master explains the ancient belief with no further comment, however, as if steeped only in the ancient world he is explaining. In one instance Godebert does step beyond the needs of bare interpretation and gives this gloss on Ovid's mention of the Milky Way: 'Since the gods called by Jupiter came to his palace by the Milky Way, therefore he describes it here in passing: on this subject there are many fables which one can see here and there among the poets. But the true reason for its whiteness and brilliance which gives it the appearance of milk is given by Cicero in the *Dream of Scipio* when he says that [the Milky Way] is placed in the middle of very many very bright stars by whose light and splendor it is illuminated'.[86] Godebert's evidence for the true explanation rests on another classical authority—and therein lies the justification for the excursus.

Godebert's most digressive remarks take the form of references to other ancient texts, which further serve to familiarize the pupils with antiquity. When Ovid describes the silver age, when men first took shelter and cultivated the land, Godebert points to some controversy: Virgil maintained that Ceres taught men agriculture while Tibullus claimed that Osiris had.[87] Eutropius, on the other hand, reports that Saturn, 'when he came to Italy from Greece taught those uncivilized populations to build houses and cultivate the land, while before then they had lived in caves and huts thatched with leaves and branches'.[88] Or, on the slightest provocation, Godebert discusses Lycurgus' first use of trumpets to rouse the army for battle.[89] Although it is possible that Godebert draws some of his classical cross-references from his own reading and education, it is more likely that, as in the few cases where I have been able to identify a source, he relies on printed compendia of classical knowledge. In addition to Polydore Vergil for the beginnings of agriculture, Godebert probably found his reference to Hippocrates's

Aphorisms 3 on the ill effects of the unequal seasons of the silver age in Caelius Rhodiginus's *Lectiones antiquae*.[90] In a single instance Godebert refers to a modern text, Alciato's emblem book, to confirm the ancient tradition that laurel is sacred to Apollo because it enables his oracles to know the future and interpret dreams.[91] Godebert also mentions at the end of his comment on dolphins a contemporary proverb about the slipperiness of the dolphin's tail, which is applied to those who attempt tasks beyond their strength.[92] Overall, however, Godebert's digressions serve primarily to broaden a pupil's knowledge of classical texts. The difficulty for the lecturer may lie in the effort required to make such cross-references: like the etymologies Godebert supplies, they are concentrated near the beginning of the text.

Godebert offers his widest range of comments as contributions to the understanding of the text, which is what I believe we should take to be his 'grammatical' commentary. He explains words and passages, both individually and contextually. He also works to reconcile Ovid's statements with his own philosophical and religious beliefs. Godebert strives above all to teach familiarity with, not distance from, the mental world of the ancients.

III

Godebert steps beyond even this broad definition of his post as 'perfecter' of grammar in the third class and devotes an equal, if not greater, number of comments to discussing the text for its form rather than its content. In brief notes, which sometimes duplicate Longolius's, Godebert signals forty-four occurrences of rhetorical figures, of twenty different types, including anaphora, antithesis, apostrophe, epexegesis, epiphonema or exclamation, metaphor, metonymy, periphrasis, prolepsis, prosopopoeia, preterition, similitude, and synecdoche.[93] Most of these can be found described and classified as figures of 'diction', 'locution', 'construction', or 'embellishment' in introductory works of rhetoric.[94] Since Godebert explains only a few of them, one must presume that his pupils were already familiar with their use. The students' learning process was still under way, however. At one point Guyon gives without reference to the text, presumably as a reminder, an example of a similitude, which is also carefully designed as a lesson for aspiring orators: 'similitude: just as the same sun both melts wax and hardens mud, thus the same speech makes some better and others worse according to the diversity of their character'.[95] Godebert defines the hypallage of the first verse of the poem,[96] and twice reminds the class that a hyperbole exceeds the belief of all men, or the common belief of men.[97] He belatedly explains the hypotyposis: in line 344 he comments that '[Ovid] explains by hypotiposis the signs and effects from which Deucalion and Pyrrha could perceive the end of the flood, that is when the mountains emerged from the waters, the trees showed themselves and finally the flat earth was uncovered',[98] but he only defines the term in line 455: 'a hypotiposis tells the thing openly so that it seems to be placed under the eyes'.[99] Guyon's shorthand mention of 'expositio sive epithsegesis', referring to Ovid's more detailed explanation of the place of water in line 37, helps to identify the latter term as a probable error for 'epidiegesis' or 'repeated narration'.[100]

More elaborately, Godebert explains why Ovid's description of the silver age as 'worse than' the golden age is an improper use of terms: 'This is a catachresis. For the comparison is made with the golden age which was quite devoid of wickedness; thus when he says "worse" he means "less excellent".'[101] Godebert also points to a 'short ἀνακεφαλαίωσις, that is a summary of all those things that he [Ovid] has presented generally until now on the separation of chaos into the four elements'.[102] In one case Godebert directly builds on the lectures on Ringelberg's *Rhetoric* that he may have delivered only shortly before,[103] pointing out Ovid's use of *amplificatio*, in describing both the cupidity of men (*amplificatio ab affectis*) and, a few lines below, the injustice and impiety of men in the iron age.[104]

Godebert's eagerness to notice rhetorical figures does not extend to an awareness of their importance for poetry in particular. In fact, to judge from the plodding paraphrase throughout the lessons, Godebert is fundamentally uninterested in poetry as a genre. Only once does Godebert refer to a figure as specifically poetic: when Neptune is described as rising from the sea with shoulders covered with purple, Godebert calls attention to a 'poetic synecdoche'.[105] Less explicitly, he recognizes in 'iusserat' a 'Homeric phrase'.[106] In his introductory comments at least Godebert places Ovid among a pantheon of Greek and Latin poets, and in this context mentions Ovid's 'elegance and charm':

As Virgil followed Homer, Hesiod and Theocritus, and Horace followed Pindar, thus here also Ovid followed in these fifteen books the famous Greek Partheus Scius [Parthenius of Chios] who had earlier written a work with this same argument. Although because of his exile he was not able to put his hand to them one last time, nonetheless because of their elegance and charm, [these books] pleased the natural dispositions of the Greeks so well that they did not hesitate to translate them in their language and to accommodate them to their use.[107]

This passage is heavily indebted to the introductory remarks by Jacobus Micyllus in the 1565 edition of Regius's commentary on the *Metamorphoses*.[108] Godebert's concern to establish the dignity of his subject by showing it to be both an imitation of a Greek source and in turn translated into Greek itself is formulaic and his words of praise for Ovid's poetic style in this context sound rather flat. More heart-felt at least is the single passing comment of appreciation for Ovid's verses within the commentary: 'Ovid here has prolonged this whole story to tell the transformation of Lycaon which he describes artfully (*affabre*) in these verses and which he sets forth precisely'.[109]

On the 'grammatical' issue of content, however, Godebert regularly identifies the beliefs, or 'fictions', that he finds characteristic of poets. In addition to the fables about the Milky Way against which Godebert warned above, it is a device of the poets (*fingitur a poetis*) to distinguish between two orders of gods, the major gods and the demi-gods,[110] to tell the story of the giants,[111] and of Briareus the giant with one hundred hands in particular,[112] or to speak of Aeolus as god of the winds.[113] Godebert thus relegates many basic tenets of ancient mythology to the status of poetic fable, and maintains a distance, if not explicitly between his own time and that of the ancients, then at least between the world of the ancient poets and that of the ancient philosophers, the boundaries of which, as we have seen, could extend into Godebert's own personal convictions. But Godebert is here again concerned with the content rather than the form of poetic texts, as in the one instance he gives of a poetic use of terms: 'Olympus is a mountain in Thessaly of such great altitude that it seems to touch the sky with its peak so that poets often use it as the term for the sky itself'.[114]

In addition to providing grammatical commentary similar to Godebert's, Regius notices figures of speech and, like Godebert, identifies beliefs and usages that are characteristic of poets, although he shows somewhat more awareness of poetry as a form.[115] But Regius offers no parallel for Godebert's more sophisticated type of rhetorical and low-level dialectical analysis which, on Mignault's showing as well, appears typical of the later, Northern Renaissance. The Dutch Longolius, for example, shares Godebert's interest in classifying the types of arguments used by Ovid; his notes are so brief, however, that Godebert's commentary remains independent of them as it integrates the technical aspects of material reserved for later classes in a familiar narrative summary. Although Godebert's comments are primarily summaries of Ovid's text, they also provide a running analysis of Ovid's strategies of presentation, classifying in more or less technical terms the role of each passage in Ovid's argument.

On the one hand, Godebert gradually introduces his pupils to different types of arguments, 'ab effectis', 'a circonstantijs locorum, personarum' and so on, using in these cases technical terms which are not covered in the introductory handbooks of rhetoric included in the *Sammelband*, but appear in manuals of dialectic like Melanchthon's. Godebert does not explain these terms, but combines them neatly with ordinary usage that serves the same purpose. On the other hand, in many comments Godebert does not use technical terms, but monitors Ovid's presentation of his subject in simple yet precise words. Perhaps more than the dialectical terms themselves, it is Godebert's persistent low-level commentary on Ovid's argument that has the most lasting impact. At least one quarter of Godebert's total of 254 comments describe the function of a passage in Ovid's text: here the poet sets out the order he will follow, here he explains, describes, there he adduces as a cause, declares, defines, proves, concludes, exaggerates or makes probable. Beyond mere summary these verbs fit each passage into a non-technical classification of arguments which constitutes a rhetorico-dialectical, although not a fully developed dialectical, analysis.

Godebert's comment on the beginning of the *Metamorphoses* immediately establishes its order and purpose:

In order to have docile and attentive readers, [Ovid] puts forward in the beginning, in the fashion of illustrious poets, those things with which he will deal in the whole work. Then he implores the help of the gods without which nothing excellent can be done. Finally he enters upon the narration and reaches back to the origin of the world to carry it up to his own time.[116]

The analysis of exordia is not unusual, however, and Regius gives almost exactly the same commentary for the passage, including the concern for having 'receptive and attentive readers'. The deeper source for both commentators lies in the conventional discussion of exordia in manuals of rhetoric. Thus Ringelberg's *Rhetorica* admonishes that 'it is appropriate whenever the opportunity allows throughout the oration to make [the listeners] attentive, well disposed and receptive, but especially in the exordium'.[117] Twice in his manuscript annotations on the *Rhetorica* Guyon repeats Ringelberg's precept. For Godebert to begin the *Metamorphoses* with such a clear reference to the text which was studied perhaps immediately before is a neat pedagogic manoeuvre.

If Godebert's analysis of Ovid's opening verses is traditional, his continued monitoring of Ovid's presentation is not. Thus in line 5 Godebert notes that Ovid 'begins the narration',[118] and in the next line that he 'describes chaos in two ways', first through the changes wrought on the forms that were not part of the initial chaos, and secondly from those things which are now seen distinctly although they were once intermingled in chaos throughout the world.[119] Ten lines later Ovid 'describes Chaos in another way, from its deformity'.[120] As Ovid moves on to describe the creation of the world, Godebert follows closely: 'he begins to explain the composition of the world by distinguishing the elements'; then he 'explains the order of the elements' and 'after the order of the elements, he briefly sets forth the nature of the individual elements taken one by one for their specific characteristics'.[121] These comments obviously serve to summarize the text; their role as rhetorical analysis is discreet. Nevertheless it is also clear that Godebert analyses Ovid's text in greater structural detail and with more precision than Regius, who gives this comment on the corresponding passage: 'he distinguished the four elements, made the earth round and fitted it with various things'.[122]

Unlike Regius, Godebert notes the tactics used by Ovid for greater rhetorical effect. 'Ovid amplifies the unhappy and miserable condition of the iron age and what kind of war blazed up among men of this age, to which the use of gold above all inflamed them.'[123] Godebert is perhaps concerned that his pupils not lose their admiration for the Greeks based on Ovid's description of the ills of the iron age. But exaggeration is a recognized rhetorical tactic, which, according to Godebert, Jupiter uses to describe his fear of human wickedness[124] and Apollo to tell his love to Daphne.[125] Godebert also notes that by describing dolphins swimming amid the forests, Ovid 'exaggerates the calamity of the flood with respect to the transformation of nature; for dolphins usually live in the water, not in forests'.[126] Godebert's description of Ovid's argument continues consistently throughout the text, and figures more prominently as the coverage continues, primarily because other types of commentary, which would often require more research on Godebert's part, become less frequent.[127] Indeed this type of commentary is ideally suited to the unprepared lecturer, as it requires only some experience.

Godebert ventures more explicitly into the art of persuasion, using technical terms from dialectic when he formally identifies the places (*loci*) on which an argument is based. When, after describing the appearance of the earth with its fourfold division into forest, mountain, valley or plain, Ovid speaks of the formation of water, Godebert comments on the symmetry in the 'places' of his description: 'just as he described the nature of the earth, first from its qualities, then from its different parts, thus he proceeds to air, and treats as its parts cloud, lightning and wind'.[128] A more common *locus*, 'from effects', appears ten times in Godebert's commentary, for example when Ovid concludes that the invention of shipping was the greatest evil of the iron age from its effects.[129] *Loci* include most types of circumstances. When Ovid describes the council of the gods, Godebert notes that 'he portrays the council of the gods which Jupiter has called from the circumstances of place and people and things which seem most worthy of note'.[130] Godebert also signals the *locus* 'from comparison' when Ovid compares the flood to the inundation of the Nile.[131] Finally Godebert notes five instances of the argument 'from related/added things', for example in the way Ovid describes how fitting it was for the cruel Lycaon to be turned into a wolf: 'he shows *ab adiunctis* that Lycaon was not changed into something very different, since the signs and traces of his earlier form remained'.[132]

Godebert is most at ease with this rhetorico-dialectical commentary in analysing the speech of Jupiter to the assembled gods. This is not surprising given the greater emphasis of his class, both in principle and in practice, on prose orations like those of Cicero rather than on poetry. First, Jupiter's silencing of the audience before his speech is the occasion for Godebert's single explicit precept on rhetoric: '[Ovid] means that Iupiter performed the office of orator when he told the gods about the crime of Lycaon, for moderation not only of voice, but of gesture is required in an orator.'[133] Godebert then notes 'the exordium of the speech'[134] and points out how Jupiter too follows the principles of Ringelberg's *Rhetoric*, even within the body of his speech:

In order to make his listeners attentive and well-disposed [Jupiter] promises that he will say and explain to them openly and in detail those things which he thought they most wanted to know, what crime Lycaon had perpetrated against him and what punishment he had received for it.[135]

Just as he had traced the structure of Ovid's opening narrative, Godebert now follows the elements of Jupiter's story, noting how he 'begins to tell and set forth' Lycaon's crime and describes the time 'from the circumstances', that he arrived at Lycaon's palace at dusk.[136] Jupiter then clinches his argument for the punishment of men by reasoning that if he himself was attacked by Lycaon, so too would the demi-gods who lived on earth be the victims of human cruelty; Godebert notes that Jupiter 'proves [his point] by an argument from the lesser to the greater'.[137] These *loci*, from circumstances (of persons, of place or of time), effects, adjuncts, or from lesser to greater, were all long-established tools of analysis by the sixteenth century, common to the lists of places since Aristotle and Cicero. Melanchthon includes them in his manual of dialectic, as they no doubt feature in many other humanist manuals that are not associated with a particular 'system'.[138] It is the innovation of Godebert's generation of humanists to include them in classroom commentary on Ovid, a text previously studied for its moral lessons, its ancient *realia* or poetic value. In these comments Godebert moves beyond the rhetorical manual of Ringelberg and borrows terms from dialectic to make his analysis more rigorous. Godebert does not venture far into dialectic, however: unlike Mignault he does not use syllogistic reasoning and does not evaluate the validity of Ovid's arguments.

Godebert is particularly concerned to trace Ovid's theme throughout the text. He points out the different kinds of metamorphoses in book I. Godebert includes the transformation of chaos into order, the changes of the different ages one into the other, the disappearance of the giants at their death, and the appearance of snakes from the warm moisture after the flood as further pieces of Ovid's

argument,[139] in addition to the more obvious cases of form-changing
in Lycaon and the stones thrown by Deucalion and Pyrrha, or in
Daphne and Io. Godebert also shows Ovid's skill in making his
descriptions of transformations more persuasive. In some cases Ovid
strives to make the differences between the two states more apparent, for example in order to distinguish the iron age from the
preceding ones Ovid opposes as much as possible its vices with the
virtues of the other ages.[140] In the actual descriptions of shape-
changing, on the other hand, Ovid seeks to make the metamorphosis
seem more probable by establishing similarities between the two
states. Thus Ovid 'describes the true metamorphosis and transformation of Daphne into a laurel tree by adding the distribution of the
different parts of her body which changed into the various parts of
the tree'.[141] Similarly 'in order to make the transformation into men
of the stones thrown by Deucalion and Pyrrha more probable,
[Ovid] explains by name the way in which all the parts of the stones
were changed into other similar parts, thus the humid and earthy
parts into flesh, the harder and more solid parts into bones.'[142]
Almost every aspect of Ovid's text is thus analysed as part of his
tactic of persuasion.

Finally, Godebert is interested in the overall construction of the
narrative and the use of transitions between successive stories,
particularly at the end of the book when the metamorphoses succeed
one another with no necessary logic. As soon as the chronological
account ends, after the flood:

[Ovid] concludes with the reason and the causes for which the earth irrigated
by the waters of the flood produced so many kinds of animals. In this way
there is a παρασκεύασις. That is a preparation to explain the victory which
Apollo accomplished over Python whom he killed with his arrows.[143]

A few lines later Ovid describes how Apollo's triumph led to the
institution of the Pythic games, whose winners were at first crowned
with oak leaves and later with wreaths of laurel. Godebert points out
that this is the perfect opportunity to tell of Daphne's metamorphosis into a laurel tree: 'Ovid took the occasion to recite this fable here
because he had just spoken of the laurel which first was born from
Daphne the daughter of Peneus.'[144] Finally Godebert notes that the
transition between the story of Daphne and that of Io is based on the
description of the place where Peneus gathered all the other rivers to

console him; only Inachus, the father of Io, was missing. So the description of the plain in which Peneus flows is not irrelevant for 'the poet starts out from topography, that is the description of the place'.[145]

Since antiquity the *Metamorphoses* had been admired for their inventive transitions.[146] It is not surprising then that Ringelberg should choose from the very text assigned by Godebert an example of transition by the use of digression:

When Ovid told the fable of Daphne . . . in order to move to the fable of Io, he recalls that all the rivers came together to console the father of Daphne, except the father of Io who was prevented by his own grief for his daughter who had been changed into a heifer. That is why his statement that all the rivers came together is a digression: that is, it serves nothing for [Ovid's] undertaking, for the metamorphosis of things, except to connect the fables.[147]

Just as when Ringelberg had discussed exordia, both Regius and Godebert made similar comments derived from standard manuals of rhetoric like his, so too on the issue of transitions which Ringelberg discusses, Regius closely parallels Godebert's commentary.[148] Regius notes that the poet describes Tempe, the valley of the Peneus, 'in order to connect Io's story to the preceding one'. Although Regius does not mention a transition to Ovid's story about Python, he notes more clearly than Godebert that Ovid's description of the origin of animals from the mixture of water and earth is inserted in order to announce Daphne's metamorphosis.[149] He also mentions the more obvious juxtaposition of the Pythian games and Daphne's story of the origin of the laurel.

IV

Godebert's comments are not of interest because they are original, but precisely because they are not. The notes Pierre Guyon left in his copy of Ovid's *Metamorphoses* provide an extensive picture of his classroom experience, in over 250 individual comments, fewer than half of which are presented here. Although his sources vary he follows the general approach of the earlier commentator Regius on most issues concerning grammatical analysis, that is, the interpretation of the meaning of the text. Godebert's rhetorical commentary on figures of speech is more detailed than Regius's, but not fundamentally different. Godebert and Regius also share the rhetorician's interest in certain key features of the text, notably its exordium and its transitions, which are discussed in the standard manuals of rhetoric, and are the object of Godebert's explication to the same class of Ringelberg's *Rhetoric*. Where Godebert departs from Regius, however, he shows us what is distinctive about college teaching in late sixteenth-century Paris. Regius offers no parallel for Godebert's continuous low-level dialectical analysis of Ovid's argumentation, which rather corresponds in intent if not in the level of explication to Mignault's Ramist lectures on Horace's *Odes*. Godebert also includes technical dialectical terms when analysing the *loci* of Ovid's arguments, most successfully in the case of a speech within the poem. He thus prepares his students for instruction in the upper forms of the college, and less immediately, for the argumentative professional world awaiting them.[150]

Program in History of Science
Department of History
Princeton University
Princeton NJ 08544 USA

REFERENCES

1. Anthony Grafton, 'Teacher, Text and Pupil in the Renaissance Class-Room: A Case Study from a Parisian College', *History of Universities*, 1 (1981), 37–70.
2. Grafton, 'Teacher, Text and Pupil', 50.
3. For a preliminary analysis of the annotations studied here and the reproduction of a number of pages see Ann M. Blair, 'Lectures on Ovid's *Metamorphoses*: The Class Notes of a Sixteenth-Century Paris Schoolboy', *Princeton University Library Chronicle*, 59 (1989), 117–44. I am grateful for permission to reuse some material published there. For brief descriptions see also Scott Carlisle, 'Renaissance Education', *Princeton University Library Chronicle*, 49 (1988), 296–7, and the H. P. Kraus rare book catalogue, *Books and Documents of the Sixteenth Century*, catalogue no. 146 (New York, 1987), pp. 54–5, which includes the reproduction of one page. The book was purchased by Princeton University Library from Kraus in spring 1987 through the efforts of Stephen Ferguson, Curator of Rare Books.
4. For the most recent work in this lively area of research see, on France: Roger Chartier, Dominique Julia and Marie-Madeleine Compère,

L'Education en France du XVIe au XVIIIe siècles (Paris, 1976); George Huppert, *Public Schools in Renaissance France* (Urbana, Ill., 1984); and for a slightly later period L. W. B. Brockliss, *French Higher Education in the Seventeenth and Eighteenth Centuries* (Oxford, 1987), ch. 3; on Germany: Anton Schindling, *Humanistische Hochschule und freie Reichstadt: Gymnasium und Akademie in Strassburg 1538–1621* (Wiesbaden, 1977); Gerhard Menk, *Die Hohe Schule Herborn in ihrer Frühzeit (1584–1660)* (Wiesbaden, 1981); on Italy: Paul Grendler, *Schools and Schooling in Renaissance Italy: Literacy and Learning 1300–1600* (Baltimore, Ma., 1989); and on humanist education more generally, Anthony Grafton and Lisa Jardine, *From Humanism to the Humanities* (Cambridge, Mass., 1986).

5. See Gabriel Codina Mir, S.J., *Aux sources de la pédagogie des Jésuites* (Rome, 1968), pp. 99–109.

6. For a concise presentation of the goals of a humanist education in the later, Northern Renaissance, see James McConica, 'The Fate of Erasmian Humanism', in Nicholas Phillipson (ed.), *Universities, Society and the Future* (Edinburgh, 1983), pp. 37–61.

7. On the division of classes at the Collège de Clermont see Gustave Dupont-Ferrier, *Du Collège de Clermont au Lycée Louis-le-Grand* (Paris, 1921), i. 215–16. He reports that the second class at Clermont was devoted to poetry.

8. In particular the third class would learn the different elements of a speech: 'exordium, narratio, argumentatio, loci communes, amplificatio etc'. Schindling, *Humanistische Hochschule*, p. 193.

9. The greater number of Greek texts studied in Mignault's class is no doubt in part the consequence of the more advanced level of the first class. On the other hand, it may also reflect Mignault's Ramist convictions; Ramus was the first master to introduce Greek in the curriculum on the same footing as Latin according to Codina Mir, p. 88.

10. In some cases the master may have requested their publication himself. See Grafton, 'Teacher, Text and Pupil', note 13, p. 63.

11. On Brumen see P. Renouard, *Imprimeurs et libraires parisiens du XVIe siècle*, Fascicule 'Brumen' (Paris, 1984), pp. 34–8. Although Guyon's text of Ovid's *Metamorphoses* was published by Denys du Pré, Brumen published a bibliographically identical text in the same year. See Renouard, p. 96.

12. This work is attributed to C. Plinius Secundus, although today 'almost everything about this set of brief lives is disputed—author, title, contents, date, sources' according to Leighton D. Reynolds, *Texts and Transmission: A Survey of Latin Classics* (Oxford, 1983), p. 149.

13. Ioachim Fortius Ringelberg, *Rhetorica* (Paris, Gabriel Buon, 1561); *Compendium libri secundi, tertij et quinti Institutionum Oratoriarum M. Fabii Quintiliani*, Iacobo Lodoico Strebaeo auctore (Paris, Denys du Pré, 1570); Cicero, *De optimo genere oratorum opusculum* (Paris, Veuve

P. Attaignant, 1557); Cicero, *Oratio pro M. Marcello* (Paris, Thomas Brumen, 1569); Cicero, *In M. Antonium Philippica Nona* (Paris, Denys du Pré, 1570); Cicero, *Pro lege Manilia oratio* (Paris, Denys du Pré, 1571); Cicero, *Oratio pro O. Ligario* (Paris, Denys du Pré, 1569); Cicero, *Post reditum in Senatu oratio* (no title page or colophon), paginated ff. 17–27, evidently excerpted from a larger work; Ovid, *Metamorphoseon liber primus* (Paris, Denys du Pré, 1570); Ovid, *Elegiae aliquot in gratiam puerorum selectae, ex libris quatuor de ponto* (Paris, Denys du Pré, 1568); Virgil, *Aeneidos liber secundus* (no title page or colophon), paginated ff. 1–16; L. Florus, *De gestis Romanorum libri quatuor* (Paris, Denys du Pré, 1568); C. Plinius Secundus, *De viris illustribus liber, qui vulgo Cornelio Nepoti adscribitur* and Suetonius, *De claris grammaticis et rhetoribus liber* (Paris, Vascosan, 1551); *Compendium Ioannis Despauterij de Syllabarum quantitate* per Ioannem Pellissonem excerptum (Paris, Denys du Pré, 1570).

14. This collection of moral aphorisms in poetic form was widely read in the Renaissance. See S. K. Heninger, *Touches of Sweet Harmony* (San Marino, Cal., 1974), pp. 259–63.

15. On Guyon's French cursive hand, see below and note 35.

16. His two mottoes are reported in Henri Tausin, *Dictionnaire des devises ecclésiastiques* (Paris, 1907), pp. 91 and 222, and in Laurence Urdang *et al.*, *Mottoes* (Detroit, Mich., 1986), pp. 135, 430 and 812. 'In labore quies' was the motto of Robert, cardinal de Lenoncourt and bishop of Châlons-sur-Marne, Metz, Embrun and archbishop of Arles, who died in 1561 (Tausin, p. 91). 'Virescit vulnere virtus' was used by Antoine Duprat, chancellor of France under Francis I, archbishop of Sens and bishop of Albi and Meaux, who died in 1535 (Tausin, p. 222). The alliterative phrase was quoted by Nonius Marcellus from the *Annals* of the Roman poet Furias Antias and was also the motto of a number of British noble families, for example of David Count of Mansfield (1573–1628) (Urdang *et al.*, pp. 135, 182). On the theory of devices in this period and their use, especially by the nobility, for expressing 'permanent or temporary *personae*' see Daniel S. Russell, *The Emblem and Device in France* (Lexington, Kentucky, 1985), for example p. 74. Since they are so widespread, these expressions cannot be identified with a particular family or geographical region that could shed light on Pierre Guyon.

17. 'Pone modum rebus, nimium ne fide secundis. / Quae dedit haec eadem sors tibi tollet opes. / Quid tibi si gemmas omnes cumularis et aurum? / Et tua tartareis mens crutietur aquis? / Ex libris Petri Guyoni et amicorum.'

18. Dupont-Ferrier (note 7), I, 63–5.

19. Ovid, *Metamorphoseon liber primus cui doctissima Lactantii accesserunt argumenta, cum annotationibus Longolij longe utilissimis* (Paris, Denys du Pré, 1570). All references to this work will be made by folio number only.

20. Gilbertus Longolius of Utrecht (1507–43), a physician by profession, prepared a number of editions and commentaries of classical authors and is mostly known today as the annotator of Erasmus's *De civilitate*. See *Contemporaries of Erasmus*, ed. Peter Bietenholz, 3 vols. (Toronto, 1987), II, 342.

21. Ann Moss, *Ovid in Renaissance France: A Survey of Latin Editions of Ovid and Commentaries Printed in France Before 1600* (London, 1982), p. 41.

22. The *Metamorphoses* is admittedly a fairly stable text. The edition used by Godebert none the less presents a number of minor differences from modern editions, and contains two extra lines—between lines 547 and 548: 'Quae fecit ut laedar, mutando perde figuram', and between the middle of line 700 and the middle of line 701: '. . . tibi nubere nympha volentis / Votis cede dei . . .' As neither of these extra lines is the object of Godebert's commentary, when referring to line numbers in the text I will ignore them and follow the line numbers in the text of the Belles Lettres edition, ed. Georges Lafaye (Paris, 1928).

23. Much of this brief sketch of Ovid commentaries in the sixteenth century is drawn from the helpful work by Ann Moss (note 21).

24. Henri Lamarque, 'L'édition des oeuvres d'Ovide dans la Renaissance française' in *Ovide en France dans la Renaissance* (Toulouse, 1981), 13–40, p. 15.

25. Regius's appointment as professor was interrupted (1486–1503) by a competitor, Giovanni Calfurnio. From Padua he moved on to a professorship at the University of Venice; he died in 1520. In general see *Contemporaries of Erasmus*, III, 134. Despite the vagaries of his career, Martin Lowry calls him 'one of the most esteemed classical scholars at the university of Padua', in *The World of Aldus Manutius, Business and Scholarship in Renaissance Venice* (Ithaca, N.Y., 1979), p. 188. His prominence is further attested by the fact that along with Niccolo Leoniceno Tomeo he figured as a character in the dialogue of Pomponio Gaurico *De sculptura* (1504); see D. de Bellis, 'La vita e l'ambiente di Niccolo Leoniceno Tomeo', *Quaderni per la storia dell'Università di Padova*, 13 (1980), 37–75, p. 48; and by the epigrams issued at his death, as recorded in Antonio Medin, 'Raffaele Regio a Venezia: epigrammi per la sua morte', *Archivio veneto-tridentino*, 1 (1922), 237–44. Unfortunately the commentaries he published on Ovid and on selected passages of Persianus, Quintilian and Pliny have not been studied.

26. Moss, p. 71.

27. Moss, pp. 40–1.

28. The interleaved folios in Guyon's *Sammelband* are of a different weight than the printed pages, which suggest that Guyon supplied his own paper to be interleaved with the printed text by the binder.

29. For the first line 'In nova corpora / fert / animus / mutatas / dicere / formas', the paraphrase runs: 'in novas effigies et species / desiderat /

mens mea / conversas / explicare, describere / figuras et imagines, cum rerum tum personarum' (f. 2r.). In all quotes I have tried to render Guyon's text as accurately as possible, without noting minor discrepancies with classical usage. Guyon sometimes doubles consonants without need (*collere*) or conversely reduces consonants that are usually doubled to a single consonant (*exagerat*); he uses '-e' for '-ae' and his punctuation is erratic. It may be possible to draw some conclusions concerning the pronunciation of Latin in sixteenth-century France from Guyon's spellings, but as they are not always consistent, it is perhaps best to see in them the influence of the fluid state of French orthography at the time.

30. Guyon writes for example, without any obvious relation to the text: 'Cum vitium prodest peccat qui recta facit. Quant pour faire une petite faute lon peut faire ung grand bien peche grandement qui faict le petit bien' (first interleaved folio facing f. 3r.). Or later: 'Ille sibi non bene consulit qui medicum instituit suum heredem. Cestuyla est bien abusé qui constitue pour son héritier son médecin. Ut enim citius eius opibus fruatur facile eum ad mortis viam ducet' (interleaved folio facing f. 4v.). The latter saying is proposed as a subject for discussion, but is not actually discussed, by Laurent Joubert in *Erreurs populaires* (Bordeaux, S. Millanges, 1578), in the appendix entitled 'Mélanges d'autres propos vulgaires et erreurs populaires': 'Si c'est folie, comme on dit vulgairement, de faire héritier son médecin.'

31. Codina Mir, pp. 81–2. In the notes taken by Guyon on the *Metamorphoses* there is one reference to a vernacular term, *ilex* (holm-oak) 'is a kind of oak that bears acorns [which] the French call *hieuse*.' 'Ilex species est quercus est glandifera Galli vocant hieuse' (l. 112; f. 4r.).

32. From the ink patterns on a few pages annotated in red rather than the usual black ink (since faded to brown), it seems that the class did not annotate the text line by line or sentence by sentence immediately after paraphrasing it. Rather the paraphrase would run ahead over about 18 lines before the class returned to comment in detail on the lines they had just covered. In other words when Guyon picked up his red ink, the first passage he paraphrased was 18 lines ahead of the first word he commented on in the margin, and similarly when he returned to black ink a few pages later, the paraphrase 'turns brown' 18 lines after the commentary does (ff. 5–7).

33. Perhaps, pressed for time, Godebert hoped to read through as much of the text as possible without stopping to comment. It is also possible, however, that Guyon simply failed by the end to enter his lecture notes as usual at the end of each lesson. I deduce that Guyon copied over his notes at leisure after each lesson from the neat and regular hand and the frequent instances of tapered paragraphs, which require knowing in advance the precise number of words to arrange.

34. For ll. 689–697, Guyon provides paraphrase for the following expressions: Arcadiae gelidis in montibus / ... celeberrima Nonacrinas // ...

eluserat ... sequentes // ... Ortygiam studiis ... colebat / ... ritu quoque cincta Dianae / falleret et credit posset ... si non / corneus. He passes over difficult words like hamadryadas and Latonia and breaks up grammatical groups like 'Ortygiam ... deam' and 'studiis ipsaque ... virginitate' (ff. 14v–15r.). Perhaps Guyon filled in only what he could manage in the final hour of the class.

35. See note 30 for examples of proverbs. There are also some marginal annotations in this French cursive, in texts where there are few annotations (Cicero's *De optimo genere oratorum*, selections from Ovid's *De ponto*, and Despautère's *De quantitate*), and at the beginning of heavily annotated works (the *Compendium* of Quintilian, Cicero's *Post reditum in Senatu* and *Pro lege Manilia*, and the *Aeneid*) in which the hand turns to italic after a few pages.

36. Discouraged by Erasmus, dictation was forbidden in some colleges, but widely practised in others, according to Codina Mir, pp. 123–4. Since it is likely that most of the notes were written in the margins only after class, it is virtually impossible to determine whether they were taken under direct dictation or whether Guyon recomposed each paragraph of commentary himself on the basis of more fragmentary class notes. However, Guyon's aural misunderstandings—for example Guyon comments on 'ignis' while the text in fact reads 'in his' (1. 425; f. 9v), or writes 'adeo' for 'a Deo' (l. 5; f. 2r; note 118 below) and 'cludelitas' for 'crudelitas' (l. 151; f. 5v; note 104 below)—and other minor grammatical errors suggest that the notes represent Godebert's lectures delivered at near dictation speed without serious reworking by Guyon.

37. I will provide the closest parallels I have found for Godebert's comments in the notes. I have used Calepinus, *Dictionarium octo linguarum* and Gesner, *Onomasticon propriorum nominum* published together (Basel, Henricpetri, 1584). Although posterior to Godebert's lectures, this edition offers some valuable parallels. Each successive edition of Calepinus's dictionary incorporated generally minor additions over earlier ones.

38. As a basis for comparison with Godebert's notes I have used the commentary of Regius, the most prominent humanist commentator on Ovid. Published in over twenty French editions between 1496 and 1528 (Moss, p. 28), Regius's commentary continued to appear in Italy later in the century. I have selected an edition printed in Venice in 1565, *Metamorphoseon libri XV ... Regii explanatio ... cum novis Iacobi Micylli ... additionibus* (Venice: Gryphius, 1565), because it offers the best example of specific borrowing that I have found, from the introductory remarks in this edition by Jacobus Micyllus to Godebert's own introductory remarks on Ovid; see below, notes 107–8. Godebert may have had access to this edition in a college library; the library of the Collège de Clermont for example reached 18,000 volumes by the late sixteenth century, see Dupont-Ferrier, i. 123.

Collation with an earlier, French edition of Regius's commentary in *Metamorphoseos libri moralizati cum pulcherrimis fabularum principalium figuris* (Lyon, 1518), reproduced (New York and London, 1976) reveals that the edition of 1565 is somewhat richer, offering for example more background on ancient accounts of the creation, alternative etymologies and suggestions for textual emendation. These differences do not affect my argument, but I will provide folio numbers from the 1518 edition in parentheses to correspond to the passages I cite from the edition of 1565 and will indicate discrepancies when they occur.

39. The relationship between rhetoric and dialectic is well-known to be fraught with tensions and ambiguities in this period. In principle, and these are the definitions that I will use, dialectic dealt with modes of reasoning, in particular syllogisms, while rhetoric described and sought to emulate Ancient tactics in persuasion. The Ramist method proposed to reduce rhetoric to elocution and pronunciation alone by transferring invention and disposition, which were traditionally a part of rhetoric, into the field of dialectic. At the same time, as Godebert's commentary shows, terms discussed in manuals of dialectic could also be used in rhetorical analysis. Between a strictly rhetorical analysis (focusing on the identification of tropes or of the parts of an oration for example) and a full-fledged dialectical analysis (seeking to lay bare the logical structure of an argument and its flaws) Godebert performs a kind of rhetorico-dialectical, or what I will call low-level dialectical, analysis, which identifies the role of different arguments in the text and classifies them into *loci* without evaluating their validity and conclusions. For more on rhetoric and dialectic in this period see Wilbur S. Howell, *Logic and Rhetoric in England 1500–1700* (Princeton, 1956); Lisa Jardine, *Francis Bacon and the Art of Discourse* (Cambridge, 1974), ch. 1; Wilhelm Risse, *Die Logik der Neuzeit* (2 vols; Stuttgart, 1964); and concerning France in particular Kees Meerhoff, *Rhétorique et poétique au XVIe siècle en France* (Leiden, 1986), and articles in Peter Sharratt (ed.), *French Renaissance Studies 1540–70* (Edinburgh, 1976).

40. For a brief but evidently similar example of the pedagogical implementation of dialectical analysis in two textbooks see Lisa Jardine, 'Humanism and the Sixteenth-Century Cambridge Arts Course', *History of Education* 4 (1975), 16–31, p. 26.

41. 'Coricidas nymphas: Corycum antrum e Parnasi nymphis sacrum. unde Corycides nymphae dicuntur. est autem forma patronymica pro possessiva.' Regius, p. 17 (f. xxii recto); 'Cephisidas undas: Cephisus fluvius est ex Parnasi radicibus fluens, unde patronymicum finxit poeta.' Regius, p. 18 (f. xxiii recto).

42. 'Dic Themi: ... est autem vocativus graecus Themi.' Regius, p. 19 (not in edition of 1518). Godebert, by contrast, does not discuss the form of the word but its function and meaning: 'Dic Themi: Apostrofe est ad Themidem, qua eam rogat, ut propaginis hominum reparandae ratio-

nem doceat, quam ut magis excitet eius clementiam et mansuetudinem ei ob oculos ponit' (l. 379; interleaved folio facing f. 8v.).

43. Regius made an important contribution to philological scholarship in positively rejecting in 1491 the traditional attribution to Cicero of the rhetorical treatise *Ad Herennium*. He was the first to do so, although Lorenzo Valla had already expressed some doubts on the issue. See Harry Caplan (ed.), *Ad Herennium* (London and Cambridge, Mass., 1954), p. ix.

44. 'Sic est legendum, non Amphitrites, ut quidam asserentes pro Neptuno poni.' Regius p. 2 (f. iii verso).

45. 'Amphitrite is the daughter of Ocean and the nymph Doris, the wife of Neptune used here by metonymy for the sea; she is called thus from ἀμφιτρίβω because she rubs away at the earth from all sides.' 'Amphitrite filia est Oceani et Doridis Nymphae Neptuni uxor hi [for hic] vero per metonimiam pro mari ponitur sic vero nominata est ἀπὸ τοῦ ἀμφιτρίβω quia terram undique atterat' (l. 14; f. 2v.). Compare with Gesner, *Onomasticon*: 'Amphitrite: Oceani et Doridos filia, quae fingitur a Poetis esse uxor Neptuni: et per metonymiam ponitur pro mari. Nomen deductum est ab ἀμφιτρίβειν: hoc est a circunterendo, quod mare terram undique terat et lancinet' (p. 27).

46. 'Iritare: provocare, stimulare. per simplex r autem scribitur. nam irritare per duplex r significat vanum et irritum facere' (Regius, p. 21). In the edition of 1518 Regius writes only: 'irritare: provocare, stimulare' (f. xxv recto).

47. 'Nectar dicitur esse deorum potus, sicut ambrosia eorumdem cibus habetur' (l. 111; f. 4r.); 'Muscus est herba humilis exiguorum foliorum quae in locis humidis et aquosis nasci solet, cuius gravis est odor' (l. 374; interleaved folio facing f. 8v.); 'Murex piscis est ex concharum genere ex cuius sanguine fit purpura' (l. 332; interleaved folio facing f. 8r.); 'Iugerum est illud agri spatium quod unum par bonum [for boum] toto die arare potest' (l. 459; interleaved folio facing f. 10r.); 'Pellex est ea quae cum viro uxorem habente concubuit' (l. 622; f. 13r.). Compare with Regius: 'Muscus herbula est minutissima, in locis humidis nascens' [p. 18 (f. xxiii recto)]; 'Iugerum: tantum terrae dicitur, quantum par boum die uno exarare potest' [p. 21 (f. xxv recto)]; 'Innato murice: Est autem murex concha, ex cuius sanguine purpureus conficitur color' [p. 17 (f. xxii verso)]. Calepinus disagrees on the last point: 'murex: piscis marinus ex concharum genere, a purpura diversus' (p. 847).

48. The etymological discussions concern words in ll. 5, 14, 64, 189, 198 and 283. Perhaps the effort of this additional research became more of a burden as the class wore on.

49. 'Caelum: Ea mundi regio quae quatuor elementis [for elementa] super eminet coelum vocatur, vel quia syderibus et stellis tanquam gemmis celata sit, vel quia sit concava, graeci enim κοῖλον concavum vocant vel quia haec omnia inferiora celet et contineat' (l. 5; f. 2r.). Compare with Calepinus: 'Uno nomine dicitur tota illa mundi pars, quae est supra

elementum ignis, quam philosophi Aethera appellant: ita dictum a celando, hoc est, occultando: quod inferiora omnia celet, et tegat: sive a stellarum imagine, quae in eo quodammodo caelatae apparent. Ambrosius lib. Hexam. Coelum, quod impressa stellarum lumina habeat, quasi Caelatum appellatur: sicut argentum, quod signis eminentibus refulget, caelatum dicimus. Varro caelum, quasi κοίλον, hoc est, cavum, dictum putat: et sic per oe diphthongum scribendum videtur' (p. 168). Regius omits the explanation from 'celare' in the edition of 1565 (p. 2), as well as that from 'κοίλον' in the earlier edition (f. ii recto).

50. 'Lucus proprie significat sylvam in cedrum [for inceduam] in qua quoniam sol minime luceret, per antifrasim lucus nominatus' (l. 189; interleaved folio facing f. 6r.). Later Godebert explains the term again, emphasizing its divine inhabitants: 'lucus est sylva incedua id est cuius arbores propter religionem non seduntur [for ceduntur] in quibus Driades Nymphae habitant' (l. 301; interleaved folio facing f. 7v.). Compare with Calepinus: 'Lucus: locus arboribus consitus, Deo alicui consecratus: a luceo per antiphrasin dictum, teste Servio, eo quod non luceat: quum enim nullae illic arbores propter religionem caederentur, opacus et sine luce erat' (p. 766). Regius does not discuss the term.

51. 'Zephirus quasi Zoiphoros idest vitam ferens, ab occasu equinotiali flat, latini eum vocant favonium' (l. 64; second interleaved folio facing f. 3r.). Compare with Gesner: 'Zephyrus: ventus flans ab occasu aequinoctiali adversus subsolanum quem Latini favonium appellant' (p. 314). Regius gives the same explanation, p. 5 (f. vi verso).

52. 'Tridens sceptrum Neptuni est quod ita appellatur quia tres dentes, et cuspides habeat' (l. 283; f. 7v.).

53. 'Terra feras: Ferarum nomine omnia brutorum animalium genera intelligit quae in terris versantur, sic dicta quoniam toto impetu ferantur' (l. 75; f. 3r). Godebert does not generalize beyond Ovid, although in a similar passage Regius attributes this use of *fera* to poets in general. 'Ferae . . . a poetis tamen frequenter pro omnibus brutis ponuntur. Ferae autem dictae sunt quia toto corpore ferantur.' Regius, p. 6 (f. vii recto).

54. 'Aethera: nomine Aetheris modo coelum modo ignem intelligit, qui propter minimam qua constat gravitatem. Idcirco hic omnis ponderis expers dicitur, cum tamen revera coelo sit gravior, quo etiam inferiorem locum occupat' (l. 68; second interleaved folio facing f. 3r.).

55. 'Non passim: non significat Poeta his verbis aliquam regionis aeris partem ventis carere, sed potius innuit unum et eundem ventum per totum aerem non vagari et unumquenque certo ac deffinito loco esse constitutum' (l. 57; second interleaved folio facing f. 2v.).

56. 'Gelidoque pavens dedit obscula [sic—text reads oscula] saxo: saxum intelligit ex quo ara composita erat, hoc autem ideo gelidum vocat propter ignem defficientem, qui aquis diluvij extinctus fuerat' (l. 376; interleaved folio facing f. 8v.).

57. 'Deucalion lachrimis ita Pirrham: . . . hic vero Pirrham Sororem suam appellat non quod eius vere soror esset, cum Epimethei patrui esset filia, sed quod illam tanquam sororem suam unice diligeret' (l. 350; f. 8r.).

58. 'Qui quanto est pondere: Si aer non esset levior terra quam gravior est igne, videtur non debere longius distare a terra quam ab igne quod tamen minus est consentaneum veritati si naturalis situs et singulorum elementorum locj spectetur, sed hoc ideo dicit, proptereaquod terra cum aqua creduntur propter quorundam animalium commoditatem unicum veluti corpus constituere, et eundem locum occupare' (l. 52; second interleaved folio facing f. 2v.).

59. 'Ultima possedit: Videri posset his primo obtuitu sive aspectu tertium locum inter elementa terrae assignare, quae tamen prae summa gravitate ultimum occupat sed si exacte res inspiciatur facile apparebit ex verbis Ovidij tertium locum aquae tribui quam dicit terrae extremam superficiem omni ex parte contingere' (l. 31; first interleaved folio facing f. 3r.).

60. 'Hi versus multos diu torserunt, multis ansam dederunt Ovidium reprehendendi, tanquam naturae elementorum parum conscium.' Regius, p. 5 (not in the edition of 1518).

61. Regius tries to resolve the passage by adducing the conclusion of his teacher Alexander Philomenus Lugensis who concluded that the passage meant that air was heavier than fire by as much as water was lighter than earth. 'Pondus aquae levius, tanto est onerosior igne. Quae lectio penitus quadrare videtur erit enim sensus, aerem tanto graviorem esse igne quantum aquae pondus elementum terrae levitate praecedit.' Regius, p. 5.

62. See Judson Boyce Allen, *The Friar as Critic: Literary Attitudes in the Later Middle Ages* (Nashville, Tenn., 1971), p. 87.

63. 'Deerat adhuc et quod dominari: Quoniam statim post discreta atque separata quatuor elementa, homo orbis cultor et habitator factus est, hic duplicem eius tradit originem, unam quae a Deo summo rerum omnium authore promanavit quae prorsus cum veritate est consentanea quam etiam sacrae scripturae probant atque confirmant. Alteram quae a Prometeo profluxit qui ex terra atque aqua fluviali aspersa hominem ad Dei imaginem prius effinxisse et deinde surrecto igne e caelo illi animam indidisse fertur quae fabulosa est et erroris plena' (l. 77; f. 3v.). Compare with Regius: 'Ultimus animalium homo ex terrae limo ad imaginem, et similitudinem Dei fuit creatus, sive a Deo totius mundi opifice, quod verum esse constat, sive a Prometheo Iapeti filio, quod poetae finxerunt. . . . sed cum fabula sit, minime mirandum est, si longe a veritate abest' [p. 6 (f. vii verso)].

64. 'Vix ita limitibus discreverat: secundam Metamorphosim id est transformationem explicat, ad creationem animalium spectantem cum enim Dei providentia omnia elementa inter se distinxisset, et unicuinque [for unicuique] quod naturae erat accommodatum attribuisset, postea

certis animalium formis et imaginibus eadem exornavit' (l. 69; f. 3r.).

65. 'His quoque: Divinam providentiam Poeta commendat, cuius consilio venti diversis atque oppositis partibus aeris sunt constituti, ne si forte una conssent [for coissent] vehementissimis flatibus totam mundi machinam vertisset [for vertissent]' (l. 57; second interleaved folio facing f. 2v.). Godebert further insists on the point, repeating two lines below: 'Diverso flamina tractu: Per tractum aeris plagam intelligit a qua unusquisque ventorum flat, caeterum hic obiter tangit Poeta cur divina Providentia singulis ventis certa loca assignavit e quibus suos flatus emitterent, ne videlicet si multi conssent [for coissent] inter se coniunctis viribus impetum facerent atque ita quascunque orbis partes subverterent' (l. 59; second interleaved folio facing f. 3r.).

66. 'Contentique cibis: Aetatem auream commendat a continentia, sobrietate et abstinentia eorum qui illius [Saturni] tempore vivebant, qui videlicet, nullos alios requirebant cibos, quibus vescerentur, praeter eos quos tellus etiam inculta his suppeditabat' (l. 103; f. 4v.).

67. At a point where Ringelberg mentions the transition between the two stories as interesting for its use of digression. See below note 147.

68. 'Etenim Cyllene: Cylene vel Cylenus nomen etiam montis est in Arcadia ubi Maia a Iove compressa Mercurium peperit, qui idcirco Cylenus vocatur quamvis alij existiment enim istud nomen adeptum fuisse ex eo quod a Cylene nympha educatus fuerit' (l. 217; interleaved folio facing f. 6r.). Compare with Gesner, who also indicates his source, 'Cyllene: Mons Arcadiae, in quo Maja a Iove compressa, Mercurium peperit, ut autor est Virgil. lib. 8 Aen.' (p. 109). The reference is to *Aeneid* VIII, ll. 138–9.

69. 'Fatidicamque Themim: Themis filia Caeli et terrae cum Iovis nuptias fugeret, ab eo in Macedonia compressa est. Haec autem ante Apollinem Oraculis praefuit, et idcirco hic fatidica dicitur' (l. 321; interleaved folio facing f. 8r.). Compare with Gesner: 'Themis: Coeli et terrae filia fuit, quae Iovis nuptias fugiens, ab eo in Macedonia compressa fuit' (p. 291).

70. 'Cephisidas: Cepisis sive Cepifis fluvius est Beotiae non longe distans a radice Parnassi montis Iuxta quem Themis Dea reddebat oracula unde eius aquae a Poetis dictae sunt fatidice' (l. 369; f. 8v.).

71. Grafton, 'Teacher, Text and Pupil', pp. 51–2.

72. 'Inde ubi libatos: in more Posithum erat, apud Antiquos ut priusquam dijs sacrificarent, aquis sese abluerent quibus omnia sua vitia, crimina detegi et obliterari credebant' (l. 371; interleaved folio facing f. 8v.). Compare with Regius: 'antiqui templa ingressuri deosque precaturi (id quod nos quoque facimus) prius se aqua aspergebant et lavabant: quam consuetudinem Deucalion et Pyrrha diis supplicaturi servarunt' [p. 18 (f. xxiii recto)].

73. 'Numen habetis: antiqui existimabant aliquod numen inesse fluminibus, et idcirco ea religiose collebant' (l. 545; interleaved folio facing f. 12r.).

74. 'Taedas exosa: periphrasis est nuptiarum vel etiam est metonimia signum pro signato, solebant enim antiqui novis nuptijs quinque taedas accenses [for accensas] praeferre' (l. 483; f. 10v.). For another example of Renaissance interest in ancient wedding rites, see the discussion of Ben Jonson's 'masque of union' in D. J. Gordon, *The Renaissance Imagination*, ed. Stephen Orgel (Berkeley, Cal., 1975), pp. 157–84, esp. pp. 174–9.

75. 'Tyranni: hoc nomen apud veteres honorificum erat, idemque significabat quod nunc apud nos Regis nomen, at vero quum qui eo nomine vocabantur sua potestate in populi pernitiem abusi sunt inde factum est ut tyrannus pro crudeli homine usurpetur' (l. 276; f. 7v.). Compare with Regius: 'tyranni sui: regis sui. tyrannus namque apud antiquos in bonam quoque accipiebatur partem, ut paulo ante scripsimus' [p. 15 (f. xxi recto)]. This is a common observation; see for example the scholia by Reinhard Lorichius on Aphthonius's example of the commonplace 'contra tyrannum': 'Verum Tyrannus olim dicebatur fortis et dominus bonus plenam in subditos potestatem habens. . . . Postea viribus imperij per superbiam coeperunt abuti. Unde tyranni nomen ad eos restrictum est, qui per insolentiam abutuntur imperijs et Rempublicam opprimunt, rediguntque in servitatem.' Aphthonius, *Progymnasmata* . . . *cum luculentibus et utilibus in eadem scholijs Reinhardi Lorichij Hadamarij* (London, Henricus Middeltonus, 1572), f. 97v.

76. 'Attonitum tanto: Poeta Augusti captat benevolentiam commemoratione caedis Iulij Caesaris avunculi sui quae ab eius coniuratis in Senatu Romano misere facta est ubi ille tribus et viginti vulneribus confossus est, ut scribit Suet. Tranq. in eius vita' (l. 202; interleaved folio facing f. 6r.). The reference is to Suetonius, *Life of Caesar* I, 82. See below for more on the rhetorical device of 'captatio benevolentiae'.

77. Regius, p. 13 (f. xvii recto–verso).

78. 'In hoc autem potissimum primo libro Ovidius non modo Poetam sed Philosophum quoque agit, accurate enim tractat ea quae ab antiquis Philosophis de primo [for prima] mundi origine elementorum distinctione, aetatum divisione actoris denique orbis Ornatu literis prodita fuerunt' (folio facing f. 2r.).

79. See Simone Viarre, *La survie d'Ovide dans la littérature scientifique des XIIe et XIIIe siècles* (Poitiers, 1966).

80. Grafton, 'Teacher, Text and Pupil', pp. 52–3.

81. 'Venae peioris: Vena non tantum est corporis animalis in qua sanguis continetur sed etiam terrae in qua sunt quidam meatus quibus metalla sunt conclusa' (l. 128; f. 5r.). In a later passage Godebert notes that such veins can also be found in stones: 'quae modo vena: in terra atque in lapidibus sunt quaedam venae meatus in quibus videlicet aquae portio continetur sicut in his includitur sanguis quibus corpus hominis constat' (l. 410; interleaved folio facing f. 9r.). Compare with Regius: 'Nam venae non tantum animalium dicuntur sed etiam metallorum' [p. 9 (f. xi verso)].

82. 'Intremuit: sub terra multi vapores et aquae in meatibus quibusdam latent e quibus dum exitum querunt atque adeo erumpunt, tanta vi concutiunt terram ut ea non tantum moveri sed hiare plerumque videatur' (l. 284; f. 7v.).

83. 'Quippe ubi: causas generationis talium animalium explicat, humorem videlicet et calorem ex quibus iusta ratione inter se contemperatis res omnes oriri philosophi scribunt' (l. 430; f. 9v.).

84. 'Utque duae dextra: Corpus ipsius terrae secundum suam latitudinem et longitudinem in quinque partes dissecat quas sive regiones sive plagas cosmographi nominant, earum omnium quae media est propter nimium solis ardorem ab hominibus habitari non potest quae idcirco torrida vocatur. Aliae duae ab ea utrinque longissimae remotae sunt, quae propter nimiam a sole distantiam frigore perpetuo rigent, quas idcirco frigidas vocant, duae reliquae inter polas, a parte utraque sitae, quia nec minus propinquae sit [for sunt] nec etiam minus ab eo remotae sunt aerem temperatum habent quae eam ob causam dicuntur temperate' (l. 45; second interleaved folio facing f. 2v.).

85. On the decisive impact of the discovery of the New World on geography see W. G. L. Randles, *De la terre plate au globe terrestre: une mutation épistémologique rapide 1480–1520* (Paris, 1980).

86. 'Est via sublimis: quoniam omnes Dij a Iove vocati per viam lacteam eius Palatium adierunt, idcirco hic eam obiter describit: de qua multe referuntur fabulae, quas passim apud Poetas videre licet. At vero certam rationem candoris eius et fulgoris qui lactis quandam speciem reffert, Cicero explicat in somnio Scipionis cum ait eam in medio permultarum stellarum lucidissimarum esse constitutam, quarum lumine et splendore illustratur' (l. 168; interleaved folio facing f. 5v.). Compare with Regius: 'Lacteum circulum describit, per quem ad regiam Iovis iter diis esse ait. eum vero circulum Graeci galaxiam vocant ἀπὸ τοῦ γάλακτος: hoc est a lacte, unde et Latini lacteum appellarunt. nam candidus esse videtur. de quo si quis plura videre cupit, legat Macrob. in somnium Scipionis' [p. 11 (f. xvi recto, although the Greek term is transliterated)].

87. 'Semina tum primum: Cererem agrorum collendorum rationem primam invenisse atque hominibus tradidisse Virg. aperte scribit lib. 1⁰ Georgic. his verbis: Prima Ceres ferro mortales vertere terram instituit. Attamen Tibullus id adscribit Osiri Iovis filio Egiptiorum Regi his versibus: Primus aratra manu solerti fecit Osiris / Et teneram ferro sollicitavit humum' (l. 123; interleaved folio facing f. 5r.). Compare with Polydorus Vergilius Urbinas, *De rerum inventoribus libri octo* (Lyon, Ant. Gryphius, 1586), III, 1: 'Agriculturam primum omnium, teste Diodoro in I. Osirim, qui et Dionysius dicitur, reperisse ferunt. Affirmat item Tibullus, ita scribens: Primus aratra manu solerti fecit Osiris, / Et teneram ferro sollicitavit humum / Primus inexpertae commisit semina terrae, / Pomaque non notis legit ab arboribus. . . . Sed omnium primam Cererem, quae, uti Ciceroni lib. II de natura

deorum placet, a gerendis frugibus, quasi Geres, nominata est, mortales agriculturam docuisse testatur Virgil. in I. Georgicorum sic scribens: Prima Ceres ferro mortales vertere terram/Instituit,' pp. 215–16. The references are to Cicero, *De natura deorum* II, 26, paragraph 67; Vergil, *Georgics* I, l. 147, and Tibullus *Elegies*, I. 7 11. 29–30.

88. 'Et glacies astricta tum primum: Tempore aetatis argentae propter nimiam aeris inclementiam coacti fuerunt homines domos aedificare ut a talibus iniurijs securi esse possent: caeterum quo in tempore primum inceperit est controversia, multi enim historiographi, inter quos est Eutropius scribunt Saturnum cum in Italiam e Graecia venisset, rudes illi [for illic] populos rationem Domorum aedificandarum terraeque collende docuisset [for docuisse] cum antea ipsi in speluncis et casulis ex frondibusque velgultisque [for virgultisque] contextis habitarent' (l. 120; interleaved folio facing f. 5r.).

89. 'Non tuba directi: Primus omnium Licurgus tubas et lituos in exercitibus adhiberi iussit, atque statuit quibus militum animi ad ineundum certamen, et fortiter in suos hostes irruendum magis excitarentur. ut refert Plut. in Institutis Laconicis' (l. 98; f. 4v.). The reference is to Plutarch, *Moralia* 238B, section 16.

90. 'Et inaequales autumnos: Autumnos inequales vocat propter inconstantem naturam tum aestatis tum hyemis inter quae interpositi sunt proptereaquod videlicet aliquando frigoribus contrahantur nonnunquam etiam diffundantur caloribus, id quod Hippocrates 3. Aphorismorum lib. multorum morborum iudicium, esse scribit' (l. 117; interleaved folio facing f. 5r.). Compare with Caelius Rhodiginus, *Lectionum antiquarum libri xxx* (Geneva, Philippus Albertus 1620), XXX, 10, col. 1680: 'Hippocrates medendi arte nunquam satis laudatus libro Sententiarum tertio: Per autumnum (inquit) acutissimi, atque exitiosissimi accidunt magna ex parte morbi, ver saluberrimum est atque non exitiosum. Eum locum summus auctor Galenus ad verbum sic interpretatur, ubi tempora idoneum omne retinent temperamentum, ver utpote temperatum per ea saluberrimum erit, at acutissimos morbos et exitiosissimos, quantum in ipsammet temporis vim et naturam agitur, autumnus importat. Si quidem ver maxime temperatum modificatumque est: per autumnum vero primum quidem eadem die modo frigus, modo aestus antepollet.' The reference is to Hippocrates, *Aphorisms* III, 9.

91. 'Daphne is the daughter of the river Peneus or as others would have it, of Ladon and earth as poets imagine since trees are born from water and earth. But Apollo is reported to have loved her because the seers whose god he is use [laurel] to announce things to come and to explain dreams; it is sacred to Apollo for this reason. On which subject read Alciatus near the end of his emblems where he treats of trees.' 'Daphne Peneia: Daphne filia est Penei fluminis aut ut alij volunt Ladonis et terrae quod ideo Poetae fingunt quoniam ex terra et aqua nascuntur Arbores. Hanc autem amasse fertur Apollo quia vates quorum ille

Deus est, in denuntiandis rebus futuris maxime in explicandis insomnijs utuntur, quae ob id Appollini sacra est. De qua lege Alciatum circa finem suorum emblematum ubi agit de arboribus' (l. 452; interleaved folio facing f. 9v.). The reference is to Alciato, *Emblemata* (Lyon, G. Rovillius, 1564). 'Laurus: Praescia venturi laurus fert signa salutis. / Subdita pulvillo somni vera facit. Aliud: Debetur Carolo superatis laurea Poenis: / Victrices ornent talia serta comas' (p. 225).

92. 'Delphines: ... Est aut [for autem] Delphini Piscis cuius impetus in natando est pernicissimus quod manifestum est hoc proverbio: Delphinum natare doces, quod torquetur in eos qui se doctiores erudire docent. Eius vero cauda adeo est lubrica, ut Proverbio locum fecerit Delphini caudam ligas quo uti solemus in eos qui rem factu difficilem, suisque viribus maiorem aggrediuntur' (l. 302; interleaved folio facing f. 7v.). For the beginning of the comment see note 126. Compare with Calepinus: 'Delphinum natare doces ... in eos competit, qui monere quempiam conantur in ea re, in qua quum sit ipse exercitatissimus, nihil eget doctore. Delphinum cauda ligas: in eos, qui quippiam in cassum conantur, propterea quod delphinus cauda sit lubrica, nec ea parte teneri queat: aut quod cauda sit valida, cujus agitatione fertur et naves aliquando subvertere, ut hac parte sit invictus. Quadrabit et in eos qui ea via quempiam aggrediuntur, qua nequaquam possit superari' (p. 357). The deeper source is Erasmus, *Adagiorum Chiliades quatuor et sesquicenturia* (Lyon: haeredes Sebast. Gryphii, 1558), who gives the same text as Calepinus, p. 186.

93. Anafora l. 367; anthitesis [sic] l. 19; anthonomasia l. 424; apostrofe l. 379; epexegesis l. 507; epifonema sive exclamatio l. 363; figura anthitheta [sic] l. 345; metafora, ab animalibus ll. 281, 420; metonymia ll. 14, 134, 187; perifrasis ll. 91, 98, 106, 131, 170, 338, 483; prolepsis ll. 190, 504; prosopepeia [sic] l. 342; praeteritio l. 214; similitudo, duplex l. 492, triplex ll. 505, 539; synedoche [sic] ll. 134, 174, 332, 354. I mention later: anakephaleosis l. 32; catachresis ll. 115, 184, seu metafora l. 420; epithsegesis l. 37; exegesis sive amplificatio ll. 138, 151, 275; hyperbole ll. 108, 153, 203, 338; hypallage l. 1; hypotiposis ll. 344, 455.

94. As in P. Mosellanus, *Tabulae de schematibus et tropis in Rhetorica* (Antwerp, Henricus Loeus, 1571); see also Philip Melanchthon, *Elementorum rhetorices libri duo* (Frankfurt, haeredes Christiani Egenolphi, 1579), pp. 227–50. Of the figures noted by Godebert, these works do not mention: anakephaleosis, epexegesis, epithsegesis/epidiegesis, exegesis.

95. 'Similitudo: sicuti idem sol et ceram calefacit et lutum condurat ita eadem oratio et alios reddet meliores et alios deteriores pro ingenij eorum varietate' (f. 9r.). Along with the proverbs mentioned above (note 30) this passage which is not directly related to the text gives evidence of an oral discussion which is not entirely transcribed in the notes.

96. 'Nova corpora: Hipallage id est Oratio inverso rerum ordine com-

plexa, naturalis enim ordo postulabat ut ita diceret corpora in novas formas mutata' (l. 1; f. 2r.).

97. 'Ad sydera: hiperbore [sic] id est oratio excedens omnium hominum fidem' (l. 153; f. 5v.); also 'Totusque perhorruit: hiperbole oratio excedens communem hominum fidem' (l. 203; interleaved folio facing f. 6r.); for 'replet: hiperbole' in l. 338, interleaved folio facing f. 8r., no more explanation is given.

98. 'Collesque exire: per hypotiposim explicat signa et effecta ex quibus Deucalion et Pirrha diluvij finem percipere potuerunt, videlicet cum montes sese erigere ex aquis, arbores item se ostendere, terra denique plana detegi' (l. 344; f. 8r.).

99. 'Viderat adducto: Hypotiposis rem enim ita aperte narrat ut prope oculis subijci videatur' (l. 455; interleaved folio facing f. 10r.).

100. 'Iussit et ambitae: expositio est sive epithsegesis, explicat enim sententiam apertius de aquae situ et loco prolatam his verbis circumfluus humor ultima possedit' (l. 37; first interleaved folio facing f. 3r.).

101. 'Deterior: Catachresis fit enim comparatio cum aurea aetate quae tamen omnis nequitiae expers fuit, itaque cum deteriorem dicit minus praestantem significat' (l. 115; interleaved folio facing f. 4v.).

102. 'Sic ubi dispositam: Brevis est ἀνακεφαλεωσίς, id est complexio eorum omnium quae hactenus generaliter de distinctione chaos, in quatuor elementa protulit' (l. 32; first interleaved folio facing f. 3r.).

103. The subscription at the end of Ringelberg's *Rhetorica* is dated 8 May 1571, while the subscription at the beginning of Ovid's *Metamorphoses* is dated Monday 14 May 1571. Although we cannot know exactly how Godebert conducted his class, and in particular if he taught more than one text simultaneously, these subscriptions indicate that references to Ringelberg in Godebert's commentary on Ovid are probably intentional reinforcements of material covered earlier.

104. 'Sed itum est in: est exegesis id est amplificatio avaritiae hominum ab eorum affectis ipsi enim non contenti frugibus ac segetibus quas culta terra his proferebat omnia metallorum genera ex imis terrae visceribus cum plurimis gemmis eruerunt' (l. 138; f. 5v.). 'Neve foret terris: amplificatio est nequitiae et impietatis eorum qui ferreae aetatis tempore vixerunt, quorum tanta fuit saevitia et cludelitas [for crudelitas] ut non modo in se ipsos arma sua distringerent et contorquerent, sed bellum quoque summo Iovi inferre auderent' (l. 151; f. 5v.). *Amplificatio* is explained in Ringelberg on f. 16v. and is the object of marginal annotations which discuss Cicero's use of *amplificatio*.

105. 'Tectum humeros: sinedoche Poetica, hoc est habens humeros tinctos' (l. 332; interleaved folio facing f. 8r.). The comment really applies to the words that precede the expression that Guyon has singled out: 'innato murice'.

106. 'Iusserat: frasis homerica' (l. 281; f. 7v.).

107. 'Ut Virgilius Homerum, Hesiodum, Teocritum et Horatius Pyndarum, ita hic quoque Ovidius Partheum Scium Graecum poetam clarissimum

qui eiusdem argumenti opus antea contexuerat immitatus est his
quindecim libris, quibus quamvis propter suum exilium extremam
manum imponere non potuerit, tamen propter elegantiam et venusta-
tem, Graecorum ingenijs ita placuerunt, ut eos in suum sermonem
convertere et suorum usui accommodare non dubitarint' (folio facing
f. 2r.).

108. 'Quo quidem opere exemplum Parthenii Chii poetae imitatus dicitur,
qui idem argumentum iam antea Graeco poemate tractasse fertur. Sic
et Virgilius, Homerum, Hesiodum et Theocritum, Horatius Pindarum:
Valerius Apollonium itemque alii alios imitati sunt. Tanta autem huius
operis gratia etiam apud Graecos fuit, ut idem ex Latino sermone, in
suum versibus transtulerint.' Ovid, *Metamorphoseon libri XV . . . Regii
explanatio . . . cum novis Iacobi Micylli . . . additionibus* (Venice,
Gryphius, 1565), 'Jacobi Micylli in titulum libri Metamorphosis
annotatio' facing p. 1. For more on this edition see note 38.

109. 'Ego vindice: totam hanc historiam Ovidius hic protulit ad declaran-
dam Lycaonis transformationem quam his versibus affabre depingit et
ad unium [for ad unguem] exponit . . .' (l. 230; f. 6r.).

110. 'Plebs habitat diversa: duplex Deorum ordo a Poetis fingitur unus
Deorum maiorum gentium quales sunt Jupiter et Neptunus qui ex
utroque parente Deo nati sunt. Alter minorum gentium quos semideos
sive Heroas appellamus, hi altero parente Deo, altero mortali geniti
sunt quales fuisse creduntur Hercules Romulus et Eneas' (l. 173;
interleaved folio facing f. 5v.).

111. 'Affectasse ferunt: gigantes finguntur a Poetis terrae filij nullo patre
creati qui cum longo tempore terras multis caedibusque multoque
hominum cruore commaculassent Iovem ipsum e celo deturbare et
coelesti imperio privare conati sunt . . .' (l. 152; f. 5v.).

112. 'Centum: Numerus certus pro incerto est. Gigantes autem centimani
appellant [for appellantur] idest permultas manus dicuntur habere,
quod et ad iniuriam inferendam paratissimi et etiam potentissimi sunt
qualis apud Poetas fingitur esse Briarius' (l. 183; interleaved folio
facing f. 5v.).

113. 'Aeolii: Aeolus a Poetis fingitur ventorum custodie praefectum [for
praefectus] esse atque in eos imperium habere ut scribit Virgilius libro
primo Aeneid.: "Vasto Rex aeolus antro, / Luctantes ventos, tempesta-
tesque sonoras, / Imperio praemit, vinclis, et carcere frenat" ' (l. 262; f.
7r.; *Aeneid* I, ll. 52–4).

114. 'Summo delabor: Olympus Thessaliae mons est tantae altitudinis ut
suo fastigio celum pertingere videatur unde fit ut a Poetis saepe pro
ipso coelo usurpetur' (l. 212; interleaved folio facing f. 6r.).

115. See in note 53 for example Regius's remark on the poetic use of 'fera'.
Regius also comments, where Godebert does not, on the opening
invocation and the parenthesis that follows and studies the stylistic
devices by which 'an insipid meaning is effected in an elegant way'. 'Dii
coeptis: invocatio; nam vos mutastis et illas: parenthesis est, caussam

invocationis continens; ... est enim emphasis, qua plura innuuntur, quam exprimantur. Minime vero imperitorum quorundam expositio est admittenda, putantium deos in varias figuras esse mutatos, a poeta significari, eoque sic esse ordinandum: Nam vos mutastis et illas. quo quidem modo sensus ex eleganti insulsus efficeretur. periret enim illa emphasis pulchra, quae per copulam, et, aperte demonstratur. sed huiusmodi acuti sensus ab istis detractoribus stolidis, ingenioque carentibus non percipiuntur' [p. 1 (f. i verso)].

116. 'In nova fert animus: Ut dociles atque attentos habeat lectores, more clarorum Poetarum initio proponit, quibus de rebus toto opere sit acturus. Deinde auxilium Deorum implorat, sine quo nihil quidquam egregium fieri potest. Postremo Narrationem aggreditur, eamque a prima orbis origine repetit ad sua usque tempora producturus' (l. 1; f. 2r.). Compare with Regius: 'In nova fert animus: consueverunt Heroici poetae in principiis statim operum suorum proponere primum, quibus de rebus sint in toto opere tractaturi, deinde invocare, tertio loco narrare. Quanquam Graeci fere propositionem cum invocatione coniungant. Eam consuetudinem Ovid. quoque in huius operis initio servat. Nam et brevissime ea, de quibus est scripturus, proponit; et deos ut sibi adesse velint, rogat et narrationem ab ipso mundi primordio orditur. 'in nova' est, inquit, mihi animus describendi mutationes corporum in novas figuras. Hac autem praepositione, quae summam eorum continet, quae in toto opere tractantur, et *dociles et attenti* lectores efficiuntur' (my emphasis) [p. 1 (f. i verso)].

117. 'Etenim per totam orationem data occasione facere licet *attentos, benevolos ac dociles* [auditores—supplied in interlinear paraphrase] sed maxime in exordio.' Ringelberg, *Rhetorica* (Paris, Gabriel Buon, 1561), f. 10r. The expression is repeated twice in the corresponding manuscript notes: 'Licet in divisione sicut in alijs omnibus partibus orationis aliquando liceat oblata occasione ad causae commoditatem, benevolentiam, et docillitatem et attentionem parare non idcirco tamen ipsa censenda sunt minus propria exordio... Dicere etiam possumus propriae [sic] captari benev. attent. et docillitatem in exordio in alijs vero partibus orationis tantum renovari' (f. 10v.).

118. 'Ante mare: a prima mundi constitutione transformationum narrationem aggreditur, sequens Hesiodi sententiam qui in Theogonia scribit primum omnium fuisse quoddam chaos ex quo postea Coelum et quatuor elementa deducta fuerint, Platonis etiam Opinionem probat et Stoicorum qui mundum adeo [for a Deo] factum esse crediderunt. Ab Aristotele vero discentit [for dissentit] qui non modo deffendit mundum esse aeternum, sed etiam ingenitum. Transformatio nihil est aliud quam mutatio ab una in aliam formam, ex quo facile est intelligere, transformationem quandam factam esse, cum ex Chao indigesta molle compositus est hic mundus qui ob pulchritudinem et eximium ornatum κοσμος a Graecis nominatur' (l. 5; f. 2r.).

119. 'Unus erat etc.: Quoniam Chaos principium mundi esse dicit idipsum

nunc describit duplici ratione, primum per mutationem formarum quibus illud corpus impolitum carebat quamvis enim omnes omnium rerum formae in eo essent, ita tamen erant confuse ut prorsus non apparerent, deinde ab his rebus quae nunc distincte conspiciuntur, in toto orbe cum antea essent in Chao permixtae' (l. 6; f. 2v.).

120. 'Sic erat instabilis: alia ratione describit Chaos videlicet, ab eius defformitate quia nempe res quae in eo conservate erant sua praestantia et pulchritudine erant destitutae et quoniam elementa inter se confusa, propter contrarias qualitates, quibus sunt praedita continuum inter se bellum atque praelium gererent' (l. 16; interleaved folio facing f. 2v.).

121. 'Nam caelo terras: Mundi compositionem explicare aggreditur per distinctionem earum rerum, quae in Chao permixtae erant et confuse unde colligere possumus mundi originem nihil aliud esse, nisi secressionem formarum quas inter se confusas Chaos complectebatur' (l. 22; interleaved folio facing f. 2v.). 'Ignea convexi vis: Ordinem elementorum explicat, cuius ratio ducta est a diversa eorum qualitate. Ita quemadmodum propter summam levitatem ignis supremum ita quoque terra propter summam gravitatem, in infimum locum optinerit [for obtinerit], aer vero et aqua ob mediam naturam utriusque qualitatis participem inter eadem interiecta sunt, ita ut aer propter maiorem levitatem aquae superemineat' (l. 26; interleaved folio facing f. 2v.). 'Principio terram: supra elementorum ordinem breviter exposuit, nunc particulatim vero et [sigillatim crossed out] atque speciatim singulorum elementorum naturam, variasque eorundem affectiones et qualitates describit initio ducto ab ipsa terra omnium infima a qua gradatim ad ea quae superiora sunt elementa assendit [for ascendit]' (l. 34; first interleaved folio facing f. 3r.).

122. 'Principio terram: Posteaquam, inquit, chaos in quattuor elementa distinxit, effecit ut undique terra foret rotunda, variisque rebus institueretur.' Regius, p. 4 (f. v verso).

123. 'Crepitantia: exagerat infelicem et miseram ferrae aetatis conditionem et quod bellum tum temporis inter homines, exarserit ad quod eos potissimum auri utillitas inflammavit' (l. 143; f. 5v.).

124. 'Qua: argumentum est a comparatione quo exagerat, atque exacerbat facinus in se admissum a Lycaone cuius quidem omnes fere mortales erant conscij. Illud viro magis execrandum esse docet magisque horrendum quam scelus quod gigantes in se patraverunt proptereaquod hi soli bellum contra se struxerant at vero in crimen Lycaonis omnes prope incumbunt eique navant operam' (l. 183; interleaved folio facing f. 5v.).

125. 'Tunc quoque visa decens: calamitatem suam exaggerat, ab Amoris sui incremento ait enim suis crutiatibus hoc accessisse incommodum, quod cum Daphne a se aufugere coepisset multo formosior ac ellegantior quam antea sibi visa fuisset, quoniam vento agitatis eius vestibus

contigerit nudatum eius corpus aspicere atque intueri' (l. 527; interleaved folio facing f. 11v.).

126. 'Delphines: exagerat calamitatem diluvij a mutatione naturae rerum,
Delphines enim in aquis degere solent non in sylvis' (l. 302; interleaved
folio facing f. 7v.). The end of the comment is quoted in note 92.

127. As noted above, there are no etymologies after l. 283; quotes from
other classical texts also stop at l. 281, while the commentary continues
smoothly to l. 580 and sporadically on to l. 630. Godebert consistently
explains proper names throughout, however.

128. 'Imminet his aer qui etc: sicut naturam terrae descripsit, tum ab eius
qualitatibus, tum etiam ab eiusdem diversis partibus idem exequitur de
aere, cuius tanquam partes constituit, nubes, fulmina et ventus' (l. 52;
first interleaved folio facing f. 3r.).

129. 'Vela dabat ventis: Argumento ab effectis ducto maximam ferrae
aetatis fuisse hominum declarat ex eo praesertim quod ad quaerendas
ex peregrinis regionibus opes navium usum excogitaverint atque earum
auxilio maria navigarint, cum tamen ventorum naturam non satis
adhuc perspectam haberent' (l. 132; f. 5r.).

130. 'Ergo ubi marmoreo: Deorum consilium quos Jupiter convocaverat
exprimit a circonstantijs loci et personarum atque rerum quae in eo,
notatu digne videbantur' (l. 177; interleaved folio facing f. 5v.).

131. 'Sic ubi deseruit madidos: locus est comparationis, confert enim Nili
inundationem cum diluvio, ut inde appareat quemadmodum post Nili
inundationem multa animantium genera in Aegipto reperiuntur humi
serpentia: ita quoque post diluvium permagnam et habundantem
eorum multitudinem ex aqua relicta productam esse' (l. 422; f. 9r.).

132. 'Veteres: ab adiunctis indicat non valde alienam licaonis fuisse transformationem cum in eo pristine formae signa et vestigia remansissent'
(l. 237; f. 6v.).

133. 'Voce manuque: oratoris officio functum Iovem significat cum apud
Deos de Lycaonis scelere diceret, non enim in oratore tantum vocis,
sed gestus moderatio requiritur' (l. 205; interleaved folio facing f. 6r.).

134. 'Non ego pro mundi: Exordium est orationis qua usus est Jupiter apud
Deos ut illis indicaret et exponeret saevitiam et crudelitatem Lycaonis,
hic vero attentionem primum parat a rei de qua dicturus est gravitate
deinde benevolentiam a persona sua et benigno in homines probos
animo quos dicit se velle a tali calamitate et feritate eripere' (l. 182;
interleaved folio facing f. 5v.).

135. 'Quod tamen: ut attentos suos ac benevolos habeat auditores pollicitur
se dicturum et eis explicaturum aperte et copiose ea quae scire illos
maxime velle existimabat quodnam videlicet facinus in se Lychaon
admisisset deinde quodnam de eo suplicium sumpsisset' (l. 210;
interleaved folio facing f. 6r.).

136. 'Contigerat nostras: incipit Iupiter narrare et exponere factum
Lychaonis ut manifestum faciat Dijs quos in consilium vocaverat,

quam execranda vitia ab hominibus terram incolentibus patrarentur imprimis quidem dicit se a caelo coactum fuisse in terras descendere, ut omoris [for rumoris?] qui de hominum sententia circonferebatur veritem [for veritatem] experiri posset' (l. 211; interleaved folio facing f. 6r.). 'Crepuscula: a circonstantia tempus describit quo Regiam Lycaonis ingressus videlicet crepusculo vespertino cum sol sese sub orizonte occultare incipit' (l. 219; f. 6r.).

137. 'An satis o superi: argumento a minori ad maius probat necessario sibi perdendos esse omnes homines qui Lycaoniam exercent in terris crudelitatem quoniam si illi permitterentur diutius vivere, reliquos omnes terrarum incolas qui minime perversi sunt opprimerent cum ipsi non dubitarint sibi Deorum summo incidijs [for insidijs] structis necem inferre' (l. 196; interleaved folio facing f. 6r.).

138. See Philip Melanchthon, *Erotemata dialectices* (Wittenberg: Iohannes Crato, 1556), pp. 300–18.

139. Metamorphosis of the ages: 'Jupiter antiqui: Primam calamitatem argenteae aetatis proponit a metamorphosi et mutatione antiqui status temporis. Nam cum aurea aetate tempus eodem semper esset statu, temperato ex modico calore et frigore; statim initio Regni Iovis, quo aetas argentea coepit, annus distinctus est in quatuor partes, qualitatibus diversas Hyemem, Autumnum, ver et aestatem' (l. 116; interleaved folio facing f. 5r.), and 'In quorum: praedictis virtutibus vitia maxime contraria opponit ut metamorphosis facilius appareret, et apertius ab alijs aetatibus praecedentibus ferrea distingueretur' (l. 130; f. 5r.). Metamorphosis of the giants: 'In faciem vertisse: declarat transformationem gigantum cum enim hi a Iove fuissent trucidati et gravissimis terrae aggeribus obbruti ex eorum cruore prodierunt infiniti prope perversi homines impietatem erga Deos et omne horrendum facinus perpetrantes' (l. 160; interleaved folio facing f. 5v.). Metamorphosis of warmed water into life forms, especially snakes: 'Caetera Diversis telus animalia formis: Explicata tota ratione diluvij causis quae omnibus a quibus illud traxit originem, nunc aggreditur ad explicationem earum transformationum quae post huiusmodi diluvium supra terram contigerunt tum enim ex putredine aquae supra eam stagnantis et solis calore continuo in eam agente permulta animantia praesertim humi grassientia [for grassantia] serpentes excitati sunt' (l. 416; interleaved folio facing f. 9r.).

140. See preceding note, comment for l. 130.

141. 'Mollia cinguntur: explicat veram metamorphosim et transformationem Daphnes in laurum adhibita distributione singularum partium eius corporis quae in alias partes lauri conversae sunt' (l. 549; interleaved folio facing f. 12r.).

142. 'Et terrena fuit: ut magis probabilem faciat lapidum a Deucalione et Pyrrha post terga iactorum in homines transmutationem nominatim declarat quo pacto quaeque lapidum partes in alias similes converse fuerint humide enim et terrenae in carnem, Duriories vero et

magis solide in ossa conversae sunt' (l. 408; interleaved folio facing f. 9r.). By contrast, Regius summarizes Ovid's description of the transformation without identifying it as a persuasive tactic: 'Terrenae, inquit, partes lapidum molles et humidae in corpus fuere conversae; solidae vero et durae in ossa; venae autem in venas.' Regius, p. 19 (f. xxiii verso).

143. 'Ergo ubi: concludit qua ratione et quibus ex causis terra aquis diluvij irrigata, tam multas animalium species protulerit. Hic autem quaedam est παρασκεύασις. id est praeparatio ad explicandam victoriam quam Apollo de Pythone peperit eo sagittis a se interfecto' (l. 434; f. 9v.).

144. 'Primus amor Phoebi Daphne Peneia: Daphnes fabulam instituto suo accommodat, ea enim aliquando in laurum transformata est, tunc videlicet cum Apollo eius forma excellenti captus dum illam fesse fugientem persequeretur imploraret parentum auxilium ut sibi adversus Apollinis inhonestos conatus succurrent: Huius autem fabulae hoc loco recitande occasionem, inde sumpsit quod nuper de lauro loqutus sit quae ex Daphne Penei filia primum orta est' (l. 452; interleaved folio facing f. 9v.).

145. 'Est nemus Aemonia: Io filiam Inaci fluminis Jupiter adamavit et compressit eamque ne id resciret Iuno in vaccam albam mutavit verum rem suspicata Iuno eam ab Iove dono impetravit, Argoque cui centum erant oculi custodiendam tradidit, sed eius sortis misertus Juppiter Mercurium misit qui Argum interficeret hunc interfectum Iuno convertit in Paonem eiusque centum oculos caude apposuit. Orditur autem Poeta a topographia hoc est loci descriptione' (l. 568; f. 12r.).

146. George Kennedy, *The Art of Rhetoric in the Roman World 300 B.C.– A.D. 300* (Princeton, 1972), p. 416.

147. 'Ovidius, quum narrasset fabulam Daphnes, quo pacto erat mutata in laurum, uti commode transiret ad fabulam Ius, omnia flumina convenisse memorat ad patrem Daphnes consolationis causa, praeter patrem Ius, qui domestico impeditus erat luctu propter filiam, quae conversa erat in iuvencam. Quod itaque dixit confluxisse illuc fluvios, digressio est: quae nihil quidem ad institutum, hoc est, ad rerum Metamorphosin pertinet: nisi quod fabulas connectit.' Ringelberg, f. 9r. The marginal annotations on this subject include summaries of the stories of Daphne and Io (f. 7v) and this discussion of Ringelberg: 'digressio videtur potius ad rei ostentationem quam ad utillitatem causae esse comparatam praesertim cum contineat ea que extrinsecus assumuntur nec ipsi causae propriae assumpti. Quinque vero ob causas ea ab oratore fieri solent. Ad transeundum ad rem diversam a causa cuius videlicet explicatio, non nihil adiumenti ei afferre potest:—ad exorciandum narrationem propriam;—ad laudandum aliquam personam;—ad amplificandum crimen quod quidem ei cum propria narratione communis est;—ad describendum aliquem locum. Quae omnia orator praestare duntaxat debet cum causae suae prodesse possunt' (f. 7r.).

148. On the transitions to the story of Daphne: 'Cetera diversis: Reliqua, inquit, animalia ex terra humida et sole calefacta orta sunt, id quod fieri posse facile Aegyptus est documento. nam post Nili inundationem glebae in varias animalium figuras commutantur. haec autem iccirco a poeta inseruntur ut commodius Daphnes in laurum metamorphosin cum superioribus connectat.' Regius, p. 19 (f. xxiii verso). And 'Nondum laurus erat: concinne mutationem sequentem cum superioribus connectit. assignans enim caussam, cur pythiorum victores esculeam coronam acciperent, laurum (qua postea, qui, vicissent, fuere coronati) nondum fuisse ait, sicque describit.' Regius, p. 21 (f. xxiv verso). On the transition to the story of Io: 'Est nemus Aemoniae: Tempe, amoenissimam Aemoniae vallem, describit poeta, quod commodius ἰοὺς, Inachi amnis filiae, metamorphosin in iuvencam cum superiore connectat.' Regius, p. 26 (f. xxvii recto, with the Greek characters transliterated).

149. Godebert notes only that poets believe that trees are born from water and earth, see note 91.

150. I would like to thank Anthony Grafton, Jean Céard and Francis Goyet for their help and valuable comments, and Stephen Ferguson of the Princeton University Library for making this study possible in the first place.

The University of Alcalá de Henares from 1568 to 1618: Students and Graduates

Benoît Pellistrandi

Between 1498 and 1517 the Cardinal Archbishop of Toledo, Francisco Jiménez de Cisneros, founded the university of Alcalá on the banks of the Henares, some thirty kilometres north-east of Madrid. The site, at the heart of Castile, was central if austere. Surrounded by other foundations of the same period or a little earlier—Toledo, Seville, Granada, Onate, Osuna, Valencia, Siguenza—Alcalá's importance lay in the privileges and protections which it enjoyed and which were ratified by Pope Alexander VI and the Spanish monarchs Ferdinand and Isabella.[1]

The university's first decrees were drawn up in 1510 and those which regulated the life and studies of the *colegios pobres* appeared in 1513. Finally, a definitive version of the constitutions and statutes of the *Colegio mayor y Universidad San Ildefonso* was issued on 17 October 1517.[2] This period of the founding of the university came to an end, appropriately enough, three weeks before the death of Cardinal Cisneros.

The university of Alcalá followed in the Parisian collegiate tradition and organized itself around the *Colegio mayor* of San Ildefonso.[3] Cisneros endowed the college with thirty-three scholarships which were to benefit students of theology, canon law and medicine. These *colegiales* held therefore at least the degree of bachelor of arts, the prerequisite for attendance at the higher faculties which taught theology, canon law and medicine. Initially chosen by Cisneros himself, these scholars gradually took over university positions as they fell vacant. Each 17 October, the eve of the opening of the university year, they elected the rector of the college who was also to function as rector of the university. Other colleges took their place in this university institution, but instead of the seven schools for teaching grammar which were originally planned, only the colleges of San Isidore and San Eugenius saw the light of day. The cardinal–founder also linked San Ildefonso to the collegiate church of Saints Justo and Pastor of Alcalá, thus offering students the possibility of an ecclesiastical career which would begin with a church living. Such was the university institution envisaged by Cisneros.[4] Marcel Bataillon's observation that 'en vérité, Saint Ildephonse est le siège d'une aristocracie universitaire' shows both the ideal which lay behind Cisneros's creation of this centre of learning and the inherent risk of deviation from his original plan.[5]

The abundance of source material and the character of the founder have led historians to examine this first stage of the history of Alcalá in particular, encouraged by the originality of the creation.[6]

The founding of the university of Alcalá entailed the setting up of a fully self-contained ecclesiastical teaching institution comprising facilities for primary, secondary and higher education. This was as much a work of church reform as a renaissance of theological studies. The project of the polyglot Bible which was undertaken there indicates the partnership which Cisneros intended to promote between textual study and theology. The introduction of nominalism and the coexistence of the three theological 'schools' of Thomism, Scotism and nominalism reveal Cisneros's intention: to make Alcalá into a centre of research. This almost Erasmian notion shows that the traditional form of theological studies in Spain was being challenged; indeed, Alcalá was setting itself up as a rival to Salamanca. Alcalá's fundamental achievement lay in the study of texts and the grooming of competent clerks, an accomplishment which deserves to be mentioned as an active contribution to the Spanish Catholic 'pre-Reformation'.

Times changed. Catholicism was buffeted by the same spiritual and intellectual winds which rocked the political unity of the empire of Charles V. The conflict which was taking root and which was to redraw the map of European spirituality no longer allowed for the luxury of more subtly defined religious positions. Erasmianism was no longer acceptable. Once the inquisition set out to find those— whether from near or far—who were likely to favour heresy, among the first to be seized were a number of former or incumbent professors of Alcalá: Hernan Nunez, who had worked on the Bible project, Dionisio Vazquez, the titular holder of the chair of holy scripture, Ramirez, professor of rhetoric, Hernan Vazquez and Albornoz, canons of the church of San Justo, and Miguel Torres, ex-rector of another college at Alcalá, the Trilingual college. In 1545 Melchor Cano arrived at the university and rehabilitated Thomism. With this the spirit of the 'first Alcalá'[7] was destroyed and the university was reintegrated into the Salamantine theological tradition.[8]

This detailed account has been necessary to understand the development of the intellectual and spiritual ethos of the university of Alcalá and to see that by 1568 we are no longer concerned with a pioneering university, but rather a university like any other. Like any other? The proof of this proposition will be found in an examination of the matriculation and degree registers which permit us to uncover Alcalá's standing in relation to its direct rivals, the universities of Salamanca and Valladolid.

In choosing as our period of observation the half century which spans from 1568 to 1618, we are immediately forced to analyse our findings in the context of the so-called 'educational revolution' of the sixteenth and early seventeenth centuries. Now that the history of higher education has moved away from a mere description of institutions, attention has become focused on the social history of student populations, the analysis of the cultural influence of the university and its role in moulding élites.[9] Today, to study the workings of a university in the modern period is to take stock of the pattern of student attendance, in other words, to answer the following questions: Who were the students? How many were there? How did they get there? What did they do there? What did they learn? Which faculties did they attend? To which careers were they destined?[10]

It was from this starting-point that Lawrence Stone was led to develop the idea of an 'educational revolution' during this period. He found that in England between 1560 and 1640 student numbers doubled and ultimately reached the record rate of 2.5% of the 17-year-old age group.[11] Richard Kagan, in his work on the universities of Castile, found the same pattern of exceptional student growth within the same chronological limits.[12] To examine the *libros de matricula* and the *libros de grados* of the university of Alcalá de Henares between 1568 and 1618 is, then, to provide detailed data of the history of a particular institution in this seminal period which can then be used to flesh out and if necessary modify assumptions about the overall pattern of student attendance which are already an historical orthodoxy.[13] It is appropriate to begin by drawing the territorial map of the university of Alcalá to discover whether we are concerned with a university which recruited nationally, or rather an institution of only regional importance. This analysis of recruitment must be undertaken for each faculty—arts, medicine, canon law and theology— taking care, of course, to note the variations in student numbers in each of the faculties which in turn affected the overall balance of the university. Then we will look at degrees: how many were taken? Did the pattern change over time? And finally, was there a process of professionalization of studies?

1. Growth in student numbers: breakdown by faculty

Until now the only figures we have had for the university of Alcalá were those supplied, at ten-year intervals, by R. Kagan. These, for the period 1550–1620, are as follows:[14]

1550	1560	1570	1580	1590	1600	1610	1620
2567	3030	3217	3208	3066	2736	2640	3632

It can be seen that there is an increase of 25% between 1550 and 1570 followed by a stagnation, a fall in the dark years of the beginning of the seventeenth century and then a reversal in this trend which brings us to the highpoint of the year 1620. Our own results, taken at five-year intervals, are as follows:

1568	3501 enrolled students
1573	3153
1578	2629
1583	3415
1588	3805
1591	2885
1598	3002
1603	2671
1608	2781
1613	3192
1618	3252

With a few slight discrepancies, one can see the same general pattern. The early date at which the threshold of 3,000 students was crossed is noteworthy: this occurred in 1560 according to Kagan or 1568 according to our findings. We both agree that numbers remained around or above this mark until the end of the century. Similarly, the trough of the years 1600–1610 may be detected in both tables, as well as the fact that the threshold of 3,000 was crossed again thereafter.

The results which can be extracted from Luis Enrique Rodriguez's thesis on Salamanca show the same low in the number of registrands in the first decade of the seventeenth century at Spain's premier university: 5,060 students in 1597, 4,141 in 1598, 4,080 in 1599 and 5,137 in 1604. From 1611 to 1620 however the figures remain steadily above the threshold of 5,000 students.[15] The dramatic events of the end of the sixteenth and beginning of the seventeenth centuries account for these results: the plague decimated the Basque provinces, Navarre, Old and New Castile as well as the Asturias, Galicia and Portugal.[16] These were the foremost areas of recruitment to the two universities. There is therefore nothing surprising about this fall in student numbers in 1600; indeed, the speed with which student numbers regained their former level may indicate that the social strata which supplied the university population were better able than most to escape the epidemic.

Viewed in the wider context of the Castilian university network, Alcalá was, in terms of the size of its student population, the second university after Salamanca. Valladolid was the third, but substantially behind with only about 1,700 students.[17] Out of the total figure of 18,000 for all Castilian students in 1590, Salamanca comprised 36.8%, Alcalá 21.5% and Valladolid 9.5%. In total, these three principal universities accounted for more than two thirds of the student population in the Crown of Castile. Here then is a first global statistic.

A richer source of analysis is provided by the breakdown of student numbers at Alcalá by faculty. Table I below shows the results.

Surprising developments emerge: the overall balance between the faculties was overturned in half a century.

The collapse in the number of students at the grammar schools — San Isidore disappeared from the matriculation register in 1617[18] — and the growth of the faculty of canon law are the two major events which emerge from this table. There is also another, less obvious,

Table 1: Breakdown of Student Numbers by Faculty

Year	Grammar	Arts	Medicine	Theology	Canon Law
1568	1370	1148	105	395	483
	39.1%	32.8%	3.0%	11.3%	13.8%
1573	1066	1017	106	497	467
	33.8%	32.2%	3.4%	15.8%	14.8%
1578	596	1048	97	437	451
	22.6%	39.8%	3.7%	16.6%	17.1%
1583	635	1526	141	588	525
	18.6%	44.7%	4.1%	17.2%	15.4%
1588	571	1687	167	739	641
	15.0%	44.3%	4.4%	19.4%	16.8%
1591	425	1275	115	518	552
	14.7%	44.2%	4.0%	17.9%	19.1%
1598	380	1261	88	567	706
	12.6%	42.0%	2.9%	18.8%	23.5%
1603	339	1178	104	469	581
	12.7%	44.1%	3.9%	17.5%	21.7%
1608	258	1244	117	438	724
	9.3%	44.7%	4.2%	15.8%	26.0%
1613	252	1420	119	520	882
	7.9%	44.5%	3.7%	16.3%	27.6%
1618	239	1318	159	515	1021
	7.3%	40.5%	4.9%	15.8%	31.4%

but intimately connected with the first two. This has to do with the preponderant share taken by the major faculties, i.e. those of medicine, theology and canon law. Their share went up from 28.1% of all matriculands in 1568 to 52.1% in 1618. Can this trend be taken to indicate a professionalization of the university of Alcalá? Certainly the network of grammar schools outside the universities grew and made those inside redundant. Some grammar schools were of municipal origin, others were linked to the Society of Jesus. The latter were the greatest challenge to the grammar schools attached to the universities. Indeed, Jesuit colleges often took the place of municipal schools which had been abandoned, without regret, by the municipalities. Such was the case at Guadalajara, 30 kilometres from Alcalá, in 1619.[19] Thus Richard Kagan was able to write: 'With Castile's major universities out of the picture, the Society of Jesus quickly became the leading organizer of secondary education in Hapsburg Spain.'[20] Did the university of Alcalá thereby become an authentic institution of higher education as what we would today call secondary education was gradually eradicated from the university sphère? Perhaps. On the other hand, the undiminishing importance of the faculty of arts, a generalist not a professional faculty, would seem to suggest that this view requires some qualification.

One thing is definitely clear: after 1568 the university of Alcalá rapidly cut its ties with its humanist roots. The studies especially promoted at Alcalá during the Cisnerian period of the university are reminders of the organic tie which linked theology with philology, and of which the polyglot Bible was such a clear expression. According to Robert Richard: 'L'Université d'Alcalá se plaît à revenir aux Pères de l'Eglise, aux lumières de l'Eglise universelle, comme aux gloires de l'Eglise hispanique: saint Jérôme, saint Ambroise, saint Augustin, saint Grégoire sont ses grands maîtres.'[21] What are these 'glories' of the ancient church if not a symbolic expression of the importance given to the written word? It seems to us, therefore, that still more than the particular importance given to the faculty of theology, evidence of the loyalty of Alcalá to the principles and vision of its founder is given by the numbers in the grammar schools as opposed to those of the faculty of arts. What can we make of this half-century after 1568? The grammar schools came to account for only a negligible part of the university population. The students following courses of study in rhetoric, that is to say those at the Trilingual college, were only two in 1618 as opposed to 102 in 1568.

One cannot help but be struck by the chronological coincidence between this development and the reforms of the Counter-Reformation laid down at the Council of Trent. The end of Spanish Erasmianism can be illustrated in many ways: in the hardening of attitudes towards the followers of Erasmus, in the *auto-da-fé* of Valladolid—that spectacular eradication, in May and September 1559, of communities which were more or less Lutheran, but definitely heterodox[22]—in the implementation of the Index by the General Inquisitor Valdés, and in the decision to deny Spanish students the opportunity of the *peregrinatio academica*. But the end is also illustrated in the revolution in matriculation figures at Alcalá. Between 1568 and 1618 the philological vocation was abandoned.[23]

This is all the more noticeable in that Alcalá is the only one of the three great Castilian universities where an alteration in the balance of its faculties can be clearly discerned in the decades after 1570.

Exact comparison with what happened at Valladolid and Salamanca is impossible because of the absence of reliable data for
Alcalá before 1560. However, the general picture seems clear. At
Valladolid the only observable change is that of an increase in the
strength of the faculties of law.[24] Similarly, at Salamanca civil law
grew in importance as theology noticeably regressed (from 13.7% of
all matriculands in 1598 to 9.9% in 1618) but that is all.[25] At these
two universities the share of the higher faculties in 1616–1618 was
75.2% at Valladolid and 84.3% at Salamanca. Above all their
professional orientation was illustrated by the dominant presence of
students of law. The predominance of the faculties of canon law over
those of civil law will also have been noticed. This was in part a
reflection of ecclesiastical and university ways of thinking, but also,
and more importantly, of the organization of legal studies and the
different opportunities open to a graduate of civil law as opposed to
one of canon law. 'En effet,' writes Jean-Marc Pelorson, 'le baccalauréat en droit canon ouvre l'accès à la licence ou au doctorat dans
la même discipline, grades exigés pour la plupart des prébendes et
dignités ecclésiastiques alors que les grades correspondant en lois n'y
suffisent pas. D'ailleurs, dans certaines universités, l'obtention d'un
double baccalauréat est plus rapide si l'impétrant a commencé par le
droit canon: à Salamanque depuis 1594, un an d'études complémen-
taires suffit, alors qu'il faut deux ans de plus pour le bachelier
légiste.'[26] Alcalá tended, then, to lose its atypical character and to
fall into line with the dominant model, that of Salamanca. This
became all the more the case at the close of the period in the 1620s
when civil law, expressly forbidden by Cisneros, entered the university curriculum. But let us not adopt Cisneros's prejudice against
legal studies. Theological thought was enriched by the incursions of
law, since the issues with which it was thereafter forced to grapple
were no longer more or less abstruse speculations, but real problems
which demanded concrete answers. It is sufficient to recall the
example of Las Casas and the rights of the Indians. The so-called
school of theologian-jurists at Salamanca began with theological
speculations and ended with new norms in law. This development of
the second half of the sixteenth century took place, be it noted, at the
university of Salamanca, a traditional university which was able to
take up the challenge which the creation of Alcalá had represented.[27]

2. The geographical background of students at the University of Alcalá

In looking at the geographical background of the student-body we shall utilize information gathered from the *libros de matricula* which shows the places of origin of the students. Primarily, the records provide data about the students' dioceses. The question is to discover whether Alcalá's recruitment was regional or national. Here, as before, comparisons with Salamanca are inevitable. First a word on the methodology used in constructing the following tables is necessary. Some of the names of dioceses were illegible—363 out of 34,286, or 1.05% of the total, which may be considered negligible. A more serious difficulty lies in the fact that some students inscribed their place of origin as *complutense* or *complutensis, compluto* being the Latin name for Alcalá. This proportion of students varies between 3.85% and 9.5%. We included these students in the figures given for the three dioceses of New Castile—Toledo, Cuenca, Siguenza—while recognizing that in so doing we might make some mistakes. This assumption rests on the discovery that the highest percentage of 'complutense' students recorded in any year during the period (9.50%) corresponds to the lowest enrolment figure for New Castilian students (51.4%). Logically, therefore, the two sets of indices belong together. Following the practice of L. E. Rodriguez, we amalgamated the dioceses of Old Castile and León as those areas were geographically, historically and politically united. In the same way, we grouped together the dioceses of Calahorra and Pamplona. The former had under its jurisdiction Rioja itself and the Basque provinces of Biscaye and Guipúzcoa; the latter contained Navarre. In this way we obtained a geographically coherent northern entity. It must be noted here that individual dioceses varied greatly in size. The diocese of Toledo was immense.

Table 2 below gives the figures for the five most important regions which supplied students to Alcalá.

Apparently, the shift in the numerical balance between the faculties was also accompanied by a noticeable change in the pattern of geographical recruitment. This was not revolutionary but none-theless one can detect a geographical narrowing in Alcalá's area of intake. The bastion of recruitment was New Castile, whereas Old Castile appears to have been well and truly under the influence of Salamanca and Valladolid. It will be observed that there was a

Table 2:　The Regional Distribution of Students

Year	New Castile	Old Castile León	Navarre Calahorra	Aragon	Andalusia
1568	51.9%	18.5%	11.2%	6.2%	3.75%
1573	58.6%	13.8%	10.5%	4.55%	3.45%
1578	62.8%	11.5%	10.5%	4.45%	3.15%
1583	60.9%	13.1%	11.6%	3.25%	2.35%
1588	61.5%	15.1%	9.8%	4.2%	2.4%
1591	60.7%	15.9%	12.1%	3.25%	1.7%
1598	61.95%	14.7%	9.3%	2.25%	2.25%
1603	58.2%	12.8%	10.05%	6.15%	2.20%
1608	60.95%	13.6%	9.0%	5.4%	2.55%
1613	63.5%	9.4%	8.6%	6.95%	2.05%
1618	64.9%	8.7%	9.9%	5.05%	1.6%

steady 10% contingent of students from the dioceses of Pamplona and Calahorra. Students from Aragon were scarce between 1583 and 1598 but in the first years of the seventeenth century made up around 5%. The Andalusian contingent steadily declined. Alcalá's recruitment became, in a word, more provincial. The predominance of New Castile was first and foremost that of the local diocese of Toledo. In 1568, 32% of students came from the immediate vicinity; in 1618 this proportion was 38.8%. In contrast, at Salamanca in 1614 only 14.2% of the students came from the diocese itself, admittedly a diocese of modest size compared with Toledo.[28]

Thus, at the same time that Alcalá was becoming a university like any other and losing its particular Cisnerian flavour, its recruitment came to be drawn from a more regional pool. If we compare the two maps, one showing the regional distribution of the students of Salamanca and the other that of the students of Alcalá de Henares in the years 1613-1614, the truly national character of Salamanca emerges clearly. Apart from Catalonia, the kingdom of Valencia, and those of Murcia and the Asturias, all the other regions sent their students to Salamanca. On the other hand, one can see very clearly the regional dependence of Alcalá; in global terms, Alcalá was the university of the Castilian *Meseta* and not even of all the *Meseta* either.

These tendencies are confirmed if we move to an examination of the areas of recruitment of each faculty (see the tables in the appendix).

In 1618, 85.8% of grammar school students came from the dioceses of Toledo, Cuenca and Siguenza. One can link this phenomenon to the professionalization of the university as the study of grammar became the monopoly of institutions of secondary education. The network of secondary colleges became increasingly dense. No longer was there any need to go to Alcalá for one's first Latin letters. The same explanation could be advanced for the growing regionalization of recruitment to the faculty of arts. In 1568, 48.4% of students came from New Castile; in 1618 this contingent made up 63%. Apart from the dioceses of Pamplona and Calahorra, all regions saw their share reduced. In contrast, at Salamanca, in 1614, only 47.2% of arts students came from the dioceses of León and Old Castile, and this was a higher number than average for students from Old Castile.[29] The comparison leads us yet again to emphasize the difference between Salamanca, which may be considered as having a national recruitment, and Alcalá which became a university of regional importance.

A similar phenomenon can be observed in the higher faculties. Of all the faculties, medicine was the most unusual in terms of the geographical origin of its students. What is immediately striking is the large share taken by Andalusia between 1568 and 1613, if that share had apparently fallen by 1618. In 1573, 17.5% of Andalusian students were enrolled in medicine. Ten years later 20 of the 81 Andalusian students of Alcalá were to be found in the faculty. In the normal course of events, the south of the Iberian peninsula sent many students to the faculties of medicine. At Alcalá, in 1578, the Portuguese made up 4.1% of all registrands, in 1608 3.4%; in 1618 the Valencians made up 3.1% of the faculty total. Similar patterns can be observed at Salamanca.[30] Should we see this predominance of southerners as a hangover from the long Muslim occupation? Did the scientific centre at Córdoba leave long-lasting imprints in Andalusia which would explain, in part, the presence of these Andalusian students in the faculties of medicine?

In the theology faculty, however, there was a continued regionalization of recruitment. In 1568 there was a fairly good regional distribution of students and New Castile accounted for only 41.5% of registrands. Then this percentage rose to approach an average of 60%, reaching its highest point in 1598 with 63.1%. Alcalá's specialization in the first half of the sixteenth century was more likely to attract a national recruitment. The fact that Alcalá reintegrated itself into the dominant tradition of which Salamanca was the epitome made for a decrease in the interest that one might have had in going there. Nevertheless, the share of students from New Castile in the faculty was, in 1618, still 6.3 points lower than the average. Oddly enough, at Salamanca, a dependence on regional recruitment was more noticeable in the theology faculty than in any other. In 1614, 47.1% of theological students came from the neighbouring dioceses of Old Castile and León—as against an average of 38.8% for all Salamantine registrands. Did there remain, then, the faint hint of a theological powerhouse at Alcalá? Was there still something peculiar about the faculty such as a strong reputation which would draw students from further afield?

The last of the three higher faculties to be considered is that of canon law. First of all, it is worth noting that the university of Alcalá was handicapped in its ability to attract law students by the absence of a faculty of civil law. A student did not have the opportunity to graduate *in utroque iure*. The two law courses were, however, complementary and allowed for a career in either church or state. During the course of the period under consideration more than 60% of the students of canon law came from New Castile. The least renowned of the higher faculties at Alcalá, it was also the one with the most marked regional composition. In fact, the proportion of New Castilian students at the faculty of canon law was, from 1568, higher by nearly ten points than that for the university as a whole. This gap was to narrow: by 1618 it was no more than 3 points. In the same period this faculty moved from 13.8% of all registrands to 31.4%. Its growing share of the university as a whole made it directly responsible for the overall regionalization which has been observed. In contrast, at Salamanca, the very centre of legal studies where the two faculties accounted for 70.9% of registrands in 1618,[31] recruitment was less regional in character. Should we be surprised by this? From the beginning of this breakdown by faculty, we have observed how Salamanca can be considered as a university of national importance in the period, whereas Alcalá lost this quality, if indeed it ever had it, given that sources do not exist for the years 1517–1558.

The tendency towards an enlargement of the area of recruitment for the university of Salamanca is striking and contrasts with the regionalization of Alcalá (see map). This, in our opinion, is the significant sign of the health of a university. Not that we would be forced to conclude that Alcalá was heading for a decline—it was

Regional Distribution of Students at the University of Salamanca 1614–1615

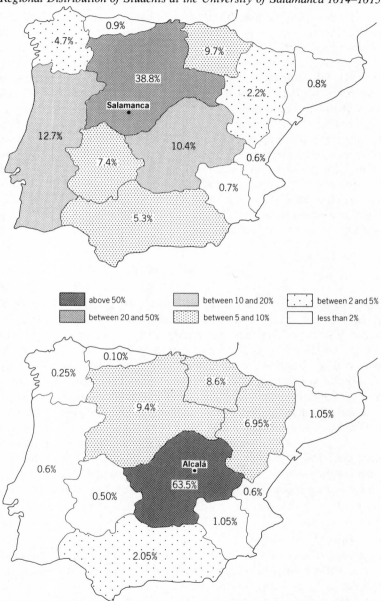

Regional Distribution of Students at the University of Alcalá 1613–1614

never more than the outstanding second of the Castilian universities but it seems indisputable that its apogee came rather in the first half of the sixteenth century. A perusal of the *libros de matricula* for the years 1568–1618, if it does not show a numerical decline, does indicate that a numerical threshold was reached by the university of Alcalá. All evidence suggests that the university had become a university of the diocese of Toledo, a sort of 'super-seminary'. Henceforth it would respond to the higher educational needs of its region, that is to say roughly Toledo and the southern fringes of Old Castile (the diocese of Segovia). Thereby it fitted itself into an intricate university network in which Valladolid was the university of the dioceses of Burgos and Palencia and Santiago de Compostela the university of Galicia. At Oviedo a university was set up to meet the requirements of the Asturias. Alcalá was the university of New Castile, while Salamanca, at the summit of this network, was the one university of national recruitment.

3. Degrees and graduates

Up to now our statistical investigation has only given us a superficial picture of the university of Alcalá. In response to the demands of social history, which require that the links of the university with society be shown, it is now necessary to describe the university in terms of its function as a centre of degree conferment. The large number of students demonstrates the need which existed for graduates in contemporary society: the educational revolution was the product of a demand for officials on the part of state and ecclesiastical bureaucracies. An examination of the *libros de actos y grados* will not shed light on these new needs.[32] On the other hand, these sources do reveal how many degrees were conferred each year, and they do throw light on the relative popularity of different types of degree, and the importance of each faculty as a centre of professional training.[33]

3.1. Degrees at Alcalá
Our objective is to provide a clear account of examinations and degrees at the university of Alcalá. What were they? How much did they cost? How many degrees were conferred each year? Only the faculties conferred degrees, hence the grammar schools have no

place in our investigation. It will be remembered that in order to follow a course of study at one of the three higher faculties, it was necessary to be at least a bachelor of arts.

There were three sorts of degree offered by the faculty of arts: the baccalaureate, licence and masters degrees. The baccalaureate was passed in June; the licence generally in December. These two degrees were given collectively. For the masters degree a specific examination was required. A baccalaureate and licence cost approximately 85 reales or around 2,890 maravedi. These figures translated, in 1600, into the equivalent of 425 kilos of bread. The masters degree was even more expensive. To start with the authorities of the university—rector, chancellor, deans, secretaries, beadles and masters of ceremonies—shared out between them 195 reales. On top of this the future master of arts had to present a hat and pair of gloves, or the equivalent in money, i.e. 6 reales, to each of the *cathedraticos* of the university. By consulting a statement of salaries paid out to the professors in 1606, we have been able to establish that there were seven *cathedraticos* in theology, six in canon law, six in medicine, eight in arts, four in rhetoric, three in Greek, and two in Hebrew. There were in addition six masters of grammar. The applicant needed therefore to spend 216 reales. His expenses did not even end there: he also had to satisfy, with two reales, all doctors of theology and all masters of arts, whose number we do not know. At the very least, a masters degree cost 411 reales or 13,974 maravedi.[34] In 1606 the *cathedraticos* of the principal chairs of theology earned 200 ducats a year or 80,000 maravedi. But a master of grammar, who was a master of arts, earned only 30,000 maravedi.[35] Thus, the cost of a masters degree was half the annual salary which one could expect to earn with such a degree. It should be noted that once the degree was obtained, the student could become a regent without necessarily abandoning his studies. A licence or a doctorate then: these were luxuries which it was necessary to be able to afford. In other words, if degrees were expensive this led many students to take their degrees from a less prestigious, and therefore less expensive, university.[36]

In medicine the student was considered a bachelor if he successfully passed the *tentativa*. This examination cost 34 reales plus 5 reales per doctor present at the oral examination. In general, these were two or three in number, so let us say a student, on average, needed to spend 15 reales under this head, plus 5 florins for the university. The total came to 2,335 maravedi.[37] Before obtaining his licence, the bachelor needed to pass three examinations called *principios*. The first two *principios* cost 20 reales, the third 34; or in total 123 reales—4,182 maravedi. To obtain a licence in medicine, it was then necessary to prove one's Old Christian origins. The faculty of medicine therefore set up a *limpieza de sangre* inquiry to look into the lineage of the candidate's parents, to ensure that he had not committed any misdemeanour, and that he had followed the course of the faculty. Next he would pass the examination which was called *Alfonsina* and finally that of the licence itself. The *Alfonsina* cost 1,360 maravedi and the licence 13,053 maravedi. This was 4.5 times the cost of a licence of arts degree.[39] The doctorate, which was sometimes bestowed very soon after the licence, was the ultimate medical accolade. It symbolized the new physician's acceptance by his peers. In the end a doctorate in medicine came to 29,000 maravedi, or a full year's salary for a master of grammar.

In the theology faculty, the process was long. It took six years of attendance at the faculty to become a bachelor, and two more to graduate as licentiate. The doctorate came immediately afterwards, providing, of course, that one had been able to cover such a large expense. The obstacles were not only financial ones: they showed themselves in the rigour of the examinations—examinations which preserved at Alcalá, as well as at Valladolid and Salamanca, the classical outline of *lectio, disputatio* and *praedicatio*. The similarity between the theological course as outlined in the statutes of the university of Alcalá and that of the Sorbonne is a similarity which stems from the fact that the Paris faculty was the model.[40] For an ordinary baccalaureate, there was first the *tentativa*, then the *principios* which were four in number—the examination consisted of an exposition on Peter Lombard's *Sentences*. Having passed the third *principio* the student was considered a trained bachelor. Between examinations, he would have attended all the proceedings of the faculty of theology for two years, and preached on two occasions. The total cost of this baccalaureate was 4,352 maravedi. The fourth *principio*, like the *quodlibeto, parva et magna ordinaria* and *Alfonsina,* was an intermediate stage between the baccalaureate and licence. Each of these examinations entailed a cost of 26 reales or, in total, 3,536 maravedi.[41]

These theological examinations which led to a licence consisted of an oral presentation of work written by the candidate upon which the examiners would comment. The first—*parva ordinaria*—was on a subject chosen by the candidate; the second—*magna ordinaria*—concerned the development of a case of conscience. The *quodlibeto* brought the student face-to-face with the doctors of the university, the chapter of the collegiate church of San Justo and San Pastor, the clergy of Santa Maria, the monks of the San Francisco monastery and the rector of the university: all these ecclesiastics would submit theological cases to him. The *Alfonsina* was the most difficult part of the proceedings. It was modelled on a method in use at the Sorbonne and was indeed known as the *Sorbonica*. It began at 6 in the morning and lasted all day, and consisted of the student making a theological study of a 'high and difficult subject' on which the candidate was required to answer all sorts of questions.[42]

Having come through each of these stages successfully, the student could think of presenting himself for the degree. If he did so, a doctor of the faculty of theology was charged with an *limpieza de sangre* investigation in the course of which he had to go in person to the candidate's place of birth and undertake a genealogical investigation *in situ* to be able to guarantee that the student held the status of an Old Christian.[43] The awarding of degrees took place only every two years. Candidates were examined by all of the doctors of theology. Each examiner received 4 reales. The faculty, its professors, chancellor, secretaries and masters of ceremonies also needed to be paid. In all, this would come to 3,845 maravedi.[44] Over four years the total cost was, therefore, 11,733 maravedi. For the doctorate, the last possible stage, the examinations were twofold. First came the *vesperias* which took place in the evening during which time a discourse was read on a 'serious and difficult subject' which was followed by a *vexamen*, a fierce counter-attack. The next day came the installation of the candidate into the doctoral ranks. This ceremony would set him back at least 20,000 maravedi.[45]

In the context of the development of the state, jurists were pushed by a favourable wind and the impression contemporaries had of them was that they were closely linked to the university. The jurist 'apparaît à ses contemporains comme une sorte d'étudiant prolongé, un homme d'études, indélébilement marqué par les livres et les cours de sa formation première.'[46] A degree in canon law was a key which opened the door to the possibility of entry into the hierarchy of the *letrados*. As in the other faculties, the degrees given by the faculty of canon law were the baccalaureate, licence and doctorate. Only the licence consisted of two stages, the *repeticiones* and the licence itself. 'Les examinateurs décernant la licence tenaient compte en général de trois éléments: les services d'enseignement rendus par le candidat, la démonstration d'un travail personnel sur un sujet choisi par lui et exposés lors des *repeticiones* . . . et une interrogation finale sur deux questions de droit tirées au sort.'[47] According to our calculations, a baccalaureate cost at least 2,700 maravedi, the *repeticiones* 1,550 maravedi, and the licence 16,200. A doctorate entailed, then, an investment of 33,000 maravedi, an enormous sum.[48] Those who obtained their licence and went on to take a doctorate had hopes of a career in the high echelons of administration, whether of church or state. Indeed, as Jean-Marc Pelorson reminds us, the licentiate and doctoral degrees were those expected of most ecclesiastical prebendaries. The requisite expense to obtain these degrees was, it was hoped at any rate, an investment which would bring substantial returns.[49]

To sum up and conclude this discussion, here are the degrees with their costs given in a table (the figures are in maravedi):[50]

Degrees	Arts	Medicine	Theology	Canon Law
Bachelors	2890	2335	4352	2700
Licentiates	2890	13053	11733	16200
Doctors	13974	29000	20000	33000

Total: the estimate in ducats is an approximation

	Arts	Medicine	Theology	Canon Law
maravedi	19754	44388	36085	51900
ducats	50–55	120	95–100	140

A question which needs to be asked at the end of this examination but before looking at the number of graduates is: what purpose did degrees serve? This theme brings us back to the question of the *letrados*, a group of fundamental importance for understanding sixteenth- and seventeenth-century Spain.[51] J. A. Maravall has explained the socio-political rise of the *letrados* in terms of the need of the continually expanding modern state for professional competence. This was the age of the birth of bureaucracy. But by emphasizing the central organs of government, Maravall gives too great a weight to the higher echelons of the *letrados*, those who had earned at least a licence and more often a doctorate at university. Quite rightly, historians such as J. M. Pelorson or A. Molinie-Bertrand remind us that the universities also produced a crowd of non-graduate *infra-letrados*. Forming the great anonymous mass of the student body, these *infra-letrados* also crowned their short stay at university with a real, if only locally important, success: as a barber in Oviedo, a schoolmaster at Orense, a scribe in Toro, etc.

3.2. An Attempted Evaluation of the Number of Graduates

We have now looked at the different sorts of degrees in some detail, and also at the examinations which needed to be passed in order to attain them. It remains, therefore, to discover how many degrees were awarded each year, which is possible thanks to the work undertaken on the years already examined. This method is valid because it complements the statistical approach to student numbers and, despite its limitations, will allow us to complete our picture of Alcalá.

Richard Kagan raises the question of degrees in the last chapter of his book. He restricts himself to an estimate of 1,200 baccalaureates, 150 to 175 licences and 50 to 60 doctorates as the number of degrees awarded each year by the Castilian universities. It is his belief that 80% of these degrees were taken at one of the three major universities—Salamanca, Valladolid and Alcalá—which, it will be remembered, accounted for more than two thirds of all students in the Crown of Castile.[53] If so, this confirms their near-monopoly. But, putting generalizations to one side, let us look at the specific case of Alcalá.

The following table gives the number of graduates as a percentage of the total number of registrands for each given year. These figures are for all faculties, but the total number of registrands does not include students from the university grammar schools for whom degrees were not relevant.

The tendency is one of decline: we move from one student out of six to one out of ten. But the percentage only tells us about students who obtained their degrees in those years. To establish with certainty the percentage of students who graduated from the university, it will be necessary to select one age group and follow its members until they disappear from the matriculation registers. Nevertheless we do get a rough indication from these percentages. Against the

Year	% of graduates	number of graduates/ registrands
1568	16.47	351/2131
1573	13.63	421/3087
1578	15.93	324/2033
1583	16.58	461/2780
1588	15.42	499/3234
1591	13.57	334/2460
1598	12.77	335/2622
1603	14.02	327/2332
1608	12.04	304/2523
1613	10.71	315/2940
1618	9.95	300/3013

substantial figures which emerge from the *libros de matricula* must
be set the smaller number of graduates. Here there is a noticeable
decline over the 50 years which have been examined. It is especially
perceptible from 1600. Did selection procedures become more
rigorous? Let us take the case of the arts faculty. Its degree course
took four years. It was the only faculty whose students were
inscribed in the matriculation registers according to their stage of
progress, and so each year of study is clearly distinguished. Thus the
figures for the freshmen in any one year can be compared with the
figures for annual registrands in subsequent years which will give us
an idea of the drop-out rate—a weeding-out process which reflected
both the abandonment of studies and the phenomenon of *peregrinatio academica* between the universities of Spain. The results of a
sample study are given below as indices, the first year being used as
the base year of 100.

Year	1st level	2nd level	3rd level	4th level
1568	100	72.6	48.7	34.3
1588	100	64.4	54.7	37.4
1603	100	72.3	46.9	39.5
1608	100	54.9	41.1	26.5
1613	100	68.5	39.0	34.4
1618	100	56.5	38.7	34.7

Despite the slightly artificial calculations, one can detect the same pattern of selection, mainly observable in the transition from the first to second years. There was always an average success rate of 36% by the end of the course. As well as examining these figures, let us also look at the number of degrees awarded by each faculty as shown below:

Table 3:   Breakdown of Degrees of the Faculties of Alcalá

Faculty of Theology

Year	Bachelors	Licentiates	Masters	% of all students in the faculty
1568		8	8	2.0
1573	6			1.2
1578	5	7	8	3.0
1583	11	3	2	2.4
1588	13	11	11	3.2
1591	4		2	1.2
1598	5	12	10	3.0
1603	6		1	1.5
1608	5	11	12	3.9
1613	12	1	1	2.5
1618	3	12	8	2.9

Faculty of Canon Law

Year	Bachelors	Licentiates	Masters	% of all students in the faculty
1568	25	5		6.2
1573	19	5		5.1
1578	11	6	2	3.8
1583	14	6		3.8
1588	18	6		3.7
1591	9	8	1	3.1
1598	11	15	5	3.7
1603	22	5	1	4.6
1608	21	14	1	4.8
1613	28	7		4.0
1618	35	2		3.6

Faculty of Arts

Year	Bachelors	Licentiates	Masters	% of all students in the faculty
1568	205	84	7	25.8
1573	174	180	24	37.2
1578	162	96	20	26.5
1583	234	149	21	26.5
1588	279	130	24	25.7
1591	183	85	20	22.6
1598	154	96	36	22.7
1603	152	126	7	22.6
1608	136	87	23	19.8
1613	135	107	14	18.0
1618	129	86	19	17.8

Faculty of Medicine

Year	Bachelors	Licentiates	Masters	% of all students in the faculty
1568	16		1	16.2
1573	11	2	2	12.3
1578	15		1	16.5
1583	19	4	3	16.3
1588	18			16.8
1591	19	4	3	20.0
1598	6			6.8
1603	7	1	1	7.7
1608	6			5.1
1613	9	2	2	9.3
1618	14			8.8

While the faculties of theology and of canon law gave out very few degrees in proportion to their student numbers, a relationship which remained virtually static, the arts and medical faculties awarded fewer and fewer degrees. Yet the degrees awarded by the former two faculties were precisely those necessary for a career in administration. In general, the graduates were scholars of San Ildefonso College. They were among the richest. The lowering of the proportion of graduates is attributable to the lessening of the number of degrees awarded by the faculty of arts.

Arguably, there was a process of professionalization in the

university of Alcalá over the period, a phenomenon which is linked to the rise of the higher faculties in the university-system as a whole, which we noted earlier. By the term 'professionalization' is meant the transformation of the university into a centre for conferring degrees on an élite already assured of entry into the service of either church or state. This is not to say that the university's function as an educator of students of all kinds was reduced or that it ceased to exist except in the form of the *Colegio Mayor* of San Ildefonso. Rather, there was a kind of contradiction between the two functions, a contradiction which was surely promoted by the élitist system of the *colegios mayores*, and which is illustrated by the rising social differentiation between the *letrados* and the *infra-letrados*. This contradiction, which was at the root of the 'blockage' of both educational and social mobility in Spain after 1600, might be one explanation for the decadence of the universities in the seventeenth and eighteenth centuries. The degrees which allowed for entry into a professional career were distributed in decreasing proportion to the number of students, as in the case of baccalaureates in canon law. This was also the case with degrees in the arts faculty. The share of bachelors declined from 17.8% of the total of arts students in 1568 to 9.8% in 1618. But the number of licentiates always remained between 6.5% and 10% of the total while masters degrees were more and more numerous between 1573 and 1598, and only afterwards declined in popularity. Here too we could consider the faculty to have been becoming more professionalized since the directly professional licence and masters degrees continued to be awarded in a fairly constant fashion and remained largely unaffected by the depression in baccalaureate degrees. It will be observed, too, that doctorates were very rare in medicine and canon law. This was because in order to follow a career in medicine or law it was not necessary to be a doctor. To become a doctor was to choose a university career. In theology on the other hand nearly all licentiates became doctors. Later they frequently became professors at Alcalá.[54]

We must take care, however, not to exaggerate this trend towards professionalization. It is only discernible because the proportion of graduates to students falls over the period. One of the causes of this decline must lie in the excessive cost of degrees. As a result students from Alcalá went to take their degrees elsewhere. Thereby the hierarchical division of the Spanish university system previously referred to was reinforced: Salamanca was at the summit, with Alcalá and Valladolid just below it, followed by the whole network of 'backwoods' universities. And another network, the terribly efficient one of the Jesuits, must not be forgotten.

At the turn of the seventeenth century students who succeeded at Alcalá were less numerous, but they might progress further. It seems therefore that during this period studies were becoming less and less a vehicle of upward social mobility. Constraints on the earlier 'educational revolution' were beginning to make themselves felt. In particular the 'revolution' was being brought to a halt through the 'closure' of the *colegios mayores*. These colleges, initially envisaged for poor students, were turning into nurseries of high-level administrators. Places were no longer being awarded according to the guidelines set out in the university statutes but according to family influence and other forms of power pressure. And it seems that this process of social exclusion spread to the university as a whole. One needed to be rich, to have social connections: a whole network of conditions which could only be met by one group.

A final general comment must be made about degrees: how many degrees were distributed each year for the whole of the Crown of Castile? Richard Kagan speaks of 1,200 baccalaureates, 150 to 175 licentiates and 50 to 60 doctorates. Let us look at the case of Alcalá for three years 1568, 1588 and 1618. If we take the total number of degrees, without distinguishing between the faculties, we get the following figures:

Year	Baccalaureates	Licentiates	Doctorates
1568	246	97	16
1588	328	147	35
1618	181	100	27

These figures contradict Kagan's. If, as he proposes, we accept that 80% of all degrees were awarded by the three great universities, and if we assume that the percentage-share of each of these universities will be proportionate to their relative student numbers, we can suppose that: Alcalá annually awarded 25% of the degrees of the Crown. Let us use the coefficient of 0.25 to extrapolate the number of degrees awarded nationally. Here are the results:

Year	Baccalaureates	Licentiates	Doctorates
1568	46	390	64
1588	1312	588	140
1618	724	400	108

We have obtained figures which deviate markedly from those offered by Kagan. What should we make of this? Must we accept that the three major universities had a virtual monopoly of licentiate and doctoral degrees, a percentage of 90% or more? Should we take Alcalá's share up to 40%? By so doing we would be able to reduce the national figures to 242 licences in 1568, 367 in 1588, and 250 in 1618. But unless we become involved in all sorts of arithmetical manipulations—whose arbitrariness must be emphasized—we cannot but question Kagan's figures. His assertion that the Castilian universities never awarded more than 170 licences a year is contradicted by our findings for Alcalá alone, with 187 licences granted in 1573. This demonstrates the importance of the work which still needs to be done in penetrating the inner workings of the 'educational revolution'.

4. Conclusions

Having come to the end of this study, let us remind ourselves of the questions asked of the matriculation figures of Alcalá de Henares and summarize the answers which have been found.

1. How many students were at the university of Alcalá between 1568 and 1618?

The number of enrolled students was around 3,000 with the arithmetical average 3116.9. The greatest number was in 1588 when there were 3,805 students and the smallest in 1578 with 2,629 registered students. The fluctuations which have been observed do not indicate a steady movement in either direction. This demonstrates convincingly, in our view, the early blossoming of student numbers in sixteenth-century Spain compared with numbers in England and probably elsewhere.

2. What was the balance between the different university faculties?

More than the rise in the number of students of canon law, the decline in student numbers at the university's grammar schools seems to us to indicate a change in the spirit of Alcalá. The new Catholic orthodoxy which came into being at the end of the sixteenth century favoured the return of Thomism and led to an abandonment of all Erasmian theological thought. This development was only encouraged by the development of a rival network of municipal colleges.

3. What were the regions of recruitment for the students of Alcalá?

By 1568 there was already a predominance of students from the three dioceses of New Castile—Toledo, Cuenca and Siguenza. This tendency became more pronounced in the following decades, so that the university became primarily a regional university.

4. Degrees at Alcalá

An examination of the *libros de actos y grados* enabled us to look at the number of degrees awarded each year. The arts faculty awarded the great majority of degrees. The explanation for this is to be found in the cost of degrees in the higher faculties.

This summary enables us to see the limits of our work and to bring attention to further research which is needed. Only a prosopographical study, if not exhaustive then at least broadly representative, could enable us to delve deeper into the problems raised. To take the true measure of the 'educational revolution' it is necessary to uncover the traces of the mass of unknown students who, upon leaving university, took their place in society. The *letrado* became a familiar figure in society: what was his status? What became of his children? Did he better himself socially? In order to find out we must give back 'la voix aux sans voix'. The heavy silence of the forgotten must be penetrated and all those who together formed the humus of the 'educational revolution' must be found.[55]

Ecole Normale Supérieure
Rue d'Ulm
Paris

REFERENCES

1. Gomez de Castro, A., *De rebus gestis a Francisco Ximenio Cisnerio, Archiepiscapa Talentana* (Alcalá, 1569); edited and translated into Spanish by Oroz Reta, as *De las hazanas de Francisco Jiménez de Cisneros* (Madrid, 1984).
2. Torre Y Del Cerro, A. de la, *La universidad de Alcalá, datos para su historia* (Madrid, 1910).
3. Codina Mir, G., *Aux sources de la pédagogie des Jésuites, le modus parisiensis* (Rome, 1968).
4. Torre Y del Cerro, and Bataillon, M., *Erasme et l'Espagne* (Paris, 1937), chapter 1: 'Cisneros et la pré-réforme espagnole', pp. 1–75; esp. pp. 14–16: 'Les destinées de la nouvelle Université sont confiées à un petit essaim de théologiens, constitué à Salamanque et qui, le 26 juillet 1508, prend possession de la *ruche neuve*. De là va naître le collège Saint Ildephonse. Le 6 août, par délégation du Cardinal fondateur, Pedro de Lerma, docteur sorbonique, Abbé de SS Juste et Pastor et chancelier désigné, nomme, conjointement avec Pedro de Carderia, chanoine de Tolède, les cinq premiers membres du collège, et ceux-ci élisent leur recteur et leurs conseillers qui désormais sont les magistrats de cette république et qui nomment avant la Saint-Luc, vingt autres *colegiales*. C'est un trait remarquable que cette association du Collège avec la Collègiale des SS Juste et Pastor. ... Les deux communautés étaient organiquement liées, dès le début, par un acte de confraternité. Et là ne s'arrêtait pas, dans l'esprit de Cisneros, leur association: avant de mourir, il fit à la Collégiale une donation de 25 millions de maravédis pour améliorer les prébendes existantes et en créer 29 nouvelles (17 canonicats et 12 rations) à condition que le recrutement s'effectuât parmi les Maîtres en théologie et les Maîtres ès arts de l'Université; innovation inspirée de Saint Pierre de Louvain qui donna à la Collégiale d'Alcalá un caractère unique et lui valut de changer son titre en celui de Magistrale. L'Université d'Alcalá se propose donc de fournir aux innombrables bénéfices de l'Eglise espagnole une élite de prébendés, et pour qu'il y ait au moins un lieu où, à titre d'exemple, les bénéfices sont donnés au mérite, les canonicats de la Magistrale seront une récompense toujours présente sous les yeux des étudiants. Il faut ajouter qu'une bourse de *colegial* à Saint Ildephonse constituait déjà une prébende enviable ... En vérité, Saint Ildephonse est le siège d'une sorte d'aristocratie universitaire.'
5. The Spanish system of the colegios mayores—there were six in the whole peninsula: four at Salamanca, one at Valladolid, the last at Alcalá—has given rise to several studies, the most complete of which to date is that of Ana Maria Carabias Torres entitled *Colegios Mayores, Centros de Poder* (Salamanca 1986). This study of the major colleges at Salamanca shows how there developed, over the course of the sixteenth

century, a kind of 'caste' feeling which can first be detected in the demand for *limpeza de sangre* and subsequently developed into an acute sense of belonging to a privileged body. Also, recruitment of the *colegiales* no longer followed the procedures laid down in the edicts of the founders, usually of the fifteenth century (San Ildefonso's college at Alcalá was the last of these) but was rather determined by the dictates of the great families, the recommendations of former pupils, or particularly powerful outside pressures. The *letrados* of the golden age found the *colegios mayores* a remarkable instrument of both social and political mobility and of strengthening this upward mobility. Jeanine Fayard's thesis, *Les Membres du Conseil de Castille à l'époque moderne 1621–1746* (Paris, 1976) should be consulted with regard to this subject. This gives a good illustration of the power of the *colegiales* and of the role of the *colegios mayores* in the creation of a political élite whose recruitment was increasingly restricted.

6. Bataillon, ch. I, pp. 1–75; pp. 11–13 offer a brief analysis of the originality of Cisneros's creation at Alcalá: 'La création de l'Université de Alcalá ne fut pas autre chose que la mise sur pied d'un organisme complet d'enseignement ecclésiastique: élémentaire, moyen et supérieur. . . . Dès son avènement à l'archevêché de Tolède, Cisneros avait conçu le projet de rénover l'enseignement théologique espagnol par l'introduction du scotisme. . . . La création *ex nihilo* avait cet avantage, au moins, de permettre le libre développement de l'institution nouvelle. Salamanque s'était émue et avait fait tous ses efforts pour décider Cisneros à rattacher la fondation qu'il projetait à l'antique université castillane. Peine perdue. Il ne s'agissait pas de compléter Salamanque, encore moins de l'imiter pour lui faire concurrence. L'université qui s'élevait devait être animée d'un autre esprit. Autonome d'abord, autant que possible, elle sera gouvernée par le recteur électif du collège Saint Ildephonse sans contrôle disciplinaire d'un écolâtre épiscopal. A côté du recteur, l'autorité transcendante qui seule peut donner l'investiture de la science sera incarnée par un chancelier, chargé, comme à Paris, de la collation des grades. . . . Mais la grande originalité d'Alcalá, c'est dans l'absence de Faculté de Droit. Salamanque et Valladolid suffisaient amplement pour fournir des juristes à toute la monarchie espagnole. Et Cisneros n'a que mépris pour la chicane, beau mépris dans lequel communient alors les enthousiastes de l'humanisme profane et les restaurateurs de l'antiquité sacrée. La théologie déterminera toute l'orientation de son Université, sa raison d'être. Comme à regret, il y fait une petite place au droit canon, et comme la faculté des Arts, vestibule de la théologie, est aussi l'indispensable préparation à la médecine, cette science nécessaire à la république ne sera pas non plus bannie d'Alcalá: deux chaires lui seront réservées où Avicenne alternera avec Hippocrate et Galien. Mais de la grammaire aux arts libéraux et des arts de la théologie vivifiée par l'étude directe de la Bible, telle est la voie droite et royale pour les jeunes gens que Cisneros voulait voir

affluer à Alcalá de tous les diocèses d'Espagne, et retourner plus tard à ces diocèses pour constituer les cadres d'une Eglise plus digne du Christ.'

7. Bataillon, ch. 9: 'Persécution des Erasmistes'.
8. Beltran de Heredia, V., 'La teologia en la Universidad de Alcalá', in *Miscelanea Beitran de Heredia. Coleccion de articulos sobre historia de la teología española* (Salamanca, 1973), iv. 61–157; id., 'Vicisitudes de la filosofia aristotelica en Alcalá', Ibid., 159–173. Also Martinez Albiach, A., *La universidad Complutense segun el Cardenal Cisneros, 1508–1543* (Burgos, 1975); and Andres, M., *La Teología española en el siglo XVI* (Madrid, 1976).
9. *Les universités européennes du XVIème au XVIIIème, Histoire sociale des populations étudiantes.* The most recent statement of the 'new' university history is D. Julia and J. Revel (eds.), 2 vols. (Paris, 1986–9).
10. Some of the earliest attempts to address these questions appeared in Stone, L. (ed.), *The University in Society*, 2 vols. (Princeton, N.J., 1975).
11. Stone, L., 'The Educational Revolution in England 1560–1640', *Past and Present*, 28 (1964), 41–79.
12. Kagan, R. L., 'Universities in Castile', *Past and Present*, 44–71; and Kagan, *Students and Society in Early Modern Spain* (Baltimore, Ma., 1974).
13. Let us turn to an inventory of the archives which have been consulted. In 1843 the university of Alcalá moved to Madrid along with its archives. The whole collection is now to be found at the *Archivo Historico Nacional* (AHN). These archives of Alcalá, as well as those of the small university of Siguenza, closed in 1837, form the collection of the *Universidades* section at the A.H.N. A catalogue of this collection was compiled by C. Gutierrez. We consulted the registration books for the years 1568, 1573, 1578, 1583, 1588, 1591 (but not 1593 because of another work in progress), 1598, 1603, 1608, 1613, 1618. That is to say, the books shelved from 434-F to 444-F. These registers, bound in the nineteenth century, are 29–30 cm by 10.5–11.5 cm. Why the chronological boundaries of 1568–1618? The other volumes (from 1553 to 1563) are rotten and illegible. For the same reason we were unfortunately unable to start before 1568. This observation allows me to express my surprise at the figures put forward by R. Kagan for the years 1550 and 1560. For the year 1550, R. Kagan would not have been able to consult the *libros de matricula* since these have been missing for some time; a catalogue of the collection *Universidades* of the *Archivo Historico Nacional*, published in the 1950s, does not mention them. As for 1560, are we to believe that the decay was not as advanced in the years 1968–70, the years of Kagan's research? In any case, it is the negligence of the A.H.N. which should be held to account. As for the *libros de actos y grados*, we consulted the books shelved at 399-F, 400-F and 401-F. The folios are numbered. For each degree awarded the names of the examiners, rector and that of the examinee are given, as well as the date

of the examination held. The text is in Latin. In the margins the name(s) of the examinee(s) and kind of degree awarded were hastily scrawled. An exclusive reliance on this marginalia could make for errors; there are occasional discrepancies between the information given in the text and that in the margins. In such cases we have followed the candidate further to eliminate mistakes.

14. Kagan, *Students and Society*, p. 249.
15. Rodriguez San Pedro Bezares, L. E., *La Universidad Salmantina del Barroco. Periodo 1598–1625*, 3 vols. (Salamanca, 1986).
16. Bennassar, B., *Recherches sur les grandes épidémies dans le Nord de l'Espagne à la fin du XVIème siècle* (Paris, 1969).
17. Kagan, *Students and Society*, p. 252.
18. A.H.N., *Libro de Matrícula*, 444-F.
19. Kagan, *Students and Society*, pp. 50–55. It is worth noting that student numbers for all the grammar schools which were linked to the universities went down in the second half of the sixteenth century. At Valladolid, according to Kagan's figures, 231 were enrolled in 1567 and only 61 in 1616. At Salamanca there was a similar fall from 1320 in 1571 to 227 in 1615. (The apparent precision of these figures is misleading. They should be taken rather as indicators of shifts than real and absolute numbers.)
20. Kagan, *Students and Society*, pp. 50–51. 'On the other hand, those universities which attempted to teach Latin on their own ran into serious trouble. With skilled masters wanting, the faculties of grammar at the universities of Alcalá and Salamanca, both of which were staunch enemies of the Jesuits, lost students at a spectacular rate. In part, this decline was the result of competition from municipal schools, but the colleges of the Jesuits, expanding rapidly in the late sixteenth century dealt the decisive blow. The faculties of Latin grammar managed to survive at these universities by attracting students from the local population, but this was not enough to halt a progressive decay. One has to await university reforms in the nineteenth century, however, before these faculties were suppressed.' Continuing to develop his analysis of Jesuit teaching, he affirms on p. 55: 'And though it is only a rough estimate, the total number of students taught by the Jesuits in the Kingdom of Castile toward the end of the sixteenth century was something on the order of 10,000 to 15,000 a year, the vast majority of whom studying Latin grammar.' Other and much more precise information may be found in P. L. Lukacs, S.J., 'De origine collegiorum externorum deque controversis circa eorum paupertatem obortis', *Archivum Historicum Societatis Iesu*, 29 (1960), 189–245, and 30 (1961), 1–80.
21. Ricard, R., 'La restauration religieuse en Espagne et au Portugal', in *Histoire de l'Eglise des origines à nos jours*, under the direction of A. Fliche and V. Martin, vol. 16, R. Aubenas and R. Ricard, *L'Eglise et la Renaissance 1449–1517* (Paris, 1951), pp. 299–311.

22. Bataillon, pp. 750–4. The author explains the immediate cause of the series of *auto-da-fé* which were celebrated in Spain from 1559 and which affected Valladolid as well as Seville and Saragossa. The spectacular form which these suppressions took and their concentration in a short space of time contributed to the development of the 'Black Legend'. A hundred or so people were executed. Of the *auto-da-fé* which took place in Valladolid in September 1559, presided over by King Phillip II, Bataillon writes: '. . . dans le ressort inquisitorial de Valladolid des dénonciations affluent au début de 1558 sur une propagande 'luthérienne' occulte qui a de multiples foyers à Valladolid, à Salamanque, à Toro, à Palencia, à Logroño. Là, comme à Séville, il s'agit surtout d'un évangélisme attaché au salut par la foi seule. . . . Il est possible que ces groupes, si l'Inquisition n'était intervenue vigoureusement en 1558, fussent devenus de véritables communautés protestantes comparables à celles qui se constituent en France vers le même temps. . . . La plus grande rigueur dont on fait preuve ne signifie nullement que les inculpés fussent plus 'luthériens' qu'un Gil ou un Vergara (deux érasmisants de la première moitié du XVIème). On brûle, en 1558, des gens qui, quelques années plus tôt, en auraient été quittes pour des pénitences de courte durée. C'est que la nouvelle méthode répressive ne permet plus de sauver sa vie par une rétraction.'

23. Perez, J., *Isabelle et Ferdinand, Rois Catholiques d'Espagne* (Paris, 1988) pp. 404–415. As Joseph Perez in particular has pointed out: 'Avec le latin, les humanités font leur entrées dans le monde savant d'Espagne. L'artisan de cette sécularisation, l'humaniste par excellence au XVIème siècle, c'est le professeur de grammaire, le grammairien, un spécialiste de la langue, un professionnel qui connaît l'art de déchiffrer et lire les textes. Ortega y Gasset a raison de voir dans l'humanisme, dans une large mesure, la dictature des grammairiens; il a tort d'en conclure que l'Espagne n'a pas connu la Renaissance, c'est-à-dire la subversion, car il n'y a rien de plus subversif que la grammaire.'

24. Kagan, *Students and Society*, p. 252, table X:

The University of Valladolid

Year	Grammar	Arts	Med.	Theo.	Canon	Law
1588	7.6%	9.2%	2.0%	6.7%	44.3%	6.6%
1616	3.6%	15.4%	1.6%	6.6%	58.8%	8.2%

25. Rodriguez, iii. 83–85.

Year	Grammar	Arts	Med.	Theo.	Canon	Law
1598	9.1%	12.4%	4.2%	13.7%	52.2%	7.9%
1618	6.0%	9.7%	3.5%	9.9%	52.1%	18.8%

26. Pelorson, J. M., *Les Letrados, Juristes Castillans sous Philippe III*.

Recherches sur leur place dans la société, la culture, et l'Etat (Poitiers, 1980), p. 37. All these questions of the relations between canon and civil law in the minds of ecclesiastics and the law curriculum of the university are treated in the first part of this thesis under the section on 'Le cadre professionnel', esp. pp. 29–32.

27. Cantu, F., 'La dialectique de Las Casas et l'histoire' *Le Supplément, Revue d'éthique et de théologie morale* (Paris), March (1987), 5–26: 'A partir de leur spéculation théorique sur les principes doctrinaux, les théologiens-juristes de Salamanque parviennent à un jugement général porté sur la réalité des choses et des hommes; ils parviennent à l'énonciation d'une règle de conduite universellement valable' (pp. 8–9). The same conclusions can be found in Pelorson, 30: 'La théologie ne pouvait cependant se priver de prolongements juridiques. Tout au long du XVIème siècle, on observe une étroite complémentarité de fait entre théologie et droit. Lorsque des 'Dominicains d'avant-garde' (selon l'expression de Marcel Bataillon) comme Las Casas et Vitoria, examinent les problèmes posés par la conquête et l'évangélisation du Nouveau Monde, ils raisonnent d'abord en théologiens, mais finissent toujours par se muer en juristes.' All of these observations show how one must take absolute care not to follow Cisneros in his hostility towards legal studies.

28. Rodriguez, iii. 202–203.
29. Ibid.
30. Ibid., 201.

Year	Portugal	Old Castile	Andalusia	Estremadura
1604	32.0%	26.7%	9.0%	8.9%
1614	44.7%	16.7%	8.6%	7.4%
1624	45.3%	16.4%	5.9%	8.5%

31. See note 25.
32. For an account of this growing demand, see Pelorson and Fayard.
33. A further source is A.H.N., 525-F, *Reforma de Don Gomez Capata, Obispo de Carthagena*, Alcalá, 1578.
34. *Reforma . . .*, fo. 32r and fo. 33r.
35. A.H.N., 868-F, fos. 104r–121v.
36. Kagan, *Students and Society*, p. 246, cites the example of the theologian and poet Fray Luis de León.
37. For these calculations, here are the monetary equivalents: 1 ducat = 375 maravedi (3.52 gr of gold); 1 florin = 365 maravedi (3.43 gr of gold); 1 real = 34 maravedi. See *Historia Social y Económica de España y America*, ed. J. Vicens Vives, vol. III, *Imperio, Aristocracia, Absolutismo* (Barcelona, 1957), pp. 47–50.
38. *Reforma . . .*, titulo L, fo. 43 r.
39. *Reforma . . .*, titulo LI, fos. 44 r–v.
40. Andres, M., pp. 56–57. This affinity with the theology faculty of Paris

should not surprise us since we know that Cisneros took his inspiration from the Sorbonne. For a comparison, see D. Julia, R. Chartier, M. M. Compère, *L'Education en France du XVIème au XVIIIème siècles* (Paris, 1976); ch. 9 'Les Universités: d'une cléricature à une autre', esp. pp. 261–263, 'Les grades, de la *disputatio* à l'examen'.

41. *Reforma* . . ., titulo XLV, fo. 37 v.
42. Andres, M., pp. 56–57.
43. *Reforma* . . ., titulo XLVII, fos. 39 r–v and fo. 40r; the candidate must be 'vieux chrétien, lui, son père et sa mère et ses grands-parents paternels et maternels, et tous ses ascendants en ligne directe, sans trace ni tâche d'hérétique, juif, more, confessos ou de quelque autre secte nouvellement convertie'.
44. Ibid.
45. *Reforma* . . ., titulo XLVIII, fos. 45 r–v.
46. Pelorson, p. 44.
47. Ibid., p. 38.
48. *Reforma* . . ., titulo LIII, fo. 49 r and titulo LIIII, fos. 50r–v.
49. Pelorson, p. 31.
50. Monetary equivalents in modern times present an almost insuperable difficulty to the non-specialist historian. A comparison of the cost of degrees in different European universities, if it is to be a genuine comparison, is also extremely difficult to effect, not least because the question of comparing standards of living enters into the equation. Some elements of comparison with the University of Paris can be made through Laurence W. B. Brockliss, 'Patterns of Attendance at the University of Paris, 1400–1800' in *Histoire sociale des populations étudiantes*, ii. 504–505, and for the University of Padua and the *Studium* of Venice through R. Palmer, *The Studio of Venice and its Graduates in the Sixteenth Century* (Padua, 1983), pp. 31–34: 'Examinations and Degree Ceremonies in Venice'.
51. Maravall, J. A., *Estado moderno y Mentalidad social, siglos XV a XVII*, 3rd edn., 2 vols. (Madrid 1986), ii. pt. v: 'Los medios de accion del Estado'.
52. Molinie-Bertrand, A., *Au Siècle d'Or, l'Espagne et ses hommes* (Paris, 1986). The author offers a detailed account of the census of 1591 which brings out the different 'notables' who were recognized as such in their towns or villages. Such references are erratic but allow one to get a sense of the social standing of the *infra-letrado*.
53. Kagan, *Students and Society*, p. 246 and note 16.
54. Such was the case, for example, of Luis Montesino, a student at Alcalá from 1567 to 1574 and a salaried professor in 1606, A.H.N., 868-F, fos. 104r to 121v.
55. This article sums up the work undertaken under the supervision of M. Bernard Vincent at the university of Paris VII, in 1987–1988.

Appendix: Regional Distribution of Students

The following twelve tables give a detailed breakdown of the regional background of students at the university of Alcalá. Their construction is a direct result of the analysis of the matriculation registers for the years 1568, 1573, 1578, 1583, 1588, 1591, 1598, 1603, 1608, 1613, 1618. In the text we grouped together Old Castile and León for geographical and historical reasons, but also because Luis Enrique Rodriguez San Pedro Bezares did so in his thesis on Salamanca. In the tables will be found the detailed breakdown which allows us to understand the exact share which the dioceses of Old Castile as opposed to those of León accounted for.

The first two tables give figures for the whole university, the ten others give, respectively, data for the grammar schools of San Isidore and San Eugenius as well as the Trilingual college, the faculty of arts, that of medicine, of theology and, finally, of canon law. In this arrangement we followed the order of the *libros de matricula*. We first constructed a table which gives the results in absolute numbers, then a table which transforms these findings into percentages. Many students were inscribed as coming from *Complutense* or *Complutensis*. This refers to the Latin name of Alcalá: *Compluto*. The proportion of all students coming from the town varies from 3.85% to 9.50%. In Table 2 in the text we added these students to the totals for the three dioceses of New Castile (i.e. Toledo, Cuenca and Siguenza), even though obviously this could lead to error. Our decision was justified by virtue of the fact that the highest percentage of students from *Compluto* (i.e. 9.50%) coincided with the lowest percentage figure (51.4%) for students coming specifically from New Castile. No other explanation for the low figure in this instance could be found.

The category of 'Nullius Diocesis' refers to villages which were under the control of Military Orders. These were the orders of Santiago, Calatrava, Alcántara and of San Juan. These territories are situated in Estremadura and in the southern part of the Kingdom (La Mancha or Andalusia).

Under the classification 'foreign' we have grouped Italians, French, Irish and Flemish together indiscriminately. They were too few in number to enable us to undertake a detailed analysis.

Under the heading 'Canaries' we have also included the Balearic islands. The share of the two islands was more or less even. Here again, the small numbers concerned did not seem to us to merit a detailed analysis.

As for the 'unidentified' category, these consist of either students whose entries were incomplete in some respect—name of town, monastery, etc. given without a corresponding diocese—or for whom the name of diocese was illegible either because of indecipherable paleography or else because of deteriorations in the *libro de matricula*.

Ia. Geographical Background of All Students at the University of Alcalá

	1568	1573	1578	1583	1588	1591	1598	1603	1608	1613	1618
Andalusia	131	109	83	81	92	49	67	59	71	66	52
Asturias	8	8	8	4	12	7	2	2	6	3	9
New Castile	1674	1716	1482	1755	2194	1606	1697	1445	1583	1889	1909
Complutense	145	132	169	324	147	144	163	111	112	137	202
Old Castile	612	404	281	418	535	427	397	329	363	280	260
León	36	31	22	31	41	33	44	13	16	20	24
Estremadura	48	34	15	18	15	18	32	28	12	16	22
Galicia	11	3	7	6	9	6	19	10	5	8	6
Murcia	23	18	17	27	37	21	32	19	16	33	47
Navarre Calahorra	392	332	276	397	374	350	278	268	251	274	321
Aragon	218	144	117	110	160	94	68	164	151	221	164
Valencia	24	12	4	17	31	11	11	26	19	19	29
Catalonia	9	16	11	17	15	13	19	16	8	34	27
Nullius Diocesis	87	80	80	110	109	79	117	121	123	127	113
Portugal	5	17	17	9	11	12	24	13	19	19	17
Foreign	23	5	12	23	12	8	16	8	18	13	19
Canaries	3	—	5	—	—	—	4	1	2	5	2
Unidentified	55	89	28	65	11	7	12	17	15	29	35

Ib. Geographical Background of All Students at the University of Alcalá

	1568	1573	1578	1583	1588	1591	1598	1603	1608	1613	1618
Andalusia	3.75%	3.45%	3.15%	2.35%	2.40%	1.70%	2.25%	2.20%	2.55%	2.05%	1.60%
Asturias	0.22%	0.25%	0.30%	0.10%	0.30%	0.25%	0.05%	0.07%	0.20%	0.10%	0.30%
New Castile	47.8%	53.7%	56.4%	51.3%	57.6%	55.7%	56.5%	54.1%	56.9%	59.2%	58.7%
Complutense	4.10%	4.20%	6.45%	9.50%	3.85%	5.00%	5.40%	4.15%	4.00%	4.30%	6.20%
Old Castile	17.5%	12.8%	10.3%	12.2%	14.0%	14.8%	13.2%	12.3%	13.0%	8.75%	8.00%
León	1.00%	1.00%	0.85%	0.90%	1.10%	1.15%	1.45%	0.50%	0.60%	0.60%	0.75%
Estremadura	1.37%	1.05%	0.60%	0.50%	0.40%	0.60%	1.05%	1.05%	0.45%	0.50%	0.65%
Galicia	0.31%	0.10%	0.25%	0.15%	0.25%	0.20%	0.65%	0.40%	0.20%	0.25%	0.20%
Murcia	0.65%	0.60%	0.65%	0.80%	1.00%	0.70%	1.05%	0.70%	0.60%	1.05%	1.45%
Navarre Calahorra	11.2%	10.5%	10.5%	11.6%	9.80%	12.1%	9.30%	10.0%	9.00%	8.60%	9.90%
Aragon	6.20%	4.55%	4.45%	3.25%	4.20%	3.25%	2.25%	6.15%	5.40%	6.95%	5.05%
Valencia	0.68%	0.40%	0.15%	0.45%	0.80%	0.40%	0.35%	1.00%	0.30%	0.60%	0.90%
Catalonia	0.25%	0.50%	0.40%	0.45%	0.40%	0.45%	0.65%	0.60%	0.30%	1.05%	0.85%
Nullius Diocesis	2.50%	2.55%	3.05%	3.25%	2.85%	2.70%	3.90%	4.55%	4.45%	4.00%	3.45%
Portugal	0.14%	0.54%	0.65%	0.26%	0.30%	0.40%	0.80%	0.50%	0.70%	0.60%	0.50%
Foreign	0.65%	0.15%	0.45%	0.67%	0.31%	0.30%	0.53%	0.30%	0.65%	0.40%	0.58%
Canaries	0.08%	—	0.20%	—	—	—	0.13%	0.04%	0.07%	0.15%	0.06%
Unidentified	1.60%	2.80%	1.05%	1.90%	0.30%	0.25%	0.40%	0.65%	0.55%	0.90%	1.05%

IIa. Geographical Background of Students at the Grammar Colleges

	1568	1573	1578	1583	1588	1591	1598	1603	1608	1613	1618
Andalusia	28	18	13	9	13	7	1	4	5	7	
Asturias	1	3	4	.3	3	1	1			1	
New Castile	674	645	338	356	334	242	218	201	174	150	125
Complutense	77	47	93	84	54	54	54	48	36	48	80
Old Castile	278	114	54	62	54	38	35	26	11	12	11
León	14	9	2	8	7	1	9	2	1	1	2
Estremadura	13	12		3		2	5	4	1		1
Galicia	6	1		2	1		5			1	
Murcia	8	6	1	5	1	2		1	1	1	
Navarre Calahorra	152	114	49	69	69	52	32	21	14	12	9
Aragon	66	51	23	8	12	8	6	6	4	6	
Valencia	9	3		1	5	2	1	6		2	1
Catalonia	2	5	1	4	2	1	1				
Nullius Diocesis	15	22	10	9	11	12	9	11	7	8	3
Portugal	2		1	1	1	1	3	2	1	1	8
Foreign	2		3	9	2			2		1	4
Canaries				1					1		2
Unidentified	24	22	6	9	1	2	1	4	2		2

IIb. Geographical Background of Students at the Grammar Colleges

	1568	1573	1578	1583	1588	1591	1598	1603	1608	1613	1618
Andalusia	2.05%	1.70%	2.20%	1.40%	2.30%	1.60%		1.20%	1.90%	2.80%	
Asturias	0.07%	0.30%	0.70%	0.50%	0.50	0.25%	0.30%			0.40%	0.40%
New Castile	49.2%	60.5%	56.7%	56.0%	58.5%	56.9%	57.4%	59.3%	67.5%	59.5%	52.3%
Complutense	5.60%	4.40%	15.6%	13.2%	9.40%	12.7%	14.2%	14.1%	13.9%	19.0%	33.4%
Old Castile	20.3%	10.7%	9.00%	9.80%	9.50%	8.90%	9.20%	7.60%	4.20%	4.70%	4.60%
León	1.00%	0.80%	0.30%	1.20%	1.20%	0.25%	2.40%	0.60%	0.40%	0.40%	0.80%
Estremadura	0.95%	1.10%		0.50%		0.50%	1.30%	1.20%	0.40%	0.40%	0.40%
Galicia	0.45%	0.10%		0.30%	0.20%		1.30%	0.30%	0.40%	0.40%	
Murcia	0.60%	0.60%	0.15%	0.80%	0.20%	0.50%			0.40%	0.40%	
Navarre Calahorra	11.1%	10.7%	8.20%	10.8%	12.0%	12.2%	8.40%	6.20%	5.40%	4.70%	3.80%
Aragon	4.80%	4.80%	3.80%	1.20%	2.10%	1.90%	1.60%	1.80%	1.50%	2.40%	
Valencia	0.65%	0.30%		0.10%	0.90%	0.50%	0.30%	1.80%		0.80%	0.40%
Catalonia	0.15%	0.50%	0.15%	0.60%	0.35%	0.25%	0.25%			0.40%	
Nullius Diocesis	1.10%	2.00%	1.70%	1.40%	1.90%	2.80%	2.35%	3.20%	2.70%	3.20%	1.25%
Portugal	0.15%		0.15%	0.15%	0.20%	0.25%	0.25%	0.60%	0.40%	0.40%	3.30%
Foreign	0.15%		0.50%	1.40%	0.35%			0.60%		0.40%	1.60%
Canaries		0.10%		0.15%					0.40%		0.85%
Unidentified	1.75%	2.80%	1.00%	1.40%	0.20%	0.50%	0.50%	1.20%	0.80%	0.85%	0.85%

IIIa. Geographical Background of Students at the Faculty of Arts

	1568	1573	1578	1583	1588	1591	1598	1603	1608	1613	1618
Andalusia	39	38	19	22	32	19	28	21	30	21	19
Asturias	4	2	2	1	6	3	1	1	5	1	2
New Castile	522	525	574	761	950	718	708	609	680	813	790
Complutense	33	32	35	136	27	32	36	11	27	26	40
Old Castile	204	148	140	216	302	190	199	172	149	136	114
León	11	14	10	10	21	14	14	2	7	8	8
Estremadura	22	11	3	4	7	8	12	9	6	7	7
Galicia	2	2	3	1	6	5	4	7	1	1	1
Murcia	7	8	13	13	10	4	14	3	8	14	15
Navarre Calahorra	143	121	128	212	178	190	137	158	164	153	155
Aragon	86	52	61	53	82	50	31	89	92	120	78
Valencia	11	2	1	8	7		4	3	8	8	5
Catalonia	3	5	6	2	5	3	4	10	3	21	7
Nullius Diocesis	39	28	30	55	43	30	52	66	48	67	54
Portugal	2	7	7	5	5	3	8	7	7	6	7
Foreign	4	1	5	6	2	5	7	1	4	6	2
Canaries		1		1			1	1		2	2
Unidentified	24	19	12	22	4	2	1	8	5	10	12

IIIb. Geographical Background of Students at the Faculty of Arts

	1568	1573	1578	1583	1588	1591	1598	1603	1608	1613	1618
Andalusia	3.40%	3.70%	1.80%	1.45%	1.90%	1.50%	2.20%	1.80%	2.40%	1.50%	1.50%
Asturias	0.35%	0.20%	0.20%	0.05%	0.35%	0.25%	0.08%	0.08%	0.40%	0.07%	0.15%
New Castile	45.5%	51.6%	54.8%	49.9%	56.3%	56.3%	56.1%	51.7%	54.6%	57.2%	59.9%
Complutense	2.90%	3.15%	3.35%	8.90%	1.60%	2.50%	2.85%	0.95%	2.15%	1.80%	3.00%
Old Castile	17.8%	14.5%	13.3%	14.1%	17.9%	14.9%	15.8%	14.6%	12.0%	9.60%	8.60%
León	0.95%	1.40%	0.95%	0.65%	1.25%	1.10%	1.10%	0.15%	0.55%	0.55%	0.60%
Estremadura	1.90%	1.10%	0.30%	0.25%	0.40%	0.60%	0.95%	0.75%	0.50%	0.50%	0.50%
Galicia	0.15%	0.20%	0.30%	0.05%	0.35%	0.40%	0.30%	0.60%	0.08%	0.07%	0.08%
Murcia	0.60%	0.80%	1.25%	0.85%	0.60%	0.30%	1.10%	0.25%	0.65%	1.00%	1.10%
Navarre Calahorra	12.4%	11.9%	12.2%	13.9%	10.5%	14.9%	10.8%	13.4%	13.2%	10.8%	11.8%
Aragon	7.50%	5.10%	5.80%	3.50%	4.90%	3.90%	2.45%	7.50%	7.40%	8.50%	5.90%
Valencia	0.95%	0.20%	0.10%	0.50%	0.40%		0.10%	0.25%	0.65%	0.55%	0.40%
Catalonia	0.25%	0.50%	0.60%	0.15%	0.30%	0.25%	0.30%	0.85%	0.25%	1.50%	0.50%
Nullius Diocesis	3.40%	2.75%	2.85%	3.60%	2.55%	2.35%	4.10%	5.60%	3.85%	4.70%	4.10%
Portugal	0.15%	0.70%	0.65%	0.30%	0.30%	0.25%	0.65%	0.60%	0.55%	0.40%	0.55%
Foreign	0.35%	0.10%	0.50%	0.40%	0.10%	0.40%	0.55%	0.90%	0.30%	0.40%	0.15%
Canaries		0.10%		0.05%			0.08%	0.08%		0.15%	0.15%
Unidentified	2.10%	1.80%	1.15%	1.45%	0.25%	0.15%	0.08%	0.70%	0.40%	0.70%	0.90%

IVa. Geographical Background of Students at the Faculty of Medicine

	1568	1573	1578	1583	1588	1591	1598	1603	1608	1613	1618
Andalusia	12	19	12	20	18	6	11	8	12	9	2
Asturias	1				2	1					
New Castile	46	40	35	58	86	57	42	54	62	61	83
Complutense	8	12	13	13	12	10	7	9	8	13	8
Old Castile	14	8	12	19	16	12	8	14	10	6	15
León	1	1	1		1	2		1		1	1
Estremadura		1		2			1	2	1	1	4
Galicia				2							1
Murcia			2		1		1	1			2
Navarre Calahorra	6	11	9	9	8	8	8	5	8	6	13
Aragon	8	4	4	8	9	6	4	5	6	9	11
Valencia		1	1		1	1			1		5
Catalonia								1	1	2	2
Nullius Diocesis	3	1	3	5	9	4	3	1	3	2	7
Portugal	1	2	4	2	1	2	2		4	2	4
Foreign	1		1		1		2	2			
Canaries											
Unidentified	4	6		3	2			1	1	7	1

IVb. Geographical Background of Students at the Faculty of Medicine

	1568	1573	1578	1583	1588	1591	1598	1603	1608	1613	1618
Andalusia	11.4%	17.9%	12.4%	14.2%	10.8%	5.20%	12.5%	7.70%	10.2%	7.55%	1.25%
Asturias	0.95%				1.20%	0.85%					
New Castile	43.8%	37.7%	36.1%	41.1%	51.5%	49.6%	47.7%	51.9%	53.0%	51.2%	52.2%
Complutense	7.60%	11.3%	13.4%	9.20%	7.20%	8.70%	7.95%	8.65%	6.85%	10.9%	5.05%
Old Castile	13.3%	7.55%	12.4%	13.5%	9.60%	10.4%	9.10%	13.5%	8.55%	5.05%	9.45%
León	0.95%	0.95%	1.05%		0.60%	1.75%		0.95%		0.85%	0.60%
Estremadura		0.95%		1.40%			1.15%	1.90%	0.85%	0.85%	2.50%
Galicia				1.40%							0.60%
Murcia			2.05%		0.60%		1.15%	0.95%			1.25%
Navarre Calahorra	5.70%	10.3%	9.30%	6.40%	4.80%	6.95%	9.10%	4.80%	6.85%	5.05%	8.15%
Aragon	7.60%	3.75%	4.15%	5.70%	5.40%	5.20%	4.55%	4.80%	5.10%	7.55%	6.90%
Valencia			0.95%		0.60%	0.85%			0.85%		3.15%
Catalonia								0.95%	0.85%	1.70%	1.25%
Nullius Diocesis	2.85%	0.95%	3.10%	3.55%	5.40%	3.50%	3.40%	0.95%	2.55%	1.70%	4.40%
Portugal	0.95%	1.90%	4.15%	1.40%	0.60%	1.75%	2.25%		3.40%	1.70%	2.50%
Foreign	0.95%		1.05%		0.60%		2.25%	1.90%			
Unidentified	3.80%	5.65%		2.15%	1.20%			0.95%	0.85%	5.90%	0.60%

Va. Geographical Background of Students at the Faculty of Theology

	1568	1573	1578	1583	1588	1591	1598	1603	1608	1613	1618
Andalusia	36	22	22	14	16	9	8	12	9	9	10
Asturias	1	1	1		1	1		1		1	1
New Castile	155	251	246	294	435	294	333	243	240	281	282
Complutense	9	18	15	46	33	20	25	16	15	16	20
Old Castile	54	71	37	73	82	78	60	55	63	53	47
León	5	3	8	1	6	8	5	6	1	3	3
Estremadura	5	6	10	6	3	1	8	10	3	6	6
Galicia	1		2				2	1	3	3	2
Murcia	4	2	1	3	13	10	9	6	2	7	7
Navarre Calahorra	57	46	57	76	79	52	57	48	47	58	55
Aragon	27	26	17	27	32	17	17	35	25	48	41
Valencia	2	3	2	2	9	4	3	14	5	5	7
Catalonia	4	5	3	7	7	6	13	3	2	6	8
Nullius Diocesis	14	8	8	9	12	12	16	15	15	10	12
Portugal		8	3	1	5	2			2	6	3
Foreign	1	2	1	4	2		3	2	2	2	2
Canaries				1			2				
Unidentified	5	30	4	24	4	4	6	2	5	6	9

Vb. Geographical Background of Students at the Faculty of Theology

	1568	1573	1578	1583	1588	1591	1598	1603	1608	1613	1618
Andalusia	9.10%	4.40%	5.00%	2.40%	2.15%	1.75%	1.40%	2.55%	2.05%	1.75%	1.95%
Asturias	0.25%	0.20%	0.20%		0.10%	0.20%		0.20%		0.20%	0.20%
New Castile	39.2%	50.5%	56.3%	50.0%	58.8%	56.7%	58.7%	51.8%	54.8%	54.0%	54.7%
Complutense	2.25%	3.60%	3.40%	7.80%	4.45%	3.85%	4.40%	3.40%	3.40%	3.10%	3.90%
Old Castile	13.7%	14.3%	8.50%	12.4%	11.1%	15.0%	10.6%	11.7%	14.4%	10.2%	9.10%
León	1.25%	0.60%	1.80%	0.20%	0.80%	1.55%	0.90%	1.30%	0.20%	0.60%	0.60%
Estremadura	1.25%	1.20%	2.30%	1.00%	0.40%	0.20%	1.40%	2.15%	0.70%	1.15%	1.15%
Galicia	0.25%		0.40%				0.35%	0.20%	0.45%	0.60%	0.40%
Murcia	1.00%	0.40%	0.20%	0.50%	1.75%	1.95%	1.60%	1.30%	0.45%	1.35%	1.35%
Navarre Calahorra	14.4%	9.30%	13.0%	12.9%	10.7%	10.0%	10.0%	10.2%	10.7%	11.1%	12.0%
Aragon	6.85%	5.20%	3.90%	4.60%	4.30%	3.30%	3.00%	7.45%	5.70%	9.25%	8.00%
Valencia	0.50%	0.60%	0.40%	0.35%	1.20%	0.77%	0.50%	3.00%	1.15%	1.00%	1.35%
Catalonia	1.00%	1.00%	0.70%	1.20%	0.95%	1.15%	2.30%	0.65%	0.45%	1.15%	1.55%
Nullius Diocesis	3.55%	1.60%	1.80%	1.50%	1.60%	2.30%	2.80%	3.20%	3.40%	1.90%	3.35%
Portugal		1.60%	0.70%	0.20%	0.70%	0.40%			0.45%	1.15%	0.60%
Foreign	0.25%	0.40%	0.20%	0.70%	0.25%		0.50%	0.40%	0.45%	0.40%	0.40%
Canaries				0.20%			0.35%				
Unidentified	1.25%	6.00%	0.90%	4.10%	0.55%	0.77%	1.05%	0.40%	1.15%	1.15%	1.75%

VIa. Geographical Background of Students at the Faculty of Canon Law

	1568	1573	1578	1583	1588	1591	1598	1603	1608	1613	1618
Andalusia	16	12	17	16	13	8	20	14	15	20	21
Asturias	1	2	1						1		6
New Castile	277	263	291	294	389	295	396	338	427	584	629
Complutense	18	23	13	45	21	22	41	27	26	34	54
Old Castile	62	63	38	48	81	111	95	75	84	73	73
León	5	4	1	12	6	6	16	2	7	7	10
Estremadura	8	4	2	3	5	7	6	3	1	2	4
Galicia	2		2	1	2	1	8	2	2	3	2
Murcia	4	2		6	12	5	8	8	5	11	23
Navarre Calahorra	34	40	33	31	40	48	44	44	64	45	89
Aragon	31	11	12	14	25	13	10	29	24	38	34
Valencia	2	3		4	9	4	3	3	5	4	11
Catalonia		1	1	4	1	3	1	2	2	4	10
Nullius Diocesis	16	21	29	32	34	21	37	28	50	40	37
Portugal		2	2	1		4	11	3	5	4	2
Foreign	1	3	3	5	3	1	5	1	3	4	5
Canaries		1		2		1	1		1	3	
Unidentified	6	12	6	8			4	2	2	6	11

VIb. **Geographical Background of Students at the Faculty of Canon Law**

	1568	1573	1578	1583	1588	1591	1598	1603	1608	1613	1618
Andalusia	3.30%	2.60%	3.80%	3.05%	2.00%	1.45%	2.80%	2.40%	2.10%	2.30%	2.05%
Asturias	0.20%	0.40%	0.20%						0.15%		0.60%
New Castile	57.3%	56.3%	64.5%	56.0%	60.7%	53.4%	56.1%	58.2%	59.0%	66.2%	61.6%
Complutense	3.75%	4.90%	2.90%	8.60%	3.30%	4.00%	5.80%	4.65%	3.60%	3.85%	5.30%
Old Castile	12.8%	13.5%	8.40%	9.10%	12.6%	20.1%	13.4%	12.9%	11.6%	8.30%	7.10%
León	1.05%	0.85%	0.20%	2.30%	0.95%	1.10%	2.30%	0.35%	0.95%	0.80%	1.00%
Estremadura	1.65%	0.85%	0.45%	0.60%	0.80%	1.25%	0.85%	0.50%	0.15%	0.20%	0.40%
Galicia	0.40%		0.45%	0.20%	0.30%	0.20%	1.15%	0.35%	0.30%	0.35%	0.20%
Murcia	0.80%	0.40%		1.15%	1.90%	0.90%	1.15%	1.40%	0.70%	1.25%	2.25%
Navarre Calahorra	7.05%	8.60%	7.30%	5.90%	6.20%	8.70%	6.20%	7.60%	8.60%	5.10%	8.70%
Aragon	6.40%	2.40%	2.65%	2.65%	3.90%	2.35%	1.40%	5.00%	3.30%	4.30%	3.30%
Valencia	0.40%	0.65%		0.75%	1.40%	0.75%	0.40%	0.50%	0.70%	0.45%	1.10%
Catalonia		0.20%	0.20%	0.75%	0.15%	0.55%	0.15%	0.35%	0.30%	0.45%	1.00%
Nullius Diocesis	3.30%	4.50%	6.45%	6.10%	5.30%	3.80%	5.25%	4.80%	6.90%	4.50%	3.60%
Portugal		0.40%	0.45%	0.20%	0.60%	0.70%	1.55%	0.50%	0.70%	0.45%	0.20%
Foreign	0.20%	0.65%	0.65%	0.95%	0.15%	0.20%	0.70%	0.15%	0.40%	0.45%	0.50%
Canaries		0.20%		0.40%	0.15%	0.20%	0.15%		0.30%	0.70%	
Unidentified	1.25%	2.55%	1.35%	1.50%			0.55%	0.35%	0.15%	0.35%	1.10%

The Politics of Professorial Appointment at Leiden, 1709*

Maarten Ultee

'As long as there's death, there's hope.'
(comment on the tenure system, attributed to
Nicholas Murray Butler)

In mid-January 1709, Petrus Hotton, Professor of Botany in the medical faculty of Leiden University, died. On February 18, after a remarkably brief interval, the Curators of the University and *Burgemeesters* of Leiden appointed Herman Boerhaave as Hotton's successor. In time the appointment appeared fully justified, as Boerhaave became one of the greatest medical teachers of the age. He gave his inaugural lecture on March 20, and soon acquired an international reputation, attracting many foreign students to Leiden. Boerhaave showed an almost superhuman capacity for work. He lectured four to five hours a day, four days a week; he treated patients, took care of the botanic garden, and served as vice-chancellor of the university in 1714 and 1730. In 1715 he proposed to revive clinical teaching of medicine; in 1718 he added the professorship of chemistry to his duties. Only in 1729 did he resign from the chairs of botany and chemistry, while keeping the professorship of theory of medicine until his death in 1738. Admiring students, biographers, and historians of medicine have agreed that his influence was great in his own university and at Edinburgh and Vienna, the leading medical schools of the later eighteenth century.[1]

What is remarkable about Boerhaave's first appointment as professor in 1709 is that he knew so little about the subject: botany. A. G. Morton in his *History of Botanical Science* notes that

Boerhaave firmly held the conviction that medicine must be linked with, and make full use of, all relevant branches of natural science. After his appointment in 1709 to the chair of medicine and botany at Leiden, this conviction, reinforced by the fact that superintendence of the botanic garden was part of his duties, led him to a more serious study of botany than he had yet undertaken . . .[2]

Indeed, Morton reports Boerhaave's claim that he 'had botanized in the polders and dunes as a student, using as a guide the local flora of Paul Hermann, then Professor of Botany at Leiden, but had not bothered to attend Hermann's lectures.'[3] Professor G. A. Lindeboom, author of the standard biography of Boerhaave, admitted that

It was more unusual that he had no qualifications whatever to teach the subject at the time when he took it over. He had no specialized knowledge of it, and neither had he ever displayed any particular interest in it. The assignment was in fact an accidental one resulting from his having to be given the chair vacant as a result of Hotton's death.[4]

More bluntly: 'When Boerhaave was appointed in 1709 to the chair of medicine and botany, he was then no botanist.'[5] We should not be surprised at the appointment of a professor without qualifications in the field: we can think of similar cases. At other early modern universities social criteria seem to have been as important as knowledge of the subject. Most professors at Siena belonged to the local aristocracy that dominated the town council, and at Padua some appointments were made without regard to subject: in 1709 Giovanni Poleni was appointed to teach astronomy on the basis of his experiments with the barometer and a calculating machine.[6] There were similar examples, not only in Italy but also in England and the United States, well into the nineteenth century. When Henry Adams was appointed to teach medieval history at Harvard in 1870, he had never studied the subject.[7] During Charles Darwin's time at Cambridge, the Woodwardian Professorship of Geology was elective: in 1818 Adam Sedgwick had boasted in his campaign, 'Hitherto I have never turned a stone; henceforth I will leave no stone unturned.'[8] And he was elected!

Yet Lindeboom's statement does draw our attention to the circumstances of Boerhaave's appointment. When Boerhaave resigned two of his chairs in 1729, he noted that despite the speedy action by the Curators and *Burgemeesters* twenty years earlier, there had been competition from at least one other scientist. Discussing his own possible successors, Boerhaave said that 'in Zurich there still lived Johann Jacob Scheuchzer, who had been proposed at the time when he, Professor Boerhaave, was appointed to the chair of botany, but he had to say that the said gentleman was over sixty years of age and, as far as he knew, not conversant with chemistry.'[9] This point has been largely overlooked by historians. Lindeboom asked,

Who could have proposed Scheuchzer as Hotton's successor in 1709? The archives contain no mention of the matter whatever. If Boerhaave had not himself mentioned the incident in 1729, it would have been completely forgotten. It is very improbable that Scheuchzer's name was put forward by the Curators, and it seems very likely that the proposal came from the faculty or from some group within it.[10]

Lindeboom thought that the faculty may have wanted a qualified botanist instead of Boerhaave, a lecturer in medicine active in private practice and in chemistry. Among the other professors there was a hint of professorial jealousy at the lucrative fees Boerhaave collected for his lectures. Yet this article will argue that more than mere jealousy was involved in the competition for Hotton's chair. Recent research suggests that it may be necessary to modify our views about Boerhaave. By placing his appointment into the historical context of Leiden University in the seventeenth and eighteenth centuries, we shall show that there was widespread international interest in the professorship of botany in 1709. Professional interests and local politics played important roles in the appointment. We shall see why the university archives are reticent: our particular focus will be on the competition between Boerhaave and Scheuchzer, and the efforts of their friends. Through correspondence we shall rediscover the more worldly activities of the Republic of Letters, the scientific fraternity in early modern Europe.

During the seventeenth century, the newly-founded Dutch universities quickly attracted students from all over Europe.[11] Their appeal was based partly on the prosperity and relative calm of the Dutch Republic while other areas suffered the ravages of the Thirty Years' War, civil strife, political and religious persecution. Philosophical and scientific ideas flourished—Descartes, Spinoza, Locke, Bayle, and many other thinkers lived and worked among the Dutch. They enjoyed the freedom to publish their writings with the thriving printing houses of Amsterdam, Leiden, The Hague, Rotterdam, and Utrecht. There were vigorous intellectual debates about Cartesianism and theology, and Dutch university faculties were often sharply divided on the acceptance of new ideas in the curriculum. The University of Leiden, founded in 1575, struggled to maintain strict Calvinist orthodoxy.[12] This university was supported financially by the States of Holland, who appointed three Curators; together with four *Burgemeesters* of Leiden, they constituted the governing college. The board had tried to assert their autonomy quite early in some celebrated cases of faculty appointments and dismissals.[13] Occasionally they expressed concerns about the teaching of new ideas: in 1647, the board prohibited all mention of Descartes in Leiden theses, public lectures, and disputations.[14] Known supporters of Descartes were still appointed to the faculty, but in 1676 the Curators made a list of twenty forbidden philosophical propositions not to be discussed publicly or privately. By that time only conservative theologians were appointed, thanks in part to the increasing influence of Stadholder William III, a former student of the university who became even more powerful as king of England in 1688/89. During the 1690s, William arrogated to himself the fictitious title of 'Opper-Curator' [Super-Curator]. He manipulated the States of Holland to choose his agents as Curators, and all professorial appointments required his approval.[15] It is clear that the administrators of Leiden University wished to avoid controversy. The intellectual attraction of progressive ideas had to be balanced against local interests in preserving good order and pleasing the Stadholder-King.

Control of the universities and many other Dutch institutions remained local. The central government of the Republic or the provincial states might pass resolutions affecting the circulation of ideas and information, but enforcement was ultimately in the hands of municipal authorities. Thus printed works that gave offence to the interests of religion or state might be forbidden in one town but allowed to circulate freely in another.[16] At the same time that some religious or philosophical opinions were forbidden at Leiden, for example, they were tolerated at Amsterdam. The decentralized nature of the Dutch state with its relative intellectual freedom was repeatedly noted by foreign observers and the Dutch themselves.[17]

The medical faculty at Leiden in the late seventeenth century had five professorships, which was large by Dutch and European standards. Other Dutch universities had only two or three professors to cover all of medicine; at German universities in the eighteenth century three was the usual number.[18] The Curators and *Burgemeesters* of Leiden had decided in 1681 to have only four regular chairs. Theodore Craanen, the fifth professor at that time, taught philosophy and medicine, and Carel De Maets, the teacher of chemistry and ordinary professor in medicine since 1672, was only granted the right to sit in the faculty of medicine in 1679.[19] In addition to teaching theory of medicine, individual professors were assigned responsibilities in anatomy, botany, chemistry, and clinical practice. The medical professors at Leiden were a precarious elite: the death or departure of even one of them required careful action by the college of Curators and *Burgemeesters*. To uphold the reputation of their university, they had appointed many foreign professors, and they organized searches throughout Europe for suitable candidates.

In the early 1690s there was high turnover and a definite shortage of medical teaching staff at Leiden. In 1689, after the death of Lucas Schacht, who had held the chair of *praxis medicinae* for twenty years, the Curators did not immediately hire another professor. They ultimately offered the post to the renowned Archibald Pitcairne of Edinburgh in November 1691; he did not come until April 1692, and left the following year.[20] When the chemist De Maets died in 1690, his eventual successor Jacob Le Mort was given charge of the chemistry laboratory but not immediately offered a chair. The anatomist Anton Nuck, appointed in 1687, died young in 1692. By 1693, the University of Leiden had only two medical professors left—Charles Drélincourt (institutes and anatomy) and Paul Hermann (botany). The Curators then tried in 1694 to appoint two new professors at once, making offers to Abraham Cyprianus from Franeker and Johannes Conrad Brunner, physician to the Elector Palatine and Professor at Heidelberg. But Cyprianus declined; Brunner, an alumnus of Leiden, wanted to know more about the salaries and privileges of the professors. Consequently the posts went to local candidates: Frederik Dekkers, a physician of Leiden, and Govert Bidloo, the successor to Anton Nuck at the Surgical and Anatomical College in The Hague. Unfortunately Dekkers was not a very inspiring teacher, but Bidloo was a brilliant anatomist. He had also recently changed his politics and cultivated the favour of the Stadholder-King, becoming general superintendent of physicians in Holland in 1690 and physician in ordinary to William III in 1701.[21] Bidloo was often absent on duty with his royal patient, causing him to neglect both clinical and anatomical teaching. The botanist Hermann died in 1695. Despite the rapid appointment of his successor Petrus Hotton, a physician who had worked in Leiden in 1679 and assisted Frederik Ruysch at the Amsterdam botanic garden, matters at Leiden worsened when Drélincourt died in 1697. Meanwhile, student enrolments in the medical faculty at Leiden declined.[22]

Facing a financial crisis aggravated by bad management, the Curators sent one of their number, Hubertus Rosenboom, to speak with William III, 'in order that he may be properly informed of the decay of the Academy'.[23] The Curators and Burgemeesters wished to restore the former glory of the university, 'under the approbation of H.M. of Great Britain as *oppercurator*', noting that 'the great decline of studies in medicine has taken place primarily because all the departments of the said faculty are not properly supplied.'[24] They proposed to promote the chemist Le Mort to a chair, and wanted to offer another professorship to Brunner. When no action was taken, in 1698 the board again complained to William about the 'indispensable necessity' of hiring 'eenige celebre mannen' [several famous men] and obtaining 'een behoorlyke subsidie' [a proper subsidy] from the States of Holland.[25] On this occasion negotiations with Brunner dragged on for another year, and Le Mort's promotion was blocked by William III. Eventually the States did give the university an extraordinary sum of 20,000 *gulden* to cover the deficit, and in 1699–1700 the board made other attempts to recruit foreigners, among them Theodor Zwinger III, professor of medicine at Basel.[26]

The sad state of medical education at Leiden in the 1690s coincided with Herman Boerhaave's student days. He matriculated at Leiden in 1684 and began studies in philosophy and theology, perhaps intending to follow his father's profession in the church. By 1689 his intellect and skill in disputation were evident in public orations, including an attack on Pierre Gassendi's views on the ethical theories of Epicurus—for which the Curators gave him a gold medal.[27] The following year, 1690, Boerhaave defended a Cartesian thesis on the distinction between body and soul, and became a doctor of philosophy. By then his interest had turned to medicine. He began attending medical lectures in Leiden, in particular Anton Nuck's public dissections. Professor Lindeboom has argued, however, that Boerhaave did not learn very much from the faculty; instead, Boerhaave's private reading of ancient and modern classics and his own vivisection experiments on dogs were the foundation of his medical knowledge.[28] As the professors of medicine at Leiden had played only a minor part in Boerhaave's education, he did not feel obliged to take his M.D. there. Indeed, in 1693 Boerhaave took his medical degree at Harderwijk, a smaller university where the fees were lower.[29] For the next eight years, he had a private practice in Leiden. In 1701, however, the Curators of Leiden University rectified some of their staffing problems by hiring Boerhaave, not as a professor, but as *Lector Institutionum Medicarum* (lecturer in theoretical medicine) for a term of three years. Boerhaave was embarked on his academic career.

At the same time, Johann Jakob Scheuchzer of Zurich was also studying and practising medicine.[30] Scheuchzer was born in 1672 to a family of municipal officials and doctors: his father was *Stadtarzt* but died suddenly in 1685. Johann Jakob studied at the *Carolinum*, the elite secondary school; he then had three years of instruction from private tutors to prepare for university. He became interested in botany, geology, and paleontology, and started making field trips to the Swiss countryside. In 1692, with the help of a scholarship from the city fathers, Scheuchzer was able to join two friends going to study at the University of Altorf near Nuremberg. It was a requirement of their scholarships that they take letters of recommendation to prominent scholars and keep an *Album Amicorum* in which these scholars would write, proving that the students had fulfilled the terms of their grants. Before leaving Zurich, the three students visited Pieter Valkenier (1641–1712), well-connected Dutch envoy to the Swiss Confederation, who gave them a letter to his friend Johann Christoph Wagenseil (1633–1705), professor of law and oriental studies at Altorf. Receiving a warm welcome, Scheuchzer at first had favourable impressions of the German university. He was pleased with his courses in chemistry, botany, philosophy and physics, but found that theoretical medicine and anatomy left much to be desired—in one year, he reported, he had dissected 'no more than one cat and two calf's heads'.[31] Confronted with the shortcomings of the university, Scheuchzer, like Boerhaave, felt obliged to study the sciences independently, and he established friendships with other observers of nature. By the summer of 1693, Scheuchzer had resolved to continue his studies in the Dutch Republic at the University of Utrecht. Thanks to his sound advance preparation and concentrated study, he was able to take his medical doctor's degree at Utrecht after only five months in residence, in January 1694.

Scheuchzer then returned to Zurich and occupied himself with alpine travels, botany, numismatics, and other scientific studies while awaiting an official appointment. At the end of 1695 he became physician to the city orphanage, and shortly afterwards he was named curator of the municipal library and keeper of the cabinet of curiosities. He also gave private lessons in medicine and natural sciences, wrote scientific treatises and edited a literary journal. Within a few years he won recognition as a member of the German *Akademie der Naturforscher*. Scheuchzer's desire for promotion is evident from his first contacts with the Royal Society of London, which agreed to publish his reports of alpine botanical expeditions. Isaac Newton and John Woodward contributed personally to the costs of engraving plates for this work. Soon he was in regular correspondence with Woodward, Hans Sloane, William Sherard, and other English luminaries.[32] Scheuchzer knew the English language well enough to translate Woodward's *Natural History of the Earth* into Latin (1703), which made the geologist's writings accessible to a wider European audience. Yet despite official support for his expeditions, Scheuchzer felt unduly constrained in his home town. He told one surprised correspondent that the Protestant ministers in Zurich regarded mathematics as a source of heresies.[33] His friends abroad helped him look for suitable employment elsewhere, and urged him to seek other posts.

Petrus Hotton's death in 1709 did not come as a surprise to Boerhaave or Scheuchzer. In fact it was eagerly awaited. On his modest short-term appointment as *lector*, Boerhaave naturally looked for a better position. His lectures were successfully drawing students, and his first publications attracted favourable notice. In 1703 the Curators of the University of Groningen approached him with an offer of a professorship, and about the same time he was on the short-list of candidates at Franeker as well. But Boerhaave was willing to stay in Leiden—if the Curators and *Burgemeesters* would make it worth his while. They were unable to appoint him to a chair right away, however, for by then there were five professors of medicine—Bidloo, Dekkers, Hotton, Le Mort (finally promoted after William III's death), and Bernhard Albinus, former physician to the King of Prussia and professor at Frankfurt-am-Main, who had been appointed in 1702. But the board was able to raise Boerhaave's salary by 50 per cent, and promised him the first vacant professorship in the faculty of medicine. He was also allowed to deliver a second inaugural oration. In return, Boerhaave promised to decline other offers. Jan van den Bergh, secretary to the Curators, appears to have been the middleman who arranged the deal.[34] This type of bargaining between university curators and professors was common among those most in demand—professors of theology, law, and medicine. The experiences of two theologians illustrate the point. Frederick Spanheim of Leiden received a call to Heidelberg in 1681, and Melchior Leydecker one from Utrecht to Groningen in 1689; but both professors remained in their posts, at higher salaries.[35] In the summer of 1708, when the sixty-year-old Hotton fell ill, the forty-year-old Herman Boerhaave had good prospects of advancement. He had just published two influential textbooks: *Institutiones Medicae*, on physiology as an introduction to medicine (1707); and *Aphorismi*, 1,479 aphorisms on pathology, summing up contemporary knowledge (1708).

As for Scheuchzer, he was also well informed about Leiden. His old patron the Dutch diplomat Pieter Valkenier had returned to The Hague in 1704. Friends since 1692, Valkenier and Scheuchzer wrote to each other frequently, monthly in 1708, even more often in 1709. On July 20, 1708, Valkenier reported Hotton's illness and promised, 'when he comes to die, I shall do all I can, with Mr. Cuper, to put you in his place.'[36] Gisbert Cuper (1644–1716), *burgemeester* of Deventer, Deputy from Overijssel, Field Deputy from the States-General to the army of Marlborough in 1706, was another influential correspondent of Scheuchzer.[37] An amateur of classical learning and collector of antiquities, Cuper was connected to the international Republic of Letters: he was in touch with Leibniz, Abbé Jean-Paul Bignon of the Paris Academies, the learned critic Jean Le Clerc, the botanist William Sherard and other members of the Royal Society. Above all, Cuper's opinion carried weight with the Curators of Leiden; he had successfully recommended a candidate for another chair.[38] Thus Johann Jakob Scheuchzer's influential Dutch friends and his outstanding record of botanical publications gave him reasonable expectations of gaining the Leiden professorship.

The winter of 1708–1709 was unusually severe. At London the Thames froze over, and the frost lasted for weeks. Communications across the North Sea were interrupted when ships froze in their harbours. In this dreadful season Hotton died. Pieter Valkenier received the first notice on January 13 (n.s.), when Hotton's brother-in-law and nephew told him.[39] Immediately Valkenier contacted

Cuper and urged him to act on Scheuchzer's behalf at Leiden. The Dutch botanists Simon Beaumont and Frans Kiggelaar also supported Scheuchzer, as did Maurits van Beverhorst, *praelector* in anatomy at the Surgical and Anatomical College in The Hague. But the attitude of the Curators and *Burgemeesters* would be crucial. Despite the cold, Valkenier was determined to find out how they stood. In all there were seven members of the board. Valkenier knew four of them well: the Count of Wassenaer-Obdam, Hubertus Rosenboom, Herman van den Honert, and Jan van den Bergh. The backgrounds of these men are quite revealing.

Jacob, Count of Wassenaer, Lord of Obdam (1635–1714),[40] was the son of a well-known admiral. Although he had received the degree of Doctor of Laws from the University of Oxford in 1670, Wassenaer pursued a military career. He joined the army and commanded a regiment of cavalry at Seneffe (1674); later he fought in the battles of the Nine Years' War and the War of the Spanish Succession, but he resigned when he was not made field marshal in 1704. A curator of Leiden since 1690, he also carried out diplomatic missions to France, England, Brandenburg, and the Palatinate. In early 1709, the Count of Wassenaer, the most prominent of the Curators, was at Dusseldorf when Hotton died.

Hubertus Rosenboom (1634–1722),[41] President of the *Hoogen Raad* in Holland, Zeeland, and West-Friesland since 1691, had long been a strong Orangist and facile servant of William III. Rosenboom was sent as *Maître des Requêtes* to deal with Amsterdam in 1674; that same year he married into the regent elite. Rosenboom served as a liaison officer between the board and the Stadholder-King, although his quarrelsome nature often made him unpopular.[42] In the 1690s he had long-running disputes with his colleagues about timely announcements of meetings, attendance, and whether university documents could be taken away from Leiden. By December 1698, William III intervened personally at Rosenboom's request, ordering the board to consider university business seriously and to settle their differences.[43]

Herman van den Honert (1664–1730),[44] *Burgemeester* of Dordrecht, had received his law degree at Leiden in 1666. In 1670 he entered the town government of Dordrecht, following his father's footsteps. Despite his family connection with the old regents, he was continued in office by William III in 1672. In 1675 he even married Anna de Witt, eldest daughter of the late Johan de Witt, generally regarded as the leading representative of the interests of regent oligarchy against Orangist claims. Van den Honert held a series of legal and municipal posts, and had been a curator of Leiden since 1703.

Finally, Jan van den Bergh (1664–1755),[45] *Burgemeester* of Leiden and secretary to the Curators since 1693, would play a key role in making the appointment. Like van den Honert, he had studied law at Leiden and took his doctorate there in 1688. Van den Bergh was active in local government and chosen 21 times as *Burgemeester* of Leiden. He entered the *Raad van State* in 1704, and was a Field Deputy to Marlborough's army in 1706, at the same time as Cuper. While it would be fair to regard van den Bergh as representing the interests of Leiden, three other *burgemeesters* of the city were also present at the Curators' meetings; consequently the magistrates' influence in university affairs was always considerable.[46]

On January 18 Valkenier wrote Scheuchzer that he would be seeing two 'seigneurs de Leiden qui sont astheure [=à cette heure] ici, et qui sont de pouvoir.'[47] Valkenier thought that the Curators would not rush the appointment. He suggested Scheuchzer obtain from the Zurich authorities the title of *professor*, because the University of Leiden did 'not like to take doctors for professors; it would be even better if [the title] could be back-dated. You will recall that I mentioned it some time ago.' Valkenier also wanted confirmation that Scheuchzer had taken his doctor's degree at Utrecht, which he thought would be seen positively. Hotton would be buried on the morrow. Meanwhile Valkenier awaited an answer from Cuper. Valkenier's enthusiasm knew no bounds: 'No doubt you know, Sir, that the professor of botany always resides in the house in the botanic garden, and I have been told his salary is 1800 Hollands florins. Oh, what pleasure I shall have, to see you well established in this country!' His letter closed with a reference to two learned journalists, Jacques Bernard and Jean Le Clerc. Bernard, editor of *Nouvelles de la République des Lettres*, was a professor at Leiden, and planned to review Scheuchzer's treatises on fish and grasses. As for Jean Le Clerc of Amsterdam, author of the *Bibliothèque Choisie*, Valkenier did not know whether he would comment on Scheuchzer's works, but he would find out that day.

Cuper was no slouch either: on January 19 he wrote two letters recommending Scheuchzer—one in Dutch for his erstwhile fellow field deputy Jan van den Bergh, the other in French for the Count of

Wassenaer, whom he had known professionally since the 1690s. In both letters Cuper mentioned his correspondence, proving Scheuchzer's 'learning, good humour, and everything that is required in such a professor'. Scheuchzer was well known in Switzerland, Germany, England, France, and Italy; Cuper urged Wassenaer to enquire about his reputation among learned men in the employ of the Elector Palatine.[48]

We can understand the delightful effect all this news had on Scheuchzer. His friends were organizing a campaign to secure him the prestigious chair at Leiden, and he responded with energetic letter-writing of his own. Scheuchzer wrote to Valkenier on January 25 and 29, February 9, 12, 16, 23, and 27; he also wrote for support to Cuper, Beaumont, Volder, Woodward, Sloane and the Royal Society. Scheuchzer hoped, too, that his colleague Theodor Zwinger III in Basel would provide a reference. Zwinger himself had been offered an appointment at Leiden nine years earlier, but had declined on account of his weak health—or perhaps, as the Curators and *Burgemeesters* of Leiden suspected, because he was only trying to obtain better conditions for himself at Basel.[49] Now he declined to write for Scheuchzer on the grounds that two of his patrons in Holland were dead, and the third was no longer active on his behalf; thus he did not think his recommendation would be of much use to Scheuchzer. None the less, he sent his best wishes for success.[50] Whether Zwinger was merely trying to avoid writing an awkward letter of reference, or had a more embarrassing personal interest in the chair, was then unclear to Scheuchzer.

In London there were more positive stirrings for Scheuchzer. On January 25 (o.s., February 5, n.s.), Dr John Woodward wrote to his friend and translator in Zurich:

There's a rumour here that Dr. Hotton is dead; and, if so, the Botanic Chair in Leyden is vacant. I should rejoice you were settled in it: and to have a man of your learning and worth so much nearer me. I have wrote [sic] to my friends in Holland by this post, and have prevailed with some other gentlemen of interest here to do the same to theirs. I do it with caution, because I'm not certain he is dead. I have wrote particularly to Mr. Valkenier: and question not but you will do the same. As I know no man in Europe so well qualified to fill that chair as yourself, so I have not been wanting in making that known to all I have wrote to.[51]

This was a surprisingly generous action by Woodward, who could be irascible at the best of times: in the same letter he continued his long-running campaign of denigration against Hans Sloane, 'a man of no learning or merit.' Woodward had also received a letter from Cuper with questions about his *Natural History of the Earth*: 'He is no great judge of those matters; but however, I treat him very civilly. Indeed I have the more reason to do so, because he treats me in like sort: and seems greatly pleased with the main of that work.'[52] On the same day Woodward prepared a Latin letter of recommendation suitable for Valkenier to send to the Curators: it described Scheuchzer as the leading botanist in the tradition of Ray, Plukenet, Tournefort, and Hotton, well suited for the professorship at Leiden, centre of the learned world.[53]

Valkenier wrote to Scheuchzer again on February 5. He had received Cuper's favourable recommendation to the Count of Wassenaer and was aware of Cuper's contact with Jan van den Bergh. Valkenier had spoken with deputies from Leiden who were attending a meeting of the States in The Hague, and he established that one Curator, President Rosenboom, favoured Scheuchzer. He knew that another Curator, Burgemeester van den Honert of Dordrecht, was coming to the States and expected to talk with him soon. Valkenier also reported the latest gossip on Boerhaave's attitude:

It was thought that Mr. Boerhaave would claim this post, for he is already a lecturer at the Academy, and he has promises for the first vacant [chair] in medicine; but since he is a great physician and no botanist whatsoever, people believe he will not seek it.[54]

Caspar Commelin, a well-known botanist of Amsterdam, was reportedly not interested in the Leiden job; thus at that moment Valkenier thought the only serious candidates were Scheuchzer and an unnamed doctor from Danzig [possibly Johann Philipp Breyne, a correspondent of Sloane and Scheuchzer]. Valkenier still believed the Curators would take several months to make the appointment, and he assured Scheuchzer that everything possible was being done for him. 'You already have patrons here, and I hope you will have even more.'[55] Meanwhile he would keep his eye on the journals for reviews of Scheuchzer's works: owing to the ice, he had no news from Le Clerc.

Ten days later Valkenier reported, 'Our affairs are still going well at Leiden.'[56] The number of candidates had increased, however. Boerhaave had made his interest known, and was the strongest, 'because he has many friends thanks to his large medical practice, even though he has done little in botany.' Dr Goris, Valkenier's former secretary at Frankfurt, had asked him not to support Scheuchzer, but he was easily put off. While Commelin might have carried the day at Leiden, his employers at Amsterdam had raised his salary and persuaded him not to apply. Valkenier knew then that van den Bergh was orchestrating the Boerhaave campaign; indeed in retrospect it appears that van den Bergh had been a friend and patron of Boerhaave since the early 1690s, even before Boerhaave had taken his medical degree.[57] Meanwhile Count Wassenaer-Obdam had made enquiries about Scheuchzer at Dusseldorf as Cuper suggested. He received a very positive report from Dr Johannes Conrad Brunner, candidate in the earlier Leiden professorial searches between 1694 and 1700. To add weight to the dossier, Valkenier sent to Leiden all his copies of Scheuchzer's works, an excerpt from Scheuchzer's last letter, and Woodward's recommendation. He had done as much for Scheuchzer as he could have done for himself. Yet to ensure his success, Valkenier also promised the Curators and *Burgemeesters* of Leiden that if Scheuchzer was appointed he (Valkenier) would endow them with a fine cabinet of fossils. This would please them greatly, Valkenier thought, for they knew he had a rich collection.

   The professorship at Leiden was not only prestigious, but also lucrative: in Valkenier's opinion, one of the best, as shown by Hotton's salary and benefits: 1,400 *livres* in pay, 300 *livres* for correspondence, 600 more from promotions and other student fees, and city tax exemptions on wine and beer—all told worth 1,000 French *écus*, and the house in the botanic garden.[58] This was a very high salary by European standards, although it should be noted that at Leiden the payment of salaries was sometimes deferred when the university was in financial straits: in the summer of 1709, for example, Bernard Albinus complained that his salary was five quarters in arrears.[59] Valkenier and Woodward recognized that such a plum would not fall from the tree without powerful shaking. They enlisted their friends and anyone else who might have influence. From London Woodward wrote he had spoken with 'Mr. Hop, son of the Great Treasurer of Holland [another colleague of van den Bergh in the administration of the Southern Netherlands]. He is of Leyden: and has wrote most pressingly in your favour: as has also the Dutch Envoy here, who is my very good friend.' With the usual geological metaphor, Woodward declared, 'I neither lost time, spared interest, or left any stone unturned, to promote the affair.' Indeed he had made Scheuchzer's cause known to English botanists and to the Royal Society, even soliciting the secretary, his enemy Hans Sloane, to write officially to Leiden. 'Upon the whole I am fully persuaded you will have the professorship, and most passionately wish it,' Woodward wrote.[60]

Alas, by the time that Woodward's second round of letters had crossed the icy North Sea, the Curators had met and offered the chair to Boerhaave. Valkenier apparently heard from Rosenboom and Wassenaer-Obdam about the deliberations on February 18.[61] 'A great debate' had taken place. Of all the candidates only Scheuchzer and Boerhaave were considered seriously, and Boerhaave had won because of his many friends at Leiden. They argued that by promoting Boerhaave to professor the University could save the 600 florins of his salary as lecturer; furthermore, they would not have to pay the moving expenses of a foreigner. (Pitcairne, who came from Edinburgh in 1692, had cost them 770 florins, and even Hotton's move from Amsterdam in 1695 had come to 250 florins.[62]) Besides, the Curators had promised Boerhaave the first vacant chair in medicine; if they did not promote him now, he would go elsewhere, taking along a good number of students, particularly the English, Scots, and Irish, who were almost all in his classes. The effects on the University and city of Leiden would be devastating. It was thought Boerhaave could teach botany adequately, and when one of the chairs in theoretical medicine became available, he could be transferred: these chairs paid even better—1,000 *écus* not counting college fees, promotions, etc. Then there would be a new opening for a botanist. Valkenier and his allies could not hide their dismay that local interests had prevailed, though there was some consolation that Scheuchzer's name was now much better known in Holland. Jacques Bernard's lukewarm comments of his treatises in *Nouvelles de la République des Lettres* for December 1708 had appeared at the booksellers just as the decision was made, but its effects were probably marginal. Jean Le Clerc's strongly favourable review in *Bibliothèque Choisie* would be taken more seriously.[63]

Further conversations with President Rosenboom gave Valkenier more insight and hope. Rosenboom was pleased that Scheuchzer would be willing to give his collections to the University if appointed to the chair. He emphasized that Boerhaave had been appointed only *provisionally* ('ce n'est que provisionellement') to the chair in botany. We may wonder whether Scheuchzer benefited from having the irascible Rosenboom as his fervent supporter. At the board meeting, Rosenboom protested vigorously when he saw that *Burgemeester* van den Honert of Dordrecht was taking the side of the Leiden officials. Considering Boerhaave's lack of teaching experience in botany, and the bad weather that season reducing university income, Rosenboom insisted that the Curators reserve the right to elect another professor of botany and pay Boerhaave only 400 florins more than his present salary of 600, thus a round 1,000 guilders to start. He thought Boerhaave was really waiting for the even more lucrative chairs held by Albinus, Dekkers, and Le Mort: so Scheuchzer would have another chance at the botanical professorship on the same terms as Hotton. There was reason to take heart. When the happy day came that Scheuchzer was appointed at Leiden, the Curators would never refuse him permission to lecture on his collections. On the contrary, they would *request* such lectures 'because this Academy is a University.'[64]

Scheuchzer's response to this news can be seen in the letters of consolation and advice he received. He was praised for his great modesty and stoic acceptance of fate. His friends encouraged him to keep working and aspiring to Leiden. Woodward had offered to give Leiden yet another collection of fossils to favour Scheuchzer's appointment: once again he wrote, 'I will leave no stone unturned to promote your esteem there.'[65] He also advised Scheuchzer to dedicate his next book to Cuper, and to inscribe one of the plates to the Archbishop of Canterbury—hoping that these gestures could be turned to service. Scheuchzer himself told friends there might be some difficulty about his leaving Zurich. This was a matter of concern, for other Swiss [e.g., Zwinger] had declined offers of Dutch professorships, placing their supporters in an embarrassing position. Yet, anticipating our age of litigation by unsuccessful candidates, Scheuchzer requested from Leiden an official note of the decision; he also wanted to know if, as rumour had it, Zwinger had been considered.[66] Valkenier doubted whether the registers of the Curators would mention Scheuchzer's name, 'because our style in these cases is very brief.' Rosenboom confirmed that the Curators kept no record of their discussions on personnel matters, expect in the case of ministers of religion; the resolutions simply reported the name of their choice to fill the vacant chair.[67] Consequently we can understand why Lindeboom found no mention of the debate in university archives. Zwinger's name had come up nine years earlier, but his supposed ill health and refusals had caused the Curators to look elsewhere. In 1709 his name was not even mentioned until the day after Boerhaave was chosen: then a French refugee brought Rosenboom a letter of recommendation for Zwinger from Paul Reboulet, a French refugee minister at Basel. Since the matter was settled, Rosenboom kept the letter and allowed Valkenier to read it. Rosenboom was all the more confident that Scheuchzer would eventually be appointed to Leiden with a double title, the freedom to write natural history of the Netherlands, and opportunities to take all the classes and field trips he wanted—as long as the university's finances did not suffer![68]

The reaction of the learned world in general to Boerhaave's promotion ranged from surprise to disappointment and outrage. At Leiden the medical faculty did not appear overjoyed with their new colleague. Boerhaave's inaugural lecture on March 20, 1709, differed markedly from those of his predecessors Hermann and Hotton: they had talked about botany, a subject he thought better to avoid. Instead he spoke about simplicity as the hallmark of true medicine: it was an elegant and well-received address, with praise for the great scientists and doctors, Louis XIV as patron of learning (and this in wartime!), the Curators and *Burgemeesters*, his teachers and students. But, as Lindeboom notes, 'he passed over the [medical] faculty in complete silence.'[69] Three weeks later President Rosenboom and Pieter Valkenier heard that Boerhaave was 'extremely embarrassed' by his new professorship and felt obliged to ask for help from botanists and apothecaries, including Frans Kiggelaar of Amsterdam, one of Scheuchzer's supporters. This may have been Boerhaave's way of flattering his opponents and making friends, but some had doubts whether he would live up to expectations.[70]

Learned correspondence was essential to the work of early modern scientists, particularly botanists, and Boerhaave duly joined the established international Republic of Letters. His friendships may be explored in the surviving documents of these vast networks. Unfortunately for us, it was Boerhaave's custom to destroy his incoming letters after he had answered them.[71] Thus we are all the more dependent on his friends who saved incoming letters, and sometimes drafts of outgoing letters as well.

Scheuchzer himself sent Boerhaave a polite Latin letter of con-

The University Botanic Garden at Leyden. Illustration in Van der Aa, Les Délices de Leyde, *1712. The residence of the Professor Botanices is seen in the right upper corner.*

gratulation, eliciting a warm response. They began a botanical correspondence.[72] By the time Valkenier visited Boerhaave at the garden in Leiden in September 1711, this friendship was well established. Exchanges of books and specimens between Boerhaave and Scheuchzer continued into the 1720s.[73] Boerhaave's first letters to Hans Sloane and William Sherard also date from 1709. Both of these letters are flattering, to put it mildly.[74] Boerhaave explained that the Curators had desired him to take over Hotton's post, and as head of the botanic garden he wished to exchange seeds and plants. He gave thanks for the contributions Sloane and Sherard had made in the past, and hoped they would continue to enrich Dutch science.

Sloane and Boerhaave sent each other brief notes accompanying gifts and letters of introduction as their friends travelled back and forth between Leiden and London: one of these notes, in 1736, introduced Linnaeus to Sloane.[75] Sherard, another prominent botanist, was farther away from Leiden in 1709. He was serving as consul for the English Turkey Company at Smyrna. Sherard had visited Leiden and stayed with Hermann at the professor's house in the botanic garden; later he edited Hermann's manuscripts for publication. He had been corresponding with Sloane, Cuper, and Scheuchzer for some years, but he had not heard of the deaths of his friends Plukenet, Tournefort, and Hotton until April, when he received two letters from Scheuchzer. Sherard's reaction to the appointment of Boerhaave was far from favourable: he told Scheuchzer he was

angry that the Curators of Leiden have so little regard for merit, and for the honour of their Academy. I know Mr. Boerhaave, but I would never have believed that he would claim that professorship, or that if he had, they would have chosen him. If it is only until he is transferred to another one, I hope that he will be promoted quickly, and that the wounds to botany will be healed by your succession.[76]

Sherard had a low opinion of most European botanists, who were constantly seeking after novelty and ignoring the discoveries already made. 'One can say about them, that like the Spaniards, they ruin themselves by their great discoveries, and that botany in their hands is like ancient Rome—*ipsa viribus suis ruit* [it collapses by its own strength].' He hoped that Johann Jakob Scheuchzer and his brother Johann would 'save botany from the barbarism that threatens it.'[77] Boerhaave could not have known of Sherard's outburst when he wrote to the consul for the first time a month later. Nor would Sherard have been likely to foresee the growth of a warm friendship between them. Over nearly twenty years the healing qualities of letters were augmented by exchanges of books and specimens, the discovery of common interests and common friends in the Republic of Letters, and personal visits.[78]

And what of Scheuchzer? Unsuccessful in his quest for Leiden in 1709, he continued to apply for other posts. In 1710 he heard rumours that the Leiden Curators wanted to hire Bernoulli from Basel.[79] In 1711 Valkenier told Scheuchzer of a possible opening at the academy of Duisburg, under the jurisdiction of the king of Prussia.[80] The following year there were prospects at Utrecht. Nothing came of any of these projects, but in 1712 Leibniz did help Scheuchzer get a serious offer of a job as physician to Tsar Peter the Great. The salary of 800 roubles (400 gold ducats) was attractive, and Scheuchzer would work together with Erskine and Bruce, two Scottish doctors. Leibniz was always keen to develop contacts with Russia and the East: he thought that Scheuchzer could perform valuable services to the Republic of Letters by finding out about nature and art in '*terra virgine*, not yet cultivated by the learned. Besides, you could make discoveries through contacts with the Tartars, Uzbeks, Persians, Mongols, and even Cathay or China.'[81] Given the choice between Russia and Zurich, however, Scheuchzer hesitated. Russia was at war, and following the Tsar would mean an itinerant life, far from family. Coincidentally, the Swiss cantons were quarrelling again: Scheuchzer found himself called into service as a military doctor in the ensuing Toggenburg War. He had already been appointed professor of mathematics at the Carolinum in 1710, and on balance he decided to stay in Zurich. He became better known as a scientist than as a physician. According to Brendan Dooley, when Scheuchzer was considered for a professorship in medicine at Padua in 1714, the *Riformatori* asked whether he 'had ever had any interest in healing at all.'[82] Later, he declined a professorship of mathematics at Padua in 1720, and he died as a respected citizen at Zurich in 1733.

We may conclude that the process of professorial appointments in eighteenth-century Leiden was not at all gentlemanly. With well-organized lobbying, the gathering of letters of reference, self-promotion in journals, patronage and political influence, the procedures resemble our own. The complexities of this case suggest that further investigation into appointments at other early modern universities may be quite rewarding. At Padua candidates sometimes were hired for one chair as a stepping-stone to another, or because they had technical skills useful to the Venetian Republic.[83] The teachers at Padua in the later eighteenth century were generally mediocre, although the university still enjoyed a reputation for paying high salaries by Italian standards. New chairs were created, and teachers of great merit received extra stipends.[84] At Montpellier, selection procedures were supposedly more open, as candidates for chairs presented sample lectures to members of the faculty and municipal officials. Yet the unruly Montpellier students were highly critical of their professors, some of whom taught poorly or not at all.[85] At Basel, the faculty and town councillors divided into three groups; each group voted for one of the candidates who had been declared eligible. The candidate with the most votes was appointed, and in case of tie selection was by lot. Whether this system resulted in the best appointments may be questioned: the Basel professoriate was marked by quasi-hereditary dynasties, and even the native Leonhard Euler, arguably the most distinguished mathematician of the century, was never appointed there.[86] Hiring processes in the newer medical faculties may also have differed from those in older ones, with more opportunity for local patronage and influence at recent foundations such as Edinburgh and Leiden. Municipal councillors and candidates were well aware of market forces: professorial salaries were supplemented by class fees that provided an incentive to attract students, very much in the city's interests.[87]

The objections to Boerhaave's appointment raised by botanists in 1709 may well represent increasing tendencies toward specialization and the evolution of independent disciplines. As we have seen, the choice of Boerhaave was a triumph for local patronage and local interests, however much it may have been justified afterwards by his teaching and scientific accomplishments. Boerhaave, the *honnête homme*, can also be seen as a figure of generalized encyclopedic learning who contained within himself all medical knowledge worth knowing. By 1719 this workaholic had a near-stranglehold on the medical faculty, occupying 60 per cent of the chairs. Instead of appointing additional professors, the Curators and *Burgemeesters* saved money by allowing Boerhaave to accumulate the titles, paying him more, but in total less than separate professors would have earned. When this particular sun was shining, there was not much room for other luminaries. The crucial role of Boerhaave in Leiden was shown in 1722, when he fell ill and was bedridden for 5 months; on his recovery in January 1723, the citizens and students celebrated with public fireworks. The cultural historian Busken Huet saw an economic motive for these festivities; the biographer Lindeboom thought them 'the spontaneous expression of cordiality and joy.'[88] Well-beloved Boerhaave may have been, but when advancing age and infirmity led him to resign two of his chairs, he seems to have had more regard for chemistry than for botany or medicine. In terms of Boerhaave's legacy, it is surely paradoxical that the medical faculty at Leiden fell to second rank just when other schools that adopted its methods flourished. Willem Frijhoff has suggested that any positive 'Boerhaave effect' in attracting students was temporary at best in an age of decline: as new medical schools were founded and expanded elsewhere in Europe, there was less reason for students to flock to Leiden.[89]

Finally, when an important professorship was at stake, the international scholarly fraternity, the Republic of Letters, could mobilize quickly, even before the body was cold and buried. A change of government such as the Glorious Revolution of 1688 or the death of William III in 1702 might also call for dramatic measures by curators and candidates—campaigns to get and keep lucrative posts. There were close links between knowledge and power in the early modern period, and historians of universities are in an excellent position to explore them.

Department of History
The University of Alabama
Tuscaloosa, Alabama 35487-0212
USA.

REFERENCES

*I wish to thank the National Endowment for the Humanities, the Bankhead Fund, and the Research Grants Committee of the University of Alabama. I am grateful for comments from the Toronto Colloquium on the History and Philosophy of Science and Technology, and the Dutch History Seminar of London. Particular thanks go to Koen Swart, William Schupbach, Naomi Rogers and Lesley Cormack.

1. Much work on Herman Boerhaave has been done by G. A. Lindeboom. His biography, *Herman Boerhaave: The Man and His Work* (London, 1968) [cited here as *Life*] and a brief summary in the *Dictionary of Scientific Biography* 2:224–228, are essential starting points. Lindeboom edited three volumes of *Boerhaave's Correspondence* (Leiden, 1962–1979); other letters remain unpublished. See also *Boerhaave and His Time*, papers read at the International Symposium in Leiden, 1968 (Leiden, 1970); Lindeboom's *Boerhaave and Great Britain* (Leiden, 1974); and *The Age of Boerhaave* (Leiden, 1983) by H. Bots, P. Hoftijzer, C. W. Schoneveld, C. Willemijn Fock, and A. M. Luyendijk-Elshout. Recently Harm Beukers has cast doubt on the

seriousness of Boerhaave's commitment to clinical teaching: 'Clinical Teaching at Leiden from Its Beginning until the End of the Eighteenth Century,' *Clio Medica*, 21 (1987–88), 139–52.

2. A. G. Morton, *History of Botanical Science* (London, 1981), 237.

3. Ibid., 277, n. 12.

4. Lindeboom, *Life*, 86.

5. *Life*, 315.

6. Brendan Dooley, 'Science Teaching as a Career at Padua: the case of Giovanni Poleni,' *History of Universities*, 4 (1984), 121.

7. '... I am to teach medieval history, of which, as you are well aware, I am utterly and grossly ignorant ... I gave the college fair warning of my ignorance, and the answer was that I knew just as much as anyone else in America knew on the subject and I could teach better than anyone that could be had.' Henry Adams to Charles Milnes Gaskell, quoted by Ernest Samuels, *The Young Henry Adams* (Cambridge, Mass., 1948), 204.

8. Adam Sedgwick, *Life and Letters*, eds. J. W. Clark and T. M. Hughes (2 vols.; Cambridge, 1890), 1:52, cited by Gertrude Himmelfarb, *Darwin and the Darwinian Revolution* (New York, 1959; 1967), 41.

9. *Boerhaave Corr.*, 2:408; *Life*, 80, quoting from *Bronnen tot de geschiedenis der Leidsche universiteit*, P. C. Molhuysen, ed., 10 Feb. 1725–8 Feb. 1765, Rijks Geschiedkundige Publicatiën 48 (The Hague, 1921), 5:69–70. Actually Scheuchzer was 57, four years younger than Boerhaave.

10. *Life*, 80.

11. See the works of Paul Dibon; C. Louise Thijssen-Schoute, *Nederlands Cartesianisme* (Amsterdam, 1954); F. L. R. Sassen, 'The Intellectual Climate in Leiden in Boerhaave's Time,' *Boerhaave and His Time*, 1–16; Maarten Ultee, 'The Place of the Dutch Republic in the Republic of Letters of the Late Seventeenth Century,' *Dutch Crossing* 31 (1987), 54–78.

12. On Leiden University, see the volumes of *Bronnen* in Rijks Geschiedkundige Publicatiën; also J. J. Woltjer, *De Leidse universiteit in verleden en heden* (Leiden, 1965); *Leiden University in the Seventeenth Century: An Exchange of Learning*, ed. Th. H. Lunsingh Scheurleer and G. H. M. Posthumus Meyjes (Leiden, 1975). L. van Poelgeest is preparing a dissertation on the university during the ancien régime.

13. The autonomy of the Leiden curators is discussed by E. M. Meyers, 'De Leidsche Universiteit als zelfstandig lichaam,' in *Pallas Leidensis MCMXXV*, A. R. Zimmerman *et al.* (Leiden, 1925), 39–65; J. J. Woltjer, 'De positie van de Curatoren der Leidse Universiteit in de zestiende eeuw,' *Tijdschrift voor Rechtsgeschiedenis* 38 (1970), 445–96; and J. van den Berg, 'Willem Bentinck (1704–1774) en de theologische faculteit te Leiden,' in *Bestuurders en Geleerden*, S. Groenveld *et al.* (Amsterdam, 1985), 169–77. On the appointment of foreign professors, see D. Nauta, 'Het Benoemingsbeleid met betrekking tot de Hoogleraren in de theologie in de Nederlanden tot ongeveer 1700,' *Nederlands*

Archief voor Kerkgeschiedenis 63 (1983), 42–68. More detailed study of the Leiden professors has been proposed by D. J. Roorda and A. J. Looyenga, 'Het Prosopografische onderzoek naar de Leidse hoogleraren 1575–1815,' *Bulletin Werkgroep Elites* 5 (1983), 30–2.

14. Sassen, 2.
15. See the exhibition catalogue by W. Otterspeer and L. van Poelgeest, *Willem III en de Leidse universiteit* (Leiden, 1988).
16. Simon Groenveld, 'The Mecca of Authors? States, Assemblies and Censorship in the 17th Century Dutch Republic,' *Too Mighty to be Free: Censorship and the Press in Britain and the Netherlands*, Britain and the Netherlands, vol. 9 (Zutphen, 1987), 63–86. Occasionally the regents did try to ban offensive pamphlets: see Craig E. Harline, *Pamphlets, Printing, and Political Culture in the Early Dutch Republic*, Archives Internationales d'Histoire des Idées 116 (Dordrecht, 1987), esp. ch. IV, '*Libelli Non Grati:* Pamphlets and the Political Culture of Control,' 111–33.
17. On the strength of particularism, see J. L. Price, 'The Dutch Republic and its Internal Tensions,' *Culture and Society in the Dutch Republic during the 17th Century* (New York, 1974), 16–40.
18. W. T. M. Frijhoff, *La Société Néerlandaise et ses Gradués. 1575–1814* (Amsterdam/Maarssen, 1981), 280, citing figures for 1811. Cf. Thomas Hoyt Broman, 'The Transformation of Academic Medicine in Germany, 1780–1820,' Princeton University Ph.D. Dissertation, 1987 [U.M.I. order no. 87-16883], 17.
19. J. W. van Spronsen, 'The Beginning of Chemistry,' in *Leiden University in the Seventeenth Century*, 337.
20. G. A. Lindeboom, 'Pitcairne's Leyden Interlude Described from the Documents,' *Annals of Science* 19:4 (1963), 273–84. Anita Guerrini, 'Archibald Pitcairne and Newtonian Medicine,' *Medical History* 31 (1987), 70–83.
21. G. A. Lindeboom, 'Govert Bidloo,' *Dutch Medical Biography* (Amsterdam, 1984), 135–9.
22. Sassen, 10–11; J. Dankmeijer, 'Is Boerhaave's Fame Deserved?' *Boerhaave and His Time*, 23–4; *Life*, 29–33.
23. Res. Curatoren, 8 May 1697, *Bronnen*, 18 Feb. 1682–8 Feb. 1725, Rijks Geschiedkundige Publicatiën, 45 (The Hague, 1920), 4:157. Otterspeer and Poelgeest, 15–16.
24. Res. Curatoren, 18 May 1697, *Bronnen*, 4:158.
25. Board's complaints, Res. Curatoren, 1 Feb. 1698, *Bronnen*, 4:161.
26. William's approval of Brunner, Res. Curatoren, 8 July 1698, *Bronnen*, 4:167; search for other foreign profs. med., 3 June 1699, ibid., 4:175; contacts with Zwinger, 9 May–20 Sept. 1700, ibid., 4:182–4. Otterspeer and Poelgeest, 16. Van Spronsen, 339–40; *Life*, 50, 60, 109.
27. Sassen, 5. This oration has been translated and published by E. Kegel-Brinkgreve and A. M. Luyendijk-Elshout, *Boerhaave's Orations* (Leiden, 1983).

28. *Life*, 34–7.
29. *Life*, 38–43.
30. The principal sources for Johann Jacob Scheuchzer are his manuscripts, kept at the Zentralbibliothek, Zürich. For a guide, see Rudolf Steiger, 'Verzeichnis des wissenschaftlichen Nachlasses von Johann Jakob Scheuchzer (1672–1733),' *Vierteljahrsschrift der Naturforschenden Gesellschaft in Zürich* 78 (1933), 1–75. Note also Steiger's dissertation, *Johann Jakob Scheuchzer (1672–1733) I. Werdezeit (bis 1699)*, Schweizer Studien zur Geschichtswissenschaft, Band 15 (1927), 1–152; no other vols. published. The article by P. E. Pilet in *Dictionary of Scientific Biography*, 12:159, contains inaccuracies.
31. Steiger, *Werdezeit*, 31.
32. Scheuchzer's letters to Sloane are at the British Library; those to Sherard at the Royal Society, London. Their letters and those of Woodward to Scheuchzer are at the Zentralbibliothek, Zürich [ZBZ].
33. Valkenier to Scheuchzer, 23 Dec. 1710, ZBZ, MS H 306, s. 221.
34. *Life*, 62–3.
35. Spanheim at Leiden, *Bronnen*, 4:36. Leydecker at Utrecht, *Acta et Decreta Senatus Vroedschapsresolutien en andere bescheiden betreffende de Utrechtse academie*, G. W. Kernkamp (ed.) (3 vols.; Utrecht, 1936–40), 2:108.
36. Valkenier to Scheuchzer, 20 July 1708, ZBZ, MS H 306, s. 128.
37. Cuper's manuscripts are at the Algemeen Rijksarchief [ARA] and Koninklijke Bibliotheek [KB], The Hague. See Ultee, 'Place of the Dutch Republic.'
38. On Cuper's recommendation, Johannes Heyman, *predikant* at Smyrna, was appointed professor of oriental languages at Leiden. The curators' correspondence with Heyman appears in the published *Bijlagen* for 1707–1709, *Bronnen*, 4:*109–*121. See also Cuper's correspondence with Heyman and van den Bergh at KB and ARA.
39. Valkenier to Scheuchzer, 18 Jan. 1709, ZBZ, MS H 306, s. 97.
40. 'Wassenaer,' *Nieuw Nederlandsch Biographisch Woordenboek* [*NNBW*], 2:1524–5.
41. J. E. Elias, *De Vroedschap van Amsterdam 1578–1795* (Haarlem, 1903), I:365.
42. 'Because of his manipulations and sharp tongue, Rosenboom had the knack of quickly making himself hated in every company in which he appeared.' Otterspeer and Poelgeest, *Willem III*, 15.
43. Molhuysen, editor of the *Bronnen*, noted the dispute began soon after Rosenboom's appointment in 1694, p. 119, n.1, but found it mysterious. He published some related documents, including the letter from William III, 10 Dec. 1698, Bijlagen, *67–*68; Res. Curatoren, 15 Dec. 1698, *Bronnen*, 4:168–9.
44. 'Honert,' *NNBW*, 8:816.
45. 'van den Bergh,' *NNBW*, 4:116–7.

46. Wolters, 'De positie van Curatoren;' Nauta, 'Het Benoemingsbeleid;' Lindeboom, *Life*, 64.
47. Valkenier to Scheuchzer, 18 Jan. 1709, ZBZ, MS H 306, s. 97.
48. Cuper to van den Bergh, 19 Jan. 1709; Cuper to Wassenaer, 19 Jan. 1709, ARA, Legatie Archieven, Zuidelijke Nederlanden, 3632 (provisional classification).
49. See Molhuysen's note to Res. Curatoren, 20 Sept. 1700, *Bronnen*, 4:184.
50. Zwinger to Scheuchzer, 21 Feb. 1709, ZBZ, MS H 319, no. 219, pub. by Marie-Louise Portmann, *Die Korrespondenz von Th. Zwinger III mit J. J. Scheuchzer 1700–1724* (Basel, 1964), no. 180, pp. 138–9, 260–1.
51. Woodward to Scheuchzer, 25 Jan. 1708 [o.s. = 5 Feb. 1709 n.s.], ZBZ, MS H 294, s. 179.
52. Ibid.
53. Copy in ZBZ, MS H 294, s. 183.
54. Valkenier to Scheuchzer, 5 Feb. 1709, ZBZ, MS H 306, s. 101.
55. Ibid.
56. Valkenier to Scheuchzer, 15 Feb. 1709, ZBZ, MS H 306, s. 94.
57. Lindeboom stated that van den Bergh helped Boerhaave get a job in the university library in the early 1690s; later Boerhaave told another curator 'that he was especially indebted to Mr. van den Bergh, who had brought him to the University.' *Life*, 50, citing *Bronnen*, 5:63.
58. Hotton's salary of f 1000 ordinary and f 400 extraordinary was set by Res. Curatoren, 28 Feb. 1695, *Bronnen*, 4:131. This was three times as much as the salary of most French medical professors, who seldom received more than 1,000 *livres* in basic pay: R. Chartier, M. M. Compère, and D. Julia, *L'Éducation en France du XVIe au XVIIIe siècle* (Paris, 1976), p. 260. In 1725 it was thought a student at Leiden would need 500 guilders per year for his food and lodging. *Life*, 57.
59. *Bronnen*, 4:244; *Life*, 57.
60. Woodward to Scheuchzer, 8 Feb. 1708 (o.s.), ZBZ, MS H 294, s. 185. Scheuchzer had written to Sloane that Cuper and Valkenier were proposing him as Hotton's successor, British Library, Add. MS 4041, f. 290, but Sloane seemed less than enthusiastic. Later he told Scheuchzer, 'I did what I could for you with the people of interest in Holland that were of my acquaintance for your succession to Dr. Hotton and am very sorry it did not succeed.' 15 March 1708 (o.s.), ZBZ, MS H 296, s. 48.
61. Valkenier to Scheuchzer, 22 Feb. 1709, ZBZ, MS H 306, s. 103.
62. Lindeboom, 'Pitcairne's Leyden Interlude,' 278. Hotton, Res. Curatoren, 8 Nov. 1695, *Bronnen*, 4:134.
63. [Jean Le Clerc], *Bibliothèque Choisie 17* (1709): 185–210, art. IV. Valkenier and Cuper may have orchestrated this review. Le Clerc mentioned Valkenier's cabinet of curiosities on p. 187; and on p. 192 he wrote, 'C'est encore à l'illustre Mr. Cuper à qui j'en suis redevable.' Cuper had corresponded with Le Clerc since 1689, and occasionally supplied material for his journals. Le Clerc's review ends with a plea for

the establishment of public museums of natural history: 'des Magasins Publics, où l'on pût voir toutes les productions de la Nature rangées en bon ordre,' p. 209.

64. Valkenier to Scheuchzer, 8 March 1709, ZBZ, MS H 306, s. 119.
65. Woodward to Scheuchzer, 20 May 1709, ZBZ, MS H 294, s. 199.
66. Valkenier to Scheuchzer, 15 and 26 March, 12 April 1709, ZBZ, MS H 306, ss. 105, 107, 111.
67. Valkenier to Scheuchzer, 12 April 1709, s. 112.
68. Valkenier to Scheuchzer, 12 April 1709, s. 113.
69. *Life*, 81–5. This 'Oration on the simplicity of purified medicine' appears in E. Kegel-Brinkgreve and A. M. Luyendijk-Elshout, *Boerhaave's Orations*. They consider whether Boerhaave's flattery of Louis XIV may have been inspired by a desire to become a member of the French Academy of Sciences, 'but it does not seem quite in keeping with Boerhaave's character as we know it,' p. 328, n. 79.
70. Valkenier to Scheuchzer, 12 April 1709, s. 111.
71. Lindeboom, *Corr.*, 1:4.
72. Scheuchzer to Boerhaave, 2 March 1709, ZBZ, MS H 150b, s. 257 (draft). Boerhaave to Scheuchzer, 24 March 1709, ZBZ, MS H 305, s. 449. Other letters pub. by Luigi Belloni, 'Aus dem Briefwechsel zwischen Herman Boerhaave und Johann Jakob Scheuchzer,' in *Circa Tillam, Studia Historia Medicinae Gerrit Arie Lindeboom septuagenario oblata* (Leiden, 1974), 83–106.
73. Valkenier to Scheuchzer, 8 Sept. 1711, ZBZ, MS H 306, s. 237; Boerhaave to Scheuchzer, 12 Dec. 1720, Gemeentearchief, Leiden, pub. by Lindeboom, *Corr.*, no. 154, 2:24–6.
74. Boerhaave to Sloane, 26 Aug. 1709, British Library, Add. MS 4042, f. 43, pub. *Corr.*, no. 94, 1:164–5; Boerhaave to Sherard, 24 Sept. 1709, Royal Society, pub. *Corr.*, no. 19, 1:44–5.
75. Sloane did send Boerhaave more substantial comments on his published case-history, *Atrocis, nec descripti prius, morbi Historia* (Leiden, 1724), letter of 17 Nov. 1724, Gemeentearchief, Leiden, pub. *Corr.*, no. 110, 1:180–7.
76. Sherard to Scheuchzer, 12 July and 27 August 1709, ZBZ, MS H 294, s. 39.
77. Ibid., s. 40.
78. Boerhaave to Scheuchzer, Royal Society, pub. *Corr.*, 1:38–162.
79. Valkenier to Scheuchzer, 23 Dec. 1710, ZBZ, MS H 306, s. 221.
80. Valkenier to Scheuchzer, 2 Oct 1711, ZBZ, MS H 306, s. 239.
81. Leibniz to Scheuchzer, 7 Dec. 1712, ZBZ, MS H 309, s. 31.
82. Dooley, 'Science Teaching,' 121, citing Archivio di Stato, Venice, *Riformatori dello Studio di Padova*, filza 81, 5 Jan. 1714.
83. Dooley cites Morgagni's near-acceptance of a chair in philosophy before receiving one in anatomy, and Jacob Hermann's recommendation of Nicolas Bernoulli for his skill in hydraulic architecture, 121–2.
84. Maria Cecilia Ghetti, 'Struttura e Organnizazione dell'Università di

Padova dalla metà del '700 al 1797,' *Quaderni per la historia dell'Università di Padova* 16 (1983): 71–102, esp. 78–82.

85. Colin Jones, 'Montpellier Medical Students and the Medicalisation of 18th century France,' in Roy Porter and Andrew Wear (eds.), *Problems and Methods in the History of Medicine* (London, 1987), 57–80, esp. 67–9.

86. Albrecht Burckhardt, 'Ueber die Wahlart der Baseler Professoren, besonder im 18. Jahrhundert,' *Basler Zeitschrift für Geschichte und Altertumskunde*, 15:1 (1916), 28–46; *Geschichte der Medizinischen Fakultät zu Basel 1460–1900* (Basel, 1917), 195–238.

87. See Anand C. Chitnis, *The Scottish Enlightenment: a Social History* (Totowa, N.J., 1976), 151–2; J. B. Morrell, 'The University of Edinburgh in the late Eighteenth Century: Its Scientific Eminence and Academic Structure,' *Isis* 62 (1971), 165. My thanks to Talisman Ford for this reference.

88. *Life*, 128. The devotion of foreign students to Boerhaave is illustrated by Albrecht von Haller and Johannes Geßner, two Swiss pupils who thought his renown fully justified. See their published diaries: *Haller in Holland: Het Dagboek van Albrecht von Haller van zijn verblijf in Holland (1725–1727)*, G. A. Lindeboom, ed. (Delft, 1958), 37+. *Johannes Geßner's Pariser Tagebuch 1727*, Urs Boschung, ed. (Bern, 1985), 62–3, citing Geßner's letter to Scheuchzer, 31 July 1727, ZBZ, MS H 337, ss. 325–8: Boerhaave was 'wahrlich ein Mann nach Verulamischer Norm!'

89. Frijhoff, *La Société Néerlandaise*. Douglas Guthrie, 'The Influence of the Leyden School upon Scottish Medicine,' *Medical History* 3 (1959) 108–22. A. M. Luyendijk-Elshout, 'De medische faculteit van Edinburgh in de 18e eeuw,' *Spiegel Historiael* 12:2 (1977): 105–9. Guenter B. Risse, 'Clinical Instruction in Hospitals: the Boerhaavian Tradition in Leyden, Edinburgh, Vienna and Pavia,' *Clio Medica* 21 (1987–88): 1–20. In the 'Boerhaave period' (1701–1738), 122 Irish medical students went to Leiden. Later the number fell, and the length of the typical Irish student's stay also decreased. Before the 1760s, he stayed two years or more and 'was in effect a genuine Leyden student. After that date the student pursued his studies elsewhere, and often went to Leyden only for the time necessary to enable him to perform the acts required for the degree.' E. Ashworth Underwood, 'The First and Final Phases of the Irish Medical students at the University of Leyden,' in E. O'Brien (ed.), *Essays in Honour of J. D. H. Widdess* (Dublin, 1978), 16–17. The Trinity College School of Medicine opened in 1711. T. P. C. Kirkpatrick, *History of Medical Teaching in Trinity College Dublin and of the School of Physic in Ireland* (Dublin, 1912), 76–78.

Noetics, Tractarians, and the Reform of the University of Oxford in the Nineteenth Century*

H. C. G. Matthew

The University of Oxford in the first half of the nineteenth century faced *in micro* the challenge which the British governing class faced *in macro*: was it possible both to preserve Anglican hegemony and to remain 'National'? That hegemony was profoundly entrenched by law and by custom both in the national parliament and in the senior university, though, significantly as we shall find, at the national level annual Acts of Parliament gave a degree of civic accommodation to those who did not attend the established church.

Oxford University made no such concession. All its members had this in common, that they had subscribed to the Thirty-nine Articles at the moment of matriculation, and had taken at the same time an oath upon the Act of Supremacy. As Edward Hawkins, later to be Provost of Oriel, put it in 1822: 'the benefits of academical education are restricted to professed members of the Church of England, by the intentions of our Founders, and the laws of the land.'[1] All resident members of the University were thus self-proclaimed members of the Church of England,[2] as were non-resident members — who continued, as we shall see, to hold very considerable power through their permanent right to vote in Convocation, the University's 'Parliament'. Moreover, the University acted as a seminary, in the sense that more of its graduates went on to be clergymen of the Church of England (and without much further training) than to any other profession. Any change in the status of the University thus involved complex consequences for Church and State, and called into question the identity and character of each. The effect of this questioning, this need to define and justify, was to have explosive consequences for all involved. Hawkins implicitly stated both the strength and the difficulty of the University: 'It is a National

Institution, I admit, but having a direct reference, never hitherto forgotten, to the National Church';[3] but if the position of the 'National Church' changed *vis-à-vis* the political nation, where did that leave the University?

Undergraduates at Oxford were not only required to be members of the Church of England; they were, since the new Examination Statute of 1800, required to be taught as such. Whatever else they studied, they were to study religion persistently: by the statute, 'at every examination, on every occasion, the Elements of Religion, and the Doctrinal Articles ... must form a part'.[4] Even a man like Hawkins, in the Oxonian context a moderate reformer, defended the requirement that undergraduates must attend Holy Communion and communicate. To those who objected, pleading unwillingness or unworthiness, he answered that the usual reply 'must in every College, I apprehend, how long soever it may be deferred, or in whatsoever terms it may be conveyed, be the *necessary* reply to them, "If you are not in a fit state to receive the Sacrament, you are not fit to be a member of this Society" '.[5]

The condition of entry to the University was thus the acceptance of what F. D. Maurice called 'conditions of thought',[6] rather than proof of ability. The reform of 1800—'modernizing'[7] though the introduction of a defined syllabus and a system of examination by classes was in effect, however conservative the objectives of its promulgators—thus also reinforced the religious and establishmentarian emphasis of the University. The view put about by the Tractarians in the 1830s, that the Oxford of their youth had been bereft of religion, was a travesty. Indeed the opposite might well be argued, that the requirement of thorough and persistent examination in religion could hardly in a university not arouse intellectual inquiry both into what was being taught—the activity which the Tractarians especially deplored—and into the institution which required that it should be taught. Quite apart from the general political pressures which were encouraging scrutiny of the relationship of the University to the nation, Oxford had, by her actions in 1800, written in her own catalyst of change.

In the context of the repeal of the Test Acts in 1828, of Roman Catholic Emancipation in 1829, and of the general movement of reform signified by the Representation of the People Act of 1832, the affairs of exclusively Anglican universities could not be expected to avoid scrutiny. Reform in Oxford, while it had its own character and pace, was also therefore a particular example of a general case.[8] It was also a sharp and distinctive example. Though the old constitution had preserved the rhetoric of an hegemonic establishment, a rhetoric which had experienced considerable revival in the early years of the century, its theoretical disabilities were in some measure alleviated, particularly in the case of non-establishment protestants, by a series of toleration, relief, and indemnity acts.[9] But this was not so with respect to entry to Oxford University. There subscription meant what it said, and the remnants of the establishmentarian constitution defined the character of the university in a way that, even before the reforms of 1828–1832, they had in considerable measure largely ceased to do in wider English civil society. In Oxford, the rhetoric of the Anglican confessional constitution fused precisely with the reality. Oxford University thus represented (in a form starker than Cambridge)[10] what was coming to be seen as an anomaly—a confessional university in an increasingly non-confessional state. The powerful reaction to the secularizing tendencies of the French Revolution had produced in Oxford a greater emphasis on Anglican confessionalism, indeed a revival of it, in contrast to Germany where equally conservative forces had secularized in order to survive.[11]

In Oxford, the reforms of 1828–1832 produced four general categories of reaction and allegiance. Briefly and simply put, these were: 1. resistance to change, on traditionalist lines (most High Churchmen and most Evangelicals); 2. the putting forward of a general case to counter 'liberalism', this case including and triggered by the special case of Oxford University (the Tractarians); 3. prudential liberal-conservatism, with limited change from within the University, without admitting the principle (Noetics such as Hawkins and, *pace* the Tractarians, Hampden); 4. assertive reformism, encouraged from within but probably eventually to be imposed from without (the Broad Church liberals of the 1840s and 1850s).

It is the purpose of this article to examine attitudes to change through the two groups most notoriously involved in the debates about it, the Noetics and the Tractarians, and to suggest that for each category the experience forced changes in position which are, at least at first glance, paradoxical.

As with any intellectual party, group or movement (the term Tractarians preferred), both the Noetics and Tractarians pose considerable difficulties of prosopographical definition. 'Noetics' was the name given to the group based in Oriel College in the 1820s, which has been described in three brilliant books, Duncan Forbes' *The Liberal Anglican Idea of History* (1950), Richard Brent's *Liberal Anglican Politics. Whiggery, Religion and Reform 1830–1841* (1987), and Pietro Corsi's *Science and Religion. Baden Powell and the Anglican Debate, 1800–1860* (1988). The term derives from the Greek 'noesis' ('characterized by, or consisting in, mental or intellectual activity'). Copleston, Whately, Thomas Arnold, Hawkins, and Hampden were their best-known names. They were the intellectual leaders of reform in Oxford University in the 1820s, but they attempted no expression of common identity through association with a particular publication, and their view of religious comprehension, which we will examine later, logically precluded acting as a party. Yet, with the advantage of retrospect, a degree of commonality can be seen, and the Noetics or Liberal Anglicans should not be too disaggregated.[12]

The better-known 'Tractarians' (as they came to be called), on the other hand, should not be presented as more coherent in objective than they were. They had an institutional cohesion to the extent that they contributed anonymously (but fairly publicly in that knowledge of authorship was not closely guarded) to a series of publications, *Tracts for the Times*, which was from the first intended to be controversial and combative. But recent scholarship has tended to emphasize the differences between the leading protagonists—Keble, Newman, Pusey—and to show that on questions as fundamental as the reformation, the early fathers and consequently the nature of authority in the Church, their positions were markedly different.[13] Moreover, since J. H. Newman left the University and the Church of England (in that order), the history of the 'Movement' is in part a history of disintegration. As Newman wrote of it: 'And so it proceeded, getting stronger and stronger every year, till it came into collision with the Nation, and that Church of the Nation, which it began by professing especially to serve'.[14] It was questions of the definition of the University which shaped the character of this 'collision'. At the time, and especially in the years 1833–1836, Tractarians and High Churchmen seemed to act together in reaction to the Whig government, with John Keble an exemplar of both traditions. This unity was, however, misleading and, as Peter Nockles' thesis has shown, there were significant differences between the two approaches. The High Churchmen characterized traditional

Oxford Toryism. Though in the person of William Palmer of Worcester College they produced two of the finest scholarly works of the period, *Origines Liturgicae* (2 vols. 1832) and *A Treatise on the Church of Christ* (2 vols. 1838), they found it increasingly difficult to do more than enunciate a sense of betrayal: betrayal by the Tractarians for Romanizing, by the Tory Party for liberalizing, by the Chancellor of the University, the Duke of Wellington, for urging the University to reform itself.[15]

These differences were obvious enough. None the less, there is a sense in which it is useful to speak of the Tractarians as a party in the University. They were perceived as acting together in the 1830s, and, especially in Oxford affairs, they intended to do so.[16] It was this attempt at corporate action in reaction to political change, especially in its likely effects on the University, which both brought the 'movement' together and in the course of the 1830s exposed to it the implications of intellectual positions only partially appreciated. Members of the Oxford Movement used the changes and proposed changes in the University to reach definitions of their own positions. The University became a testing ground for theories of orthodoxy, history, and theology and, in the course of this process, the 'Movement' fell apart.

It is, therefore, dangerous to accept Tractarian historiography— so abundant and so self-confident—as 'normative' and to see, as Tractarians themselves saw (and as their apologists have continued to see) other approaches as aberrant. Rather, the history of the University shows the extent to which Tractarian opinions were uncertain and shifting, starting with a powerful reaction to what they understood to be objectives of liberalism, and ending with considerable accommodation of it in its political form.

Thomas Arnold, a leading Liberal Anglican, in discussing what the term 'history' meant, remarked: 'The general idea of history seems to be, that it is the biography of a society. It does not seem to me to be history at all, nor simply biography, unless it finds in the persons who are its subjects, something of a common purpose'. Referring specifically to the history of universities, he said: 'History has to do with that which the several members of each of these societies have in common: it is ... the biography of their common life. And it seems to me that it could not perform its office, if it had no distinct notion of what this common life consisted'.[17]

It was the attempt of these 'several members' to reach agreement about what their common life *should* consist of which was to give rise to the crises of the 1830s and 1840s. Bitter and violent as were the struggles, which spilled over into almost every aspect of Oxford University life including its sermons, there is a very important point to be made about them at the start. With a very few exceptions they were successfully contained within the university and the church: there was no English disruption. Some men left the Church of England and the University, but they did so in dribs and drabs; the Sheldonian witnessed nothing like the procession of 451 ministers led by Thomas Chalmers out of the General Assembly in Edinburgh on 18 May 1843, eighteen months before the abortive attempt to censure Tract XC. The Scottish Disruption was a salutary warning to the Church of England in Oxford. Pusey and Keble, not Newman, were the characteristic Tractarians. It is too easy to forget this basic point—that the history of the University in one of its most quarrelsome periods serves above all to illustrate the remarkable cohesion of the English governing class, and its ability to reconcile widely differing intellectual positions through continued 'unity of action'.

This sense of unique national purpose, usually taken to be a defining characteristic of Broad Churchmen, in fact I think went very wide, and acted as a point of unity, not definable in rational terms, at a time when intellectual differences would suggest on paper complete disintegration. A purely intellectual history of the period would leave the reader baffled as to how the University or the Church could continue to exist. A 'union of action', a common practice rather than a common belief, was advocated by Arnold as the necessary cohesive element of a society, and so it eventually proved to be with Oxford University. But this was not to be until attempts at a common belief had been shown to be so disruptive as to be unacceptable.

The term 'university' poses problems of definition, rather of the same sort as does the 'Church of England'. Indeed, each of the terms which concern us—State, Church, University—are what may be called 'essentially contested'.[18] Since all the members of the University were also members of the State and of the Church, it is not surprising that definition of the latter terms took priority. Thus we find that most of the protagonists in the debate about what Oxford was and what she should become were also, and indeed primarily, principals in the dispute about definitions which were necessarily antecedent to those of 'university'. It is no more an accident that Palmer's *Treatise on the Church of Christ*, Gladstone's *The State in its Relations with the Church* and F. D. Maurice's *The Kingdom of Christ* were all published in 1838, six years after the passing of the Reform bill, than that the 'Hampden row'[19] followed it by four years. For all related to the *grand bouleversement* of British politics, begun by the repeal of the Tests in 1828, of which the Reform Bill seemed, especially to those in Oxford, an apocalyptic apotheosis. What is curious is that attempts at theoretical definition occurred only after religious pluralism in the national constitution had been permitted by statute. The arguments for hegemony followed its political abolition. In a context in which the formal monopolistic underpinnings of the Anglican establishment had been partially dismantled, the winning of the argument for a continuing religious and cultural hegemony took on a new importance.

Because the crisis of Oxford seemed part of a crisis for the nation, works on Oxford as a separate entity, or on the character of a university, are rarely found.[20] It was left to Newman a generation later and in the calmer times of the 1850s to write his *Discourses on the scope and nature of university education* (1852, later called *The idea of a university defined and illustrated* 1873), a work of liberal spirit (in one sense of the word) of which the crusading Newman of the 1830s would hardly have been capable.

What then was this university? The University of Oxford consisted in one sense of a body of resident fellows as defined by the Laudian Statutes, almost all of them clergymen of the Church of England, and of matriculated undergraduates of various sorts; but these fellows, and undergraduates and others were members of colleges which had in our period, many held, virtually subsumed the University—in the same way though not to the same extent in which Trinity College, Dublin, had almost completely, though not technically, subsumed the University of Dublin. These colleges were private foundations, many of them governed by custom rather than statute. In another sense the University was, in normal times, almost a metaphysical conception; for Masters of Arts, registered as holding that degree and paying certain fees, were entitled to vote in Convocation, to which all proposed changes to University statutes had to be referred. The majority of Convocation, therefore, was not resident in Oxford, had no responsibility either for executing the statutes that it might pass or for coping with the difficulties left when

proposed changes were rejected. Its purpose was to enable the
expression of national rather than private or local opinion about the
University's affairs.

This 'external university' was to play a central role in the shifts of
opinion of the 1830s and 1840s, expression of its opinion in debates
and votes in Convocation being greatly facilitated by the growth of
railways. Many of the most important disputants and behind-the-
scenes advisers in the 1830s were members of the 'external' rather
than of the resident university: the Keble brothers and the 'Hackney
Phalanx' on the one side,[21] Arnold, Whately, and Copleston on the
other, had left Oxford by 1830.

The University was linked to the state by its Members of
Parliament, by crown appointments, by its relationship to the
'Church of England' by law established, and by a rather uncertain,
ultimate control by the crown over statute change. Its degrees were
passports to ordination in the Church of England and to various
other positions.

All this is obvious and no doubt familiar, but when taken together
goes to show how complex any reform might be, what a range of
interests and opinions it would necessarily provoke. The University
claimed a national status, and was granted it, but its arrangements
and the dominance of colleges encouraged localism and self-refer-
ence of an extreme sort. Like the Church of England, an institution
of this sort could only function if its own members conceived its role
historically, approached its structural idiosyncrasies sympatheti-
cally, and saw it as an aspect of the British constitution, that strange
admixture of principle, custom, and anomaly. Newman's famous
remark, that the Church of England had no inventory of its
treasures,[22] was grossly a-historical: it was a living inventory.

Like the constitution, there might be first principles, but they were
inferred rather than stated, save the one: the subscription on
matriculation to the Thirty-nine Articles of the Church of England.
This seemed a defining principle, and Subscription to the Articles
was therefore the action from which almost all the controversies
directly or indirectly took their form. When W. E. Gladstone was
admitted to the University in 1828, he accurately noted in his diary:
'matriculated, taking the oaths, & subscribing to the Articles &
Statutes'.[23] The question of the articles' Subscription became for
Oxford what Roman Catholic emancipation had been for the British
constitution, and this was no accident for the intellectual and
political debate about both was intricately intertwined.

Roman Catholic emancipation had been a defining issue in national life at least since 1815. It was the public issue on which the Noetics of Oriel gained their notoriety. Their view of emancipation had in fact two rather different sources and consequences, represented in the writings of Richard Whately and Thomas Arnold.

The dominant mind amongst the Noetics in Oxford was Richard Whately, though he owed much—intellectually if not politically—to Copleston, as he made clear in his edition of Copleston's *Remains*.[24] Whately was appointed Principal of St Alban Hall by the Whiggish Chancellor, Grenville, in 1825. Whately's works and actions exercised a powerful influence on both Noetics and some Tractarians.

In Whately's view, the Christian Church, in marked contrast to the Jewish theocracy, had 'no secular power';[25] it should exercise 'no secular coercion',[26] it should not, even where it had the means, impose conformity save on its own members. He launched, in his anonymous *Letters on the Church* (1826), a powerful attack on Warburtonianism[27] (i.e. Church acceptance of State defence in exchange for integration and loss of independence): the presence of bishops in the House of Lords was 'a disaster; Church property should only be protected in the same sense as any corporation's property was protected; the Church must regain its own voice through a revival of Convocation: 'The connexion such as it now subsists, between the State and the Church, which some, both statesmen and churchmen, from confused or partial and imperfect views of the subject, are so anxious to maintain, is not only in principle unjustifiable, but is, in every point, inexpedient for both parties'.[28] This applied to the state as well as the Church, because, by exclusively favouring a narrowly-defined Church of England, Roman Catholics, whose faith Whately and Arnold saw as the expression of the depravity of human nature and original sin in an unadulterated form, were encouraged to feel alienated and would be encouraged to permanent degradation. Hence the improvement towards grace which the Church of England represented was made less likely by the Roman Catholics' civic disaffection.

This is, for the most part, a startling view of Church–State relations by a man often described as a Whig. 'I have come to the discovery that I am a divine-right Tory', Whately noted in 1820;[29] he attacked Whiggery for the view that there was any mutual accountability between Church and State.[30] On the other hand, he deplored certain aspects of divine-right toryism and in his hostility to the apostolic principle was not-at-all a High Churchman. Thus Whately found common ground with the Whigs on a number of issues, including Roman Catholic emancipation and university reform, and was appointed Archbishop of Dublin by Grey in 1831, but he should really only be seen as a Whig in the sense that contemporaries regarded him as one.[31] His *Letters on the Church* need only apostolicity added to lead straight to Hurrell Froude's notorious *Tract 59*.[32] As Whately was not a Whig, so also was he not a rationalist. His inductive philosophy attacked eighteenth-century rationalism and also the generalized deductivist propositions of most of the political economists. Whately had thus pointed the way both for the Tractarians on Church/State questions (and for Newman in the practice of questioning and defining), and for the Broad Churchmen in his inductivism.

Carried further by his colleague R. D. Hampden, Whately's inductivism led to a wholesale attack, in Hampden's Bampton Lectures of 1832, on scholastic philosophy and rationalism.[33] Reflecting in 1848 on the controversy to which those lectures eventually led, Hampden wrote: 'If there is anything to which my writings have been uniformly opposed, it is Rationalism. I have no leaning whatever towards such a mode of speculation, nor have I ever had; ... having been put on my guard against it, by a familiarity with Butler's *Analogy*'[34]—a work which, Hampden took pains to point out, he had largely been responsible for introducing as a set book in the University.

Hampden thus extended one aspect of Whately's thought: the Tractarians, and especially Newman and Hurrell Froude, another. Hampden was the quicker to see the implications of what he was doing. Newman and Froude moved painfully in the 1830s to work out the implications of Whately's *Letters* which Newman in the *Apologia* recalled as having so astonished him at the time of their publication.

Hampden had turned Whately against the schoolmen in his Bamptons; on his own terms he was hard to assail. He next turned his methodology against Subscription and the Articles. This was a shock for contemporaries, for he lifted a long-standing dispute, dating back to the 1770s, to a quite new methodological and philosophical level; for Hampden's arguments in his pamphlet on Dissenters in 1834 were not prudential or expedient, but theological. Arguing that 'no conclusions of human reasoning, however correctly deduced, however logically sound, are properly religious truths', he maintained that there was insufficient basis for exclusion of dissenters through a requirement to subscribe. Indeed the Articles, Hampden thought, in true Broad Church style, ought to be improved 'commensurate with the advances made in their scientific methods and calculated to embrace a wider extent of Christian profession, without any sacrifice of real Christian truth'.[35] But this was not an argument for pluralism of belief. Rather it was, as with Arnold, the contrary: Oxford would remain 'as it always had been a Church of England institution';[36] dissenters would attend it on Church of England terms: 'If persons of different communions are willing to conform to our discipline, and receive instruction from us, knowing that we are members of the Church of England and sincere teachers of its theological system—where can be the real objection in such a case? . . . As we believe ourselves to have the truth on our side, so we must believe the ultimate ascendancy must be to our own views'.[37]

Thus, although there would be no tests for entry, all those entering would know the character of the institution they were joining, and, once in, would receive an Anglican education: 'Instruction in the Articles themselves *is* of use; and that I suppose to continue, even though the tests be removed'.[38] Since truth would have the victory, removal of tests would be the means to an extension of Anglican influence. Hampden thus stood fully in the Arnoldian tradition of Anglican cultural hegemony. His position was really that of a prudential liberal-conservative, but it was caricatured by his opponents as being one of assertive liberalism. However, at the end of his pamphlet, a different argument is used, which quickly exposes the difficulty of the Broad Churchmen:

Besides, after all, the University is not the Church. It is only accidentally a society of church members, and considered as a literary society, it has surely no right to rest on authority, as the *foundation* of its lessons in any department of knowledge.[39]

Here, of course, was the problem, and this was the Tractarians' point. Taking the University as 'a literary society', were any limitations to opinion appropriate? Hampden believed that 'we must go back to the divinely inspired teachers of Christianity. This is our only consistent resting place'.[40] But the thrust of his century was in a different direction. It was ironic that it was the Broad Churchmen, those with the methodology of updating on 'scientific methods', whose approach now seems so anachronistic: Hampden's assumption that Oxford would remain primarily an Anglican University which would absorb and Anglicanize dissenters worked in the social context but hardly in the context of belief, and this Hampden would personally have deplored.

Hampden's complaint in the 1830s was that the Tractarians, his chief and most articulate opponents (much more articulate than the Evangelicals who also deplored him)[41] had not, for all their vast output, engaged with him on his own terms. This was, on the whole, quite true, with the possible and perhaps ambiguous exception of Newman. Pusey, particularly, during the great row of 1836 when Melbourne appointed Hampden to the Regius Chair of Divinity, tried to shoot down Hampden with antithetical authorities, not by engaging him and defeating him. Though successful in mobilizing votes against Hampden in 1836—the University voted by 474 to 90 that although a Professor and a Head of a House he should be deprived of his place on the syndicate for choosing select preachers and that he should not be consulted when a sermon was called in question before the Vice-Chancellor[42]—Pusey's approach indicated the extent to which the Tractarians were being driven into an intellectual corner. Their opposition to what the Broad Churchmen called 'scientific methods'—the teaching of modern languages, modern history, textual criticism—left them reliant on an a-historical use of texts and on dogmatism.[43] In the sense that a university was a 'literary society', the Tractarians risked having little to say about its modern character and direction, except that they disapproved of it.

Hampden in 1834 was theological in his arguments, not historical; it was left to Arnold to develop the latter dimension in his famous article 'The Oxford Malignants' (as the editor of the *Edinburgh Review* entitled it),[44] published the day of the Hampden vote in Convocation. Arnold, unlike Whately, had an idealized view of the nation-state, based on an Aristotelian teleology. Though he agreed with Whately on the apostolic succession, 'Believing that the Church has no divinely-appointed succession of governors',[45] he argued that this cleared the way to a potentially perfect unity of Church and State: 'I would unite one half of the Archbishop of Dublin's (Whately's) theory with one half of Mr Gladstone's; agreeing cordially with Mr Gladstone in the moral theory of the state, and agreeing cordially with the Archbishop in what I will venture to call the Christian theory of the Church, and deducing from the two the conclusion, that the perfect state and the perfect church are identical'.[46] Not surprisingly then, a review of Whately's *Letters* in the *Edinburgh Review* (1826)[47] called forth Arnold's first substantial statement of his comprehensive theory of Church, State and Society and of his organic view of nationality. For Arnold, therefore, the end of a society 'should be good rather than truth',[48] and this good it was the duty of both Church and State to inculcate. All Christians, though there were difficulties about Quakers, Roman Catholics, and Unitarians, could be comprehended within one national church if churchmen would but seize the moment: 'the national Church in every generation is equally invested with sovereign power to order such rites and forms of worship as it may deem expedient'.[49] It followed from this position that Subscription to the Articles at matriculation could hardly be a matter of much significance.

Whately and Arnold were both permanently out of Oxford by the time the Reform Bill passed—though Arnold returned under Whig patronage as Regius Professor of Modern History in 1840. The statesman of the Noetics was Edward Hawkins, Provost of Oriel from 1827, the famous election in which Newman supported him rather than Keble (his future fellow-Tractarian) who withdrew.

Hawkins was in terms of the university spectrum a Whig, and certain of his qualities were Whiggish. He recognized the inevitability of a degree of constitutional reform, and he attempted to guide the Hebdomadal Board towards it. He was the chief proponent of the 'Declaration' solution to the articles question by which the difficulty could be prudentially set aside by candidates for admission to the University making a general 'Declaration' of allegiance, the principle of the truth or otherwise of the Articles thus not being directly confronted. Hawkins worked from the premise he had put forward in defending compulsory attendance at college Communion: 'the question is, how to carry on the system with the least harm and the utmost good, which will consist with the *principle* of the system. And there is surely considerable range for the exercise of discretion ...'[50] In the mid-1830s, Hawkins pressed for a Declaration as minimizing injury, not a means to effective pluralism: 'it seems undeniable, that the benefit which the University derives from a religious *test*, as such, may be quite as easily secured by a

Declaration equivalent to the present Subscription'.[51] To Pusey's comment on this, 'Is the proposed substitution of a "Declaration" for "Subscription to the Thirty-Nine Articles", intended to relax our present position or no?', Hawkins replied: 'We have rather to enquire into the merits of the proposal, than the intentions of its authors'.[52]

In 1834, in the light of a series of initiatives in Parliament stopped only by the House of Lords, the Heads of Houses, led by Hawkins and encouraged by Wellington, requested Convocation to substitute a Declaration for Subscription. In May 1835 Convocation, dominated by non-resident voters, rejected the proposal by 459 votes to 57.[53] 'Some form of Declaration will, I doubt not, be at length approved' Hawkins confidently but erroneously told the Earl of Radnor in a public letter in 1835,[54] that is, he believed that self-generated institutional reform was a desirable and practical solution. Hawkins went further than mere fixing:

The ancient system of the University is at present submitted to a gradual process of change in all its most important features. We are in a state of transition from one great system to another.[55]

What the new 'great system' was to be, remained, however, undefined.

Underlying Hawkins' apparently rather simple political position was an interesting and in certain respects revolutionary theological one. In his 1819 sermon on tradition, which Newman heard him give,[56] he posited the existence of an oral tradition in the early church, as an essential complement to the written works of the fathers. It was the control, validity and relationship to formulated doctrine and potential heresy of this oral tradition which drew Newman's attention to the Arians of the fourth century, which formed the subject of his first book, published in 1833.[57] Hawkins' reliance on this sort of oral tradition meant that for him, because truth in the Church did not depend on formulaic statements, the move from Subscription to Declaration was consistent, and raised none of the sort of problems of definition which it posed for a dogmatist like Pusey.

The thrust of Noetical writings on the Subscription question was thus towards change, though the implications of their various positions led in different directions. The thrust of Tractarian writings on the university question in the early 1830s was towards rejection of change (though many accepted Catholic Emancipation), but the implication of their positions equally led them to unforeseen consequences. As Pelikan in a recent brilliant if somewhat a-historical exposition of Newman's opinions has pointed out, Newman early formulated the notion of 'economy'[58] and the notion of the possibility of the *development* of this oral tradition side by side with its periodic doctrinal formulation. Pelikan did not point out that this seed was originally implanted in a Noetical context, with the influence of Hawkins obvious. The question of Newman's intellectual debt to the Noetics requires more investigation. But it is likely to prove to be substantial, fundamental and hidden. Newman's aim in launching the 'second Reformation' of 1833 was an attack, absolutist in tone, on 'anti-dogmatic liberalism'.[59] He proceeded, however, inductively; nothing could be more inductive than his statement in the *Apologia* that he believed in God because he believed in himself.[60] Though his aim was to correct his own 'drifting in the direction of liberalism', the evolutionary view of development which seemed to be the solution to the 'difficulty' of Anglicanism was fully in the nineteenth-century liberal tradition.[61] Its oddity was not its application of evolution and development, but its eventual use to justify a need for authority. Newman's powerful reaction against liberalism in the 1830s prevented him noticing that he was associating three very different types of liberalism, and failing to distinguish between them.

First, the secular liberalism of the *Westminster Review* and the utilitarians, which sought for a pluralism of values, or at least a type of social and political organization which would permit the existence of a variety of values without a theistic legitimization. Second, the militant anti-clericalism of the Continent and especially France: it was the sight of a *tricoleur* in France which decided Newman on beginning a crusade in England. Third, the Broad Church comprehension of the Arnoldians, anti-dogmatic but powerfully Anglican, which was politically liberal in terms of the 1830s, because comprehensive changes were rejected by the Tories, but which sought an essentially conservative consolidation of national values defined in Anglican terms. By regarding the Arnoldians as a Trojan horse of utilitarianism, the Tractarians hugely confused the debate. Newman's own attempt at comprehension in Tract XC (arguing that the Articles could be read in a Catholic as well as a Protestant sense) was accompanied by no acknowledgement that the method and even the purpose of the Tract owed much to Whatelyesque or Arnoldian arguments and influences. Newman's direction was henceforth to make a break in 'unity of action' by resigning from St Mary's, the University Church, and retiring to Littlemore, a parish just outside Oxford, thus signifying his distance from Tractarians as well as Broad Churchmen.

But before reaching this position, Newman offered what was perhaps the starkest defence of subscription as an emblem of obedience and, consequently, as an antidote to liberal values in education:

The advantage of subscription (to my mind) is its witnessing to the principle that religion is to be approached with a submission of the understanding. Nothing is so common, as you must know, as for young men to approach serious subjects, as judges—to study them, as mere sciences. Aristotle and Butler are treated as teachers of *a* system, not as if there was more truth in them than in Jeremy Bentham. The study of the 'Evidences' [for Christianity] now popular (such as Paley's) encourages this evil frame of mind—the learner is supposed to be external to the system—our Lord is 'a young Galilean peasant'—His Apostles, 'honest men, trustworthy witnesses,' and the like. Milman's 'Jews' exhibits the same character of mind in another department. Abraham is a Sheik, &c., &c. In all these cases the student is supposed to look upon the system from without, and to have to choose it by an act of reason before he submits to it,—whereas the great lesson of the Gospel is faith, an obeying prior to reason, and *proving* its reasonableness by making an experiment of it—a casting of heart and mind into the system, and investigating the truth by practice. I should say the same of a person in a Mahometan country or under any system which was not plainly and purely diabolical—the religion in occupation is at least a representative of the truth; it is to him the witness of the Unseen God, and may claim, instead of scepticism and suspicion, a prompt and frank submission in the first instance, though of course the issue of the experiment would not be one of confident conviction, but of doubt, or of discrimination between one part of the system and another.

In an age, then, when this great principle is scouted, Subscription to the Articles is a memento and protest—and again actually does, I believe, impress upon the minds of young men the teachable and subdued temper expected of them. They are not to reason, but to obey; and this quite independently of the degree of accuracy, the wisdom, &c., of the Articles themselves.[62]

The view that undergraduates were, intellectually, 'not to reason, but to obey' was a view held quite consistently by the Tractarians, especially in the 1830s. But this view of the ethos of a University was hardly one sustainable in nineteenth-century England. It was also one which held potential difficulties for Tractarians. For if those who decided on the content of obedience were not Tractarian, what then followed for the Tractarian view of dogma?

In the spirit of Newman's maxim, the Tractarians opposed the introduction of subjects thought to encourage independence of thought, such as modern history (one implicit target in the passage quoted above) which was by its nature anti-dogmatic, and modern languages, which equipped students to read dangerous continental works. In these campaigns they were often joined by the Evangelicals, whose concern for the stature of the Bible encouraged a strong distrust of history and modern languages. The difficulty for Tractarians was that, while they wished to discourage what they saw as speculation, they themselves wished to pursue their own inquiries, for they by no means saw the Church of England as being, in the early 1830s, in a satisfactory condition. Thus Pusey opposed the introduction of theology as an academic subject, as exposing sacred matters to speculative inquiry,[63] but introduced a Theological Society under strict clerical control, whose study was to be conducted 'according to the peculiar character of our Church', with no paper read or subject discussed unless the society's executive committee had approved it in advance of the meeting.[64]

In the 1830s, therefore, Pusey was an unyielding defender of Subscription. But, unlike some of its defenders, Pusey was a realist. At the same time as developing his own style of Anglo-Catholicism as a distinct but loyal tradition within the Church of England, he also, assisted no doubt by that tradition's increasingly cautious view of the establishment, came to see that Subscription was unsustainable. Pusey by the 1840s conceived the battle to be between belief and unbelief. His aim with respect to the University was to save the college tutorial system,[65] which he saw as morally beneficial (if conducted by clergymen), against the development of a professorial, lecture-based system, which he regarded as a mere imparting of knowledge, and, to judge by his experience of German universities in the 1820s, probably dangerous knowledge. Thus, when he came to make his formidable assault on the Royal Commission's proposals

of 1852, which included the abolition of Subscription at matriculation, his aim was to preserve a clerically-run collegiate university.
In this cause, the outpost of Subscription to the Articles was too
exposed. Pusey withdrew from it discreetly. In his vast budget of
'Evidence' on the proposals, he did not mention Subscription, so far
had events moved him since the mid-1830s. His conclusion to his
'Evidence' was more than an echo of the Hampden view which he
had so excoriated sixteen years before: Oxford 'has to recover the
ground which she has lost by letting the education of the country to
slip out of her hands ... It is right that Oxford should embrace all
who will come to her to be educated in her way'.[66] The more
dogmatic the Pusey group of the Tractarians became in theology,
the more their preservation of a niche in the Church of England
required flexibility in other matters, and Subscription, central to
their university position in the 1830s, had become such by the 1850s.

It was left to Robert Hussey, Regius Professor of Ecclesiastical
History, to state what had been the Tractarian position but had now
become that of the unbending High Churchmen: 'the effect of the
scheme recommended by the commissioners, if executed throughout, would be (whatever might have been intended,) to separate the
University, as a place of Education, from the Church of England;
and therefore, by necessary consequence, from the profession of the
Christian Faith. For the Christian Faith, in order to be taught, must
be something definite; and that, *something definite*, can be in this
place no other than what is held and taught in the Church of
England'.[67]

We thus see how very complex is the intellectual history of the
University in the period, how lines apparently parallel and separate
are in fact crossed and tangled. We see how the view of the Oxford
Movement as an easily separable, anti-liberal variable is misleading
and anachronistic (though by the 1836 period it had become Pusey's
first aim to make it both separable and anti-liberal). We may also
note of the Noetics that nothing is more striking in their writing than
the fervour of their faith—nothing is more misleading than to
present them as incipient secularists, as is shown by their eagerness
to refute both utilitarianism and Unitarianism. Lumping them in
with the utilitarians or the Unitarians, or both, as the Oxford
Movement did from 1833 onwards, was an extraordinary mistake.

For the Noetics agreed with the rest of the University that the
resuscitation of some form of Hookerian theocracy[68] was the ideal:

they were not religious or intellectual pluralists, but rather looked to the reformulation of religious language in order that pluralism might be avoided: they sought a total explanation of the world within an Anglican theology. The Noetics' successors came to see the impossibility of such an all-embracing Anglicanism, in scientific terms in the career of Baden Powell (as Pietro Corsi's book shows),[69] in moral and historicist terms in the careers of Pattison and A. P. Stanley.

Once the area of Arnoldian comprehension had been agreed, there was to be no intellectual or religious pluralism within it; there was a world of difference between 'latitudinarianism' and comprehension. There was nothing religiously or morally pluralistic about Arnold's Rugby. In its ultimate intentions, Broad Churchmanship was as illiberal (in the Millite sense) as Tractarianism—perhaps more so. Whereas the Tractarians' latent anti-establishmentarianism allowed them an external reference point of authority, the Broad Churchmen had none beyond the national church and the individual understanding of scripture; already in Arnold's Lectures 'race' is singled out as a defining and integrating criterion for national self-awareness.[70]

Nor were the Noetics Germanizing historicists in the sense that the Tractarians imagined them. Though the Arnold group was historicist in intention and in their secular publications, they were not Biblican scholars in the historical sense, and made little attempt to use their historicism against the Bible in the way Pusey feared. The Noetics of the 1830s kept away from Biblical studies of a technical sort and even their Broad Church successors were, by Continental standards, amateurs. James Barr's argument that Jowett's reading of the Bible 'like any other book' showed he was the opposite of an historically based critic is surely right, and can be applied to many of the earlier Broad Churchmen.[71] For some of them this was an inconsistency. Arnold, for example, would have been appalled to have seen applied to the Bible the arguments of his appendix to Thucydides, and even Connop Thirlwall became alarmed at the end of his life at the length to which some took historical biblical criticism.[72] The intellectual careers of the later Broad Churchmen show that allowing a moderate study of modern languages and modern history in Oxford University—the two great bug-bears of the Tractarians—did not lead directly to the ascendancy of anti-Christ in the University.

One certainly cannot explain the dissolution of three centuries of Anglican cultural hegemony simply in terms of the Oxford crisis of the 1830s and 1840s. In some ways, especially at a European level, this crisis was anachronistic before it started. But one can argue that the form the crisis took—a bitter and divisive battle between men whose unity of action and thought remained, *comparatively*, quite considerable—left state intervention and religious and intellectual pluralism as the only possible solutions.

Contest over the character and definition of what a University might be was one aspect of a general attempt at self-definition by the various Church parties of the time. It may have helped them to clarify their thoughts about other matters, but it had not led to any agreement in theological terms about the University. Both sides were agreed that the University should be not only Christian but Anglican, but neither could persuade the other to support its definition of what an 'Anglican University' might amount to—and behind the very term 'Anglican' (or 'Church of England', for 'Anglican' was an innovation as a word, itself a product of the definitional struggles) lay the question of the national role of the University. It may well be that there was, in fact, no definition available to either side consonant with the political forces working within the nation at large.

All the battles of the 1830s and 1840s produced only a few minor statute changes: the University of 1845 was hardly formally different from that of 1828. But it was clear that attempts at reform from within had produced a stale-mate between the competing schools of religious definition. 'Only leave us to ourselves', Hawkins had asked in 1835.[73] The request implied local action and consequences. It was granted: neither Whig nor Tory governments made a move. By the 1840s the result was plain to see. The dogmatists had become more dogmatic; the advocates of Anglican comprehension had failed to persuade their colleagues that minor surrenders might produce major gains. As the Peel government moved to repeal the corn laws and thus associate the governing classes with the interests of urban industrialism, the University of Oxford stripped W. G. Ward of his degree and would have done the same to Newman but for the good sense of the Senior Proctor. 1845 showed the extent to which the University risked becoming merely sectarian.

Mark Pattison recalled that the effect of Newman's conversion in 1845 'was not consternation; it was a lull—a sense that the past agitation of twelve years was extinguished by this simple act'.[74] But as college fellows became accustomed to passing the port without imminent acrimony, it became clear that much in fact had changed. 'It is not at all easy (humanly speaking) to wind up an Englishman to a dogmatic level', Newman observed,[75] but once it had been done the effect was striking. The consequences of the rows in Oxford about University reform between 1828 and 1845 were in fact considerable.

First, the presentation of Oxford as a 'national' university was, if not ruined, severely damaged. The self-sustaining wealth of the colleges and the lack of many educational alternatives were dangerous foundations to rely on, especially given the foundation of University and King's Colleges in London. Oxford's claim to be 'a National Institution'[76] was undermined as it became nationally apparent that the University was incapable of agreeing on internal reform. Moreover, changes in the national constitution, with nonconformists and Roman Catholics admitted to a fuller participatory citizenship and Jews soon likely to be so, were not mirrored in the University, with the consequence that Oxford as 'a National Institution' by the 1840s differed significantly in membership from the political nation as represented at Westminster. What had seemed revolutionary in 1828–1832 was by the 1840s beginning to seem normative, and this left the university the more isolated.

Within Oxford the Noetics of the 1820s and the early 1830s were by the 1840s being replaced by a more coordinated group of liberal reformers, less intellectually daring but more willing to act in a coordinated way to encourage institutional reform, and to be prepared to propose much more far-reaching structural change.[77] Several of them, such as A. C. Tait and Mark Pattison, had had a passing phase of Tractarianism, against which they reacted sharply and emotionally but from which they took the Tractarians' considerably developed skills in organizing a propaganda campaign and delivering a vote. Thus in the 1840s the Tractarians found turned against themselves several of the weapons they had so effectively deployed in the 1830s.

The Tractarians' blocking of constitutional and examination syllabus reform and their refusal on dogmatic principle to accept even the most cautious reforms, in fact, by their delays, encouraged the much bolder syllabus reform of 1850. This introduced at a stroke disciplines such as modern history which the Tractarians had previously successfully excluded as dangerous and likely to encourage error. The defeat of the Tractarians in 1845 on the vote on W. G. Ward made their reversal of influence in the 'external university' (as compared with the Hampden vote in 1836) nationally explicit and, internally, made possible the liberals' victories in syllabus reform.[78] The disintegration in 1845 of the forces that had defeated reform in the 1830s cleared the way. The liberals were strong enough, in alliance with the Russell government, to win the battle of the Royal Commissions, dominating that appointed in 1850 and producing in 1852 a revolutionary report which would have 'Germanized' the University by shifting the balance of teaching from the tutors to the professors.[79] This was the risk that the Tractarians had run: in resisting all change they had created the opportunity for revolutionary change, for that is what the implementation of the 1852 Royal Commission Report would have been.

However, the removal of Newman by his conversion to Roman Catholicism in 1845 allowed a reconstitution of the Tractarian Movement by Keble and especially Pusey: the Movement to an extent moved out of the University into the parishes and ceased to assume so arrogant a tone. Under Pusey's statesmanship, Tractarianism worked within the Church of England, developing it rather than assaulting it with test and challenges of the Tract XC sort.

The way was thus cleared for the compromise of 1854. The High Churchmen and Tractarians abandoned their absolute positions. Pusey wrote an effective attack on the liberals' report and was able to cast *them* in the role of absolutists. He made an effective alliance of Tractarians, Evangelicals, and college tutors. This alliance worked with Gladstone—an Evangelical who had become a quasi-Tractarian—who was, as M.P. for the University, in charge at Cabinet level of the preparation of the Bill which was the consequence of the Royal Commission's report.[80] This chastened combination permitted a moderate reform which, from its point of view, contained liberalism by emasculating it. The colleges, though regularized and reformed, remained the dominant force in the University and the professors, though more powerful, remained fundamentally ancillary to the teaching structure of the University. Entry to the University and graduation as Bachelor of Arts was unrestricted by tests, but the degree of Master of Arts still required (until 1871) acceptance of the Articles and, by virtue of this continuing restriction, the government of the University and the Colleges remained effectively under the control of the Church of England. It was, in fact, very much the settlement Hampden had advocated in 1834. But the twenty-year interval meant that what in 1834 would have been a triumph for liberalism in 1854 seemed a disappointment. In so far as there was a definition, it was in terms of what the political nation and its governing coalition of Whigs, Peelites, and Liberals had become. The Oxford Act of 1854 reflected the political and religious character of the Aberdeen coalition: no longer assertively Anglican, but a compromise not seriously to the short or medium-term disadvantage of the Church of England. Gladstone, in his position as Chancellor of the Exchequer and coordinator of the making of the University of Oxford Bill, represented the change which his Oxonian generation had experienced and had in large measure accepted.

The period 1833–1845 showed that the battle of historicism and organicism *versus* Tractarian anti-historicist dogmatism was inconclusive. The organicists, in an age of increasing pluralism in the national context, had acted too late. The bold Arnoldian objective of the maintenance of protestant hegemony by a radical introduction of comprehension had failed. The best that could be hoped for was a temporary maintenance of authority. But this authority was based not on intellectual acceptance of the primacy of 'national religion' but on a social authority permitted by ascendancy in the public schools. The Noetics, and their successors the Broad Churchmen, initially so intellectually daring, found themselves increasingly circumscribed by the intellectual sterility of 'muscular Christianity',[81] the price they paid for social domination, and they increasingly moved towards Conservatism politically. They had hoped to offer God a modern nation intellectually and religiously Anglicanized. But as their theology waned, their public schools, the intended agents of this regeneration, represented a new form of exclusion. The apostles of organic national unity had, in their chief national social reform, created a lasting disunity in education.

Equally, the Oxford Movement had moved on from its members' alliance with the High Churchmen to a specifically *religious* exclusivism, characterized by their growing emphasis on ritualism and sacerdotalism. It recognized it had lost the attempt to preserve the University as a seminary, and to prevent what it regarded as heresy within the Church, let alone outside it. It gave up the attempt to continue the establishment of Anglicanism as the national language of the educated classes, and it settled for a 'separate tradition' solution even within the University.

Having set out in the 1830s to try to enforce orthodoxy and unity of belief, the Tractarians ironically found themselves supporting what was by the 1850s really an Arnoldian 'unity of action'. Thus having successfully prosecuted the Broad Church volume *Essays and Reviews* (1860) for heresy in 1864, a few years later they had to accept one of its contributors, Frederick Temple, as Bishop of Exeter.[82] The Tractarians found themselves relying on the Liberal party, whose tolerance had been their starting point of execration, for their existence in the Anglican church, as the Broad Churchmen, led by Tait, drove home in alliance with Disraeli's Conservative government the advantage against them in the Public Worship Regulation Act of 1874, passed to discipline the Tractarian Ritualists.

Thus the crisis over the reform of Oxford University in the 1830s led eventually to a paradox: the 'liberal' tradition of the 1830s by its intellectual failure and its social success became conservative, while the Tractarian reaction against what it saw as liberalism in the 1830s led eventually to political association with it.[83]

The High Churchmen, exponents of our first category of attitude (resistance to change on traditionalist lines), had little left to say. Their most prominent figure in University politics, Godfrey Faussett, had successfully prosecuted first the Noetical Hampden in 1836, later the Tractarian Pusey in 1843—yet all three sat, day-by-day, side-by-side, in their cathedral stalls in Christ Church bound together (until Hampden's translation to Hereford in 1848) by the 'unity of action' of cathedral and college life. The High Churchmen had emphasized human imperfectibility in Church and State, and had blamed both Arnoldian organicists for seeking perfection too enthusiastically in the temporal sphere and Newmanites for seeking it too ardently in the ecclesiastical. Palmer's preface to the third edition of his *Treatise on the Church of Christ* (1842, p. xi) is most obviously directed at Newman, but is also perhaps a comment on the Arnoldians:

Another great error consists in the formulation of a theory of optimism in the Church, irrespective of the actual declarations of revelation, or the testimony of facts. It is the most unsound theory which leads to the notion of a universal church, perfectly united in communion and faith, free from all unsoundness in doctrine and morals, and possessed of a standing infallible in all its decisions. This theory of *perfection* in the Church is wholly at variance with our experiences of the laws of creation. Imperfection is the necessary condition of human nature in all its parts and throughout the whole course of its history

But this High Church pessimism—perhaps the dominant voice within the University during the 1830s—had nothing to offer to an institution which, if it was to remain 'National', could not avoid responding to the changes in the political nation.

The Oxford Movement, in alliance at first with High Churchmen and some Evangelicals, prevented internally-generated change, and handed the fate of the University to that forum whose deficiencies it had been the first to deplore, the House of Commons. Fortunately for Oxford, the nation, in the form of its representative institutions, proved wiser than its clerical intelligentsia.

St Hugh's College
Oxford OX2 6LE

REFERENCES

*I am obliged to Dr Mark Curthoys, Dr Jane Garnett, Dr Paul Langford, and Dr John Walsh for their very helpful comments on an earlier draft of this paper.
  1. [E. Hawkins], *A Letter to the author of 'An Appeal to the Heads of the University of Oxford' upon compulsory attendance at the Communion. By a Graduate* (1822), 20. Attendance at Communion once a term was required by most colleges. Newman, who wanted the requirement abolished, regarding it as 'profanation', quarrelled with Hawkins over it; see I. Ker, *John Henry Newman* (1988), 37–8. Compulsory communion was probably at least as great a deterrent to Methodists as Subscription.
  2. This is probably a slight exaggeration, though in a sense technically true; at that time, the boundary between the Church of England and Methodism was blurred, it being not uncommon in some areas to attend both churches. How many persons subscribing at matriculation were more Methodist than Church of England unfortunately cannot be known, but it was probably a very small number. Candidates for matriculation knew that Subscription was not treated as a formality and that there would be sharp scrutiny of their religious behaviour during

their time as undergraduates. Members of protestant denominations other than Methodism (whose schism was recent and not definitive) could hardly have subscribed, nor could Roman Catholics. A traditional defence of the Church of England and Subscription was that these were self-imposed debarments, since all Englishmen were members of the Church of England. But by the 1830s, with a considerable increase in denominationalism, it was increasingly difficult to argue that this simple equation was sufficient, although it remained true.

3. [E. Hawkins], *A Letter to the Earl of Radnor upon the Oaths, Dispensations, and Subscription to the XXXIX Articles at the University of Oxford. By a Resident Member of Convocation* (1835), 17.

4. W. R. Ward, *Victorian Oxford* (1965), 13.

5. [Hawkins], *A Letter to the author*, 22.

6. [F. D. Maurice], *Subscription No Bondage, or the practical advantages afforded by the Thirty-Nine Articles as Guides in all the branches of Academical Education . . . by Rusticus* (1835), 22. Maurice, supporting Subscription as against a Declaration, argued: 'The difference between Oxford and other Universities is, not that she imposes conditions of thought upon her students, and that they assent and consent to them; for so far all institutions are alike; but that she *states* what are her conditions of thought' (ibid.). For Maurice, Subscription was an acceptance of those 'conditions of thought' necessary to proper understanding: 'I affirm not only that theological conditions of thought are useful, but that no other provision would be equally useful, or would at all meet the case' (ibid. 55–6).

7. The intention of the reforms was preservative, but the introduction of classes was the stimulus to inter-collegiate competition and marked the start of the association of the University with the dominant ethos of liberalism and equality of opportunity.

8. For the general case, see G. F. A. Best, 'The Protestant Constitution and its supporters, 1800–1829', *Transactions of the Royal Historical Society*, 5th series viii (1958), 107–27, Olive Brose, *Church and Parliament. The reshaping of the Church of England 1828–1860* (1959), and J. C. D. Clark, *English Society 1688–1832. Ideology, social structure and political practice during the ancien regime* (1985), ch. 6.

9. See Paul Langford, *Public life and the propertied Englishman, 1689–1798*, ch. ii (forthcoming).

10. At Cambridge, 'no religious test was, or ever had been, imposed upon undergraduates at matriculation' and in 1772, in the face of likely parliamentary action by statute, the requirement to subscribe to the Articles when taking a degree was replaced by a requirement to declare *bona fide* membership of the Church of England; see D. A. Winstanley, *Unreformed Cambridge* (1935), 301ff.; see also J. Gascoigne, *Cambridge in the age of the enlightenment* (1989), 202 and G. M. Ditchfield, 'The Subscription Issue in British Parliamentary Politics 1772–79', *Parliamentary History* vii (1988), 45–8.

11. See C. E. McClelland, *State, society and university in Germany 1700–1914*, ch. 4.

12. For the development of 'Broad Churchmanship' from its Noetical origins, see I. Ellis, *Seven Against Christ. A study of 'Essays and Reviews'* (1980), ch. 1.

13. See e.g. R. H. Greenfield, 'The attitude of the Tractarians to the Roman Catholic Church 1833–1850' (Oxford D.Phil 1956); David Nicholls, 'Gladstone and the Anglican critics of Newman' in J. D. Bastable, *Newman and Gladstone. Centennial Essays* (1975); and P. B. Nockles, 'Continuity and Change in Anglican High Churchmanship 1792–1850' (Oxford D.Phil 1982).

14. J. H. Newman, quoting himself, in *Apologia pro Vita Sua* (1864; references here are to the 1959 p.b. edition), 153.

15. For Wellington's role, see Ward, *Victorian Oxford*, 94.

16. See J. H. Newman, 'State of religious parties', *British Critic and Quarterly Theological Review* (1839), xxv. 406; excusing the over-enthusiasm of some of his followers, Newman adds: 'in what has been above said, about the invisible and spiritual character of the present reaction, there was no intention of denying that it may be necessarily enveloped externally ... with the dress and attributes of a school'.

17. Thomas Arnold, *Introductory Lectures on Modern History ... with an Inaugural Lecture* (1842), 4–5.

18. W. B. Gallie, 'Essentially contested concepts', *Proceedings of the Aristotelian Society* (1955–6).

19. Renn Dickson Hampden, fellow of Oriel college and a Broad Churchman, gave the prestigious Bampton Lectures in 1832 and became Principal of St Mary Hall in 1833; in 1834 his *Observations on religious dissent* alarmed the Tractarians and in 1836 attempts were made to prevent his appointment as Regius Professor of Divinity by the Whig Prime Minister, Lord Melbourne. Although his Bampton Lectures had been little queried at the time, they were used against him and after various votes, he was censured by Convocation in a series of petty indignities (although he remained, as Regius Professor, a Canon of the Cathedral). His appointment in 1847, by the Whig Prime Minister, Lord John Russell, to the bishopric of Hereford, occasioned violent Tractarian and High Church opposition and was only confirmed by election after a series of legal disputes.

20. A notable exception is Maurice, *Subscription No Bondage* which attempts directly to address the question of the relationship of the Oxford *syllabi* to the tenets of the Church of England as expressed in the Articles.

21. For the 'Phalanx', named after the part of London in which some of its members lived, see Corsi, *Science and Religion*, ch. 1.

22. J. H. Newman, *Lectures on the Prophetical Office of the Church* (1837), 30.

23. H. C. G. Matthew, *Gladstone 1809–1874* (1986), 18.

24. See 'Preface' and 'Introduction' to R. Whately (ed.), *Remains of the Late Edward Copleston D.D.* (1854).
25. *Letters on the Church. By an Episcopalian* (1826), 7. Though Whately never avowed authorship of the pamphlet, there seems little reason to doubt that he wrote it; see Corsi, *Science and Religion*, 86ff.
26. *Letters on the Church*, 44.
27. William Warburton, 1698–1779, bishop of Gloucester, defended the Whiggish eighteenth-century church settlement.
28. *Letters on the Church*, 157.
29. *Miscellaneous Remains from the Commonplace Book of Richard Whately, D.D. . . . edited by Miss E. J. Whately* (1864), 64.
30. Ibid.
31. See also Brent, *Liberal Anglican Politics*, 146ff.
32. Hurrell Froude's *Tract 59*, 'The Position of the Church of Christ in England, relatively to the state and the nation' (1835) anonymously assessed 'the *gains* and *losses*' from 'STATE PROTECTION and STATE INTERFERENCE'.
33. R. D. Hampden, *The Scholastic Philosophy considered in its relation to Christian Theology in a course of lectures* (1832).
34. Ibid. 3rd edn (1848), liii; Joseph Butler, *The Analogy of Religion Natural and Revealed, to the Constitution and Course of Nature* (1736).
35. R. D. Hampden, *Observations on Religious Dissent* (1834), 42.
36. Ibid. 41.
37. Ibid. 34–5.
38. Ibid. 36.
39. Ibid. 39.
40. Ibid. 39.
41. Though the Tractarians together with the High Churchmen led the attack, Evangelical support was an important ingredient of their support in the 1830s; ironically, Pusey's accession to the team of Tract writers made this alliance much more difficult, since his long Tracts, really different in kind from Newman' s earlier *ballons*, exasperated the Evangelicals by their comments on baptism and the eucharist. Newman's *Tract XC* (1841) was denounced by both High Churchmen and Evangelicals and the alliance of 1834–6 was by the early 1840s, if not useless, at least unreliable; see P. Toon, *Evangelical theology, 1833–1856. A Response to Tractarianism* (1979), ch. 2, and J. S. Reynolds, *The Evangelicals at Oxford 1735–1875* (2nd ed. 1975), ch. 6.
42. Owen Chadwick, *The Victorian Church* (1971), i. 119.
43. For Pusey's hostility to liberal scholarship ('the scepticism as to Homer ushered in the scepticism on the Old Testament'), see H. C. G. Matthew, 'Edward Bouverie Pusey: from Scholar to Tractarian', *Journal of Theological Studies*, xxxii (April 1981), 122.
44. [T. Arnold], 'The Oxford Malignants and Dr. Hampden', *Edinburgh Review*, lxiii (April 1836), 225–39.
45. Arnold, *Introductory Lectures*, 51.

46. Ibid. 52.
47. [T. Arnold], 'The Church of England', *Edinburgh Review*, xliv (September 1826), 490–513.
48. Arnold, *Introductory Lectures*, 39.
49. Thomas Arnold, *Principles of Church Reform*, ed. M. J. Jackson and J. Rogan (1962), 113; first published in 1833. Arnold argued that with suitable flexibility on the part of the Church of England, and a change in tone, especially towards Roman Catholics, even these denominations could be brought within the fold of the national church.
50. [Hawkins], *Letter ... by a Graduate*, 23.
51. [Hawkins], *Letter to Radnor*, 24.
52. [E. B. Pusey], *Questions respectively addressed to Members of Convocation on the subjoined Declaration* ... [1835], 2; [E. Hawkins], *Oxford Matriculation Statutes. Answers to the 'Questions Addressed to Members of Convocation'* (1835), 3.
53. Ward, *Victorian Oxford*, 97.
54. [Hawkins], *Letter to Radnor*, 23.
55. Ibid. 6.
56. Newman, *Apologia*, 102.
57. J. H. Newman, *The Arians of the Fourth Century, their Doctrine, Temper and Conduct* ... (1833).
58. At the 1983 Patristics Conference in Oxford, proceedings to be published; *audivi*; and Newman, *Arians*, 82.
59. Newman, *Apologia*, 119.
60. Ibid. 98. This is not quite the same as Leslie Stephen's view that Newman was fundamentally if unintentionally sceptical in his method of argument; see L. Stephen, 'Cardinal Newman's scepticism', *Nineteenth Century*, xxix. (February 1891) 179.
61. Ibid. 105. Under the influence of Whately, Newman believed, 'I was beginning to prefer intellectual excellence to moral; I was drifting in the direction of liberalism'.
62. Newman to Perceval, 11 Jan. 1836, quoted in H. P. Liddon, *Life of Edward Bouverie Pusey* (1893), i. 301; For the Tractarian idea that obedience, discipline, and habit are vital to the acquisition of spiritual knowledge (i.e. Newman's view given in a less authoritarian tone) see Y. Brilioth, *The Anglican Revival: studies in the Oxford movement* (1925), 237–9.
63. 'To propose a secular end for the acquisition of the knowledge of God, is to degrade God. Such study must either become trivial, or it would end in hardening the heart and in unbelief ... the new School of Theology would become a school of indifferentism to the truth'; E. B. Pusey, *Summary of Objections against the proposed Theological Statute* (1854), 8, 12.
64. Liddon, *Pusey*, i. 332ff.
65. This system did not at that time encourage the free and sometimes speculative discussion which would today be regarded as its characteris-

tic, for college teaching at that time was normally in classes, working from a text not an essay, and catechetical in character. Undergraduates might have an occasional one-to-one meeting with a college tutor, but individual instruction was carried out by the private coaches who lived in or about Oxford. These coaches, who were not formally part of the college or university teaching staff, were often more academically distinguished than their official counterparts and often wrote books on academic subjects.

66. *Report and evidence upon the recommendations of Her Majesty's Commissioners for inquiring into the state of the University of Oxford, presented to the Board of Heads of Houses and Proctors December 1, 1853* (1853). See pp. 1–173 for Pusey's 'Evidence'.

67. *Report and Evidence* (1853), 231.

68. Richard Hooker, *Treatise on the Laws of Ecclesiastical Polity*, published in eight volumes in various forms between 1594 and 1662; John Keble's edition of Hooker's *Works* (3 vols. 1836) did much to anchor the Tractarians to the Church of England.

69. Corsi, *Baden Powell*, Part III.

70. 'we have, if I may so speak, the ancient world still existing, but with a new element added, the element of the English race. And that this element is an important one, cannot be doubted for an instant. Our English race is the German race; for though our Norman fathers had learnt to speak a stranger's language, yet in blood, as we know, they were the Saxons' brethren; both alike belong to the Teutonic or German stock'; Arnold, *Introductory Lectures*, 26.

71. James Barr, 'Jowett and the reading of the Bible "like any other book" ', *Horizons in Biblical Theology* (June 1983), iv. 1–45; see also P. Hinchliff, *Benjamin Jowett and the Christian Religion* (1987), ch. 6. Jowett's contribution to *Essays and Reviews* (1860), 'On the interpretation of Scripture', while it recognized that 'the diffusion of a critical spirit in history and literature is affecting the criticism of the Bible in our own day in a manner not unlike the burst of intellectual life in the fifteenth or sixteenth century', was in fact hostile to critical and historical theory: 'No other science of Hermeneutics is possible but an inductive one, that is to say, one based on the language and thoughts and narrations of the sacred writers . . . Excessive system tends to create an impression that the meaning of Scripture is out of our reach . . . The method creates itself as we go on, beginning only with a few reflections directed against plain errors . . . such reflections are the rules of common sense . . .'

72. Forbes, *Liberal Anglican Idea*, 108.

73. [Hawkins], *Letter to Radnor*, 26.

74. M. Pattison, *Memoirs* (1885), 212.

75. Newman, *Apologia*, 251.

76. [Hawkins], *Letter to Radnor*, 17.

77. Ward, *Victorian Oxford*, ch. 7.

78. Passages from W. G. Ward's *Ideal of a Christian Church* were condemned by 777 to 386 votes, and Ward's degradation was carried by 569 to 511 votes; Ward, *Victorian Oxford*, 122.

79. Ward, *Victorian Oxford*, ch. 8 and *Report of Her Majesty's Commissioners appointed to inquire into the state, discipline, studies and revenues of the University and Colleges of Oxford, Parliamentary Papers* (1852), xxii (the Cambridge report is in *P.P.* (1852–3), xliv).

80. See Matthew, *Gladstone*, 83ff. and E. G. W. Bill, *University reform in nineteenth-century Oxford* (1973), 150ff.

81. See D. Newsome, 'Finale: Godliness and Manliness' in *Godliness and Good Learning* (1961). Thomas Hughes, *Tom Brown's Schooldays* (1857) marked, Newsome argues, the emergence of the new trend in its perversion of the Arnoldian ideal: 'when Arnold exhorted his boys to be manly, he meant that they were to put away childish things; but when Hughes portrayed Tom Brown as the paragon of manliness, he was expressing his admiration for the sort of boy "who's got nothing odd about him, and answers straightforward, and holds his head up ... frank, hearty and good natured ... chock-full of life and spirits" '; ibid. 197–8. The term 'muscular Christianity' dates from the 1850s; ibid. 198.

82. See Ellis, *Seven Against Christ*, 200ff, which gives an excellent account of the controversy and the prosecutions; legal action was taken against H. B. Wilson and R. Williams (the verdict of deprivation being set aside by the Judicial Committee of the Privy Council); Pattison, Temple, and Jowett could not be prosecuted being unbeneficed.

83. W. R. Ward, 'Oxford and the origins of Liberal Catholicism in the Church of England', *Studies in Church History*, i. 233–54 (1964).

Conference Reports

The comparative history of the foundation of universities in Europe and in Arab countries: Baghdad, 20–7 March 1989.

This very ambitious conference was organized jointly by the Paris-based Euro-Arab Summer (now renamed Itinerant) University and the Universities of Baghdad and al-Mustanṣiriyya to mark the completion of the restoration of the *medersa al-Mustanṣiriyya*, the school built beside the Tigris in Baghdad by the 'Abbāsid caliph al-Mustanṣir bi'llāh in 1234. The formal reopening of these most beautiful buildings was marked with considerable ceremony and extended hospitality. The conference, which was run with notable efficiency and punctuality, was attended by scholars from Spain, France, Britain, West Germany, Poland, Sweden, Italy, the United States, Morocco, Tunisia, Egypt, Iraq, Bahrain, and the United Arab Emirates.

Although the concept of 'dialogue' was much favoured at the conference, it was not in fact very evident in its proceedings. In particular the differences of approach between historians and non-historians and between Europeans and Arabs were so profound that constructive exchange was very difficult. Mutual understanding was the more difficult because, although the full texts of papers were not circulated in advance as planned, the tight schedule of the sessions allowed speakers only twenty minutes to summarize their contributions. Many therefore spoke at great speed, placing a heavy burden on the interpreters providing simultaneous translation into Arabic/French/English. Furthermore the time allowed for discussion at the end of each session was invariably taken up by lengthy statements largely unrelated to any historical issue raised by the preceding papers.

In a particularly compressed opening session various archaeologists discussed education in ancient Mesopotamia, reflecting the strong belief of Iraqis in a continuity between ancient and Islamic civilization in Iraq. Other sessions considered both early Islamic education (with an especially interesting description of 'teaching circles') and also the schools attached to individual mosques, notably al-Qarawiyyūn in Fez, al-Zaytūna in Tunis and al-Azhar in Cairo; the *medersa al-Mustanṣiriyya* itself, which was not attached to a mosque, was of course also discussed in detail. A Soviet scholar from Tajikistan was however unable to be present to deliver his paper on the influential schools of Bukhara. Many medieval European universities, from Coimbra to Uppsala, were described, with particular emphasis on the importance of Greek learning received via the Islamic world and of Arabic science and philosophy; some speakers also considered the development of oriental studies in European universities into modern times. The problems facing the newly established universities of the Gulf states were also frankly analysed. There were in addition several papers of a more general and non-historical nature. For the most part too much attention was given to the relative antiquity of various institutions and not enough to a real comparison of their nature and their social role. While the intellectual debt of the medieval west to the Islamic world was underlined, the institutional influence of Islamic schools on European universities was sometimes vigorously asserted but never substantiated. A fundamental difference to emerge between the interests of Europeans and Arabs was that among Arab scholars intellectual and educational questions appeared to be essentially a subject for literary rather than historical study; in particular there seemed to be no interest in the social history of education. It is to be hoped however that the great range of material presented in this conference will broaden the outlook of both Europeans and Arabs interested in the development of higher education, and will improve the prospect of a true dialogue in the future.

Ralph Evans
History of the University of Oxford
Clarendon Building, Bodleian Library
Oxford OX1 3BG

Practitioners and Medical Practice in the Latin Mediterranean, 1100–1350: Barcelona, 11–15 April 1989.

The Institució Milà i Fontanals, Conseil Superior d'Investigacions Cientifiques, Barcelona, together with the Wellcome Unit for the History of Medicine, Cambridge, arranged this most stimulating conference as an extended and intensive small-scale workshop, consisting almost entirely of the speakers. Although the title of the event suggested an emphasis on the practice rather than the theory of medicine, the relationship between the two was a natural focus for many speakers. Papers of direct relevance to the history of universities included Jole Agrimi and Chiara Crisciani, 'The epistemology of practical medicine in the *Cirurgia* and in the *Summa* of Guglielmo da Saliceto', Jon Arrizabalaga, 'University medical practitioners faced with the Black Death (1348) in Latin Mediterranean Europe: perceptions and reactions', Peter Denley, 'Sociological aspects of the medieval medical student and of his training in Italian universities', Danielle Jacquart, 'Medical practice at Paris in the first half of the fourteenth century',

Piero Morpurgo, '*Practici versus theorici.* La Polemica tra Gerardo da Cremona e i maestri salernitani', Cornelius O'Boyle, 'Relations between physicians and surgeons in Paris during the fourteenth century', Joseph Shatzmiller, 'Etudiants juifs à l'Université de Montpellier: 1348–1394', and Nancy Siraisi, 'How to write a Latin book on surgery: organizing principles and authorial devices in Guglielmo da Saliceto and Dino del Garbo'. Neither this list nor the complete programme does justice to the achievements of the conference. The extensive discussion of each paper threw up many interconnections and recurrent themes, and university historians will benefit from the whole range of the papers given when they are published in revised form.

Peter Denley
Queen Mary and Westfield College
University of London
Hampstead Campus
London NW3 7ST

The Shape of Knowledge from the Middle Ages to the Enlightenment: The Warburg Institute, London, 16–17 June 1989.

The colloquium on 'The Shape of Knowledge', held at the Warburg Institute in June, was in many ways a posthumous tribute to the innovative scholarship of Charles Schmitt who had, before his death, conceived the idea of a conference on the classification of the sciences. The moving spirits were Richard Popkin, Donald Kelly, and Constance Blackwell, who, with the active assistance of J. B. Trapp, brought the project to fruition. A mere taxonomy of the compartments of learning might on the face of it seem an academic subject of more than usually narrow appeal. But understanding the constitution of knowledge at any given time entails more than the history of philosophical sects and doctrines, since it is crucially connected with the history of education, with the processes for acquiring and transmitting knowledge, and with the interrelationship between the branches of learning. Thus the division of the sciences is central to an understanding of the intellectual past.

The conference was almost encyclopaedic in the range of topics covered, ranging as it did from the Italian school curriculum of the fourteenth and fifteenth centuries (Robert Black) to sixteenth-century logic (Luce Giard) and to Christina, bluestocking queen of Sweden (Susanna Akermann). It included a paper on Islam and the classification of knowledge (Robert Jones) and extended to eighteenth-century Hebrew studies (David Katz). The very breadth of subject matter and time was itself a challenge to the narrowness of modern disciplines and fragmentation of modern scholarly expertise. The scope of the conference represented an attempt to capture the unity of knowledge in the period leading up to the enlightenment. By providing a daily summing up together with an open discussion at the end, the organizers sought to interlink the particular specialisms of each day's contributions. None the less, particularity was a feature of the conference; every paper was concerned in some way with the factors shaping the intellectual past, be they institutional (Peter Denley on university institutions in medieval Italy), curricular (Richard Blum on the German Catholic university curriculum), or other areas' periodicals (Thomas F. Wright on seventeenth- and eighteenth-century libraries) or the impact of new ideas and methodologies (Michael Hunter on the early Royal Society, Lynn Joy on Gassendi and Diderot). Several papers were concerned to fill out the shape of learning in the past by discussing topics now excluded from or altered by modern categories of learning: 'Forgotten ways of knowing', the title of Alison Coudert's paper on F. M. van Helmont and seventeenth-century cabbalism, might equally well have served as a title to Brian Copenhaver's paper on magic and the philosophers of the seventeenth century, or Grazia Tonelli's on the Faculties of the soul in Galen and Bacon. Penelope Gouk's paper underlined the relevance of music to the history of seventeenth-century philosophy and science, a relevance deriving from the place of music on the arts curriculum.

A small minority of papers were devoted to the interrelationship of the disciplines. Of these, Charles Lohr's and Donald Kelley's demonstrated outstandingly the importance of schemes of classification as a determinant of the constitution of knowledge. Charles Lohr's paper, 'The Transformation of the Aristotelian Division of the Speculative Sciences', was primarily concerned with Jesuit teaching of the 'queen of sciences', metaphysics. His paper discussed the establishment of metaphysics as an independent science as a result of the reformation of the entire philosophical curriculum of sixteenth-century Spanish universities with the transfer of metaphysics from the theological to the arts curriculum and the abandonment of the Aristotelian aporetic framework in favour of a more loosely Aristotelian synthesis exemplified by Suarez. Donald Kelley's paper, 'History and the Encyclopaedia', was concerned with the evolution of history as a mode of thought, with the historicization of the classification of knowledge by which the static model adopted by the early humanists was transformed into the dynamic conception of an advancement of learning by later encyclopaedists. Not only did history become more prominent as one of the *studia humanitatis*, but also did its importance in defining other fields of study within the total perspective of the encyclopaedia. As a paper which explored and explained the genesis of intellectual history as a discipline, it was the key paper in a conference concerned to map the intellectual past.

The conference concluded open-endedly, discursively rather than dogmatically. This was perhaps inevitable, in view of its range. While there could have been a little more sharpening of focus by the speakers on the interrelationship of the various subject areas, it was, I think, important that the colloquium did not produce a grand schema pre-emptive of future research in the area. The conference could perhaps be described as a set of preliminary enquiries marking out directions for studying the subdivisions of knowledge in the past. The shape of knowledge outlined by the conference was that of an archaeological trench dug to determine the nature and extent of the field for future investigation.

Sarah Hutton
The Hatfield Polytechnic

The Second Biennial Conference of Historians of the Universities of the Low Countries and the British Isles: St Anne's College, Oxford, 15–17 September 1989.

Participants from Belgium, The Netherlands, Ireland, and the United Kingdom assembled for this second conference. Andrew Hope from Oxford presented a paper on William Tyndale, emphasizing how this cautious reformer was first saved by the reluctance of the Antwerp magistrates to act decisively against him before falling victim to a kidnapping plot, probably organized by an alliance of conservative English bishops with their Louvain counterparts. Dr Broeyer of Utrecht outlined the theological position of William Whitaker, whom he described as an 'Anglo-Calvinist'. Dr Upton of Birmingham presented some details of links between Scottish students and the Netherlands, showing how influential was the role of the English and Scottish staple ports in the Low Countries. For Prof. Ridder-Symoens of Amsterdam and Ghent the university of Douai has for too long been seen simply as a centre of training for English Catholic priests and should rather be viewed as an academic centre similar to other contemporary universities. Dr Robinson-Hammerstein, herself from Trinity College, Dublin, examined the careers of the early Provosts of the college, showing a conflict between the declared regional aims of the foundation and its international connections as an academic centre. The spread of Dutch legal books into Scotland was discussed by Dr Osler of Frankfurt, who brought the early results of his computer analysis of a number of library collections. Mr Colpaert of St Niklaas gave a fascinating glimpse of the life and work of Abbé Mann, the English secretary of the Theresian Academy of Brussels at the outbreak of the French Revolution. The little-known world of nineteenth-century Dutch universities was investigated by Dr Roelevink of the Hague with interesting comparisons with the position in Belgium and England. Finally, Dr

Otterspeer of Leiden gave a witty analysis of the Dutch attempts to act as honest broker between the victorious powers and the defeated central powers in the international learned societies of the post-World War I period. The conference provided stimulating discussion and valuable social contact between participants. It was agreed that the third meeting would be held in The Netherlands in 1991. Contributions to the second conference will be published. Details of future activities and of the published proceedings of the first conference can be obtained from the British organizer, Dr John M. Fletcher, Department of Modern Languages, Aston University, Aston Triangle, Birmingham B4 7ET.

John M. Fletcher

The Vocabulary of Schools and of Methods of Teaching in the Middle Ages: Rome, 20–1 October 1989.

This short conference, organized by the International Committee for the Study of the Vocabulary of Institutions for Intellectual Communication in the Middle Ages, in association with the Ecole Française de Rome and the Department of Philosophy of the University of Rome 1 — La Sapienza — was especially concerned with pre-university education and with institutions later only loosely connected with the universities. There were, however, a few papers of interest to specialists studying the history of universities. Danielle Jacquart of Paris discussed concepts of *theorica* and *practica* amongst medical teachers in twelfth-century Salerno and Victor Crescenzi examined the vocabulary used by the glossators of legal books in Bologna. Alfonso Maierù of Rome took a critical look at the use of the words '*facultas*' and '*verificare*' amongst physicians and artists at Bologna. He was especially sceptical of any attempt to attach any administrative meaning to the concept of '*facultas*'; during discussion it was pointed out that the word did, however, refer to important administrative structures in the later German and Scottish universities. Antonio García y García from Salamanca discussed regulations for schools in the Spanish peninsula and Jacques Verger of Paris attempted to isolate new and traditional usages in the wording of the early statutes and privileges of the French universities.

It is expected that the proceedings of the conference will be published. Any enquiries may be directed to Dr Olga Weijers, Royal Library, Prins Willem Alexanderhof 5, 2595 BE Den Haag, Netherlands.

John M. Fletcher
Department of Modern Languages
Aston University
Birmingham B4 7ET

Colloque historique pour le VIIe Centenaire de l'Université de Montpellier, 1289–1989: Montpellier, Faculté de Médecine, 23–4 October 1989.

The University of Montpellier is one of a handful of universities which dates from the twelfth century and whose official foundation occurred some considerable time after it had become a centre of higher learning. It was only in 1289 that the university was given papal recognition through the bull of Nicolas IV, although the faculties of law and medicine had been flourishing for over a century. For the lack of any other alternative date of foundation, however, 1289 has been generally taken to be the moment of the university's inception. The year of the bicentenary of the French Revolution was therefore also the year of the university's seven-hundreth anniversary. While the rest of France gorged itself on revolutionary memorabilia, the *Fédération historique du Languedoc Méditeranéen et du Roussillon* sensibly decided to commemorate a rather older event. The colloquium devoted to the history of the university was part of a week-long celebration of the foundation of the *studium generale* which included concerts and an ecumenical service in the cathedral.

The first day of the colloquium was primarily dedicated to evoking the history of the original university, closed, like its sister institutions in France, in September 1793 by the Convention. Although due obeisance was made to the more colourful episodes and individuals in Montpellier's medieval and early-modern past, the most interesting papers were given by Jacques Verger and Dominique Julia which placed the university in a wider national and European context. Both papers showed that until 1700 at any rate, Montpellier was a peculiarly vibrant French university for a provincial institution, drawing students from all over Europe through the significance of its medical faculty and its ecumenical spirit. It was only in the eighteenth century that it became barely distinguishable from the other twenty or so French provincial universities, except for the fact that its medical faculty was much larger than elsewhere.

Since 1793 the history of the University of Montpellier has been extremely complicated. Napoleon preferred professional schools to traditional universities, so when institutions of higher education were restored in the first decade of the nineteenth century, Montpellier eventually became the home of separate schools and faculties of medicine, pharmacy, law, science and letters, grouped together under an umbrella institution, the Montpellier academy. Under the Third Republic an attempt was made to resurrect the old university by grouping the faculties together once more, but in recent decades the great expansion in student numbers has encouraged the creation of subject-universities. Today the Montpellier academy has four universities under its administrative wing, one based at Perpignan and one especially devoted to the arts, letters and the human sciences, Montpellier III or the *Université Paul Valéry*.

It was to the history of the different institutions contained within the Montpellier academy that the second day's proceedings were dedicated. To an English observer, unaccustomed to the concept of a subject-university with its mass clientele, virtually every paper was both illuminating and fascinating. The key paper in the morning session was given by Gerard Cholvy on the faculty of letters from its foundation in 1808 until the present day. Initially (and here the faculty was no different from the others established by Napoleon outside Paris), the curriculum was extremely narrow. In the mid-nineteenth century courses were only given in philosophy, history, and Latin, French and Greek literature. Geography was taught from 1868 and Arabic in the 1880s, but it was the 1950s before any modern European languages were taught apart from Romance tongues. Numbers, too, were initially small; as late as 1894 there were only 171 students. The 1950s however saw a dramatic expansion and by the 1960s numbers had reached 7000. The creation of a separate humanities university becomes understandable, all the more that today the faculty of letters at Paul Valéry offers twenty-three different degree courses.

In the afternoon Jacques Mirouze offered a similarly sweeping study of the development of the faculty of medicine since its inception in 1803. Most participants during the second day, however, were understandably content to look at the work of particular individuals. Of particular interest for a historian of universities was Louis Secondy's paper devoted to the late nineteenth-century dean of the faculty of letters, Alexandre Germain. Generally remembered for his painstaking studies of the original university of Montpellier, it was interesting to hear that Germain was an important figure in the movement to develop the study of geography as a means to encouraging patriotic fervour under the Third Republic. Two other papers which I found especially striking were those given by Roland Andréani and Didier Mehu. Andréani's paper concerned Ferdinand Castets, a late nineteenth-century professor of modern European literature who knew no foreign languages except Italian. Otherwise uninspiring, his claim to fame lay in the way he used his university position to become a local politician and thereby anticipated a common twentieth-century development (Montpellier, it seems, is habitually governed by academics). Mehu's paper concerned a far more important figure, the ecclesiastical historian, Augustin Fliche, who taught at Montpellier from 1919 until his death in 1951. An indefatigable supporter of local history through his presidency of the *Fédération historique de Languedoc Méditerranéen et du Roussillon* and an historian with an international reputation, he remains today an ambivalent figure because of his *Pétainiste* sympathies and his association with the Vichy government.

Many of the audience had personal recollections of the developments and individuals discussed on the second day, so discussions at the end of the paper tended to be anecdotal. This, however, should not detract from the papers themselves. I was continually struck by the amount of research which had gone into particular contributions delivered by members of the Montpellier universities, not always historians and never normally working on university history. The *Fédération historique* did its best to cover every aspect of the post-1800 university's life. The only area about which little information was provided in the course of the colloquium was on research in the natural sciences, although a final paper by Michel Lacave looked at the work done at Montpellier since the 1960s. This omission was somewhat unfortunate given the fact that the faculty of science at Montpellier, at least before 1850, had a research reputation completely at variance with that of the other moribund science faculties in nineteenth-century France. It would have been useful, then, if there had been some discussion of Montpellier's contribution to the natural sciences over the last two centuries, and some attempt to analyse why there was so little research in the French faculties compared with the achievements of their German counterparts.

This, though, is to end on an unnecessarily negative note. Although to those used to the English university tradition the Academy of Montpellier may seem a peculiar animal, the institutions within its umbrella clearly inspire the same affection and loyalty as their Anglo-Saxon counterparts. There is a definite interest in the Academy in studying its history even if there is no grand project of the kind promoted at many American and British universities. As the proceedings of the colloquium will be published, the fruits of this research will eventually be available to university historians everywhere. Those wanting further information about the colloquium should contact Professor G. Cholvy at the *Fédération historique, Archives départementales de l'Hérault*, B.P. 1266, 34011 Montpellier cedex.

L. W. B. Brockliss
Magdalen College
Oxford OX1 4AU

Essay Review

Between Harvard and the Past

Phyllis Keller, *Getting at the Core: Curricular Reform at Harvard.*
Cambridge, Mass.: Harvard University Press, 1982. xi + 201 pp.

Derek Bok, *Beyond the Ivory Tower: Social Responsibilities of the
Modern University.* Cambridge, Mass.: Harvard University Press,
1982. 318 pp.

Derek Bok, *Higher Learning.* Cambridge, Mass.: Harvard University Press, 1986. 206 pp.

Why was it that when it came time for the oldest university in the United
States to celebrate its 350th birthday its president wrote a general book on
university education, *Higher Learning* (Cambridge, Mass., 1986) and Harvard University republished a charming collection of reminiscences, *The
Harvard Book* (Cambridge, Mass., 1986)?[1] During his presidency, A. L.
Lowell compared Harvard with Oxford and Cambridge. One point of
comparison is immediately obvious—Oxford has an impressive university
history project: Harvard does not. Of course it has had its great historian in
Samuel Eliot Morison. His four-volume history began with an important
collection of essays on the history of various departments of Harvard
College, *The Development of Harvard University since the inauguration of
President Eliot, 1869–1929* (Cambridge, Mass., 1930), and was followed by
The Founding of Harvard College (Cambridge, Mass., 1935), *Harvard
College in the Seventeenth Century* (Cambridge, Mass., 1936) and his survey:
Three Centuries of Harvard 1636–1936 (Cambridge, Mass., 1936). Despite
this impressive scholarship, Harvard still has no in-depth university history
for the years 1700–1869 and 1930–1980. Indeed Derek Bok seems to imply
in a revealing footnote that a history of the academic disciplines at Harvard
entails a mastery of complexities beyond the ability of one scholar's mind
and he voices no hope that any joint venture might be undertaken in the
future.[2]

It is true that Harvard has found historians since 1936. Three books have
been written on the influence of religion and moral philosophy: W. Smith's
Professors and Public Ethics, Studies of Northern Moral Philosophers before

the Civil War (Ithaca, 1956), D. W. Howe's *The Unitarian Conscience: Harvard and Moral Philosophy 1805–1861* (Cambridge, Mass., 1970), and Norman Fiering's *Moral Philosophy at Seventeenth Century Harvard* (Chapel Hill, 1981). For the history of science in the nineteenth century there is A. H. Dupree's *Asa Gray* (Cambridge, Mass., 1959) and I. Bernard Cohen's *Some Early Tools of American Science* (Cambridge, Mass., 1950). Nineteenth-century social history has been recently studied by Ronald Story, *The Forging of an Aristocracy* (Middletown, 1980) and mid-twentieth century social history by Enrique H. Lopez, *The Harvard mystique* (New York, 1979) while the continental intellectual background of Harvard teachers and students has been told by C. Diehl in *American and German Scholarship 1776–1870* (New Haven, 1978). The only systematic histories of the rise of university disciplines are Bruce Kuklick's *The Rise of American Philosophy* (Cambridge, Mass., 1977) and Paul Buck's *Social Sciences at Harvard 1860–1920* (Cambridge, Mass., 1965). There have also been three histories of Graduate Schools: *The Harvard Divinity School* (Boston, 1954) ed. by G. H. Williams, H. K. Beecher's *Medicine at Harvard* (Hanover, N. H., 1977) and *The Uncertain Profession* by A. G. Powell (Cambridge, Mass., 1980) a history of the School of Education. The book which presents the best recent overview of the university is Bainbridge Bunting's *Harvard, an architectural history* (New York, 1985). For Harvard's own self-image two histories have been key works: Hugh Hawkins *Between Harvard and American: The Educational Leadership of Charles W. Eliot* (New York, 1972) and Seymour M. Lipset and David Riesman's social history: *Education and Politics at Harvard* (New York, 1975). Harvard has not been without its books of nostalgia with *College in a Yard: Minutes by Thirty-nine Harvard Men,* ed. Brooks Atkinson (Cambridge, Mass., 1957) and *Our Harvard: reflections on college life by twenty-two distinguished graduates* (New York, 1982). All this writing has been on an ad hoc basis; only Bunting attempts any integration of material and here it is done only in the footnote references.

But what Harvard has had were Presidents who wrote about Harvard history and about education at Harvard and in the United States. A genre of apologetic literature has developed which grew up around the Presidential inaugural address—an address which took as its theme an examination of the past which was then used to interpret the present. In the nineteenth century these were published along with other speeches given at the inauguration of the President. By the time of Lowell the speech was published later in a collection of essays. While Conant's speech was not, he published several collections of lectures which served a similar purpose. Pusey returned to Lowell's formula of publishing his speeches as a collection. Of the three recent books about Harvard: Derek Bok's, *Beyond the Ivory Tower* (Cambridge, Mass., 1982) is gathered from a series of speeches and reworked to provide a coherent view and his *Higher Learning* (Cambridge, Mass., 1986) was written as a book, while Phyllis Keller's *Getting at the Core* (Cambridge, Mass., 1982) presents the debate behind the recent Harvard curriculum review and reorganization. Like other in-house publications, these books are at times panegyric and are not the matter of university history.[3] But they should not be dismissed out of hand, for not only do they tell us what Harvard wants us to know about itself, but in this case, they inadvertently reveal what has been thought about the topic of university history and its relationship to university curriculum—a not inconsiderable topic.

Derek Bok opens his book *Higher Learning* with a story about himself. Some months before his inauguration as President, he was told by an adviser that his most 'creative ideas about the future of Harvard' would come before he took office. In true Harvard style he reviewed the actions of his predecessors: Eliot, Lowell, and Conant. He notes Eliot spent the summer writing his inaugural address, Lowell taught and Conant went to Europe looking for new ideas. Bok rejects all three, the last somewhat to his own surprise—for Bok, a former Fulbright scholar, initially puzzled that he felt such a journey would not bring him the new ideas he needed. Here Bok was indirectly not only rejecting Conant's model but the model of all Harvard presidents since, at least for the purpose of this essay review, Josiah Quincy. He declares Harvard's independence from Europe, not because he perceives that the division of knowledge at Harvard is different from those in European universities, but because he sees the American university operating in an entirely different social structure. He gives three distinct reasons: 1) the relationship between the university and the government grants freedom from government control, 2) there is competition between universities which creates a different relationship among universities, and 3) the response American universities must have to their students—all these made the internal structure of the institutions radically different from European ones. The idea that universities in the United States are unique is hardly a new idea, but that there is nothing to learn from Europe and the European university experience is.

Out of the eleven presidents preceding Bok seven, Josiah Quincy, Edward Everett, James Walker, Charles Eliot, A. Lawrence Lowell, James Conant and Nathan Pusey, were writers, and some left a considerable body of published material. A survey of their writings will underline how radical Bok's break is with past perspectives. Quincy, Everett, Walker, Eliot, Lowell, Conant and Pusey all spoke of Harvard as part of and a continuance of the European intellectual and university tradition. Quincy's major contributions are the first history of Harvard: *History of Harvard University* (Cambridge, Mass., 1840) and *Remarks on the Nature and Probable effects of Introducing the Voluntary System of the Study of Greek and Latin* (Cambridge, Mass., 1841). Quincy felt that Harvard was finally coming of age because 'science and learning as an independent interest of the community' was acknowledged. Harvard, for Quincy, as for most Harvard Presidents, was a great liberating force in Western society. According to his version of events, during the Dark Ages education had been controlled by the Catholic clergy who directed the mind to suit the purposes of the church to enforce its dogmas through 'threats of the terrors in the after life'. This was followed by the dogmatism of the Protestant reformation. For Quincy only now in the present age and in the U.S. was there some freedom.[4] If Harvard's liberal virtue made it superior to European universities, its academic quality did not. The problem of how to arrange the undergraduate curriculum to include new subjects was articulated by Quincy in *Remarks on the Nature and Probable effects of the Introduction of the Voluntary System of the Studies of Latin and Greek* (Cambridge, Mass., 1841). An administrator rather than a scholar, Quincy spoke of the problems the new multiplicity of topics made for the undergraduate curriculum. Beside Latin and Greek there was History, Natural History, Chemistry, Philosophy, Physics, Astronomy, Theology, Geography, Modern Languages, English Themes and Declamations as well as Modern Oriental Literature. Academic departments as we now know them did not yet exist. The problem for Quincy was practical; he had no theory of education or principle for organizing knowledge.

Edward Everett (1846–1849) was the first President to have studied in Germany and the first American to receive a Ph.D. there. In his inaugural address[5] he proposed the establishment of a philosophy and scientific faculty to build an institutional structure similar to the European model— he succeeded only in establishing the Lawrence Scientific Institute. Like Quincy he thought of Harvard as a catalyst for change and like Eliot, Conant and Bok, Everett had an interest in general problems of education giving speeches throughout the country.[6] More sensitive to educational questions than Quincy, he commented critically on the dilemma of the curriculum of Harvard College: 'They have so multiplied the list of academic studies, that, in the period of four years assigned to the collegiate course, three months is the aggregate of the time which would be given to any one branch if equal attention were paid to all, reckoning the two ancient languages as but one study and the modern languages as another'.[7] Less censorious of the middle ages than Quincy, the classicist Everett condemned the view that false logic of the Greek cultivated by the scholastics in the middle ages caused the decline of learning. He noted that the attainment of the teacher, Aristotle, should be judged by his pupil Alexander of Macedon— yet as a Protestant he could not admit that the Greek classical tradition had been preserved by the medieval Catholic universities. As he saw it the Greek Orthodox monks kept that tradition alive and it was brought to the west at the time of Constantinople. Everett's great 'liberal force' was what he called

the 'great affair of the mind'. Great minds were a democratic force and did
not depend on heredity. During the middle ages great men like Bede, Alcuin,
and Roger Bacon were able to rise despite the fact that only the elite were in
education and 'tyranny ruled'. Much is made of Everett's failure as a
personal leader because he insisted on trying to make Harvard College itself
a moral place, but the fact is that from his presidency the question ceased to
be whether, but when the undergraduate curriculum would be modified to
allow some specialization and when the university would have the vision
and money to develop Graduate Schools of Science and Philosophy.

Under James Walker (1853–1859) the movement toward a university
structure started again. For him the university was to create an environment
which would nurture the new professional men who should provide society
with its needed leaders. Like Everett, he saw the university as a source of
change, a 'liberal force' in society. When he made his survey of Western
thought, he followed its Protestant and liberal progress from Wycliff and
fourteenth-century Oxford, to Luther and Wittenberg and finally to Harvard and the American Revolution, each movement was one toward
freedom. Yet when he looked at the present he was troubled, there was
'intellectual anarchy' and a new authority was needed to replace the old.
While he complained that the older authority was without liberty and no
progress has been possible for either the educated or uneducated, he was
vague about the new one, saying only vaguely that it must come from
'leading minds' which would be properly focused when the training in the
professions was improved. Unlike Quincy and Everett he looked at the
medieval church schools as democratic institutions where the poor scholar
had been educated according to his merit; colleges in the United States he
thought should try to imitate this pattern.[8] If the middle ages was described
to suit current religious and historical prejudices and if its description did
not relate to facts, it should be remembered that medieval history was not
institutionalized as a subject at Harvard until Charles Haskins' appointment in 1902 despite some preliminary courses by Henry Adams.

In two important ways Walker broke with the past. First he described
knowledge as organized along departmental lines (a new notion at a time
when departments were just developing) which in turn led to his admission
that it was the university not the person which must be the embodiment of
liberal education, and secondly he was markedly less moralistic than his
predecessors. Harvard students were to be selected because of their intellectual competence, not 'moral distinction'. Harvard should not spend time on
the quarter of the students who had trouble adjusting. Both the institution
of Harvard University and the curriculum of Harvard College were at a very
elementary level in 1863, the presidents of Harvard still did know how to
describe Harvard, both Jered Sparks and Walker used the words 'university'
and 'college' interchangeably.

Charles Eliot's[9] inaugural address (1869) is currently taken as the point when Harvard emerged into the modern era and one president, Nathan Pusey, edited it.[10] The address was well received not because what it said was new but because it encapsulated much that the committee established by the Overseers of Harvard had recommended. Because the papers of Walker and Hall have not been collected and the history of nineteenth-century Harvard has not been studied in depth, the changes Eliot has been thought to have suggested have been exaggerated. He restated in an incisive way much which had been said before. That there was no antagonism between literature and science was first said by Quincy, that there should be changes in the method of teaching Latin and Greek by Hill, that there should be higher standards for entering students by Quincy, that individual students had individual talents by Everett and Walker. Even his plan for more electives was not as revolutionary as it has been made to appear. By the time he took office only the Freshman had a required curriculum and only half of the courses in the next three years were required. There were new themes: 1) that Harvard had become larger and more impersonal and would become more so with an elective course system; 2) there were great economic differences between scholarship students and wealthy students, and 3) that pay and academic standards of the teaching Faculties of the university were inadequate. The fact is that those academic departments which did exist were often manned by people who were incapable of doing scholarship.[11] The speech which would signal a new direction would have to wait until 1884.

The 1884 speech, 'What is a Liberal Education?'[12] delivered at Johns Hopkins, was a masterful use of history to supply precedents for his curriculum revolution. Attacking current notions of conservatives that there had been such a thing as a fixed liberal arts curriculum in historical perspectives, he noted that some basic core of university subjects were in fact relatively new additions. Greek was new during the time of Erasmus, analytical mathematics had replaced Euclid and experimental chemistry had recently fought a battle to be included. He then went on to attack the lack of English literature, French, German, history, Political Economy and Natural Science in the current college curriculum. Eliot's basic point was that the Western university curriculum had a history of change and the current changes he was proposing were part of that tradition.

Lowell,[13] like Conant after him, was a popular undergraduate teacher, lawyer by training and historian by vocation. He wrote five undergraduate textbooks on England and European government, each of which went through from five to eight printings.[14] Lowell's view of Harvard College's curriculum was governed by two separate experiences, first his membership on the committee in the Harvard history department where the under-graduate major, History and Literature, was first formulated in 1906—this served as Lowell's model for departmental majors after he became President—and second his study of the education of the civil service *Colonial Civil Service. The selection and training of Colonial officials in England,*

Holland and France (New York, 1900). Here the idea of a general education with a final examination which qualified candidates for professional training was born. Lowell was well prepared to reorganize the curriculum of Harvard College in 1909. He had been writing about the subject since his paper 'The Choice of Electives' 1887. His inaugural[15] address began by recounting the shift from a required curriculum early in the nineteenth century to a totally elective one under Eliot. Using Oxford as his model, he pointed out how it has been the custom to let undergraduates specialize in topics since 1807. His goal was the highest development of the individual and for this to happen he thought it was necessary to concentrate the energies of the undergraduate. Equally important to Lowell was competition among the students. He extolled these virtues in 1909 at Columbia University;[16] again in his speeches he exhorted students and audiences to appreciate quality of intellect, something he believed to be appreciated in Europe and not in the United States. He felt himself in the minority naming a collection of speeches, *At War with Academic Traditions in America*, saying: 'Throughout these papers the guiding idea was to inspire in university and college life a great desire and respect for scholarship . . . for in America these seemed to the writer far undervalued'.[17]

James Conant[18] became President of Harvard in 1933, but it was not until 1943 that he established the committee which was to produce *General Education in a Free Society, Report of the Harvard Committee* (Cambridge, Mass., 1945) commonly called the *Redbook*. This report was more ambitious than anything written before or since by a Harvard curriculum committee, it was not just about the education of Harvard but also about the reordering of secondary education in the United States. Its section on the Harvard curriculum began with a criticism of the concentration and distribution requirements which characterized the Lowell curriculum. This was seen to be weak in providing 'the development of a common body of information and ideas which would be in some measure the possession of all students'.[19] They believed that each student had to understand what each field of learning had in common with all others. As Conant explained it, if the scientist looked back on the development of science it is possible to suggest that its chronology might have been accidental, and that like history and the social sciences, science should be studied by examining the 'warrant for a belief'.[20] Out of sixteen courses in the undergraduate curriculum they assigned six to the general education curriculum, one was to be in the social sciences, one in the sciences, including history of science, and one in the humanities. It was not European institutions Conant wanted Harvard to learn from but European culture. European culture held the key to the progress of the liberal free world in its war against totalitarian Communism. The model humanities course was something called Great Texts of Literature which would include Homer, one or two Greek tragedies, Plato, the Bible, Dante, Shakespeare, Milton and Tolstoy. Literature courses should cross national boundaries. In the Social Sciences a model course was Western Thought and Institutions which would include Aquinas, Machiavelli, Luther, Locke, Montesquieu, Rousseau, Adam Smith, Jeremy Bentham, and John Stuart Mill. Science was to be made accessible to the non-scientist, the principles of the physical and biological sciences were to be taught, the students were to have made available the great literature in Science, and the history of Science was to be part of Science. Conant wrote extensively on the history of Science, publishing *On Understanding Science* (Cambridge, Mass., 1947, rep. 1952) and *Modern Science and Modern Man* (New York, 1952) and editing a college textbook on science, *Harvard Case Histories in Experimental Science* (Cambridge, Mass., 1948).[21] There were to be three more courses taken in the last two years of college. As the *Redbook* said, 'Unless the educational process includes at each level of maturity some continuing contact with those fields in which value judgements are of prime importance, it must fall far short of the ideal'.[22] True to the tone of the *Redbook* Conant himself devoted his energies to the improvement of public education in the nation and in raising the standard of teachers' education. America he saw in two ways, as the leader of the Western World in the battle of the Cold War, hence the centrality of Western-European civilization in the Harvard curriculum and secondly as a country which had a duty to supply quality education to the disadvantaged. Thus educational institutions had important roles to play in society, they were repositories of culture but they also could and should be used as agents of social change.[23]

When Derek Bok looked back on Harvard predecessors he might imitate, the summer before he assumed the Presidency of Harvard, Nathan Pusey was not one. From the political point of view this was understandable. Pusey had just completed an exhausting term as President, bearing the brunt of the SDS student revolt at Harvard.[24] Yet the two men held certain views in common. They both presided over a university not only of national but international stature, both thought that this was significant, and they observed that some of the most exciting and important educational and professional innovations were happening in the Graduate School of Harvard. Central for both was the continued growth of Harvard as an independent institution in the United States. Pusey in his essay 'Leadership and the American University',[25] an address given at Brown University in 1955, drew from George H. Williams' reconstruction of the sources for the theological conception of what constituted and motivated early Harvard. He delineated the history of the concept of divine sanctions on which the university was said to define itself as the guardian of the interior life of the 'Republic of Letters'. Harvard provided the link for the idea that there was a 'transfer of learning' between antiquity and the present day. Williams' reconstruction described how the university became an autonomous institution between the Church and the State and how it took on itself the tradition of 'translatio studii' from Athens to the middle ages and Paris, to Calvin in

Geneva and finally to Increase Mather at Harvard. When retelling this history Pusey admitted that language which spoke of the teacher as a prophet standing beside the king and priest was inappropriate to contemporary realities, but that keeping the university an independent entity was as necessary in 1955 as it ever had been. Pusey reflected on Williams' idealized history and noted how recently it has been—since the time of the Civil War—that the independence of Harvard had been recognized by the State. To maintain its independence in 1955, Pusey wrote that Harvard must free itself from the economic demands of the industrial complex and the idea that a university must pay its way. The correct goal of the university, he concluded, was the 'free and disinterested and lively play of the mind'. This was not the atmosphere at Harvard when Pusey resigned in 1970 amid problems not of his own making.

It was against the background of the student disruptions that the rejuvenation of the undergraduate curriculum was ordered by Derek Bok soon after he took office. *Getting at the Core* by Phyllis Keller is the official history of the debates leading up to the new Core curriculum adopted in 1979. It was written to appear in 1982 at the same time as Bok's *Beyond the Ivory Tower*. It is a modest book chronicling the principal debates but neither setting them within the context of the history of disciplines nor collecting the original papers so that the book can serve as a source for university history. Keller divides her discussion into four parts, an historical background of the 1970 curriculum crisis, the articulation of the problem, the debate over the Core curriculum and a description of the basic ingredients. Keller, a social historian, relies on Seymore Lipset's 'Political Controversies at Harvard 1639–1974' for much of her historical background. As a result her chapter, 'A Century of Change' describes the changes from a prescribed curriculum in Eliot's youth to his 1884 reforms as a journey from oppression to freedom. In Keller's eyes even Lowell turns into a progressive: his reforms, she says, were the result of applying early-twentieth-century progressivism to higher education. Lowell would not have recognized himself. On the other hand, she summarizes the objectives of the *Redbook* well, but is less clear why this curriculum failed. It would seem it was principally caused by students and faculty who wanted to study more specific topics in greater depth. She is better at characterizing the social changes which happened at Harvard in the '50s as a result of a recruitment policy which selected students throughout the United States on other than academic grounds. The result was students who were 'unevenly prepared for college work'. These students, it was felt, needed minimum standards in College education.

In 1973 a committee under Henry Rosovsky, Dean of the Faculty of Arts and Sciences, was formed. He gathered together a committee of five faculty members, two members of the administration and two students. As told in 'The Search for a Mandate', Rosovsky was a major figure articulating the problems students experienced at Harvard. These were: 1) undergraduate teaching had been devalued by specialist faculty; 2) economic resources had to be focused so the College had not gotten its correct share of money; 3) there had been a bewildering increase in the number of department and course committees; 4) various parts of the university were felt to be in conflict with each other; and 5) introductory courses were staffed by graduate students. After much consultation Rosovsky outlined what he thought should be the educational goals of Harvard students, they should: 1) be able to think and write clearly; 2) achieve depth in some field of knowledge; 3) have a critical appreciation of mathematical and scientific methods as well as main forms of historical and quantitative analysis; 4) be familiar with the scholarly, literary, and artistic achievements of the past; 5) major religious and philosophical concepts; and 6) not be provincial. The debate on how to incorporate these points into a coherent curriculum went on between 1975–1977. Five areas were designated for the Core: Letters and Arts, History,[26] Social and Philosophical Analysis,[27] Mathematics and Sciences,[28] Foreign Languages and Culture. Unfortunately the debates are not reported in detail. One telling comment is recounted which underlines how different the attitude of Harvard is today to what it was in the nineteenth century when it worked with high schools and other colleges to establish standards for university entry. Although it was admitted that the study of a foreign language was a good thing, current requirements were said not to give enough depth for the requirement to be meaningful. The argument that to abolish the language requirement would have disastrous effects on the high schools was met with this comment: Harvard was 'unwilling to assume that Harvard degree requirements should be determined by reference to the alleged effects its actions will have on 'school systems across the country'.[29]

In 1977 a central committee met to shape the programme and by 1978 it was ready with an outline which would serve as the focal point of the faculty debate. Keller summarizes some of the arguments, but unfortunately gives only snatches of what were no doubt rather detailed arguments. One of the most interesting comments quoted in favour of a Core curriculum came from O. E. Wilson, Professor of Biology, who stated his belief in the essential coherence of knowledge. He observed that the central concepts of science were 'continuously reforming in a way so as to increase in number much less rapidly'. Unfortunately we do not learn how this observation affected, if it did affect, the way the Science courses were set up. There is so much one would like to know. Why did the historians not like the Historical Study unit? Bok was impatient with the long process of discussion. Keller reports a comment that reforming the curriculum was like 'moving a cemetery'. The Core curriculum was a modest innovation compared with earlier efforts, it did not attempt to state what was to be known, or how it was to be known, but instead underlined areas of knowledge to be studied and acknowledged that analytical techniques, be they literary criticism or mathematical analysis, were common to all fields. Modes of thought rather than a body of knowledge were the unifying component. Fascinating as the individual topics for courses are, the impression remains that the arrangement of knowledge is fundamentally ahistorical—a dramatic change of emphasis from the Conant General Education formula. However, from what one gathers both from Bok's reports and evidence from the current catalogue, the Core is alive and popular. In the beginning year of the Core of the 84 approved courses, 53 were specially created, 24 were altered versions of existing courses and 7 were transplants from the General Education Program. By 1988–1989 there were over 160 courses and a new category, General Education Electives. It would be interesting to know if the methodological approach to knowledge has affected teaching in advanced level courses.

Derek Bok's *Beyond the Ivory Tower* is a book about Ethics and the concept of institutional neutrality. By choosing Ethics, Bok is taking up again a topic that university presidents in the early to mid-nineteenth century thought their own. It was also as, Smith, Howe and Fiering attest, a subject of major importance at Harvard from the seventeenth to the nineteenth century. After this time many of the issues covered in Ethics courses became subjects for the new Social Sciences. Bok summarizes the history of the evolution of Ethics and its relation to the emerging Social Sciences and points out that ethical issues ceased to be of interest as a topic because of the natural evolution in the fields of psychology, economics, and anthropology. Initially these fields evolved from philosophy and included Ethics among the topics discussed, but as each became more scientific in its methodology, normative values were discarded and Ethics ceased to be among the topics discussed. Even in the Philosophy departments Ethics shifted its study to the study of ethical language and away from application of ethical judgements in life.

Ethical concerns by Harvard Presidents were not new in the twentieth century. Lowell and Conant used ethical terminology when they exhorted students to study. Lowell entreated students to strive for academic excellence and implied that it was their moral duty to become academically superior. Conant had two concerns, the salvation of the free world from the twin dictatorships of Fascism and Communism and the raising of national academic standards from high school students to increase opportunities for everyone for higher education. For him, better education freed students from the risk of an interest in Fascism and Communism, while raising academic standards for minority students made the United States a more moral society. Such social ethical simplicities disappeared with the student riots of the late '60s and '70s. Increasingly students demanded that the university itself act ethically in society. To save Harvard from being pushed and pulled in various directions, Bok constructed a new historical myth, one based on a mixture of historical fact and personal reflexion which he lays out in a section on 'Basic Academic Values'. 'Academic Responses to Social Problems' in section two examines the correct ethical response to 'Radical Inequality and University Admissions', 'The Study of Ethics' itself and 'Ethics and Academic Science'. He concludes in section three with 'Addressing Social Problems by Nonacademic' means where he covers the 'University and the local community', 'Taking Political Positions', and 'Accepting Gifts' and 'Boycotts'. His argument is founded on his idea of university autonomy. Bok develops a variation on the theme outlined by Williams and accepted by Pusey. Bok's autonomy is not based in the feudal autonomy of the university balanced between Church and State or between Big business and the State, but is constructed around the notion of the institutional guarantees and restraints of free speech which create an institutional neutrality. As Bok tells it, in the nineteenth century the university was a 'quiet enclave with little direct impact on the outside world'. This trouble-free existence was violated by the great benefactors in the early twentieth century who, as a price for their donations, wanted to control the opinions of the academic staff, in particular, in the economics departments. In reaction the American Association of University Professors developed to protect the right of faculty. From this movement grew the notion of institutional autonomy—autonomy in educational policy, curriculum, admissions policies and academic standards—all to be controlled by the faculty. Bok says that a kind of social contract arose which provided a freedom of speech as long as the member of the academic staff spoke on his own behalf, and not for the university. This university autonomy was in turn violated in many ways—by the Congress who in giving money after the Second World War insisted that its social goals be followed, and, most troubling to Bok, by students who wanted the university to act in an ethical way.

To maintain institutional neutrality he denied certain rights to the government. It should not 'review course materials to ensure that they do not reflect discrimination on the basis of sex' nor discourage research into some unsettling piece of knowledge or put pressure on universities to hire or fire scholars because of their opinions. What the national government has a right to do is to promote a new service, such as give money for training, but if they want the university to provide more services: to women, the handicapped or to minorities, the government should provide the money. Equally the government has a right to prevent wrongful disposal of hazardous wastes and to insist on standards of accountability for federal funds. For Bok, the university should teach Ethics but the institution itself should not be the agent of change in society except in very limited ways. Defining the correct way a university should act, Bok says, is complicated by the diverse traditions from which American universities grew—from Germany came the idea of the research professor and graduate students, from

England an emphasis on undergraduate teaching and from the United States Morill Act which established land grant colleges, the active involvement of the faculty in activities in the community, and the training of students for a rapidly developing society. This involvement in the community brings with it problems. The President or Dean must constantly vet programmes and block initiatives they deem unwise or which violate the accepted norms of society. Bok then gives a telling example of how to judge when the university should act and when it should not. While stating that scholarship programmes for Black South African students should be supported, he strongly resists attempts to pressure the Board of Governors to stop investing in South Africa (a position many have found inexplicable). Bok explains it with the following statement: 'Nevertheless, we can easily see the difference between this type of assessment and a deliberate effort to promote a particular social reform'.[30]

When Bok discusses 'Academic Responses to Social Problems', he defends his choice of the topic Racidl Inequality over 'war and peace, the preservation of the environment, the delivery of health-care and the status of women' on the grounds that this issue involves discussion of selecting students, hiring faculty and shaping the curriculum. This essay review is not about the history of discrimination of women at Harvard but one comment is relevant here: not until 1977 were women given equal access to scholarship funds at Harvard. Bok is blindly male centred and is perhaps unconscious that he justifies lowering entrance standards for black males who make up 10% of the American population, while at the same time white women who made up 51% of the population were not being given equal access to scholarship funds. Women have never been well treated at Harvard. Bok justified the lower entry standards on the grounds that Grade and Test scores are of limited value. Bok, like Keller, devalues factual material learned by students in high school, and one can see here how the laudable search for talented undereducated students got out of hand and directly led to lowered expectations of academic attainment for all high school students. This attitude has no doubt been largely responsible for the crisis currently occurring in American high schools.

What Derek Bok really cares about is the reintroduction of the teaching of Ethics. Bok divides the teaching of ethics into three. First there is the teaching which is done outside the classroom when reasoning with student activists about what the university can and cannot do. Secondly there are courses in which ethical issues naturally arise like political economy, social theory and political philosophy. Finally there is the teaching of moral philosophy. Here his interest has resulted in curriculum changes. In the 1988–1989 catalogue of the Faculty of Arts and Science, the Core curriculum lists eight courses available for beginning students. But Bok goes further; he wants training in ethics in the Professional schools of law, medicine and business schools. Here he admits there is a real problem because experts may know the Socratic method but not know Ethics. Bok calls for the creating of a strong interdisciplinary programme for students seeking careers in teaching and scholarship.

The only other issue of interest to us here is Bok's discussion of 'Technical Assistance Abroad'. Although governments and international agencies are also agencies for technical assistance abroad. Bok insists the properly organized and administered projects have a place in the university, for scholars. who teach and write about these subjects have much to gain from working overseas. Such experience offers opportunities to test prevailing theories and adapt them to include a broader range of variables.[31] This type of activity also forces scholars in different disciplines to work together and learn for different methodologies. The area in which the university is superior to government or international agencies is in the realm of education. These programs are not without their problems, however: should the university review all projects to see if they fulfil its ideal moral standard? Bok says no, this infringes on academic freedom. On the other hand, the university should insist that projects do not infringe on the university's right to have its own admissions procedures and curricula. There are real dangers in engaging in projects in totalitarian regimes. Bok rightly weighs the pro and con and does not come out with a clear answer but suggests that often the poor and oppressed in these regimes can be helped by projects, so that they should not be rejected out of hand.

Higher Learning (1986) is Bok's book about teaching in what he calls 'the multiversity'. Extrapolating on Harvard's experience, he makes qualified generalization about American Higher Education and in so doing comments about university history. In a revealing footnote he comments: 'Some readers may wonder why anyone would write about universities without discussing research ... Yet the fact is that almost no one can write comprehensively about research ... To write about the deeper questions of research across a wide spectrum of fields may be a task beyond the capacities of almost any author'.[32] Bok divides this book into five chapters: 'The American System of Higher Education', 'Undergraduate Education', 'Professional Schools', 'New Developments' and 'Prospects for Change'. Bok concentrates on what he calls the Great Curriculum Debate when he discusses undergraduate Education. As one looks back on the major forms of the Harvard curriculum from Eliot, who let new subjects flourish at a time when new divisions of knowledge were developing, to Lowell, who brought order to the newly developing departments with the major and honours system, to Conant, who tried to introduce historical and interdisciplinary courses to tie knowledge together, one sees how reasonable and historically valid each change was at the time. Each of those men was interested in organizing the entire undergraduate curriculum. Bok was not, he was just interested in providing the core integration for the beginning years of the undergraduates' intellectual life. The great debate over whether students should take a great books course, or distribution requirements or have a Core curriculum does not matter to him, what did was that the academic staff agree and be enthusiastic about the curriculum. Unlike other Harvard Presidents, Bok does not care how knowledge is organized, but he does care whether teaching in courses is good and that course materials are organized so that students can learn efficiently.

Where Bok, former Dean of the Law school, is at his best is when he discusses, albeit in a summary way, the evolution of the curriculum and teaching in the Professional Schools: the Law, Medical and Business Schools. The Law school is a very different place from the School of Arts and Sciences because it does not select its teachers from people who do research. As a result it is not well understood how the legal system works and what 'effects it has on those it purports to serve'. Most satisfactory is the teaching in the Law School. Law schools, in order to train students out of state, and because of the enormous amount of information to ingest developed the case method of teaching so that students learned how to use rules and analyse information which they could then apply to new cases. Techniques of analysis replace mastery of fact or historical understanding. In Business Schools, on the other hand, managers are not available to train graduate students and Ph.D. economists are hired. As a result, there is often little relationship between their theories and problems of management. In medical schools Ph.D.s are employed, research being the key to new medical treatment, but there remains a real problem about the enormous amount of information medical students have to learn. In this field the problem of teaching masses of factual material has not been solved, analytical reasoning techniques cannot be substituted for knowledge about how the body functions. Bok returns again to the subject of Ethics saying that despite their different subject matters, all professions have one problem in common, students and practitioners of the professions do not take the ethical problems seriously enough. In the Professional Schools ethical questions, central to the role people in the professions play in society, are not taught well, Bok believes, because too little emphasis is placed on teaching the history and problems of the professions. By neglecting to teach this subject 'faculties have overlooked an opportunity to help their students think more deeply about the vexing question of how they can find meaning in their work and career'.[33] Why history of the professions, the history of Harvard and indeed history of universities are subjects which receive no institutional support at Harvard is not a subject that we can answer here. The 1988–1989 catalogue mentions no such courses. The only department in which the history of professions is discussed in any depth is in James Conant's History of Science Department.

Derek Bok is an honest man and does not create intellectual connections when he does not see any. The Harvard of Quincy to Lowell thought of itself as an intellectual imitator of Europe, the Harvard of Conant the saviour of

Europe and inheritor of European culture. This tradition continued with less strength during Pusey's presidency. With Bok the perspective has changed. America is no longer a colony and Europe does not need saving. Harvard too has changed. During the tenure of Pusey and Bok it was transformed from a national college with Graduate Schools into an international university which not only trained undergraduates and professional students but directed major technical assistance programs, attracted international scholars onto its faculty and trained newly appointed Government officials. Bok seems to lack an intellectual context into which to place this dynamic institution. When one steps back and surveys the description of Harvard Bok gives, historical comparisons which could provide a context for Harvard do come to mind. In many ways the organization of the university with its liberal arts college and great professional schools look now, as they did not in the nineteenth century, like the medieval and Renaissance universities with their schools of philosophy and professional schools. One would like to know how the graduate schools have influenced the undergraduate cirruculum. There is another comparison with the great university centres of the past. Harvard now, like Paris and Bologna in the middle ages and Padua in the Renaissance, is a great international centre. One would like to know how that has affected subjects taught and Harvard's own perception of itself. One would like to know how Harvard's development in the twentieth century compares with that of Oxford, Cambridge, Paris and other international universities. Bok's lack of historical perspective also affects his discussion of how teaching could be improved. He rightly points out that little research has been done into effective teaching in both the College and in the Professional Schools. But to understand the disciplines people are teaching, surely they need to know how these disciplines arose and what their development tells us about how people have constructed the topic in the past. When this is understood it will be possible to understand the structure of the topic today and it will be easier to direct future work. Harvard presidents' speeches and books attest the centrality of cultural and university history to their view of Harvard and its place in the world and demonstrate how their perception of cultural history directed daily decision making, curriculum organization, and informed the cultural life of Harvard. One senses in these books a new cultural isolation, an isolation that as an American living in Europe I cannot help but regret. Books of nostalgia filled with memories of a beloved college supply pleasant and important feelings but cannot serve as a substitute for the historical and cultural perspectives which have traditionally directed Harvard.

The Foundation for Intellectual History
28 Gloucester Crescent
London NW1 7DL

REFERENCES

1. I would like to thank the Office of the President at Harvard for supplying me with the current catalogue of the *Courses of Instruction 1988–89 for the Faculty of Arts and Sciences*. It was the idea of the former editor, the late Charles B. Schmitt, that I write an essay review which would examine these books within the context of university history. I should also like to thank Peter Denley for reading the manuscript and offering many helpful suggestions.
2. Derek Bok, *Higher Learning* (Cambridge, Mass., 1986), p. 2, n. 1, see p. 250 of this article.
3. C. B. Schmitt, 'Essay Review, Three important publications for University History', *History of Universities*, Vol. IV, pp. 179–85. Schmitt outlines three main types of university history: 1) ceremonial publications, 2) scholarly, objective historical studies, and 3) published documents. The presidential inaugural address descends from the inaugural address professors gave to opening classes and the inaugural addresses of named professorships. As a genre it remains to be studied.
4. Josiah Quincy, *History of Harvard University* (Cambridge, Mass., 1840), Vol. 2, p. 445
5. Edward Everett, 'Inaugural Address', *Addresses at the Inauguration of the Hon. E. E. Everett, L.L.D.* (Boston, 1846), pp. 29–60.
6. Edward Everett, *Orations and Speeches* (2nd ed.), (Boston, 1850) vols. 1–2.
7. n. 6, Vol. 2, p. 501.
8. James Walker, 'Inaugural Address', *Addresses at the Inauguration of the Rev. James Walker, D.D., 1853* (Cambridge, 1853), pp. 33–69.
9. Eliot attracted four complimentary studies: E. Kueknemann's *Charles W. Eliot, President of Harvard University* (Cambridge, 1909), H. H. Sanderson, *Charles W. Eliot, Puritan Liberal* (New York, 1928), Henry James, *Charles W. Eliot* (2 Vols.; Cambridge, Mass., 1930) and Hugh Hawkins, *Charles W. Eliot, Between Harvard and American* (New York, 1972) and one memorial volume, *The ninetieth Birthday of C. W. Eliot* (Cambridge, Mass., 1925) containing greetings from 97 Harvard Clubs, 148 universities and colleges and 14 Learned Societies.
10. Charles W. Eliot's speeches appeared in three editions: *American Contributions to Civilization and other Essays* (New York, 1890), which went through five printings, *Educational Reform* (New York, 1899) and William A. Neilson's *Charles W. Eliot, The man and his beliefs* (New York, 1926). His inaugural address was printed in all three collections and Nathan Pusey re-edited it in C. W. Eliot, *A turning point in higher education. The inaugural address of Charles William Eliot as President of Harvard College*, intro. N. Pusey (Cambridge, Mass., 1969).
11. In languages the major effort was in translation, for example: in French, Ferdinand Bucher published English translations of French texts, see *The College Series of French plays* (8 vols.; New York, 1864–8), in Latin, grammar writing: G. M. Lanes' Latin grammar edited by M. H. Morgan (New York, 1898). There were two stars, however, Francis Bowen in philosophy see B. Kuklick, *The Rise of American Philosophy* (Cambridge, 1977), pp. 28–45, and Louis Agazziz.
12. Reprinted by Eliot in *Educational Reform*, pp. 89–122, and by W. A. Neilson, *C. W. Eliot, The man and his beliefs* (New York, 1926), pp. 39–70.
13. See Henry A. Yeoman, *Abbott Lawrence Lowell, 1856–1943* (Cambridge, Mass., 1948).

14. *The Government of England* (New York, 1908) reprinted five times, *Essays on Government* (Boston, 1889) reprinted five times, *Government and Parties in Continental Europe* (1896) reprinted eight times in five editions, *Greater European Governments* (1918–30) reprinted five times and *Public Opinion and Popular Government* (1913–30) reprinted seven times.
15. A. Lawrence Lowell, *At War with Academic Traditions in America* (Cambridge, Mass., 1934), pp. 32–45.
16. *At War*, n. 15, 'Competition in College', pp. 46–64.
17. *At War*, n. 15, p. v.
18. The only book written on James Conant is a critical attack on his work as an educational reformer by James E. McClellen, *Toward an Effective Critique of American Education* (New York, 1968).
19. *General Education in a Free Society, Report of the Harvard Committee* (Cambridge, Mass., 1945), pp. 191–2.
20. James Conant, *The Citadel of Learning* (New Haven, 1956), pp. 13–19.
21. The object of the case method was Conant's belief that contemporary science was impossible for the layman to understand, the case histories were to assist the reader to recapture a time at an early stage of science when the experimenter may know little more than the reader.
22. See note 20, *General Education in a Free Society*, p. viii.
23. One can only list his major works: *Education in a Divided World* (Cambridge, Mass., 1948), *Education and Liberty* (Cambridge, Mass., 1953), *Child, Parents and the State* (Cambridge, Mass., 1959), *Revolutionary Transformation of the American High School* (Cambridge, Mass., 1959), *Slums and Suburbs. A commentary on schools in metropolitan areas* (New York, 1961), *Thomas Jefferson and the Development of American Public Education* (Los Angeles, 1962).
24. Seymore M. Lipset, 'Political controversies at Harvard 1636–1974' in S. M. Lipset and David Riesman, *Education and Politics at Harvard* (New York, 1975).
25. Nathan Pusey, 'Leadership and the American University', *The Age of the Scholar* (Cambridge, Mass., 1963), pp. 43–52.
26. History was divided into Historical Study A which 'explain the background and development of major aspects of the modern world' and Historical Study B 'which examined in detail the complexity of controversial and transforming events in the past that do not bear directly on modern policy questions'.
27. Philosophy is centred around Moral Reasoning and Social Analysis courses which are designed 'to show how, by the use of formal theories that are tested by empirical data, one can better understand the behavior of people and institutions with respect to some important problem'.
28. History of Science which Conant thought should be used to understand scientific reasoning is shifted to History and there are courses in 'Medicine and Society in America' and 'Modern Science and Modern Societies'. The old emphasis on the evolution of scientific knowledge and the nature of scientific discovery is gone.
29. P. Keller, *Getting at the Core* (Cambridge, Mass., 1982), p. 59.
30. Derek Bok, *Beyond the Ivory Tower* (Cambridge, Mass., 1982), pp. 291–3.
31. n. 30, p. 197.
32. See n. 2, p. 2.
33. See n. 2, p. 111.

Book Reviews

Thomas Bender (ed.), *The University and the City from Medieval Origins to the Present.* New York and Oxford: Oxford University Press, 1988.

There can be no more remarkable testimony to the close bonds of the university to a city than the cover of this book (mysteriously uncaptioned) which shows the burghers of Edinburgh gathered to witness the laying of the foundation stone of their 'ruinously expensive' new eighteenth-century university building designed by Robert Adam. The volume contains fourteen fascinating and thought-provoking essays on this theme which were presented at a conference held imaginatively to celebrate the centenary of the Graduate School of Arts and Sciences at New York University in session 1986/7. Eschewing both American parochialism and the confines of their own hundred-year history, Thomas Bender and his fellow organizers put together a programme, catholic in its scope and content. The volume opens with J. K. Hyde's last scholarly work before his death, on universities and cities in medieval Italy and concludes with Nathan Glazer on New York's universities since the Second World War. The essays encompass Leiden at the peak of its prowess in the seventeenth century (Anthony Grafton), Geneva in the eighteenth century (Michael Heyd), Chicago in the nineteenth and twentieth centuries (Edward Shils), and of course New York (Daniel Hollinger). The essays are rarely self-indulgent, and when there are lists that read like Founders' Day thanksgivings they are used constructively. Stimulating as are Nicholas Phillipson's analysis of Edinburgh in the Enlightenment and Carl Schorske's description of the conservative citizens of Basle's willingness to 'fish in troubled waters' in recruiting teachers for their university as eminent as Karl Follen, later the founder of German Study at Harvard, the reader is left to ponder with the editor whether any progress has been achieved except to sound yet another historical clarion call of 'More needs to be done'. For all its quality, the book is curiously old fashioned, moulded by academics preoccupied by 'freedom' after the traumatic events of the inter-war years which saw the Humboldtian ideal debased not just in Germany but more subtly but as importantly for this study in the United States through quotas to exclude poor Jewish immigrants, understandably regularly referred to both by Nathan Glazer and David A. Hollinger. Throughout but particularly in the modern period the university emerges as an idea often with a spiritual concept that will immerse its students in *geist* essential for *bildung* (Charles McClelland on Berlin). This view that underpinned German university education, even when it had been diverted towards the narrow ambitions of the Prussian state, permeated even the Weimar Institute of Social Research at Frankfurt with its rejection of the 'fragmentation of knowledge characteristic of bourgeois *wissenschaft*' (Martin Jay). The city, likewise, emerges as a vague shifting concept sometimes with problems (Chicago and New York) that academic nostrums may help to solve but rarely with any specific higher educational needs to assist in its economic, cultural, or political progress. The reluctance to conceive of universities as purveyors of knowledge and consumers of goods and services, and cities as consumers of knowledge and purveyors of goods and services (with the notable exceptions of the opening essays by J. K. Hyde and Stephen Ferualet) is the weakness of the whole volume. For this reason the *Studiae particulare* thrown up by every city the world over to cater for its particular industrial, commercial, cultural, and political needs are referred to only obliquely and then infrequently. There is nothing here about the way the *studiae generale* (the true universities) did battle with these institutions in the nineteenth century, by seeking to capture their market and in the twentieth century emerged victorious. Sheldon Rothblatt in his essay on 'London: A Metropolitan University?' should have tackled these issues head on; but he fails not only to understand mid-nineteenth-century London with its powerful engineering industries, financial institutions, and its plethora of learned societies and institutions (both local and national); but also the nature of the non-conformist attitudes that led to the university's establishment. These criticisms are made as much to advance the debate that Thomas Bender has stimulated than to detract from this book. Rarely does the publication of conference proceedings, read in the heat of a Mediterranean summer, makes you wish you had been there. This one certainly does.

Michael S. Moss
University of Glasgow

Quaderni per la Storia dell'Università di Padova 17 (1984), 18 (1985) and 19 (1986). Editrice Antenore, Padua.

The first sixteen volumes of this impressive periodical were the subject of an essay review by Brendan Dooley in Volume 5 (1985) of this journal. The purpose of this note is simply to draw attention to the continuing work of the Centro per la Storia dell'Università di Padova as expressed through its *Quaderni*. The most recent three volumes continue the blend of biographical and institutional surveys, editions of documents, bibliography, reviews and notices which characterizes the series. Individuals studied include the fifteenth-century jurist Laura Palazzolo (by Giovanni Ronconi, vol. 17) and the humanist Gasparino Barzizza (Dieter Girgensohn, vol. 19), and the sixteenth-century physicians Giacomo Tiburzi da Pergola (Alessandro Pastore, vol. 17) and Falloppio (Giorgio Ferrari, 'L'opera idro-termale di Gabriele Falloppio; le sue edizioni e la sua fortuna', vol. 18). There are two articles by Virgilio Giormani on the growth and formalization of chemistry teaching at Padua in the eighteenth century (vols. 17 and 18). Articles on institutional history include two contributions by Piero Del Negro on the university reform of 1761 (vols. 17 and 19), a survey by Maria Cecilia Ghetti on the university between 1798 and 1817 (vol. 17), and a discussion, and inventory, of mainly seventeenth-century orations for the saints who were the protectors of the university (by Silvio Bernardinello, vol. 19). Enzo Grossato gives biographies of Paduan students who fought under Garibaldi (vol. 18), while the *Miscellanea* section abounds with biographical information about various Paduan students from all periods. The volumes continue to be meticulously indexed and thus provide an accessible as well as a learned tool for scholars.

Peter Denley
Queen Mary and Westfield College
University of London
Hampstead Campus
London NW3 7ST

Christopher Brooke and Roger Highfield, with photographs by Wim Swaan, *Oxford and Cambridge*. Cambridge: Cambridge University Press, 1988. xxv + 367 pp. £25.00.

This book is a general history of the two oldest English universities from their foundation to the present day. It is high time that the two were considered together, for the many points of similarity in their histories are as instructive as the better-publicized features that distinguish them from each other. This is an appropriate moment for such a study, with so much new work having been published on Oxford and Cambridge in recent years.

   The authors are well qualified for the task: both are leading medieval historians and each is an expert on the history of his own university. The book makes use of the most recent scholarship in the field at the time of its composition, citing a very wide range of printed sources, primary and secondary, from different periods as well as some unpublished dissertations. It is informed and thoughtful, and written in a clear and interesting manner. The university towns appear first. Two chapters, one on each, outline their histories up to the present day. The remaining nine chapters cover the development of the universities chronologically, in separate sections. The narrative is fused together very well, with a minimum of repetition or overlap. Nearly every aspect of university and college history is covered: institutional, intellectual, social, and religious. Well over 200 splendid photographs adorn the book, all but a handful by Wim Swaan. As well as being lovely to look at, they form an integral part of the history, which draws on the architectural record to illustrate wider developments.

The result is an admirably comprehensive and well-balanced treatment of a diffuse and wide-ranging topic. Some readers, no doubt, will feel that their particular areas of interest or expertise should have received more extensive coverage: I felt that more could have been written about the social phenomenon of athleticism and the games cult in the nineteenth and twentieth centuries, to which the numerous boathouses and pavilions bear witness. The authors have been scrupulously fair in the number of pages allotted to each period of the universities' history, but the years from 1920 to the present day, which have seen so many seemingly significant developments, might have merited more extensive treatment. Gonville and Caius College features perhaps a little too prominently in the Cambridge illustrations.

But these are minor points. *Oxford and Cambridge* could hardly be bettered as a general history of the two universities and it is likely to remain a standard text for a good many years to come.

John Twigg
11 Hope Drive
The Park
Nottingham NG7 1DL

Josef Polišenský *et al.* (eds.), *Alma Mater Carolina Pragensis. Charles University and Foreign Visitors.* Prague: Charles University, 1988. 231 pp. Kcs 35.50.

These forty-five travellers' accounts, the offshoot of a forthcoming history of the University of Prague, form a curious amalgam. Though richly illustrated, the collection will hardly make much appeal to the layman, since the texts are all rendered in their original languages: not just Latin, German, French, and English, but Spanish and Portuguese, Polish and Russian, even Slovene. Yet the editorial commentary, paradoxically rendered trilingually throughout (in Czech, Russian, and English), is exiguous, and the introduction too brief to do more than hint at how the Hussite tradition sustained the image of the Charles University over the centuries, and how foreign eyes may have been better able than domestic ones to discern its distinctive features, especially in times of tension. Some extracts are very short indeed, from the first, by an Italian humanist who in 1399 seems to have delivered himself of just thirteen words on the subject, to the final plaudit in 1984 from the Secretary-General of the United Nations. Others contain little direct reference to the university, rather than to the urban or cultural scene of Prague as a whole. Hard information about student life, teaching methods, and the like at the Carolinum appears, on the present evidence, almost unobtainable from this source. Such travellers as penetrated its portals rarely provide more than an often sketchy description of the library and collections. (Perhaps the most valuable comment on that score comes— quaintly—from a German denied access to them because of a recent fire, who records that most books could be saved because more than forty readers had been present when the blaze broke out—surely an impressive figure for 1801?) We are left with a handful of testimonies interesting by virtue of the fame of their authors (Swedenborg, Miranda, a famished Mozart and a weary Hegel), and a few better-informed writers: the perceptive scientist Georg Forster and the anticlerical Dutch lawyer Johan Meermann in the late eighteenth century; the Polish doctor Moszyński in the 1830s, one of the last to communicate by means of Latin; and above all the philologist, August Schleicher, whose venomous comments on conditions in the 1850s have been reproduced from a recently rediscovered manuscript (cf. the article by T. Syllaba in *Acta Universitatis Carolinae. Historia Universitatis Carolinae Pragensis*, xxviii, 1 [1988], 77–90). Near the end, amid the bathetic effusions of Soviet academicians, is one hopeful sign, in V.-L. Tapié's tribute to Josef Pekař, his 'maître incomparable', and to the merits of the Bohemian Baroque—both subjects taboo at the Caroline University in recent decades.

R. J. W. Evans
Brasenose College
Oxford

Alan B. Cobban, *The Medieval English Universities. Oxford and Cambridge to c. 1500.* Aldershot: Scolar Press, 1988. xvii + 465 pp.

With the early volumes of the History of the University of Oxford Project now safely gathered in, the time was right, if ever there could be such a time, for a single volume synthesis of our current state of knowledge of the medieval universities in England. The impressive bibliography and range of reference undoubtedly show that Alan Cobban is in a position to deliver such a work. Nevertheless, it is inevitable that the position reached remains highly provisional. The internal records of many of the colleges are still unexplored. For Cambridge this remains an acute problem and Cobban relies heavily upon his own work on the King's Hall. The *Records of Early English Drama* volumes for Cambridge, now published, would have greatly enriched the manuscript sources for everyday life in the colleges. Instead, Cobban relies on statutory evidence here, having elsewhere suggested that statutes do not reflect actual practice in the recruitment of fellows.

It is in placing the two universities in the socio-political structure of medieval England that Cobban is at his strongest. By applying quantitative methods to the issues of recruitment and career structures, he has made valuable advances in this difficult, often personalized, area. Inevitably this does not make for easy reading and is not to be recommended for the non-specialist. By insisting upon statistical data and a more exact analytical method, Cobban has certainly moved medieval university history far from its traditional reliance upon statutes and building accounts. However, by choosing to ignore the curriculum and comparative European evidence, we are left with a partial account. Furthermore, it is difficult to believe that this book will convert the non-specialist to an interest in university history and there remains a need for modern introduction to the subject. Perhaps Dr Cobban would care to oblige.

Christopher A. Upton
University of Birmingham

Damian Riehl Leader, *The University to 1546.* A History of the University of Cambridge, general editor C. N. L. Brooke, volume i. Cambridge: Cambridge University Press, 1988. xxi + 399 pp. £35.

Damian Leader's history of the University of Cambridge to 1546 should be warmly welcomed by students of medieval universities—and by many others besides. It was the offer of Leader's work which encouraged the Cambridge University Press to undertake a history in four volumes of the university from its beginnings to the late twentieth century. This first volume is to be followed by others from Victor Morgan (1546–1750), Peter Searby (1750–1870), and by Christopher Brooke, who is also the general editor of a series which will clearly make a significant contribution to the study both of European universities and of English society. The volume has been handsomely produced and carefully edited by the Cambridge University Press.

Both Brooke in his preface and Leader in his introduction note that historians in Cambridge have been much less interested in the history of their university than have their counterparts in Oxford, and Leader adds that the pre-reformation university has been especially neglected. Mullinger's history of medieval Cambridge (1873) is less satisfactory than the studies of early Oxford by Maxwell Lyte (1886) or Mallet (1924). Rashdall's work on the universities of medieval Europe (1895) dealt with Cambridge all too briefly and dismissively. Willis and Clark's architectural history of Cambridge (1886) was a fine achievement but was followed by very little further work on the medieval university, despite the early availability in print of important sources. In the last thirty or so years, however, medieval Cambridge has received a good deal of scholarly attention—most often from historians outside Cambridge. Leader has made a clear synthesis of much of this work and has been scrupulous in acknowledging his sources. This recent research has also been used by two books published within a short time of Leader's, W. J. Courtenay's *Schools and Scholars in Four-teenth-Century England* (1987) and A. B. Cobban's *The Medieval English Universities* (1988). Courtenay's concentration on the fourteenth century and Cobban's emphasis on institutional developments make these valuable complements to Leader's study of Cambridge.

In his preface Christopher Brooke disarmingly contrasts the 'great battleship' of the History of the University of Oxford (three of whose eight volumes have so far appeared) with the 'modest, serviceable frigate, sent from Cambridge'. Sheer bulk is not the only important difference between the two series; all aspects of Cambridge in each period, for example, will be covered by a single author, while the Oxford volumes are more by way of collections of studies by teams of specialists. There are characteristic strengths and weaknesses which follow from each approach. Unity of style can certainly be an advantage in a book as well written as the first of the Cambridge series. Leader's prose is clear and unpretentious and he is commendably ready to explain basic questions in a way that presupposes no specialized knowledge in the reader. A good example is his lucid exposition of the basic texts studied in the several faculties and of the student's course to his degree. Furthermore his judgement is consistently careful and well balanced.

Leader is familiar with both medieval English universities, and it is a great strength of his work that developments at Cambridge are constantly related to contemporary Oxford (references to continental universities are naturally much less frequent). Indeed so intimate is the intermixture that an inattentive reader might sometimes take an example from one university as evidence of practice in the other. In view of this altogether sensible determination to treat the English universities in parallel it was unfortunate that the first volume of the history of Oxford appeared only in 1984, when Leader's text must have been in its almost final form. A few references to the first Oxford volume (and even to the third, published in 1986) have been spliced into the finished version, but clearly it was not possible to take account of it systematically, and very occasionally Leader's Oxford sources have let him down. Thus the description of the earliest Oxford colleges suffers somewhat from following Rashdall rather than more recent scholarship, and to say that the King's Hall was the first college regularly to admit undergraduates is to evade some difficult questions about the early character of Merton, Balliol, and Exeter at Oxford. The statement that Cambridge's theology school, completed in the 1390s, is the oldest central building of the English universities seems not to take account of the congregation house built at Oxford in the 1320s.

A single author cannot treat all aspects of the university with equal expertise, and the shape of his work will naturally reflect his own particular interests. Leader's volume combines conscientious summarizing of the work of others on subjects where he is not himself especially at home with an expansive treatment of those areas which he knows best and considers to be of central importance. The institutional development and internal structure of Cambridge, its relationship to church and state and with the town of Cambridge, the recruitment and later careers of its students and its social character are presented clearly and briskly—perhaps a little too briskly in places. Leader has not really got to grips with the current debate on the careers of university men. He seems not to allow for the substantial proportion of students who did not take a degree, or for those who have left no trace in our sources, and his assumption that most arts students went into 'parochial work' may appear plausible, but it surely goes beyond the evidence. By contrast he gives an extremely helpful treatment of the relationship of university studies in grammar to the career of schoolmasters. While there is much valuable information about the endowment of colleges, their economies and the finances of the university are hardly considered. Although the extant sources dictate that major themes must often be considered more in relation to the colleges than to the generality of the university, Leader does not neglect Cambridge's hostels, which tended to be larger and perhaps better equipped than the academic halls of Oxford. He also takes pains to stress the significance of the Cambridge convents of the mendicant orders, especially before 1400 when friars may have comprised between a third and a half of all scholars. The smallness of Cambridge in the fourteenth century—perhaps less than half the size of Oxford—and its dramatic numerical and institutional growth in the fifteenth century to parity with Oxford early in the sixteenth is a theme which runs through the entire volume. Leader is at his best and most original in discussing the content of the curriculum and methods of teaching. These matters, together with a consideration of the intellectual climate of the late fifteenth and early sixteenth centuries in which they changed so significantly, occupy perhaps two thirds of his text. Although his own research has been concerned primarily with the faculty of arts he also handles theology and law very confidently and clearly. His sureness of touch deserts him momentarily in his treatment of medicine, where for example the confusion of Arabic works is compounded by the index, but he has much of interest to say on Cambridge physicians and the connection between astronomy and physic. He has made very full use of university and college statutes and of the surviving registers of both Oxford and Cambridge which record the studies of candidates for degrees in the later fifteenth and early sixteenth centuries. The category of evidence which best typifies Leader's approach—and to which a separate section of the bibliography is devoted—consists of library catalogues and other booklists, which he has analysed to estimate what texts were available in Cambridge. Furthermore his examination of surviving copies, both manuscript and printed, allows him to assess the extent to which particular texts were actually used. These materials are marshalled in conjunction with Emden's biographical register of medieval Cambridge to construct a series of intellectual biographies of Cambridge men. The intellectual character of medieval Cambridge has been its least studied aspect, and this exercise in academic prosopography is possibly the most original aspect of the volume. As at Oxford, but in contrast to continental universities, Scotism was almost unchallenged, though the works of Scotus were known mainly through commentaries, especially those of Canonicus and Andreas. Leader is unable to identify any specifically Cambridge school of thought in philosophy or theology, and observes that the friars followed the intellectual fashions of their particular orders. Again like Oxford, Cambridge produced little original thought in the fifteenth century, and the works of Aristotle continued to be taught by means of commentaries written in the previous century. But if Leader finds in medieval Cambridge no author of European reputation (leaving aside its slight claim to Scotus) he does identify many serious and accomplished scholars. Their books indicate interests which often bridged the divisions between the faculties, and practical handbooks for parochial work are found alongside more strictly academic works. Thus the extensive library of John Warkworth, master of Peterhouse 1470–1500, included Peter Lombard's *Sentences*, Aquinas, Anselm, Augustine, Origen, Gregory, Bernard of Clairvaux, Augustine of Ancona, commentaries on Aristotle and the Bible, Terence and many texts for the liberal arts, texts of canon law, several collections of sermons and some pastoral manuals; Warkworth's annotation of his books reveals a particular interest in Christological and Mariological questions.

The nature of the surviving evidence, of Cambridge's development and of the author's own interests combine to place a heavy emphasis on the end of the fifteenth century and start of the sixteenth. There is an excellent analysis of the way in which the content of the curriculum and methods of teaching were changed in these years. These changes were effected more centrally and formally, and with less resistance, than was the case at Oxford, and as early as 1488 new statutes restructured the arts course under the influence of humanist ideals. There is a most illuminating description of the profound shift of emphasis in the faculties of grammar, arts and theology in these years. Due weight is given to Erasmus's stay in Cambridge from 1511 to 1514 but it is made clear that the university had changed greatly in the years before his arrival. Not that Erasmus's admirers in Cambridge fully shared his antipathy to their scholastic predecessors, for they owned traditional commentaries on the *Sentences* alongside the works of English and Italian humanists. The replacement of the ailing 'regency' system of teaching, which relied on the lectures required of newly graduated masters, by salaried university and college lecturers was initiated rather sooner and more systematically at Cambridge than at Oxford. Leader's description of these changes is admirable. Here too he takes a biographical approach to his interconnected themes, intertwining his examination of the circle of Lady Margaret Beaufort and John Fisher or the friends and pupils of Erasmus with his account of the foundation of new colleges and the transformation of the university's teaching arrangements and curriculum.

The few decades either side of 1500 were a time of remarkable intellectual upheaval at Cambridge, but Leader shows that old and new studies and attitudes coexisted remarkably well; it was not even the arrival of Lutheranism in Cambridge but rather the ramifications of the royal divorce in the 1530s which introduced a deadly bitterness into academic disputes. Just as Cambridge acquired a European reputation for humane learning and entered the mainstream of humanist reform it was required, together with Oxford, to be the ally of Henry VIII against Rome. It benefited splendidly by ecclesiastical, lay, and royal patronage which culminated in Henry VIII's Trinity College and it assumed a new influence in the Tudor state and church, but again like Oxford it was to be subjected to ever closer interference in its affairs by the crown. In 1535 the execution of Fisher and his replacement as chancellor of Cambridge by Thomas Cromwell were followed by royal injunctions to the university which consolidated both the reform of its studies and the immediacy of royal control.

Ralph Evans
History of the University of Oxford
Clarendon Building, Bodleian Library   *Oxford OX1 3BG*

Olga Weijers, *Terminologie des Universités au XIIIe siècle*. Rome:
Edizioni dell'Ateneo, 1987. xlii + 437 pp.

Too many years ago, this reviewer, after spending several years in a detailed
study of the medieval Oxford faculty of arts, began work in the archives of
the university of Freiburg. Believing in the unity of the system of higher
education in the later middle ages, he anticipated little difficulty in understanding the medieval records of the university. Very soon, a sadder and
wiser man, convinced of the value of the comparative study of medieval
university terminology, he began to appreciate the difficulties facing those
attempting such an understanding.

Olga Weijers herself has founded the modern study of medieval university
terminology: others have investigated the use of certain special expressions,
but no general coverage of this subject has been previously attempted. This
book considers university usage under three headings: terms used by the
institutions themselves, names adopted by university personnel—teachers,
students, administrators and college members, the vocabulary of teaching—
courses and vacations, methods of instruction, and examinations and
degrees. Most terms or groups of terms are first examined, then their earliest
appearances and their semantic development from classical times are
discussed. This approach inevitably leads to some repetition and much
cross-reference. Certainly this book is not to be read for the development of
its argument, its cohesion or for its style; rather it will be used as a work of
reference and as a source of information; perhaps it could have been better
produced as an extended glossary. Nevertheless, those who use this volume
regularly will acquire quickly a thorough awareness of the practices and
policy of the early medieval universities.

Although this book does not present any overall analysis of the material
discussed, certain conclusions seem apparent. Firstly, the recognized division between southern 'legal' universities and northern 'arts' universities is
often confirmed, especially by the regular recording at this date of terms
used 'only' or 'mainly' in the Italian universities: *professor, statutarius* and
so forth. Secondly, the different usage of the English universities, and
particularly of Oxford, is clearly shown. Many words used regularly in
England—*cista, questionista, hebdomadarius, commissarius*—are unknown
or hardly known elsewhere. Thirdly, as this reviewer found, terms having a
certain meaning in one university often have a different meaning elsewhere;
even Oxford and Cambridge did not interpret the expression *congregatio
magna* in the same way. Olga Weijers begins the discussion of the varied
meanings of 'determinatio' here; by 1500 the problem of understanding the
significance of this word had become much more problematical.

Throughout this survey, there are regular comments on existing hypo-
theses and sharp observations about some interpretations: on the view that
the word 'bacallarius' is derived from an Arabic source, Olga Weijers notes:

'C'est chercher loin une solution pourtant toute proche'! Some of her interpretations may be challenged; for instance, has she properly understood the Oxford statutory reference to 'three terms' in each year? Does this record those terms when the masters lectured, whereas the year was in fact divided into *four* terms, one of which was to become the 'long vacation'?

It will be apparent that here we have a major work of reference, indispensable to all historians of the medieval universities. Who will be courageous enough to produce a similar volume for the fourteenth and fifteenth centuries?

John M. Fletcher
Department of Modern Languages
Aston University
Birmingham B4 7ET

Robert Marichal (ed.), *Le Livre des Prieurs de Sorbonne, 1431–1485*. Paris: Aux Amateurs de Livres, 1987. 303 pp.

In their minutes of the sessions of the Sorbonne assembly, the priors record the difficulties of existence in an inner-city society, recovering slowly from the impact of occupation and war. Armed personnel are everywhere; theft and violence are ever present problems. Doors have to be closed during meal times to prevent the incursions of robbers; precious vessels are locked away and the fellows substitute those made of cheaper material. Servants constantly betray their trust, absconding with college property or arranging for their accomplices to enter through gates left conveniently unlocked. Even the bread kept for the mass was not safe in the chapel. College revenues fell and the sale of books and silver goblets was considered. There were so few fellows in residence in 1436 that the Sorbonne itself agreed to pay something towards the clerks' commons 'to preserve the college and prevent the introduction of outsiders'.

Despite these problems, the college survived and has left to us this fascinating record of its daily life. Scholars accustomed to reading such minutes will not be surprised that little is noted here of academic interest; the priors were more concerned with the management of college property, the distribution of accommodation to the fellows and, above all, the maintenance of the house. This final task proved difficult. The fellows were accused of heavy drinking: Reginald de Brulle was such an alcoholic that, after ignoring warnings against causing scandal, he was declared a 'sad case', was rejected by one fellow asked to control him and finally accepted by another who was to keep him from drink until his parents collected him.

Fellows and clerks found the attraction of women irresistible: one was returned to the college after being discovered with a prostitute and with stolen property, of the college, on his person. Insults, attacks, general loutish behaviour usually involving noise, stone throwing and the tipping of urine, were endured by lecturers and fellows. College provisions, its apples, raisins, pears or wine regularly disappeared. The chief offenders were frequently the religious, including a certain abbot who had to be warned about behaviour which had shocked the college. Fines, expulsions, the whipping of junior scholars are recorded regularly by the priors.

Behind this record of widespread criminal behaviour and general misconduct, we can perceive desperate efforts to maintain the 'old way' of life. The tradition of living 'socialiter et collegialiter, moraliter et scolastice' was crumbling. Fellows frequently took their drink and meals in their private rooms, slept outside the college and ignored many of its regulations; one fellow objected to attempts to enforce the rules by protesting that his home and his books were 'in the street'. An interesting clue to the possible origins of the Oxbridge tutorial system can be found in the custom of allowing Sorbonne fellows to have students living with them in their rooms, but attending lectures elsewhere. The priors spent considerable time attempting to control the numbers and behaviour of such lodgers.

It will be apparent from this brief survey that this well-edited source provides valuable and interesting material for all interested in the varied life of Paris masters and students of the fifteenth century.

John M. Fletcher
Department of Modern Languages
Aston University
Birmingham B4 7ET

Zenon Kaluza, *Les querelles doctrinales à Paris: Nominalistes et réalistes aux confins du XIVe et du XVe siècles* (Quodlibet 2). Bergamo: Perluigi Lubrina, 1988. 204 pp.

The conflict between the ancient and modern *viae* is a set-piece of fifteenth-century university history. Zenon Kaluza's fine, richly documented study clarifies the origins, nature, motives and consequences of the conflict at the University of Paris. Kaluza focuses on two leading figures: Jean Gerson, who became Chancellor in 1395 and retired briefly to Bruges before resuming his reform of the theology faculty in 1400, and Johannes de Nova Domo (Jean de Maisonneuve or Jan van Neuwenhuyze), who taught in the arts faculty for nearly a quarter of a century (ca. 1395–1418).

In various tracts and letters, Gerson specified three 'ways' of theological thinking. His terminology became commonplace in the fifteenth century. The 'logicians' or *terministae*, whose school originated in England, denied the reality of universals outside the mind and thus dwelt upon the analysis of terms in theology. The 'Scotists', or 'metaphysicians', or *platonici*, or *phantastici*, or *formalizantes*, on the other hand, treated 'ideal reasons' as if they were separate, eternal realities. Gerson criticizes the *terministae* for their excessive use of logic in theology, and the *formalizantes* for introducing fanciful distinctions into considerations of the transcendent God. Kaluza rightly perceives that Gerson's animus against the Scotists was motivated by his concern for preserving the absolute divine simplicity, as taught by pseudo-Dionysius.

In the face of these extremes, Gerson recommended a 'third way' of *veritas communis*: the way of thirteenth-century theological masters, who maintained a moderate, balanced use of logical and philosophical notions in theology. Gerson's programme effectively excludes fourteenth-century developments in theological thinking. By deft literary analysis, Kaluza shows that Gerson's texts do not reflect any actual disputes in the theology faculty at the time of his chancellorship; rather they remember disputes that took place in the time of his own teachers' studies (ca. 1360–1380). Gerson does not engage the arguments of particular masters. His method characterizes 'doctrinal currents' by salient formulae from which a chain of (usually invidious) conclusions can be deduced. Without unfair polemic, Kaluza judges that Gerson's criticisms are based on piety, superficial in their comprehension and finally irrelevant. Nonetheless, they were influential.

Gerson seemingly was unaware of discussions in the arts faculty that took place about the time of his Chancellorship. The arts master Johannes de Nova Domo, whose writings circulated to Cologne, Louvain, and other universities, launched a relentless attack on the terminists, in particular the followers of Buridan. Against the terminists, Johannes adopted a principle that he found in Aristotle: 'contra negantem principia non est disputandum'. In his mind by denying the extra-mental reality of universals the terminists denied the first principles of logic, indeed, the object of all art and science. Likewise by denying the *modos significandi* they denied the first principles of appropriate speech in grammar. Especially insidious is the terminists' expansion of the doctrine of material supposition to the near elimination of simple suppositions. Johannes correctly perceived that this doctrine radically altered the interpretation of Aristotle and the understanding of universals, signification, etc.

Johannes de Nova Domo's attitude, like Gerson's, forecloses discussion and contributed to the sharp separation of the *viae*. Johannes wished to expel the books of the moderns from the curriculum. Like Gerson, he called for a return to the sound peripatetic teaching of thirteenth-century masters. On all points he invoked *dicta* of Aristotle, mediated by the paraphrases and interpretations of Albert the Great. For Johannes, Kaluza points out, Aristotle's words are a coded language that establishes norms by which the teachings of masters are confirmed or dismissed. Johannes understands the *licentia philosophandi* to mean that Aristotle should always be interpreted so as to conform with Catholic truth. He thus promoted a certain sacralization of Aristotle that has had a long career in Catholic thought.

Although he called for a return to thirteenth-century styles of thinking, Johannes' model of philosophy is an innovation. Kaluza characterizes it as traditionalist and apologetic, inasmuch as it defines itself in relation to a tradition that it strives always to defend, and as polemic and fideist, inasmuch as it excludes all that falls outside its definitions and routinely resorts to faith to confirm its conclusions. Johannes, in short, confers upon philosophy the dogmatic status of theology. This is a quite ironic return to the sources in the thirteenth century.

Kaluza's book contains three valuable appendices: an assembly of texts from Gerson concerning the *formalizantes*; a text from Heimericus de Campo that resumes the doctrines of the formalists; a presentation of the headings, text divisions and questions of Johannes de Nova Domo's unpublished commentary on Alexander de Villedieu.

In my judgment, Zenon Kaluza's *Les querelles doctrinales* is an exquisite study that will become a scholarly classic..

Kent Emery, Jr.
University of Notre Dame

Peter Dear, *Mersenne and the Learning of the Schools*. Ithaca and London: Cornell University Press, 1988. xiii + 264 pp.

Peter Dear's study of Mersenne's thought is the first full-length examination of this important seventeenth-century intellectual broker since Robert Lenoble's classic *Mersenne ou la naissance du mécanisme* (Paris, 1943). Scholarship in the history of science generally as well as specialized studies of seventeenth-century natural philosophy have undergone important developments in the forty-five years separating these two studies. Although Dear's book reflects many of these scholarly developments and thus adds to our understanding of Mersenne's role in the intellectual life of the first half of the seventeenth century, it by no means supplants Lenoble's magisterial work, which remains one of the fundamental studies of the origins of the mechanical view of nature.

Marin Mersenne (1588–1648) is best remembered for his role as an intellectual clearing-house of ideas in natural philosophy. He conducted a vast correspondence with almost all the major figures in natural philosophy at his time, serving a role now filled by the not-yet-invented scientific journal. His correspondence runs to fifteen published volumes, and it is an essential source for all studies of science and philosophy in the early seventeenth century. He also wrote a number of books on various aspects of natural philosophy, particularly mathematics, music, and method.

Peter Dear approaches Mersenne's work topically and chronologically by considering the ideas he expressed in his major books. In every case, Dear argues, Mersenne's approach reflected the philosophical and methodological predilections of his Jesuit education at La Flèche, the same college at which Descartes studied a few years later. In particular, Dear effectively argues that Mersenne's rejection of a physics that aimed to achieve certain knowledge of the real essences of things—a physics sought by Descartes as well as by Aristotle—had its roots in a probabilist approach to knowledge endorsed by sixteenth- and early seventeenth-century Jesuit natural philosophers. This argument extends and revises Richard Popkin's important work on the role of scepticism in early modern philosophy.

Dear gives a detailed account of a number of the topics which attracted Mersenne's attention: the relationship between physics and mathematics, especially the place of 'eternal truths' in a world freely created by an omnipotent God; the idea of a universal harmony, underlying both mechanics and music, and providing the rationale for a mechanical account of music theory; and the role of language in philosophical systems. In each case, Dear devotes considerable attention to the historical roots of Mersenne's thought, finding the most pervasive influences coming from his Jesuit teachers, from whom he also gained an appreciation of the methods of Renaissance humanism and the views of St Augustine.

Dear's book adds to our understanding of Mersenne's complex outlook by showing how his approach grew out of his educational background. By examining in detail one individual's intellectual development, it illuminates questions about the influence of education on intellectual life and about the transplantation and extension of ideas from one realm of discourse, theology, to another, natural philosophy.

Margaret J. Osler
University of Calgary

H. de Ridder-Symoens and J. M. Fletcher (eds.), *Academic Relations Between the Low Countries and the British Isles, 1450–1700. Proceedings of the First Conference of Belgian, British and Dutch Historians of Universities held in Ghent, September 30–October 2 1987.* Ghent: Studia Historica Gandensia No. 273, 1989, 161 pp.

In April 1986 the International Commission for the History of Universities proposed that three biennial conferences should be held 'to reinforce contacts between university historians and so to stimulate new research'. This collection of eight papers from the first of these conferences reflects that intention; three of the essays deal with the traditional subjects of research concerning academic relations while the remaining papers suggest new lines of possible research as well as reflecting upon recent work. The introductory paper by Peter Vandermeersch provides a useful bibliographical survey of the subject. His paper concentrates on three main areas: firstly, the printing of English books in the Low Countries; secondly, the students from the British Isles who studied at Louvain and Douai; and finally there is very brief consideration of the cross-fertilization of intellectual ideas.

Three papers deal with the traditional themes of academic relations between these countries. Dr Feenstra discusses the legal connections between Scotland and the Netherlands during the seventeenth and eighteenth centuries, although his study is not confined to that period and includes a reference to the notes made on law lectures attended by William Elphinstone at Louvain between 1431–1433. The eighteenth century is also considered in Luyendijk-Elshout's paper on William Cullen and the Leyden Medical School. Dr Van Westrienen's contribution provides a Dutch viewpoint upon the Dutch tourists who ventured to England as part of the educational Grand Tour, in preparation for their tours of France.

The remaining papers explore new fields relating to academic relations between the Low Countries and the British Isles. E. M. Braekman provides a useful comparison between the educational ordinances of the Walloon synods, in particular he compares the orders of the so-called Synod of Wesel with those of the Synod of Emden. He has also drawn together the results of four recent publications in order to provide an index of the Calvinist ministers and preachers who served in the Netherlands before 1565. The Calvinist desire to study the original texts of the Scriptures encouraged the development of Hebrew studies. Attempts to establish such studies in England were only a limited success until the arrival of Calvinist refugees escaping from persecution in the Low Countries. This area is explored by Drs Fletcher and Upton, who consider the impact that John Drusius had upon the development of Hebrew Studies at Merton College. The attitude of the Oxbridge colleges to European affairs in general is reflected in another paper which discusses three little-known anthologies of poetry written on the death of Sir Philip Sidney. The final paper provides a glimpse of the everyday life of the universities with an unrewarding comparison of the eating and drinking habits of colleges in Louvain and Oxford.

This collection of papers provides a welcome attempt to further research in the academic relations between the Low Countries and the British Isles.

Andrew Spicer
University of Southampton

Laurence Brockliss, Gerald Harriss, and Angus Macintyre, *Magdalen College and the Crown. Essays for the Tercentenary of the Restoration of the College in 1688*. Printed for the College: Oxford, 1988. 106 pp.

Magdalen's clash with James II in 1687–1688 is one of the best-known incidents in Oxford's seventeenth-century history and it has been well documented; but as a popular tale it is still too often filtered through Macaulay's spiteful narrative, and nearly a century has elapsed since the last extensive work on the subject was published. This scholarly but highly readable re-examination is therefore timely.

The book comprises three essays, one by each of the authors. Gerald Harriss surveys the relationship between the college and the crown from its foundation in 1458 to the reign of Charles II, principally with regard to royal intervention in the choice (and sometimes the removal) of presidents and fellows. This view of a single theme over such a long period is unusual and valuable, for it brings out clearly the crown's changing aims and methods over time, as well as the dilemma of the college, caught between its duty of obedience to the royal prerogative on the one hand, and its statutory obligations and dislike of outside interference on the other. The conclusions have a wider relevance to the history of the English universities in this period, though the Magdalen evidence alone might lead one to underesti-mate the influence generally of place-seekers at court in procuring fellow-ships under Elizabeth and James I.

The second piece, by Angus Macintyre, takes a fresh look at the college's battle with the king in 1687–1688, an incident deemed highly significant by contemporaries and subsequent historians. This is a blow-by-blow descrip-tion with commentary explaining the development of the king's tactics and the college's response. It too has a broader relevance for those who are interested in James's policies and the Anglican resistance to them, partly because it is a self-contained study with its own conclusions and not simply slotted into the wider picture.

Laurence Brockliss completes the volume with a detailed biographical analysis of the 30 fellows intruded by the crown, demonstrating convincingly from this that James did not take advantage of the expulsion of the fellowship to turn Magdalen into a purely Catholic seminary, though the opportunity was there to go much further in that direction than he did, and that he and his advisers probably had no consistent religious policy regarding the college. The result, unintentionally perhaps, was a hybrid, religiously mixed society, though in an age when few held up the ideal of toleration it was hardly surprising that Protestants feared the worst.

All three writers make full use of the published histories and documents concerning the Magdalen events, but these are handled critically; unpublished material from the college archives is also employed extensively, together with other pertinent printed sources. Volumes III and V of the *History of the University of Oxford* help in putting matters in context, and the authors do not seem to have been unduly inconvenienced by the absence of volume IV (1603–1688), which has yet to appear in print. Some readers, though, may be inconvenienced by the lack of an index.

John Twigg
11 Hope Drive
The Park
Nottingham NG7 1DL

John Gascoigne, *Cambridge in the Age of the Enlightenment: science, religion and politics from the Restoration to the French Revolution.* Cambridge: Cambridge University Press, 1989. xi + 358 pp.

One of the most misleading words in the English language is Oxbridge. It may have a certain currency in suggesting that Oxford and Cambridge have similar buildings, and that they enjoy a common type of humour enunciated in accents that are readily transferable. In other respects, it misleads. The two universities have, historically, been *unlike* each other. Each presents a mirror-image of the other, and, in so doing, they offer a choice of teaching methods, syllabuses, and politics to the aspiring undergraduate. As Gascoigne's book argues, this polarity was never more clear than in the eighteenth century.

Unlike recent works on Oxford, this study chooses narrow themes to examine. It deals essentially with the intellectual dominance of Newtonianism at Cambridge, its theological corollaries and the political connections which it fostered. Valuable statistics are scattered through the book, but there is no attempt to deal with the nature of college life, the social composition of the undergraduate body, or with teaching and examining methods. Within this limited scope, this is a study of some authority.

In the eighteenth century, Oxford was heavily classical in its interests, while Cambridge was mathematical. Cambridge was Whiggish for most of the century, and even admitted to a few radicals. Its alumni challenged the Test Acts, did much to foster Unitarianism, and gave a gentlemanly veneer to a number of late eighteenth-century reform movements. Oxford would have none of these things. There were non-stipendiary amateurs performing experiments in the High and the Broad, but literary men on the Cam, like Macaulay, could sigh for Oxford with some justification. According to Dr Gascoigne, one of the major factors in pointing this difference was the power of Newtonianism. Fully established as an orthodoxy by 1730, it proved hard to shift or modify. Mathematics reigned supreme. Budding botanists or the fashionable geologists of 1800 found a warmer welcome in Oxford.

Cambridge's character in the eighteenth century was formed by the happy conjunction of the publication of the *Principia* and the prominence within the Church of England of a group of Cambridge men, who found Newton's ideas the perfect complement to latitudinarian theology. For men like Tillotson and Tenison, the future of Christianity lay not in an emphasis on Revelation or authority, but in demonstrating how closely its precepts could be founded on the application of 'reason'. Theology and mathematics should be approached in the same way. According to a contemporary, 'the new philosophy ... was a latitudinarian designe to propagate new notions of divinity.' In its extreme form, this 'reason', in the view of Hoadley, would strip Christianity of its mysterious quality altogether, leaving a bishop, for example, as nothing but a layman with a crook in his hand. No wonder that the opponents of Newton felt that his ideas 'hath Made Not only so many Arians but Theists.'

Newtonianism took nearly forty years to capture Cambridge, being considerably peddled by Craige, Bentley, and Cotes. As the rules of mathematics were expressed by the light of reason, so the principles of politics and religion could be similarly discovered. Reason made men tolerant, latitudinarian, and—because Stuart divine-right monarchy was unreasonable—Hanoverian. From 1688 to 1760, Cambridge was favoured by government and intellectually chic. Then came disaster. Newtonian reasonableness held little attraction for George III. Cambridge men spoke and wrote in favour of American rebels and French Jacobins. Worst of all, in 1768, Cambridge elected a vice-chancellor who combined the terrible attributes of being erratic, politically suspect, and long lived. By contrast, in 1772, Oxford got it right for once and elected Lord North. The mirror-image of the two universities was preserved, but the mirror had been turned through one hundred and eighty degrees.

In describing the assimilation of Newtonianism into religious and political thinking, Dr Gascoigne has done the history of the eighteenth century a great service, indicating one of the major ways in which what might be called the English enlightenment differed from that in Europe. Reason did not challenge established religious and political thinking. Cambridge men accommodated it.

L. G. Mitchell
University College
Oxford

Salvador Albiñana, *Universidad e Ilustración. Valencia en la época de Carlos III.* Valencia: University of Valencia Press, 1988. 307 pp.

In the second half of the eighteenth century the Spanish universities were perceived by the 'enlightened' advisers of the crown as idiosyncratic, hidebound pedlars of outdated theoretical knowledge. In consequence, in the reign of Charles III an attempt was made from above to standardize the curriculum (through the introduction of textbooks) and to make it more relevant and practical (through the introduction in the law faculty, for instance, of courses in Spanish as well as Roman law). The reform initiative, however, was only partially successful and fundamental changes were only achieved by the liberal regimes of the nineteenth century. The aim of the book under review is to uncover the reasons for the relative failure of this reform movement by studying its operation in one particular institution.

The author believes that the key to understanding the failure lies in the attitudes of the professoriate. The major part of the book, therefore, is devoted to a study of the catedráticos and opositores who either held or aspired to hold appointments in the University of Valencia in the age of the Enlightenment (specifically 1734–1807). The author's findings, though suitably cautious and balanced, go a long way to confirming the traditional picture of the university professor of the eighteenth century. The large majority were clerics (with the obvious exception of the professors of medicine), few had any commitment to changing the curriculum, and the theologians, always the dominant group, were consumed by their own internecine quarrels over doctrinal niceties. In such a context reform could only come from outside, but at the same time could be easily stymied and could only be introduced as a compromise. Yet Valencia, the author suspects, was far less atrophied than most Spanish universities, if admittedly similar studies are not yet available. The professors at Valencia, whatever their other failings, showed a surprising dedication to teaching as a profession and a healthy, if not always academic, publishing record. In the medical faculty, furthermore, Valencia had a group of professors who kept abreast of contemporary developments and boasted international contacts. As a result, reform in Valencia, especially after 1787 with Blasco as rector, did get off the ground at least.

Albiñana's work is a scholarly and readable study to which full justice cannot be done in a short review. If any criticism can be levelled against the work, it is that much more could be surely said about the actual classroom teaching. The author is content to list the textbooks promoted in the different reform initiatives of the Caroline period and has apparently made no attempt to search out student notebooks (the fundamental source for any curricular study). It would be useful, moreover, to be given more information about student numbers at the university, even if this is obtainable elsewhere. Valencia's importance as a subject for study lies in the fact that it was one of the largest Spanish universities in the eighteenth century, one too where numbers actually rose in defiance of the national trend. It would be interesting to know what connection the pattern of enrolment had, if any, with the course of reform.

These are, however, minor criticisms. One of the great strengths of the work is that, despite its origin as a doctoral thesis, it does not just inform but offers considerable food for thought. Throughout Albiñana is keen to show the peculiarity of the Spanish Enlightenment. Spain, he insists, entered the eighteenth century hermetically sealed from the outside world. It was Europe's 'Tibet'. In consequence, the Enlightenment that developed there was necessarily a chiefly homegrown phenomenon which built on sixteenth-century Spanish humanism and was as much a movement of religious revival as one of secularization. For this reason state-led reform could only be timidly anticlerical and the reformation of institutions such as the universities only half-hearted. The crown could demand the renovation of the curriculum at Valencia but it did nothing to ensure the appointment of reform-minded professors. The appointment and support of the professoriate remained as always the preserve of the town council and the local church, both staunchly conservative institutions.

Such observations are interesting, but are they true? As described by Albiñana, the Spanish Enlightenment does not look significantly different from the movement in other Catholic countries, even France. Historians have too readily assumed that the Enlightenment was anti-Christian and militantly secular, defining the movement not by its general character but by the ideas of its most forceful and exceptional figures, such as Voltaire. Spain, then, may not be peculiar at all. What is needed is a fuller understanding of this movement of spiritual and moral renewal in both

Catholic and Protestant Europe. Studies so far suggest that the movement was far from homogeneous. Catholic baroque Christianity in particular was under attack from both optimistic humanitarians impatient of confessional wrangling and from austere Augustinians anxious to emphasize the nothingness of man. It would be useful to know where on this broad spectrum of anti-establishment religious attitudes the Spanish university reformers, like G. Mayans, are to be placed. Albinaña continually hints at their Jansenist proclivities. Were they to be found to belong in reality to the Augustinian wing of the religious reform movement, it might further help us to understand the flawed nature of university reform under Charles III. There may well have been a tension (one that Albinaña has failed to grasp) between these Augustinian educationalists and their more 'humanitarian' contacts in the Council of Castile (Campomanes, Floridablanca et alia), which would have made the formulation, let alone the implementation, of a coherent policy of university reform impossible.

L. W. B. Brockliss
Magdalen College
Oxford OX1 4AU

Dominique Julia (ed.), *Les enfants de la Patrie*, special edition of *Histoire de l'Education*, Paris, 1989. 205 pp.

It is particularly appropriate that this work should have appeared for the Bicentenary of the French Revolution, as with the new upsurge of enthusiasm for democracy, education came under considerable scrutiny at that time. The debates still continue in educational circles and history always provides valuable lessons. Dominique Julia introduces this collection of articles in that spirit, to assess the revolutionary plans in their context, their successes and shortcomings.

Bruno Belhoste contributes on the origins of the *Ecole polytechnique*. He has been fortunate in that Fourcy's now well-known history was recently reproduced in Jean Dhombres's edition and Janis Langins has produced *La République avait besoin de savants*. Belhoste has missed some recent research apart from this, but he provides interesting material on the *écoles d'application* and the role of Monge in the creation of the *Ecole polytechnique*.

Jean Dhombres, on the other hand, writes entertainingly on the mania for everything 'revolutionary', the opposition to elitist teaching at the *Ecole polytechnique* and clashes over the content of mathematics courses between 1789 and 1799. Arguments were, of course, to continue long after that, with Cauchy and Prony at loggerheads on this issue for many years. Dhombres also attempts to explain why science and mathematics received so much attention during the revolutionary years and their usefulness and application in a society being re-created. He reminds us of the role of examiners, and of the great names at the *Ecole normale*, where the aim was to spread mathematical education throughout France. Algebra was taken back to first principles and linked with geometry, but to master mathematics was a lengthy process—so a new elite emerged and a new social gulf appeared. In addition to classic sources like Hahn and Taton, Dhombres has made a thorough exploration of archive material.

Laurence Brockliss describes changes in medical education and the attempts to break down elitism and privilege within that profession. The distinction between surgeons and physicians, for instance, was abolished. Louis Liard, at the end of the nineteenth century, claimed that the modernization of the teaching in France was unequalled in Europe at that time, but Brockliss weighs up the evidence carefully and disputes the black and white conclusions and the condemnation of eighteenth-century medicine as opposed to the revolutionary approach. He reminds us, for instance, of the advantages of studying with practical experiment at Montpellier in the eighteenth century, the necessity for practical experience before entering the Nancy College of Medicine and the practical examinations in anatomy in Paris. Indeed, he provides a detailed analysis of medical practice in eighteenth-century France and the problems, such as student overpopulation in the medical faculties after the Revolution. He draws on some interesting and relatively unexplored archive material in addition to published sources.

Hans-Christian Harten refers to conflicts within the republican movement, the church, the 'protestant threat' and the effects of the Revolution on schools and teachers, varying from region to region. There were, for example, drastic fluctuations in the qualifications of teachers, and acceptance of republicanism was more widespread in areas of greater literacy. Interesting tables compare the various *départements*, the percentage swearing the constitutional oath, literacy levels, changes in place-names, cultural facilities, republican schools and authors of pedagogical and cultural works. Sources are given and interesting conclusions are drawn from the diversity of the statistics. A high level of literacy, for instance, favoured acceptance of revolutionary and cultural activity and rejection of tradition. Changes with regard to the church and increased political and cultural participation may have had greater importance than socio-economic factors.

Marie-Madeleine Compère appraises the *écoles centrales*, and attempts to tackle questions which the abundant relevant literature has left unanswered. She details the legal documents pertaining to the schools and the divergences between plans and reality. Her main topic is the teaching of classical languages, Latin, Greek and an abortive attempt to introduce Hebrew. The French language was neglected!

To complete this useful collection of articles, there are reviews of recently published, relevant books. The volume, informative in many areas, is a valuable addition to the many studies of the revolutionary period produced during 1989.

Margaret Bradley
Department of Languages, Politics and History
Coventry Polytechnic, Priory Street, Coventry CV1 5FB

Iu. D. Margolis and G. A. Tishkin, *Otechestvu na pol'zu, a rossiia-nam vo slavu: iz istorii universitetskogo obrazovaniia v Peterburge v XVIII–nachale XIX v.* Leningrad: Izdatel'stvo Leningradskogo Universiteta, 1988.

In the spring of 1983, the authors of this book published in Leningrad University's weekly paper an article titled 'How Old Is Petersburg-Leningrad University?' The answer was that the university is older than you thought. The 'traditional' answer, the authors pointed out, is that the university was founded in 1819 but they argue that in truth the university was founded by Peter the Great in 1724. This book is an elaboration of the 1983 article, attempting to justify its conclusion and explain its significance.

In the introduction and conclusion the authors argue that the question is important because it is an issue of the national historical memory, an issue touching the country's heart and soul. 'After nearly a century [buried] in the depths of history, [the truth about] this temple of learning is resurrected' (p. 12). In 1819, the university was 'renewed, but the roots of the first capital institution of higher education extend back to the eighteenth century times of Peter and of Lomonosov' (p. 219). Moreover, it is important to pay attention to the history of the university to 'satisfy the fatherland's need for historical memory, incompatible with the bureaucratic perception that, stemming from the time of Dmitri Tolstoi, suppressed the tradition of Petersburg University for a whole century' (p. 224). Early in the eighteenth century, 'Petersburg was among the spiritual and cultural centers of the time. Since then, it has traveled a difficult, and interrupted, path. But that path of glory and service for the fatherland has been traveled' (p. 225).

To explain and justify their conclusions, the authors present a history of the university's eighteenth-century predecessors, the Academy of Sciences founded by Peter the Great and the Teachers College founded by Catherine the Great. Much attention is paid to Lomonosov, who served as rector of the university, i.e. the Academy of Sciences, and as a 'true son of the fatherland' fought the influence of imported German academicians such as

Mueller and other 'enemies of Russian enlightenment' (p. 102). Much of the evidence the authors present to show that there were institutions of higher learning in St Petersburg more or less continuously since the reign of Peter the Great is well known. Some of the evidence presented is not well known. For example, the authors describe a document from 1757 that they located in the Central State Historical Archives that proposed, in some detail, a building for the university. On the reverse side of one page is a note that Lomonosov had seen the document. The plan was not funded and hence the building never came into existence, but the authors find the existence of the plan, and Lomonosov's knowledge of it, evidence of the continued existence of the university (pp. 122–6). They reject, almost bitterly, the judgment of Dmitri A. Tolstoi, the reactionary mid-nineteenth-century Minister of Education, who also was a prolific scholar who wrote thoroughly documented histories of schools and churches in eighteenth-century Russia. Tolstoi concluded that since in the eighteenth century the university had no building, no professors, and no students, it did not exist. The authors insist instead that the university was being 're-organized, not liquidated' (p. 156).

The authors grant that they have a serious 'methodological problem' to solve in order to establish the connection between the modern university founded in 1819 and its predecessors. They point out, however, that 'in the history of state institutions in Russia interruptions and great changes are common. The history of St Petersburg University is not different in kind.' Vilna University, for example, celebrated its 400th anniversary in 1979, even though the 'obscurantist policy of tsarism kept it closed 1832–1919' (pp. 16–17). Granted that there existed institutions of higher learning in St Petersburg in the eighteenth century, it does not seem that the authors have successfully solved the problem of making useful links between those institutions and the university that all agree was founded in 1819. There are much better informed, and written, studies of learning in eighteenth-century St Petersburg than this. J. L. Black, D. M. Griffiths, I. de Madariaga, Gary Marker, and Max Okenfuss recently have published works much more likely to advance knowledge of the subject than Margolis-Tishkin. More to the point, perhaps, this book is not nearly as well informed, or thoughtful, as the works of Tolstoi (1885) or S. V. Rozhdestvenskii (1910), or even Shabaeva's textbook history of education in Russia (1973).

In sum, this book is not a useful contribution to the literature on the history of the university in Russia. It does not succeed in making plausible, let alone prove, its main theme, while its control of information and sources falls much short of what others have achieved on this subject, and its muddled, repetitious exposition suggests haste, not care, in the writing. Nonetheless, it is interesting that Leningrad University published this book in 1988, in an edition of more than 8,000 copies (about four times the usual number for university press monographs of the history of schools!), to argue that 'Moscow should not claim that it is the older, senior institution', for in the eighteenth century 'both Moscow and St. Petersburg suffered the same childhood disease—weakness' (p. 19). This book may be important as a protest of Leningraders against the dominance of Moscow. Regrettably, it is not important as a contribution to scholarship on the history of Petersburg-Leningrad University.

James T. Flynn
College of the Holy Cross

G. A. Tishkin (ed.), *Ocherki po istorii leningradskogo universiteta*, vol. V. Leningrad: Izdatel'stvo Leningradskogo Universiteta, 1984.

This is the fifth volume in a series published irregularly since 1962 and contains an index of all the articles in the five volumes. It may be worth noting that the quite substantial history of Leningrad University edited by the same group of scholars who founded the series in 1962, S. B. Okun, N. G. Sladkevich, V. V. Mavrodin, and S. N. Valk, titled *Istoriia Leningradskogo Universiteta: Ocherki* (Leningrad, 1969) is not a volume in this series (some bibliographic guides to the contrary), but is a balanced history of the university while the volumes in the series present individual essays on various topics in the university's history. The current (i.e. 1984) volume is in format and material exactly like its predecessors, though the editorial 'collective' that produced it has changed almost completely since 1964. In every issue there are contributions on the development of a particular field of learning in the university, on leading figures in its history, and on the participation of the students and (sometimes or) professors in the revolutionary movement. In volume I (1962), there is an article on the development of mathematical physics, a study of the career of M. A. Balugianskii, the university's first rector, and an article on the student movement and the 'first demonstrations in 1901'. In the current 1984 volume there is a piece on the development of biology in the 1820s and 30s, one on Professor Kavelin, a liberal leader in the 1860s, and one on the participation of the university's students in the 'revolutionary movement in 1907–February 1917'.

In substance, the articles are nearly as consistent as in subject. The treatments of fields of learning are in large measure catalogues of names of scholars and publications with little analysis either of the field of learning or its political-social-cultural impact on the university or the society it served. The biographical pieces are more likely to take up questions of broader interest, such as the individuals' views about, if not role in, larger political or cultural developments. The articles on participation in the revolutionary movements provide examples that show that the university fit quite exactly into the general movement, or at least that the *Ocherki* fit quite exactly into the conceptual framework provided by the text-book or multi-volume histories of the USSR put out in the 1960s by Mysl' ('Thought', the publishing house for 'social-economic literature') or Nauka ('Learning', the publishing house of the Academy of Science). In some important ways, then, the contributions in this series are quite inconsequential. In other ways, however, they can be very useful. Many of the articles, e.g. E. M. Kosachevskaia's contribution on Balugianskii, summarize or provide a substantial introduction to a scholar's major study. Moreover, almost without exception the articles provide excellent introductions to the literature of their subjects, providing well-informed basic bibliographic guides. For example, M. V. Borisenko's article on the participation of St Petersburg University students in the revolutionary movement 1907–1917 seems particularly well suited for the sort of fruitless recitation of formulaic answers that characterized Soviet history for so long. The piece indeed begins with the standard citations of Lenin. But the piece also provides well-documented discussion of the themes of some important Soviet scholarship, e.g. Avrekh's work on the Third Duma, set in the context of a learned discussion of the periodical press of the 1920s, before Stalin's consolidation of his political power imposed not only censorship but an approved answer for all scholarly questions, together with university records, and recent Soviet dissertations. In sum, in many cases the contributions in *Ocherki* at the least provide sound guides to a literature and sources otherwise hard to discover and thus can prove extremely useful for study of the university in its first century, 1819 to the early 1920s, if not beyond.

James T. Flynn
College of the Holy Cross

Arthur T. Hamlin, *The University Library in the United States: Its Origins and Development*. Philadelphia: University of Pennsylvania Press, 1981. xiii + 271 pp.

Arthur T. Hamlin has written the first general history of American university libraries, a short, readable book based partly on the secondary literature, in which he has read widely, and partly on his own experience of nearly fifty years as a librarian in six large American libraries, the New York Public Library, and five distinguished university libraries. As executive secretary of the Association of College and Reference (now Research) Libraries in the 1950s Mr Hamlin gained broad knowledge of developments in American university libraries during the most interesting period in their history. The book is intended as 'a readable, interesting account for the mature reader outside as well as inside the profession.' The number of footnotes was kept to a minimum, but there is a list of sources on which the chapters were based and an excellent bibliography. By the author's own admission, the book is not the definitive work on the subject, but it is certainly a good, popular treatment of it. By now a number of reviews have appeared, most of which are quite favourable. A few have been critical of the book for being anecdotal and lacking in depth.

The book is in two parts, the first and shorter of which (81 pp.) is a general survey of the history of American university libraries from the beginnings—the establishment of a library at Harvard in 1639—to the 1970s. The second and much longer part (137 pp.) treats the history of special aspects of the subject—collection building, administration, finances, service to students and scholars, architecture, departmental libraries, library cooperation, cataloguing, and library technology. There are also several appendices, one of which is in very small type. The book is a bit repetitive as topics discussed in the first part are sometimes gone over again in the second.

The index passes over many things in silence, and various groups are often indexed only under their acronyms or initials. The 'Seminar on the Acquisition of Latin American Library Materials' is listed in the index only under 'SALALM'. There is a cross-reference from 'Beinecke Library' to 'Yale University', but one searches for the latter in vain, though Yale is often mentioned in the text.

There are three references in the index to the British Museum and two to the British Library Lending Division. The Bibliothèque Sainte Geneviève is mentioned twice because of its influential cast-iron stacks, and the Göttingen University library also gets two references, one because of a quotation from a letter by George Ticknor, who studied there, and one in connection with the influence of German universities, particularly Göttingen, on Johns Hopkins University in Baltimore. German university seminars are mentioned several other times in the text, but they are indexed under the word 'Seminars'. There is one reference to the Bibliothèque Nationale in the index, also to the passage on cast-iron stacks, but the text contains another interesting reference to this library. On p. 128 Hamlin says that it was probably the example of *La Société des Amis de la Bibliothèque Nationale et les Grandes Bibliothèques de France* that led Harvard to establish a friends of the library group.

Cambridge University was a great influence on Harvard in the seventeenth century, many Harvard faculty members having been Cambridge men. In later years, Gore Hall, Harvard's first separate library building, was patterned after the chapel at King's College, Cambridge, and the use of alcoves with a table in each in Wren's library at Trinity College, Cambridge, was copied both at Harvard and Yale. The index lacks a cross-reference from 'Cambridge University' to 'King's College, Cambridge' and to 'Trinity College, Cambridge'. The Bibliotheca Mediceo-Laurenziana is mentioned on p. 147 for its great influence on library architecture generally, but the index shortens the name to 'Bibliotheca Laurenziana'.

Hamlin states on p. 33 that 'As the largest library, Harvard was the first to have a conscientious and talented leader for a number of years in the person of William Harris, a distinguished entomologist who devoted himself to the library from 1831 to 1856.' This was Thaddeus William Harris, 1795–1856, who is considered by others to be the least effective librarian Harvard ever had. Hamlin calls the computerized index to medical literature, MED-LARS, the 'brain-child of the National Library of Medicine', but it would be more accurate to call it the brainchild of the late Dr Frank Bradway Rogers, the former director of this library. In connection with the computerization of medical libraries, mention might have been made of the pioneering work of Irwin Pizer in developing the State University of New York Biomedical Communications Network.

Hamlin's book is fairly well balanced, and it pulls together a good deal of useful and interesting information about the history of American university libraries. It fulfils the purpose for which it was written, though it will no doubt disappoint those who are looking for more than the short overview this book is.

Philip J. Weimerskirch
Providence Public Library

R. D. Anderson, *The Student Community at Aberdeen 1860–1939.* (Quincentennial Studies in the history of The University of Aberdeen.) Aberdeen: Aberdeen University Press, 1988. x + 159 pp.

Student life, its rituals and private codes, as well as its more conventional sociological aspects, is difficult for the historian to apprehend. The documents we have for the study of students in their habitat are too often the creation of the subjects themselves—the major sources of evidence about the student culture are student magazines, produced by a minority of a given year, reflecting the biases of that minority, subject to a degree of censorship by university administrators. Memoirs and published diaries are subject to the distortions of memory and the emendations of time. The nature of the evidence has encouraged historians of universities other than Oxford and Cambridge to view student cultures as ephemeral, matter for garnishing an administrative or commemorative account of university life—little more. R. D. Anderson has paid the whole study of students and their lives at the university the enormous compliment of a scholarly and serious study, a project which was hinted at in the final chapter of his *Education and*

Opportunity in Victorian Scotland (Oxford, 1983), and which he has undertaken at the request of the University of Aberdeen in celebration of its quincentennial.

Using the University of Aberdeen as a background, Anderson develops themes from his earlier work, covering a long period beginning with the union of Marischal and King's College under the Universities (Scotland) Act of 1858 and ending with the outbreak of the Second World War in 1939. He calls his work 'scenes from provincial life' (p. 116), reflecting not only the highly local character of student recruitment to the university throughout this period but also the affinities between students and the provincial middle class. Using the extraordinarily detailed matriculation records for the university, he demonstrates the extent to which the university recruited from the rural middle and upper artisanal class, while giving full weight to the presence of a significant minority of working-class students. Using the records of the Arts Class, as well as the student journals of the period, he traces the swift rise of a corporate identity in the newly-united university, made possible initially by the existence of a unitary Arts curriculum, which allowed for a high degree of common sentiment among students. This identity gave rise to a number of institutions which have become subsequently the model for much of English, as well as Scottish student life, including clubs, student journals, athletics and, most important, the Students' Representative Council. Anderson reminds us that, although these innovations were a response to demand for the teaching of social skills, necessary if Scottish students wished to join the British professional class, they followed a trend in student organization that could also be traced to the Continent and to the United States. To the ancient universities of England this movement owed very little.

The creation of a strong student culture based on the day student saved the Scottish universities from the problem of how to emulate the ancient universities in the provision of residence, a dilemma which was to vex the English civic universities in the early twentieth century, and which they were never adequately to resolve. The experience of Scottish students was not, however, without relevance to the English case, and the abiding value of Anderson's book is that he offers the student of British universities so many opportunities for contrast and comparison. For instance, when the first women were admitted to Aberdeen after 1889, they encountered the limitations of a corporate ideal based largely upon male solidarity—their presence gradually modified this ideal, but the conflicts it generated are reminiscent of those encountered by the first women students at the Owens College, Manchester.

The most intriguing sections of this account concern the students' response to war—primarily to the Boer War, to the First World War, and to the long hostile decade leading up to the Second World War. In their responses to the Boer War, Scottish university students mirrored the attitudes of the professional classes they expected to join, patriotic but conscious that a university education was an investment not lightly thrown away for the sake of a moment's heroism. The response to the First World War was wholehearted and tragic, the Volunteer company in which Aberdeen students were concentrated was virtually destroyed at the Battle of Loos. Fifteen ex-students, including the principal's son, were killed together. Anderson points out that in this respect, universities with Officer Training Corps were apt to feel the impact of their losses less vividly, as O.T.C. units sent their members to a variety of assignments, rather than keeping them together. In other respects, however, the experience of Aberdeen—emergency mobilization in 1914, the gradual dominance of women in student affairs, and the slow return to a semblance of normality as the war progressed—reflects that of the English civic universities.

Student response to the growing threat of war throughout the 1930s is a more complex issue, which Anderson handles with scrupulous fairness. It is hard to acknowledge, for instance, student interest in fascism, whereas student politics of the left have been well documented. Anderson's handling of the last years of his story, when the British student warily approached the coming war, reflects the great strength of this book—his meticulous use of evidence leads his readers to appreciate a culture, a mood, which varied according to the winds and weather of the outside world, but which is consistent with the unchanging realities of students' lives.

Elizabeth J. Morse
Center for Studies in Higher Education
University of California
Berkeley, CA 94720

John E. Craig, *Scholarship and Nation Building. The Universities of Strasbourg and Alsatian Society, 1870–1939*. Chicago and London: University of Chicago Press, 1984. xii + 515 pp.

In both conception and realization, this is a highly successful book. It offers a detailed but always sharp account of university life in Strasbourg between the establishment of the Reichsland of Alsace-Lorraine, in the aftermath of the Franco-Prussian war, and the beginning of the Second World War. The book falls naturally into two parts. The first is devoted to the Universität, largely the brainchild of Franz von Roggenbach. A south German Catholic, von Roggenbach saw the university that he was appointed, by Bismarck, to organize as above all a vehicle for the determined, if sensitive and necessarily slow, assimilation of Alsace-Lorraine to the German cultural tradition. The second treats the Université, whose establishment in 1919 was one of the highest symbolic priorities of France as she reacquired her 'lost provinces' and began her own process of cultural imperialism.

The contrast between these two phases is all the more instructive since, for both the Germans and the French, Strasbourg's university had a very special function in the pursuit of nationalistic objectives. At least in the early years of the German period, as Craig shows, nationalism bore fruit in the funds and talent that were drawn to Strasbourg in equal abundance. It is true that even a salary twice the going rate for an Ordinarius failed to entice Theodor Mommsen from Berlin (though he was plainly tempted). But younger men, such as Hermann Baumgarten, Wilhelm Scherer, and Gustav Schmoller (most of them still in their thirties and with reputations still to make), did respond both to their own patriotic sentiment and to a unique opportunity for both nation-building and academic career-making amid excellent facilities and with a route to the top distinctly more open than in the older German universities. Likewise, in the first flush of the French administration, professors of outstanding distinction were assembled. Among them were Marc Bloch and Lucien Febvre, both of whom taught at Strasbourg through the 1920s and early 1930s. It was during this period, in 1929, that the *Annales d'histoire économique et sociale* was born, the fruit of uncommonly close relations between disciplines, a sense of almost colonial isolation, and a mission to create a distinctive French style of scholarship that would combine German rigour with the French gift for synthesis.

Craig brings out well the fragility of the successes of the first phase in the history of each institution. By 1900 many younger Strasbourg scholars were weakening in their commitment to the vision of a German cultural crusade that had fired their predecessors: to the dismay of a recognizable 'old guard', Strasbourg was drifting towards a cosmopolitanism that left the young German minds in their charge as open to Henri Bergson and Romain Rolland as they were to Stefan George or Friedrich Neumann. After 1919, the main problem lay in the lure of Paris. Even by the mid-1920s, Etienne Gilson had drifted away to the Sorbonne, and there were signs that some early vocations were wearing thin.

It is an essential plank of Craig's predominantly political interpretation that in all this the people of Alsace were rather hapless pawns. Their role, it seems, was that of spectators of institutions that stood consistently aloof from their society. In the German period, the university was set apart by its official language (German, needless to say), a dominant protestantism, and an association with free thought; in the 1870s and 1880s, at least, this was enough to distance it from the bulk of the Catholic population. In the 1920s, by contrast, after nearly half a century of German influence, it was the university's use of French which formed the severest barrier not only to the admission of local students but also, on occasions, to the recruitment of Alsatian-born professors whose French was less than fluent.

Scholarship and Nation Building stands as a salutary reminder of the ease with which notions of the universality of learning and the transcendent internationalism of the scholarly community can be cast aside in the face of national interest. If there is a moral in this engaging story, therefore, it has at least this gloomy side. There may be no such thing as an exclusively national academic culture. But the culture that all of us in the world of learning like to believe we share is capable of an alarming degree of nationalistic distortion, not least at the hands of academics themselves.

Robert Fox
University of Oxford

George Davie, *The Crisis of the Democratic Intellect: the Problem of Generalism and Specialization in Twentieth-Century Scotland.* Edinburgh: Polygon, 1987. vi + 283 pp. £17.95.

Drawing out Leviathan with a hook has been recognized, since the Book of Job at least, as no easy matter. In the early years of this century a determined attempt was made to dethrone philosophy from its central place in the Scottish universities. In so far as it may now be treated in them as a 'specialist subject', some success attended these efforts in the end. The cost, in Dr Davie's view, has been high. In this splendidly idiosyncratic book he charts the damaging effects of the long struggle between those who 'saw . . . the Scottish universities . . . as . . . centres of *la grande culture*' and the Scottish Education Department head who wanted them to become 'first-rate training colleges for turning out . . . very efficient . . . schoolteachers for secondary education' (pp. 7, 8).

Sir John Struthers of the SED and the secondary teachers of the Educational Institute of Scotland had, at face value, a strong case. The traditional trio of subjects—logic, Latin, and mathematics—had survived from a time when the Arts Faculties had been primarily a training ground for ministers of religion. The universities north of the border were not semi-private institutions like the collegiate federations of Oxford and Cambridge: the SED, powerfully backed by the Carnegie Trust, was trying, quite legitimately, to create a state university *system* for Scotland.

We know a good deal by now about the unintended effects which are apt to flow from reforming efforts of this kind. The struggle does more harm than the eventual settlement can do good. 'Like the Church-State crisis of 1833–1843', Dr Davie writes in his prologue, 'the . . . struggle . . . not only occupied a frenzied decade (1917–1927) . . . but resulted in the break-up of a fundamental institution which had kept the Scottish people together . . .

universities turned their backs on the SED and the Scottish schools in order to join themselves, in due course, with the system of schools and universities in England, under the auspices of the Department of Education and Science.'

In 'metaphysical Scotland' organizational matters raise questions of principle. Dr Davie deals broadly with what soon became an unending series of debates. These can be summarized in his phrase (p. 61) as 'elitism versus anti-elitism, liberalism versus utilitarianism, vocationalism versus generalism'. Each of the greatest protagonists—John Burnet, Norman Kemp Smith, and John Anderson—is given a chapter to himself (though the last named left Scotland for an Australian professorship in his early thirties). Anderson forms the link with C. M. Grieve, whose poetry is examined for its philosophical implications. The last eighty pages of the book are concerned with the impact on 'Scottish philosophy' of the doctrines of Bertrand Russell, G. E. Moore, and Gilbert Ryle. A little more attention to mundane administrative matters might have been welcome: neither the UGC nor the Robbins Committee receives its correct title; but in Dr Davie's pages Edinburgh's claim to be the Athens of the North gains a fresh endorsement.

Michael Brock
St George's House
Windsor Castle

Christophe Charle and Eva Telkes, *Les Professeurs du Collège de France: Dictionnaire Biographique, 1901–1939.* Paris: Editions du CNRS, 1988. 247 pp. F160.00.

This collective biography of the ninety-five members of the *Collège de France* appointed between 1901 and 1939 is part of a wider project covering French academic life in the nineteenth and twentieth centuries. The *Collège de France* seeks to represent the highest achievement in every field of scholarship, science, and medicine, and many of the men in this volume (for they are all men) achieved eminence outside the strict academic circle. A brief introduction summarizes the data about social origins, birthplaces, careers and ages of appointment, but the editors' principle is to make each entry as full as possible, and there is much additional information which will be of value both to comparative historians and to students of the French élite. The general pattern is one familiar from other such studies. Nearly a third were born in Paris, and all but a few received their higher education there. About a quarter came from the lower middle or working class, though their fathers tended to be shopkeepers, white-collar workers or skilled

History of Universities

artisans rather than peasants or industrial workers. Among the majority of bourgeois origin, there was a bias towards officialdom and the world of teaching, and some were hereditary *universitaires* like the historian Lucien Febvre, the son and grandson of secondary teachers. But there was probably more ideological diversity in the *Collège de France* than at the Sorbonne. There was a significant number of Catholic intellectuals, including the radical theologian Alfred Loisy, and while many professors seem to have abstained rigorously from politics, others were drawn in by the Dreyfus Affair in the 1900s, and by the traumatic events of the 1930s and the Second World War. If three professors (Frédéric Joliot, Paul Langevin and Henri Wallon) were impelled into the Communist party by anti-fascist activity, another, Bernard Faÿ, was deprived of his chair for collaboration, and there were nationalists as well as Dreyfusards among the older generation. But these are only samples of what can be gleaned from this valuable work of reference, which could perhaps have no equivalent in countries with a less centralized intellectual life than France.

R. D. Anderson
University of Edinburgh

Ulrich Karpen, *Access to Higher Education in the Federal Republic of Germany*. Frankfurt/Main, Berne, New York and Paris: Peter Lang Verlag, 1988. 145 pp. sFr. 34.

As the author is aware (pp. 23–4 and 35–6), three ideas of the university inform the West German tertiary education system: the Humboldtian-elitist idea (which is still alive in the 'old' universities); the meritocratic-instrumentalist idea (which generated the technical universities and *Fachhochschulen*); and the egalitarian-comprehensive idea (from which the new universities have arisen over the last 25 years). However, there exists a contradiction between the first two ideas and the third which has been replicated in the conflict between the terms of the Higher Education Act (*Rahmengesetz*) of 1976 (which states that every German citizen with the necessary qualifications has the *right* to study at a university) and the universities' increasing need to select their students (especially in the so-called *numerus clausus* subjects such as medicine). Professor Karpen's book, besides providing much useful factual information on the West German school and university systems (pp. 6–15 and 16–33) and two long appendices containing English translations of the relevant legal instruments (pp. 60–145), also discusses the ways in which the West German authorities have tried to resolve the above conflict—by setting up a central clearing-house and defining terms of operation which are compatible with the West German Constitution (pp. 34–59). Unfortunately, the English-speaking reader who knows no German will, I suspect, find the text more than a little rebarbative. Typos abound; there is a good range of basic grammatical errors (the perfect instead of the past tense (pp. 23 and 31), 'there' for 'their' (p. 25), 'who's' for 'whose' (p. 39)); the punctuation conforms to German rather than English expectations; and there are some weird neologisms ('anticonceptive-effect' and 'study-beginners' (p. 17)). More importantly still, wide swathes of the text are couched in Germish—that strange dialect beloved of undergraduate translators which, reminiscent of Heidegger on a bad day, obscures rather than promotes meaning. Here are two examples: 'The latter one is meant to preserve to every applicant the constitutionally based right to be admitted, although others—more apt ones—are admitted earlier' (p. 50); and 'They are integrated into the planning and distribution of students-process of state institutions. One acknowledges their possibilities and accomplishments as an instrument of pluralistic competition. Due to the heavy inpact [sic] of civil rights as rights to share public offerings and the social-state-principle as a directive for the states [sic] activities—both of Federal Law-character—, problems of access to higher education in fact are mainly regulated by Federal Law, although it is the Länder, which are the "masters of the universities".' (p. 52). The author has simply not tried hard enough to render his text into real English: which is a pity, as his central discussion is very relevant to the crisis that is currently building up within West Germany's higher education system.

Richard Sheppard
Magdalen College
Oxford

Bibliography

New Projects in University History
A new Journal for the history of universities

A further sign of the growing interest in the history of universities is the establishment and successful inauguration of a new Journal from the DDR. Leipzig University has for some years been known for its concern with university history. In 1982, for example, the university organized a conference to which scholars from the United States, France, Great Britain, Hungary, and the BRD were invited; the papers were published by the university as *Die Geschichte der Universitäten und Ihre Erforschung* in 1984. Now this concern has been given a more concrete and permanent form. From 1987 the university has sponsored *Leipziger Beiträge zur Universitätsgeschichte*, an annual publication edited by a group of Leipzig historians led by Dr Werner Fläschendräger, whose lively and scholarly studies have brought much information and pleasure to those working in this field. The new Journal concentrates on the history of the University of Leipzig, on the development of its links with other universities and on the spread of its influence throughout the learned world. It is, however, expected that, as the Journal develops, contributions relating to the comparative history of other universities will be printed. The first issues show that the new publication will be especially valuable to students of the academic history of eastern Europe, with which Leipzig, of course, had very close links. The second issue of the Journal, for example, contains a survey of the influence of the university on the intellectual life of the Polish state in the fifteenth and early sixteenth centuries. The Journal also prints relevant documents and photographs and has a section for book reviews. Details of the new Journal may be obtained from the Karl-Marx-Universität Leipzig, Direktorat für Forschung, Abteilung Wissenschaftliche Publikationen, Goethestrasse 3/5, Leipzig, DDR-7010.

The Influence of the Spanish Universities in America

The University of Alcalá has organized since 1987 annual conferences to discuss the role of Spanish universities in the development of the university system of America. The conference proceedings are published. The organisers would be grateful to hear from scholars interested in presenting papers on this theme at their conferences. Financial support is available. Further details may be obtained from The Secretary, ACISAL, Casa de la Entrevista, c/San Juan 1, 28801 Alcalá de Henares, Spain.

Texts and Studies on the History of the University of Cambridge

In recent years there has been a considerable expansion of interest in the history of European universities. Nevertheless, it is widely recognized that the history of the University of Cambridge has, with certain conspicuous exceptions, been rather neglected. One problem has been the absence of a single series designed for publications concerning the history of the university. A new series is planned to remedy this problem.

It will consist of: 1. Texts of important unpublished sources concerning the university (which exist in abundance). 2. Monographs on particular topics. Under this heading occasional collections of essays by one or several authors may be included; such collections would be restricted to a single period or theme. Suggestions for volumes to be included in the series are now invited. These, and any enquiries about the series, may be addressed to the General Editor, Dr P. N. R. Zutshi, Keeper of the University Archives, University Library, West Road, Cambridge CB3 9DR. The General Editor would be particularly glad to hear of work in progress or nearing completion which may be suitable for the series.

Publications on University History since 1977:
A Continuing Bibliography

Edited by John M. Fletcher
With the assistance of Christopher A. Upton

Produced with the co-operation of the International
Commission for the History of Universities

Preface

Rapid changes in central and eastern Europe have at times made postal
communication extremely difficult and have hampered our efforts to obtain
information. However, some lists have arrived and are included in this
volume. We hope for less troublesome contacts in the future. Our contributors in Italy, P. Nardi, and in West Germany, R. vom Bruch and R. A.
Müller, have now handed the task of collecting information to other
colleagues. We thank them for their past efforts and welcome our new
contributors in these countries. May we remind readers that the five
volumes of *History of European Universities: Work in Progress and Publications*, which include bibliographical material for the years 1977–81, may be
purchased from the address below. Later lists have been published in
History of Universities, volumes seven and eight for 1988 and 1989.

The following have contributed reports for this issue; membership of the
International Commission is indicated by an asterix. A. Kernbauer
(Austria), H. de Ridder-Symoens* and J. Paquet* (Belgium and the
Netherlands), C. A. Upton (British Isles), M. Svatoš (Czechoslovakia),
J. Verger* (France), W. Smolka (BRD), L. Szögi (Hungary), D. Maffei*,
P. Maffei and G. Minnucci (Italy), J. Basista (Poland), A. García y García*,
A. M. Carabias Torres and D. L. M. Gutierrez Torrecilla (Spain and
Portugal) and N. Siraisi (USA). Copy has been prepared by Pauline A.
Fletcher and Françoise Bannister. We are most grateful to all for their work.

Readers are asked to send to us notes of any titles omitted from our lists.
We would especially request details of material in local publications not
easily accessible to us or our contributors. We would like to thank the many
individuals who have sent information to us during the past year.

Dr J. M. Fletcher
Dept of Modern Languages
Aston University
Aston Triangle *Birmingham B4 7ET* *England.*

Austria

Additions to Earlier Lists

For 1980
Merinsky, J.: Die Auswirkungen der Annexion Österreichs durch das Deutsche Reich auf die Medizinische Fakultät der Universität Wien im Jahre 1938. Thesis. Vienna.

For 1981
Shank, M. H.: Acad. benefices and Germ. univs during the Great Schism: 3 letters from Johannes of Stralen, Arnold of Emelisse and Gerard of Kalkar 1387–88, *Codices MSS. Z. f. Handschriftenkunde*, 7: 33–47.

For 1983
Binder, D. A.: *Das Joanneum in Graz. Lehranstalt und Bildungsstätte. Ein Beitrag zur Entwicklung des technischen und naturwissenschaftlichen Unterrichtes im 19. Jahrhundert*, Graz.

For 1985
Kernbauer, A.: *Das Fach Chemie an der Philosophischen Fakultät der Universität Graz*, Graz.
Hammerstein, N.: Besonderheiten d. österr. Univ.- u. Wissenschaftsreform zur Zeit Maria Theresias u. Josephs II, in *Österreich im Europa der Aufklärung. Kontinuität und Zäsur in Europa zur Zeit Maria Theresias und Josephs II*, 2 vols, Vienna (henceforth noted as *Österreich im Europa*), 2: 787–812.
Ruwet, J.: Die Reform d. Univ. Löwen 1740–80, in *Österreich im Europa*, 2: 813–46.

Publications 1987
Hirschegger, M.: *Archiv der Universitätsbibliothek Graz. Systematische Erfassung des Bestandes 1775–1945*, Graz.
Hölvényi, G.: Studenten aus Ungarn. Ihr Studium an verschiedenen Univ. im 18. Jh., in R. G. Plaschka and K. Mack eds: *Wegenetz Europäischen Geistes. 2. Universitäten und Studenten*, Vienna: 118–26.
Ortner, F.: *Die Universität in Salzburg; die dramatischen Bemuhungen um ihre Wiedererrichtung 1810–1962*, Salzburg.

Publications 1988
Egglmaier, H. H.: *Naturgeschichte, Wissenschaft und Lehrfach. Ein Beitrag zur Geschichte des naturhistorischen Unterrichts in Österreich*, Graz.
Engelbrecht, H.: *Geschichte des österreichischen Bildungswesens. Erziehung und Unterricht auf dem Boden Österreichs*, 5, Vienna.
Kernbauer, A.: *Svante Arrhenius Beziehungen zu österreichischen Gelehrten. Briefe aus Österreich an Svante Arrhenius 1891–1926*, Graz.

Weingand, H.-P.: *Die Technische Hochschule Graz im Dritten Reich. Vorgeschichte, Geschichte und Nachgeschichte des Nationalsozialismus an einer Institution*, Graz.
Wyklicky, H.: *Das Josefinum. Biographie eines Hauses*, Vienna.

Belgium and the Netherlands

Additions to Earlier Lists

For 1977
Palm, L. C.: Snellius and his Newtonian teaching in Halle, *Janus*, 64, 15–24.
Pieterse, A. G. M.: De controverse Leiden-Utrecht (The L.-U. controversy). Thesis. Groningen. (Concerns the training of colonial civil servants early 20th century).

For 1978
Feddema, H. and Muyzenberg, O. B. van den: Koloniale belangen in de acad.: hoe kwam de Utrechtse Indologieopleiding tot stand? (Colonial concern in the acad. How did studies of the Indies at U. develop their status?), in F. Bovenkerk etc. eds: *Toen en thans De sociale Wetenschappen in de jaren dertig en nu*, Baarn: 105–119.

For 1980
Schutte, O.: *Het Album Promotorum van de academie te Harderwijk*, Zutphen.

For 1981
Crane, L. ed.: *University and Reformation*, Leyden.
Steven Turner, R.: The Prussian professoriate and the research imperative 1790–1840, in H. N. Jahnke and M. Otte eds: *Epistemological and social problems of the sciences in the early 19th century*, Dordrecht: 109–21.
Trio, P.: De O.L.V.-broederschap van de scholieren van Parijs te Ieper gedurende de late middeleeuwen *c.*1330–1600 (The O.L.V. assoc. of Paris scholars at 'Ypres during the late middle ages *c.*1300–1600). Thesis. Louvain.

For 1983
Vandermeersch, P.: Een onderzoek naar de relatie stad-universiteit in de periode van het late-humanisme. Bruggelingen te Leuven en aan buitenlandse studia (An enquiry into city-univ. relations in the period of late humanism. Bruges students at L. and at foreign univs). Thesis. Ghent.

For 1985
Farge, J. K.: *Orthodoxy and Reform in early Reformation France. The Faculty of Theology of Paris 1500–43*, Leyden.

For 1986
Debus, A. G.: Chem. and the univs in the 17th cent., *Acad. analecta. Meded.* ... *wetenschappen*, 48/4: 13–33.
Felix, F.: L'enseignement de la chémie à la fac. de médecine de l'ancienne univ. de Louvain 1685–1797, *Acad. analecta. Meded.* ... *wetenschappen*, 48/4: 77–86.
Frijhoff, W.: Pieter de la Courts reisjournaal 1641–43 als ego-document (P. de la C.'s travel journal as ego-document), in *Pieter de la Court in zijn tijd 1618–85. Aspecten van een veelzijdig publicist*, Amsterdam/Maarsen: 11–64.
Gall, H. C.: *Willem Bilderdijk en het privatissimum van Professor D. G. van der Keessel* (W.B. and the p. of prof. D. G. van der K.), The Hague/Leyden. (W.B. 1756–1831, poet and lawyer, D. G. van der K. prof. at Leyden).
Le notariat en Roman Pays de Brabant et l'enseignement du notariat à l'université catholique de Louvain, Brussels. (Cat. of an exhib. at Louvain-la-Neuve 13–28 March 1986).
Meinel, C.: Die Chemie an d. Univ. d. 18. Jh. Institutionalisierungsstufen u. konzeptioneller Wandel, *Acad. analecta. Meded.* ... *wetenschappen*, 48/4: 35–57.
Rabbie, E. and Ahsmann, M.: Astraea Lugdono-Batava. A recently found poem by Hugo Grotius on Joost Swanenburch in a jurid. disput. of 1599, *Lias*, 13: 107–21.
Visser, R. P. W. and Hakfoort, C., eds: *Werkplaatsen van wetenschap en techniek. Industriële en academische laboratoria in Nederland 1860–1940* (Workshops for science and tech. Industrial and acad. labs in the Neths 1860–1940), Amsterdam.

For 1987
Bergh, G. C. J. J. van den: Iets over pub.- en privaatrecht (Something about pub. and private law), in C. Streefkerk and S. Faber eds: *Ter recognitie. Opstellen aangeboden aan Prof. Mr Van der Linden*, Hilversum: 9–17. (Considers teaching of law).
Bezemer, C. H.: Les répétitions de Jacques de Révigny. Thesis. Leyden. (J. de. R. 13th cent. prof. at Orléans).
Beukers, H.: De opkomst van het univ. onderwijs in verloskunde en gynaecologie in Ned. (The devel. of univ. instruction in obstetrics and gynaecology in the Neths), in F. J. J. van Assen etc. eds: *Een eeuw vrouwenarts*, Amsterdam (henceforth noted as *Een eeuw vrouwenarts*): 241–58.
Coppens, C.: Cadeautjes van Pighius en Tapper in een Leuvense band (Gifts

from P. and T. in one L. volume), *Ex officina*, 4: 36–52. (Of 16th century).

—— 'Steadfast I hasten': the Louvain printer Henrick van Ha(e)stens. Bio-bibliog. details, *Quaerendo*, 17: 185–204. (H. van H. came from Leyden to L. around 1600).

Dambre, W.: *August Wagener 1829–96. Een leven voor het onderwijs* (A.W. 1829–96. A life of teaching), Ghent. (A.W. prof. at Ghent).

Derez, M.: De Leuvense univ. en het spoorwezen (L. univ. and the railway), in *Mechelen, Leuven, Tienen . . . retour. Een treinreis door het verleden*, Louvain: 165–70.

Etambala Zana, A.: Un centenaire: Le Séminaire Africain de Louvain 1886–88. Docs inéd., *Les nouvelles rationalités Africaines*, 2: 301–43.

Frijhoff, W.: Zeelands univ.: hoe vaak het mislukte, en waarom (Z.'s univ.: how often it failed and why), in *Worstelende Wetenschap. Aspecten van de wetenschapsbeoefening in Zeeland*, Middelburg: 7–41.

Hammerstein, N.: *Res Publica Litteraria* oder *Asinus in Aula?* Anmerkungen zur 'Bürgerlichen Kultur' u. zur 'Adelswelt', in A. Buck and M. Bircher eds: *Respublica Guelpherbytana*, Amsterdam (henceforth noted as *R.G.*): 35–68.

Houbrechts, H.: De oprichting van de Hist. Kring: naar de vorming van een 'gens historica' 1935–40 (The creation of a hist. circle: towards the formation of a 'g. h.'), in *Liber Amicorum Dr J. Scheerder*, Louvain: 263–90.

Nieuwenhuyzen-Kruseman, A. C. and Assen, F. J. J. van: Honderd jaar Ned. gynaecol. proefschriften: met bibliog. en bijhorend register (100 yrs of gynaecol. dissertations: with a bibliog. and tables), in *Een eeuw vrouwenarts*: 259–301.

Ridderikhoff, C. M. ed.: *Deuxième livre des procurateurs de la nation germanique de l'ancienne université d'Orléans 1547–67*, 2 vols, Leyden.

Ridder-Symoens, H. de: Eigenheid in den vreemde: Studentnat. aan de Europ. univ. (Identity abroad. Student 'nations' in the Europ. univs), in *Eigen en Vreemd. Identiteit en ontlening in taal, literatuur en beeldende kunst*, Amsterdam: 137–46.

Smit, F. R. H.: *Jonkheer Mr A. F. de Savornin Lohman en de Groningse universiteit* (A. F. de S. and the univ. of G.), Groningen. (Exhibition catalogue).

Sottili, A.: Lauree Pavesi nella seconda meta del Quattrocento, in *R.G.*: 128–66.

Steenberghen, F. van: Etienne Gilson et l'univ. de Louvain, *Rev. phil. de Louvain*, 85: 5–21.

Urbain- van Tiggelen, B.: La faculté des arts de Louvain face au gouvernement autrichien, une institution sclérosée? Les réformes introduites dans l'enseignement des sciences 1715–90. Thesis. Louvain-la-Neuve.

Uyttebrouck, A.: L'invitation de Lelewel au prof. à l'univ. libre de Bruxelles 1834–35, in T. Wysokinska ed.: *Joachim Lelewel à Bruxelles de 1833 à 1861*, Brussels: 139–54.

Vandenghoer, C.: *De rectorale rechtbank van de oude Leuvense universiteit 1425–1797* (The rector's court of the old univ. of L. 1425–1797), Turnhout.

Varendonck, F.: *Henri Moke 1803–62. Leven, werk en gedachtenwereld* (H. M. 1803–62. Life, work and views), Ghent. (H.M. prof. at univ. of Ghent).

Vijftig jaar faculteit der rechtsgeleerdheid V(laamse) U(niversiteit), B(russel) (50 yrs of law studies at the V.U.B.), Antwerp.

Waterbolk, E. H.: Viglius van Aytta te Ingolstadt 1537–42 en de cartografie (V. van A. at I. and cartography), in *De historie herzien: vijfde bundel 'Historische Avonden'*, Hilversum: 165–82.

Wilde, I. de: *249 vrouwen na Aletta Jacobs. Vrouwelijke gepromoveerden aan de Rijksuniversiteit Groningen 1879–1987* (249 women after A. J. Female graduates at the univ. of G. 1879–1987), Groningen.

Zorzoli, M. C.: The career of a law prof. at the univ. of Pavia during the Spanish period, 16th–17th cents, *Tijdsch. voor rechtsgesch.*, 55: 57–66.

Publications 1988

Academische redevoering van Albert Schultens, ter nagedachtenisse van den grooten Herman Boerhaave (Acad. oration of A.S. in memory of the great H.B.), Amsterdam.

Bakker, H. A.: *Pieter Jelles Troelstra aan de Groningse Universiteit 1882–88. 'De meest studentikoze van alle studenten'* (P.J.T. at G. univ. 1882–88. 'The most student-like of all students'), Groningen.

Beukers, H.: Clinical teaching in Leiden from its beginning until the end of the 18th cent., *Clio medica*, 21: 139–52.

Bleker, J.: Med. students—to the bed-side or to the lab.? The emergence of lab.-training in Germ. med. educ. 1870–1900, *Clio medica*, 21: 35–46.

Bocke, H. etc.: *Van Jezuïetenklooster tot rechtsfakulteit. Bladzijden uit de geschiedenis van de Universiteitsstraat 1585–1988* (From Jesuit cloister to the law fac. Pages from the hist. of the U. 1585–1988), Ghent. (Cat. of an exhib. 18–27 Oct. 1988).

Boudin, H. R.: La participation de deux Belges, étudiants en théol. protestante, à la première équipe internat. de secours aux blessés militaires lors de la Campagne d'Italie en 1859, *Analecta theol. fac. Bruxellensis*, 2 (1975–85): 131–72.

——— La présence d'étudiants belges à la fac. de théol. évangélique de Genève 1839–1919, *Analecta theol. fac. Bruxellensis*, 2 (1975–85): 115–30.

——— Répertoire des étudiants originaires de Belgique ayant fréquenté les écs préparatoire et de théol. de l'Oratoire à Genève 1839–1919, *Analecta theol. fac. Bruxellensis*, 2 (1975–85): 131–72.

Braive, G.: La situation des jeunes filles à Saint-Louis dans l'entre-deux-guerres, *Facs univ. Saint-Louis (Brussels). Bull. d'inform.*, 26: 17–20.

——— Le cercle d'hist. du chanoine De Lannoy, *Facs univ. Saint-Louis*

(Brussels). *Bull. d'inform.*, 27: 13–16. (Prof. De L. organized this soc. 1910–40).

Breugelmans, K.: De hervorming van de Leuvense rechtsfac. in de tweede helft van de 18e eeuw (The reform of the facs of law at L. in the 2nd half of the 18th cent.), *Bijd. tot de Gesch.*, 71: 51–75.

Burnotte, G.: Le rôle de Henri de Dorlodot dans la fond. de l'Instit. de géol. de l'univ. cath. de Louvain, in *Résumés des mémoires de licence en histoire 1985*, Louvain-la-Neuve: 39–41.

Clercq, P. de: In de schaduw van 's Gravesande. Het Leids Physisch Kabinet in het tweede helft van de 18e eeuw (In the shadow of 's G. The L. physic cabinet in the 2nd half of the 18th cent.), in M. Fournier and B. Theunissen eds: *Het instrument in de wetenschap. Bijdragen tot de instrumentgerichte wetenschapsgeschiedenis*, Special issue of *Tijdsch. voor de gesch. der geneeskunde, natuurwetenschappen, wiskunde en tech.*, 10: 149–73.

Courtois, L.: A propos de l'admiss. des étudiantes à l'univ. cath. de Louvain 1920, *Louvain. Rev. mensuelle de l'assoc. des anciens et amis de l'univ. cath. de Louvain*, 2: 16–17.

Dehon, G.: Législation gallicane et exigences doctrinales à l'univ. de Douai à la fin du 17e s., in P. L. Neve and O. Moorman van Kappen eds: *Conservare jura*, Deventer: 23–32.

Despy-Meyer, A., Pollet, I. and Hoore,⁓ M. d' eds: *Université Libre de Bruxelles. Mai 68–20 ans déjà*, Brussels. (Cat. of an exhib. 20 April–14 May 1988).

Dievoet, G. van etc.: *Lovanium docet. Geschiedenis van de Leuvense Rechtsfaculteit 1425–1914. Tentoonstellingscatalogus* (L. d. Hist. of the fac. of law at L. 1425–1914. Cat. of an exhib.), Louvain.

Dronkers, J.: De bijd. van de groei in onderwijsdeelname aan de econ. groei 1960–80 (Educ. expansion and econ. growth 1960–80), *Mens en Maatschappij*, 63: 44–64.

Fasseur, C.: Hemelse godin of melkgevende koe: de Leidse univ. en de Indische ambtenaarsopleiding 1825–1925 (Celestial goddess or milchcow: L. univ. and the training of Indian officers 1825–1925), *Bijd. en mededelingen voor de gesch. der Ned.*, 103/2: 209–24.

Glorieux, G. and Rouzet, A.: les Velpius à Louvain. Formation d'un atelier, in M.-T. Isaac: *Ornementation typographique et bibliographie historique. Actes du colloque de Mons, 26–28 août 1987*, Brussels: 67–85. (The V. family closely assoc. with univ. of L. in 16th–17th centuries).

Gobbe, C.: La vie estudiantine à l'univ. de Louvain 1898–1914. Un printemps agité en 1914, in *Résumés des mémoires de licence en histoire 1985*, Louvain-la-Neuve: 48–50.

Groen, M.: *University Education in the Netherlands 1815–1980, Legislation and Civil Effect*, Eindhoven, 1988. (Trans. of earlier Dutch works).

Halkin, L. E.: De l'acad. calviniste de Gand à la fac. de théol. de Bruxelles, *Analecta theol. fac. Bruxellensis*, 2 (1975–85): 105–114.

Hamoir, G.: La découverte de la méiose par Edouard Van Beneden à Liège en 1883, une étape capitale de nos connaissances sur l'hérédité, in *49e congrès de la fédération des cercles d'archéologie et d'histoire de Belgique . . . Congrès de Namur. Actes* (henceforth noted as *Congrès de Namur*), 1: 251–52.

Heireman, K.: De jonge-boekdrukkunst en de Leuvense univ. (Early printing and the univ. of L.), *Ex officina*, 5: 48–61.

Herinneringen aan de Biltstraat. 's Rijksveeartsenijschool. Veeartsenijkundige Hoogeschool. Faculteit der Diergeneeskunde 1821–1988 (Memories of the B. The schl of veterinary studies under its 3 names), Utrecht.

Hoftijzer, P. G.: A study tour into the Low Countries and the German states. William Nicolson's *Iter Hollandicum* and *Iter Germanicum* 1678–79, *Lias* 15(1): 73–128.

Houtzager, H. L. etc. eds: *Kruit en Krijg. Delft als bakermat van het Prins Maurits Laboratorium TNO* (Gunpowder and war. Delft as birthplace of the Prince M's laboratory of the TH, Delft), Amsterdam.

Hove, H. van: *125 jaar ingenieursopleiding te Leuven 1864–1989. Gedenkboek* (125 years of the training of engineers at L. 1864–1989. A memorial), Antwerp/Keulen.

Kaiser, W.: Theorie u. Praxis in d. Boerhaave—Äre u. in nachboerhaavianischen Ausbildungssystemen an deutschen Hochschulen d. 18. Jh., *Clio medica*, 21: 71–94.

Lamberts, E.: Het profiel van de kath. univ. Leuven 1835–1985 (The profile of the cath. univ. of L. 1835–1985), *Onze Alma Mater*, 42(1): 63–73.

———— and Roegiers, J.: *De universiteit te Leuven 1425–1985* (The univ. of L. 1425–1985), Louvain. (Illustrated ed. of the book published in 1986).

Lamberts, H. W.: *Commentaar bij herinneringen. De Nederlandsche Handelshogeschool 1913–38. De Nederlandsche Economische-Hogeschool 1938–73* (Commentary with memories. The Dutch schl of commerce 1913–38. The Dutch high schl of econs 1938–73), Rotterdam.

Lokin, J. H. A.: Groninger civilisten uit de 19e eeuw (G. civilists of the 19th cent.), in J. Kingma: *Catalogus van de tentoonstelling 'Honderdvijftig jaar Burgerlijk Recht in Groningen'*, Groningen.

Loosbroek, T. van etc. eds: *Geleerde vrouwen* (Learned women), Nijmegen. (Considers several female univ. students and teachers).

Mahillon, P.: Les protestants et l'univ. belge, *Analecta theol. fac. Bruxellensis*, 2 (1975–85): 15–31.

Mijnhardt, W. W.: *Tot Heil van 't Menschdom. Culturele Genootschappen in Nederland 1750–1815* (For the salvation of mankind. Cult. socs in the Neths 1750–1815), Amsterdam.

Moulin, D. de: *History of surgery with emphasis on the Netherlands*, Dordrecht. (Considers also univ. teaching).

———— ed.: *'s Rijkskweekschool voor militaire geneeskundigen te Utrecht 1822–65* (The state training schl for military physicians at U. 1822–65), Amsterdam.

Naiditch, P. G.: *A. E. Housman at University College, London. The election of 1892*, Leyden.

Obert, C.: La promotion des études chez les Cisterciens à travers le recrutement des étudiants du coll. Saint-Bernard de Paris au Moyen Age, *Cîteaux*, 39(1–2): 65–77.

Otterspeer, W.: De kern van de zaak. De oude wijn, het nieuwe vat. Van de Leidse univ. en de niet te remmen voorsprong (The core of the matter. Old wine, new barrel. Concerning L. univ.; the start is not to be restrained), in D. D. Breimer etc. eds: *Het Academisch Bedrijf. De Leidse Universiteit, context en perspectief*, Leyden: 1–27.

——— Dood aan concordia, leve de eensgezindheid! De Leidse student in 1818; van academieburger tot staatsburger (Death to agreement; long live unanimity! The L. student in 1818; from academic to citizen), in P. van Zonneveld ed.: *Het Bataafsch Athene. Cultuurhistorische opstellen over Leiden 1800–50*, Leyden: 19–31.

——— Huizinga voor de afgrond. Het incident-Von Leers aan de Leidse universiteit in 1933 (H. on the verge of disaster. The Von L. incident at L. univ. in 1933), Utrecht.

Rapp, F.: Univs et principautés: les Etats bourguignons, in *Milan et les Etats bourguignons: deux ensembles politiques princiers entre Moyen Age et Renaissance (14e–16e siècles)*, Brussels: 115–32.

Ridder-Symoens, H. de: Steden en hun onderwijs (Towns and their schools), in M. van Rooijen ed.: *Steden en hun verleden. De ontwikkeling van de stedelijke samenleving in de Nederlanden tot de 19de eeuw*, 's-Gravenhage: 201–24. (Considers also universities).

Risse, G. B.: Clinical instruct. in hospitals: The Boerhaavian tradit. in Leyden, Edinburgh, Vienna and Pavia, *Clio medica*, 21: 1–20.

Roegiers, J.: De reglementering van het boekbedrijf aan de oude univ. Leuven (The regulation of the book-trade at the ancient univ. of L.), in J. van Borm and L. Simons eds: *Liber amicorum H.O.L., Vervliet*, Kapellen: 75–88.

Ruuls, A. W.: Vier vragen omtrent de disputaties, binnen het jurid. onderwijs aan de Nijmeegse kwartierlijke acad. verdedigd onder Petrus de Greve (periode 1663–76), benevens een poging tot beantwoording (4 questions concerning disputations arising out of the teaching of law in the N. acad. defended under P. de G. (around 1663–76), with an attempt to provide answers), *Batavia acad.*, 6(2): 31–51.

Segers, J.: Un portrait armorié inéd. d'Adrien van den Spiegel, prof. de médecine à Padoue 1578–1625, in *Congrès de Namur*, 1: 419. (Portrait in the Rijksmuseum, Amsterdam).

Sicking, C. M. J.: De Leidse universiteitsbiblioth. van 1587 tot? (L. univ. library from 1587 to ?), *Openbaar Vaktijdsch. voor bibliothecarissen, literatuuronderzoekers en documentalisten*, 20(5): 160–65.

Sullivan, T. J.: The 'Coll. de Cluny'. Statutes of Abbot Simon de la Brosse 1365, *Rev. bénédictine*, 98: 169–77. (Coll. of univ. of Paris).

Theys, G.: *Van van't Sestichhuis tot college van de Hoge Heuvel 1633–83* (From van't S. to the coll. 'van de H. H.' 1633–83), Amersfoort.

Tiggelen, B. van: Du règlement de la 'Camera experimentalis' à la 'schola experimentalis'. Une page méconnue de l'hist. de la fac. des arts au 18e s., *Lias*, 15(1): 129–43.

—— Les ouvrages scientif. des biblioth. de la fac. des arts de Louvain au 18e s., in *Congrès de Namur*, 1: 260–61.

20 jaar Leuven Vlaams (20 yrs of Flemish L.), in *Vlaams archief. Jaarboek van de Vlaamse beweging*, Brussels: 45–108.

ULB à la une. La Belgique et l'Université Libre racontées par la Presse, Brussels.

Verhas, M.: *Studiebeurzen van overheidswege aan studenten van de Gentse Rijksuniversiteit 1836–49* (Govt grants to students of the RUG 1836–49), Ghent.

Vink, M.: Ontloken talent: studenten aan de univ. van Amsterdam: de soc. samenstelling (soc. herkomst en sekse) 1965–85 (Full-blown talent: students of the univ. of A.: soc. composition (soc. origin and sex) 1965–85), *Mens en Maatschappij*, 63: 67–76.

Vis, G. J.: Van Groningen tot Luik. De beginjaren van het acad. handboek voor Ned. Letterkunde en welsprekendheid (From G. to Liège. The early yrs of the acad. handbook of Neths lit. and eloquence), *De 19e eeuw*, 12(3): 180–204.

Vos, L. etc. eds: *De Stoute jaren. Studentenprotest in de jaren zestig* (The daring yrs. Student protest in the 60s), Tielt.

Vrugt, M. van de: Rondom 1838. Recht en rechtsgeleerden in Utrecht (Around 1838. Law and lawyers in U.), *Jb. Oud-Utrecht*: 81–98.

Winges, M.: Deviant gedrag van studenten: verkrachters in de 17e en 18e eeuw (The deviant behaviour of students; law-breakers in the 17th and 18th cents), *Batavia acad.*, 6(1): 9–26.

Publications 1989

Altbach, P. G. and Selvaratnam, V. eds: *From dependence to autonomy: the development of Asian universities*, Dordrecht.

Bataillon, L. J.: Exemplar, pecia, quaternus, in O. Weijers ed.: *Vocabulaire du livre et de l'écriture au moyen âge*, Turnhout (henceforth noted as *Vocabulaire*): 206–19.

Braekman, E. M.: Theol. training of reformed ministers of the Low Countries, in H. de Ridder-Symoens and J. M. Fletcher eds: *Academic relations between the Low Countries and the British Isles 1450–1700*, Ghent (henceforth noted as *Academic relations*): 65–93.

Feenstra, R.: Scottish-Dutch legal relations in the 17th and 18th cents, in *Academic relations*: 25–45.

Fletcher, J. M. and Upton, C. A.: Eating and drinking in Renaissance Oxford and Louvain, a comparison of the food and drink purchased at Merton Coll. and Busleyden Coll. in the early 16th cent., in *Academic relations*: 143–58.

—— John Drusius of Flanders, Thomas Bodley and the devel. of Hebrew studies at Merton Coll., Oxford, in *Academic relations*: 111–29.

Frank-van Westrienen, A.: 'Een tourken door het landt'. Dutch tourists in 17th-cent. Eng., in *Academic relations*: 95–109.

Hamesse, J.: Le vocab. de la transmission orale des textes, in *Vocabulaire*: 168–94. (Considers methods used in univs of middle ages).

Luyendijk-Elshout, A. M.: The Edinburgh connection: William Cullen's students and the Leiden med. schl, in *Academic relations*: 47–63.

Otterspeer, W. ed.: *Leiden oriental connections 1850–1940*, Leyden.

Ridder-Symoens, H. de: Het onderwijs te Antwerpen in de 17e eeuw (Educ. in 17th-cent. Antwerp), in *Antwerpen in de 17e eeuw*, Antwerp: 221–50. (Considers also movt of A. students into universities).

—— It. and Dutch univs in the 16th and 17th cents, in C. S. Maffioli and L. C. Palm eds: *Italian scientists in the Low Countries in the 17th and 18th centuries*, Amsterdam/Atlanta: 31–64.

—— Studenten uit het Meetjesland aan europ. univ. (Students from M. at europ. univs), in L. Stockman, P. Vandermeersch and L. Pée eds: *Liber amicorum Achiel de Vos*, Evergem: 99–116.

—— and Fletcher, J. M. eds: *Academic relations between the Low Countries and the British Isles 1450–1700*, Ghent. (Individual items noted separately).

Rooden, P. T. van: *Theology, biblical scholarship and rabbinical studies in the 17th century. Constantijn l'Empereur 1591–1648, professor of Hebrew and Theology at Leiden*, Leyden. (Inform. about study of Hebrew in univs of Holland).

Upton, C. A.: 'Speaking sorrow'. The Eng. univ. anthologies of 1587 on the death of Philip Sidney in the Low Countries, in *Academic relations*: 131–41.

Vandermeersch, P.: Some aspects of the intellect. relationships between the south. Neths and Eng. in the 16th and 17th cents, in *Academic relations*: 5–23.

The British Isles

Additions to Earlier Lists

For 1978

Newman, J.: Oxford libraries before 1800, *Archaeol. jnl*, 135: 248–57.

Sutcliffe, P.: *The Oxford University Press. An informal history*, Oxford.

For 1979

Bylebyl, J. J.: The Schl of Padua: Humanistic med. in the 16th cent., in C. Webster ed.: *Health, medicine and mortality in the 16th century*, Cambridge: 335–70.

For 1980

Brundage, J. A.: Eng. trained canonists in the middle ages: a statistical analysis of a soc. group, in A. Harding ed.: *Law-making and law-makers in British history*, London: 64–78.

Dewhurst, K. ed. and trans.: *Thomas Willis's Oxford lectures*, Oxford. (Lects of prof. of nat. phil. in early 1660s).

Duncan, G. D. and Evans, T. A. R.: The medieval alumni of the univ. of Cambridge, *Past and Present*, 86: 40–51.

Mitchell, W. T. ed.: *Epistolae academicae 1508–96*, Oxford.

—— *Registrum cancellarii 1498–1506*, Oxford.

Ponting, B.: Maths at Aberdeen: devels, characters and events 1495–1717 and 1717–1860, *Aberdeen univ. rev.*, 48: 26–35, 162–76.

For 1981

Colvin, H. M.: *The Sheldonian Theatre and the Divinity School*, Oxford.

Craster, E.: *History of the Bodleian Library 1842–1945*, Oxford.

Denley, P.: The university of Siena 1357–1557. Thesis. Oxford.

Heyworth, P.: *The Oxford guide to Oxford*, Oxford.

Langins, J.: The decline of chem. at the Ec. Polytech. 1794–1805, *Ambix*, 28: 1–19.

For 1982

Baldwin, J. W.: Masters at Paris from 1179 to 1215: a soc. perspective, in R. L. Benson and G. Constable eds: *Renaissance and renewal in the 12th century*, Oxford: 138–72.

Guild, J. and Law, A. eds: *Edinburgh University Library 1580–1980*, Edinburgh.

Prest, J.: *Balliol studies*, London. (Contribs to the hist. of the Oxford college).

Schmitt, C. B.: Phil and science in 16th cent. Ital. univs, in *The Renaissance: Essays in interpretation*, London: 297–336.

Sharpe, K.: Archbishop Laud and the univ. of Oxford, in H. Lloyd-Jones, V. Pearl and A. B. Worden, *History and imagination: Essays in honour of Hugh Trevor-Roper*, London: 146–64.

For 1983

Briggs, A.: Tradit. and innovation in Brit. univs *c*.1860–1960, in W. Phillipson ed.: *Universities, Society and the Future*, Edinburgh (henceforth noted as *Universities*): 186–203.

Colvin, H. M.: *Unbuilt Oxford*, London.

Grafton, A.: From Ramus to Ruddiman: the *studia humanitatis* in a scientif. age, in *Universities*: 62–81.

Gregor, I.: Liberal educ.: an outworn ideal? in *Universities*: 145–60. (Considers civic universities).

Jones, P.: The Scott. professorate and the polite acad. 1720–46, in I. Hont and M. Ignatieff eds: *Wealth and virtue. The shaping of Political Economy in the Scottish Enlightenment*, Cambridge: 89–117.

Lyons, F. S. L.: The idea of a univ.: Newman to Robbins, in *Universities*: 113–44.

McConica, J.: The fate of Erasmian humanism, in *Universities*: 37–61.

Nuttgens, P.: Technology and the univ., in *Universities*: 167–85.

Phillipson, N.: The pursuit of virtue in Scott. univ. educ.: Dugald Stewart and Scott. moral philos. in the Enlightenment, in *Universities*: 82–101.

Phillipson, W. ed.: *Universities, Society and the Future*, Edinburgh. (Relevant items noted separately).

Slee, P.: History as a discipline in the universities of Oxford and Cambridge. Thesis. Cambridge.

Stone, L.: Soc. control and intellect. excellence: Oxbridge and Edinburgh 1560–1983, in *Universities*: 1–30.

Twigg, J. D.: The Parliamentary visitation of the univ. of Cambridge 1644–45, *Eng. hist. rev.*, 98: 513–28.

——— The university of Cambridge and the English Revolution 1625–88. Thesis. Cambridge.

Underwood, M.: Behind the early statutes, *The Eagle*: 3–9. (Of St John's Coll., Cambridge).

For 1984

Chadwick, O.: Dr Samuel Jonson and the Dixie prof. of eccles. hist., *Jnl of eccles. hist.*, 35: 583–96. (Of Cambridge University).

Dawson, J. E. A.: The foundation of Christ Church, Oxford and Trinity Coll., Cambridge in 1546, *Bull. of the inst. of hist. research*, 57: 208–215.

Goudie, A. S. ed.: *700 years of an Oxford college: Hertford College 1284–1984*, Oxford.

Hewison, R.: Footlights: *A hundred years of Cambridge comedy*, London.

Hunt, R. W. and Gibson, M.: *The schools and the cloister. The life and writings of Alexander Nequam 1157–1217*, Oxford.

Kersting, A. F. and Watkin, D.: *Peterhouse 1284–1984: an architectural record*, Cambridge.

Leader, D. R.: Teaching in Tudor Cambridge, *Hist. of educ.*, 13: 105–119.

Lovatt, R.: The first cent. of the coll. library, *Peterhouse record*: 60–73.

Morgan, V.: Country, court and Cambridge university 1558–1640: a study in the evolution of a political culture. Thesis. Univ. of E. Anglia.

Perry, G. B.: *The Bristol medical school*, Bristol.

Simcock, A. V.: *The Ashmolean Museum and Oxford science 1683–1983*, Oxford.

Stott, R.: The incorporation of surgeons and medical education and practice in Edinburgh 1696–1755. Thesis. Edinburgh.

For 1985

Bradley, M.: Civil engineering and soc. change: the early hist. of the Paris Ec. des Ponts et Chaussées, *Hist. of educ.*, 14: 171–83.

Cobban, A. B.: Elective salaried lectureships of south. Europe in the pre-Refn era, *Bull of the John Rylands library*, 67: 662–87.

Colvin, C.: A don's wife a century ago, *Oxoniensia*, 50: 267–78.

Dow, D. A.: Rival conceptions, *The coll. curant*, 74: 11–15. (Presentation to the chair of midwifery at Glasgow univ. 1853).

Geyer-Kordesch, J.: German med. educ. in the 18th cent., in W. F. Bynum and R. Porter eds: *William Hunter and the 18th-century medical world*, Cambridge (henceforth noted as *William Hunter*): 177–205. (Inform. about teaching at Germ. universities).

Hairsine, R. C.: Oxford univ. and the life and legend of Richard III, in J. Petre ed.: *Richard III. Crown and people*, London: 307–32.

Lawrence, C.: 'Ornate physicians and learned artisans.' Edinburgh med. men 1726–76, in *William Hunter*: 153–76.

Pantin, W. A.: *Canterbury College, Oxford: Documents and History*, Oxford.

Swanson, R. N.: Univs, graduates and benefices in later medieval Eng., *Past and present*, 106: 28–61.

For 1986

Chester, N.: *Economics, Politics and Social Studies in Oxford 1900–85*, Oxford.

Clogg, R.: *Politics and the Academy: Arnold Toynbee and the Koraes Chair*, London. (A. T.'s experiences as first holder of the K.C. in Greek, univ. of London).

Edwards, G. P.: Aberdeen and its classical tradit., *Aberdeen univ. rev.*, 51: 410–26.

Gratton-Guinness, I.: On the transform. of the Ec. Polytech. archives, *Brit. jnl for the hist. of science*, 19: 45–50.

Haig, A. G. L.: The church, the univs and learning in later Victorian Eng., *Hist. jnl*, 29: 187–201.

Hoyle, D.: A Commons investigation of Arminianism and Popery in Cambridge on the eve of the Civil War, *Hist. jnl*, 29: 419–25.

Woodman, F.: *The architectural history of King's College chapel and its place in the development of late Gothic architecture in England and France*, London.

For 1987

Annan, N.: The reform of higher educ. in 1986, *Hist. of educ.*, 16(3): 217–26.

Blair, J. S. G.: *History of medicine in St Andrews university*, Edinburgh.

Carter, J. J. and Pittock, J. H. eds: *Aberdeen and the Enlightenment*, Aberdeen.

Davis, V.: William Waynflete and the educ. revn of the 15th cent., in J. Rosenthal and C. Richmond: *People, politics and community in the later middle ages*, Gloucester: 40–59.

Ferrari, G.: Public anatomy lessons and the carnival: the anatomy theatre of Bologna, *Past and Present*, 117: 50–106.

Howarth, J.: Science educ. in late-Victorian Oxford: a curious case of failure, *Eng. hist. rev.*, 102: 334–71.

—— and Curthoys, M.: The pol. econ. of women's higher educ. in late 19th and early 20th-cent. Britain, *Hist. research*, 60: 208–31.

Kadish, A.: Univ. extension and the working class. The case of the Northumberland miners, *Hist. research*, 60: 188–207.

Price, D. T. W.: *Bishop Burgess and Lampeter College*, Cardiff.

Ringer, F.: Comparing 2 acad. cultures: The univ. in Germ. and in Fr. around 1900, *Hist. of educ.*, 16(3): 181–88.

Rothblatt, S.: Hist. and comparative remarks on the federal principle in higher educ., *Hist of educ.*, 16(3): 151–80.

Simon, B.: The student movt in Eng. and Wales during the 1930s, *Hist. of educ.*, 16(3): 189–203.

Sinclair, A.: *The red and the blue: Intelligence, treason and the universities*, Sevenoaks.

Slee, P.: Prof. Soffer's 'Hist. at Oxford', *Hist. jnl*, 30(4): 933–42.

Soffer, R. N.: Nation, duty, character and confidence: Hist. at Oxford 1850–1914, *Hist. jnl*, 30(1): 77–104.

—— Modern univs and nat. values 1850–1930, *Hist. research*, 60: 166–87.

Twigg, J. D.: *A history of Queens' College, Cambridge 1448–1986*, Woodbridge.

—— Ryl mandates for degrees in the reign of Charles II 1660–85: an aspect of the Crown's influence in the univ. of Cambridge, *Procs of the Cambridge Antiquarian Soc.*, 86: 105–111.

For 1988

Berkel, K. van: A note on Rudolf Snellius and the early hist. of maths in Leiden, in C. Hay ed.: *Mathematics from manuscript to print 1300–1600*, Oxford: 156–61. (R.S. 1546–1613 prof. at L. and Marburg).

Black, R.: Higher educ. in Florentine Tuscany: New docs from the second half of the 15th cent., in P. Denley and C. Elam eds: *Florence and Italy. Renaissance studies in honour of Nicolai Rubinstein*, London (henceforth noted as *Florence and Italy*): 209–19.

Brockliss, L., Harriss, G. and Macintyre, A.: *Magdalen college and the Crown: Essays for the tercentenary of the restoration of the college 1688*, Oxford.

Cook, D. J. and Mason, J.: *The building account of Christ Church Library 1716–79*, Oxford.

Crowther, M. A. and White, B.: *On soul and conscience. The medical expert and crime. 100 years of forensic medicine in Glasgow*, Aberdeen.

Denley, P.: Acad. rivalry and interchange: the univs of Siena and Florence, in *Florence and Italy*: 193–208.

Jones, P. M.: Thomas Lorkyn's dissections 1564/5 and 1566/7, *Trans of the Cambridge bibliog. soc.*, 9(3): 209–29. (Inform. about the study of med. at Cambridge).

Mayer, T. F.: A fate worse than death: Reginald Pole and the Parisian theologians, *Eng. hist. rev.*, 103: 870–91.

Nutton, V.: 'Prisci dissectionum professores'. Greek texts and renaissance anatomists, in A. C. Dionisotti, A. Grafton and J. Kraye eds: *The uses of Greek and Latin: Historical essays*, London (henceforth noted as *Greek and Latin*): 111–26.

Pearson, D.: A Cambridge bookseller's account of 1572, *Trans of the Cambridge bibliog. soc.*, 9(3): 230–47.

Tudor, H.: *St Cuthbert's Society 1888–1988*, Durham. (Hist. of Durham's non-coll. institution).

Wilson, N. G.: Vetter Fausto, prof. of Greek and naval architect, in *Greek and Latin*: 89–95. (V.F. prof. at Venice from 1518).

Publications 1989

Cahan, D.: *An Institute for an Empire. The Physikalisch-technische Reichsanstalt 1871–1918*, Cambridge.

Cobban, A. B.: The role of colls in the medieval univs of north. Europe, with special ref. to Eng. and Fr., *Bull. of the John Rylands library*, 71: 49–70.

Fletcher, J. M. and Upton, C. A.: Feasting in an early Tudor coll. The example of Merton Coll., Oxford, in D. Williams ed.: *Early Tudor England*, Woodbridge: 37–59.

Gascoigne, J.: *Cambridge in the Age of the Enlightenment*, Cambridge.

Hargreaves, J. D. and Forbes, A.: *Aberdeen university 1945–81, regional roles and national needs*, Aberdeen.

Haward, B.: Oxford Univ. Museum, *Architects' jnl*, 190(13): 40–63. (Architect. study with photos by M. Charles).

Kelly, J. N. D.: *St Edmund Hall. Almost seven hundred years*, Oxford.

Kuczynski, M. G.: The Cornish entry, *Pembroke coll. Cambridge soc. Annual gazette*, 63: 32–37. (Students from C. at P. coll. late 17th and 18th centuries).

Hammerstein, N.: The modern world, science, med. and univs, *Hist. of univs*, 8: 151–78.

Leader, D. R.: *A history of the university of Cambridge. 1. The university to 1546*, Cambridge.

Lee, D. C.: *The people's universities of the USSR*, London.

McVaugh, M. and Ballester, L. G.: The med. fac. at early 14th cent. Lérida, *Hist. of univs*, 8: 1–25.

Morrissey, T. E.: The art of teaching and learning law: A late medieval tract, *Hist. of univs*, 8: 27–74. (Instructions for students and teachers at Padua c.1400).

Rees, H.: *A university is born: The story of the foundation of the university of Warwick*, Coventry.

Rizzo, M.: Univ., admin., taxation and soc. in Italy in the 16th cent., the case of fiscal exemptions for the univ. of Pavia, *Hist. of univs*, 8: 75–116.

Ringrose, J.: The early texts of the coll. statutes, *Pembroke coll. Cambridge soc. Annual gazette*, 63: 38–52.

Turner, G. L'E.: Experimental science in early 19th-cent. Oxford, *Hist. of univs*, 8: 117–35.

Twigg, J. D.: Evolution, obstacles and aims: The writing of Oxford and Cambridge coll. hists, *Hist. of univs*, 8: 179–99.

Verger, J.: Sven Stelling-Michaud and the hist. of univs, *Hist. of univs*, 8: 201–210.

Canada

Additions to Earlier Lists

For 1977
Hammer, C. I.: The Town-Gown confraternity of St Thomas the Martyr in Oxford, *Mediaeval studies*, 39: 466–76.

For 1981
Leader, D. R.: The study of arts in Oxford and Cambridge at the end of the Middle Ages. Thesis. Toronto.

Publications 1986
Black, J. L.: *G.-F. Müller and the Imperial Russian Academy*, Kingston/ Montreal.

Despy-Meyer, A.: Les étudiantes dans les univs belges de 1880 à 1941, *Perspectives univ.*, 3(1–2): 17–49.

Stabler, E.: *Innovators in education 1830–1980*, Edmonton. (Includes essays on Mount Holyoke Female Seminary (U.S.A.) and the Open University (U.K.)).

Publication 1987
Johanson, C.: *Women's struggle for higher education in Russia 1855–1900*, Kingston.

Central and South America

Publication 1981
Valcárcel, D. ed.: *Historia de la universidad de S. Marcos 1551–1980*, Caracas.

Publication 1982
Mamerto Carro, J.: *Bosquejo histórico de la Universidad de Córdoba*, Buenos Aires.

Publication 1984
Beuch, T. M. and Melcón, A.: *Los dominicos en la Real y Pontificia Universidad de México*, Mexico.
Publication 1987
Nadai, E.: *Ideologia do progresso e ensino superior; Sao Paulo 1891–1934*, Sao Paulo.

Czechoslovakia

Additions to Earlier Lists

For 1982
Beránek, K.: Řeč Jana Antonína Scrinciho o Kosmovi a Damiánovi ve světle české barokní hagiografie (The speech of prof. J. A. S. celebrating St Cosmas and St Damian, patrons of the Prague fac. of Med.), *Zprávy Archivu Univ. Karlovy* (henceforth noted as *Zprávy AUK*), 4: 80–88.

Publications 1983
Beránek, K. ed.: *Liber decanorum facultatis philosophicae Universitatis Pragensis 1367–1585*, Prague.
———— Příspěvek k nejstarším dějinám pražských univ. kol. (The oldest hist. of univ. colls at Prague), *Acta Univ. Carolinae. Hist. Univ. Carolinae Pragensis* (henceforth noted as *AUC: HUCP*), 23, Fasc. 1: 57–63. (Summary in German).
Cach, J.: Pedagog. seminář české univ. v Praze v letech 1882–87 (The dept of pedagogy of the Czech Univ. at Prague 1882–87), *Pedagogika*, 33: 61–75.
Čornej, P.: Zdeňka Nejedlého léta učňovská a vandrovní (Prof. Z. N.'s studies and first yrs of his research activity), *AUC: HUCP*, 23, Fasc. 2: 7–42. (Summary in German).
Fajkus, B.: Přírodní vědy na filoz. fak. Univ. Karlovy v letech 1882–1900 (Nat. sciences in the fac. of philos. of the Charles Univ. 1882–1900), *Zprávy AUK*, 5: 39–68.
Fechtnerová, A. and Hojda, Z.: Vztahy pražské univ. k Vratislavi v 17. až 18. století (Relations of Prague Univ. with Wrocław), *AUC: HUCP*, 23, Fasc. 1: 65–76. (Summary in German).
Grešík, L.: Výchova vysokoškolskej intelig. na Slovensku v rokoch 1956–60 (The educ. of the educ. class in Slovakia 1956–60), *Hist. časopis*, 31: 891–911. (Summaries in French and Russian).
Kučera, J. P. and Rak, J.: *Bohuslav Balbín a jeho místo v české kultuře* (Prof. B.B. and his role in Czech culture), Prague.
Malíř, J.: Z pramenů k dějinám brněské univ. (From the sources towards a hist. of the univ. at Brno), *Universitas*, 16(5): 14–20.

Mates, P.: K problematice rozvoje vysokých škol v letech 1945–47 (The devel. of Czechoslovak univs 1945–47), *AUC: HUCP*, 23, Fasc. 2: 43–60. (Summary in German).

Petráň, J.: *Nástin dějin filozofické fakulty Univerzity Karlovy v Praze (do roku 1948)* (An outline for a hist. of the fac. of philos. of the Charles Univ. at Prague to 1948), Prague.

Polišenský, J.: Vilém Mathesius a počátky studia dějin anglo-americké lit. a kult. na Univ. Karlově (Prof. V. M. and the beginnings of the study of the hist. of Anglo-American lit. and cult. at the Charles Univ. at Prague), *AUC: HUCP*, 23, Fasc. 1: 37–54. (Summary in English).

Raková, I.: Prameny ke sporu o pražskou univ. v letech 1622–54 (Sources concerning the controversy about Prague univ. in 1622–54), *Zprávy AUK*, 5: 11–17.

Sousedík, S.: *Valeriár Magni 1586–1661. Kapitola z Kulturních dějin Čech 17. století* (V. M., a chapter of cult. hist. in 17th cent. Bohemia), Prague.

Svátek, J.: Pět akad. řečí Františka K. Halašky z let 1814–32 (5 acad. speeches of prof. F.K.H. 1814–32), *Zprávy AUK*, 5: 18–38.

Syllaba, T.: *Jan Gebauer na pražské univerzitě* (Prof. J.G. at Prague Univ.), Prague. (Summaries in German and Russian).

Urfus, V.: Slavnostní disputace na pražské filoz. fak. v r. 1688 a její básnická oslava (K otázce šlechtické intelig. v pobělohorských Čechách) (The noble intelligentsia and its role in Bohemia illustrated by the disputation in the Prague fac. of philos. in 1688), *AUC: HUCP*, 23, Fasc. 1: 27–35. (Summary in German).

Publications 1984

Duchoňová, J.: Seznam akad. funkcionářů Univ. Karlovy v letech 1945–84 (A list of acad. officials of the Charles Univ. at Prague 1945–84), *Zprávy AUK*, 6: 58–117.

Herold, V., Horský, Z. and Mráz, M.: Filoz. a přírodní vědy v době Karlově (Philos. and nat. sciences under Charles IV), in *Karolus Quartus*, Prague: 249–70.

Hlaváčková, L. and Rozsívalová, E.: *Studium a přednášky na lékařské fakultě pražské univerzity v letech 1690–1848* (The course of studies at the Prague fac. of Med. 1690–1848), Prague.

Hrnko, A. and Žatkuliak, J.: Univ. Komenského na rozhraní 50. a 60. rokov (Komenský Univ. at Bratislava at the turn of the 50's and 60's), *Hist. časopis*, 32: 593–619.

Kejř, J.: Právní vzdělanost v Čechách v době Karlově (Legal cult. in Bohemia under Charles IV), in *Karolus Quartus*, Prague: 127–34.

Krzemieńska, B.: K problematice přírodních věd v Čechách doby Karlovy (Problems in nat. sciences in Bohemia under Charles IV), in *Karolus Quartus*, Prague: 273–87.

Melanová-Kubová, M.: Založení pražské Univ. a její rozvoj za vlády Karlovy (The fndation of Prague Univ. and its devel. under Charles IV), in *Karolus Quartus*, Prague: 217–30.

314   *History of Universities*

Raková, I.: Cesta ke vzniku Karlo-Ferdinandovy univ. (Spory o pražské vysoké učení v l. 1622–54) (The controversy about Prague Univ. in 1622–54), *AUC: HUCP*, 24, Fasc. 2: 7–40. (Summary in German).

—— Přehled akad. funkcionářů pražské univ. v letech 1774–1882 (1892) (A list of acad. officials of Prague Univ. 1774–1892), *Zprávy AUK*, 6: 3–38.

Rozsívalová, E.: První asistenti na pražské lékařské fak. (The first lecturers of the Prague fac. of Med.), *AUC: HUCP*, 24, Fasc. 1: 27–37. (Summary in German).

Svatoš, M.: Seznam rektorů a děkanů bývalé Německé univ. v Praze 1882–1945 (A list of rects and deans of the German Univ. at Prague 1882–1945), *Zprávy AUK*, 6: 39–57.

Syllaba, T.: Dopisy lipských prof. Leskiena a Wislicena ke sporu o pravost Rukopisu královédvorského (The letters of profs L. and W. from Leipzig concerning the controversy of the truth of *Rukopis královédvorský*), *AUC: HUCP*, 24, Fasc. 2: 71–89. (Summary in German).

Urban, Z.: Čestný doktorát F. L. Čelakovskému z roku 1848 (The Dr h.c. degree for F.L.Č. in 1848), *AUC: HUCP*, 24, Fasc. 1: 39–44. (Summary in German).

Urfus, V.: Rektor pražské univ. Jan Jindřich Turba a jeho rodina (K postavení intelig. a úřednické šlechty v pobělohorských Čechách) (The rect. of Prague Univ. J.J.T. and his family: on the position of the intelligentsia and noble office holders in Bohemia after 1620), *AUC: HUCP*, 24, Fasc. 2: 41–53. (Summary in German).

Vávra, J.: Zapomenutá doktorská disertace o Jaroslavu Haškovi (Ke vztahům mezi posluchači a prof. Karlovy univ. za fašistického ohrožení ČSR) (A doct. diss. concerning J.H.: on the relations between profs and students of the Charles Univ. before 1938), *AUC: HUCP*, 24, Fasc. 2: 55–68. (Summary in German).

Publications 1985

Beránek, K.: Promoce v Klementinu v letech 1604–1617 (Graduation ceremonies at the Clementinum 1604–1617), *AUC: HUCP*, 25, Fasc. 1: 7–32. (Summary in German).

Havránek, J.: Studenti Univ. Karlovy na jaře a v létě roku pětačtyřicátého (The students of the Charles Univ. in the spring and summer of 1945), *Zprávy AUK*, 7: 70–134.

Herold, V.: *Pražská univerzita a Wyklif* (Prague Univ. and J. Wyclif), Prague. (Summary in German).

Kunštát, M. and Svatoš, M.: Přehled základních dat institucionálního vývoje českých vysokých škol 1348–1985 (A survey of essential data and facts concerning the instit. devel. of univs in the Czech lands 1348–1985), *Zprávy AUK*, 7: 146–73.

Litsch, K.: 17. listopad 1939 (17th November 1939), *Zprávy AUK*, 7: 46–49.

Mates, P.: Vývoj brněnských vysokých škol v letech 1945–47 (The devel. of univs at Brno 1945–47), *AUC: HUCP*, 25, Fasc. 1: 95–114. (Summary in German).

Pavlíková, M.: *Bolzanovo působení na pražské univerzitě* (The activity of prof. B. Bolzano at Prague Univ.), Prague. (Summaries in German and Russian).

Šimeček, Z.: Z počátků výuky pomocných věd hist. na pražské univ. (The beginnings of lecturing on the basic hist. disciplines at Prague Univ.), *AUC: HUCP*, 25, Fasc. 1: 33–47. (Summary in German).

Spurná, S.: Univ. Karlova a Československá akad. věd (The Charles Univ. and the Czechoslovak Acad. of Sciences), *Zprávy AUK*, 7: 135–45.

Svatoš, M.: Rozsah a původní podoba listinného fondu pražské univ. (The medieval records of Prague Univ.), *AUC: HUCP*, 25, Fasc. 2: 15–33. (Summary in German).

Tretera, I.: Casus Štěpán Doubrava: K neznámým dopisům Ernsta Macha Augustu Seydlerovi z roku 1882 (Unknown correspondence between E.M. and A.S. in 1882 concerning S.D.), *AUC: HUCP*, 25, Fasc. 1: 59–94. (Summary in German).

Vágner, P.: Uplatnění absolventů studia chemie Karlovy univ. v letech 1900–39 (The careers of graduates of the Charles Univ. in chemistry 1900–39), *AUC: HUCP*, 25, Fasc. 2: 47–66. (Summary in German).

Zilynská, B.: *Husitské synody v Čechách. Příspěvek k úloze univerzitních mistrů v husitské církvi* (The Hussite Synods in Bohemia: the role of univ. masters in the Hussite church), Prague. (Summary in German).

Publications 1986

Brožek, J. and Hoskovec, J.: K počátkům užité psychol. na Univ. Karlově (Explorations in early applied psychol. at the Charles Univ.), *AUC: HUCP*, 26, Fasc. 1: 51–62. (Summary in English).

Čornej, P.: *Rozhled, názory a postoje husitské inteligence v zrcadle dějepisectví 15. století* (Convictions and attitudes of the Hussite intelligentsia according to the historiography of the 15th cent.), Prague. (Summary in German).

Čornejová, I.: Studenti pražské univ. ve zbrani: 17.–18. století (Students of Prague Univ. in arms: the 17th and 18th cents), *Documenta Pragensia*, 6(1): 238–48. (Summary in German).

—— and Fechtnerová, A.: *Životopisný slovník pražské univerzity. Filozofická a teologická fakulta 1654–1773* (A biog. reg. of the Prague Univ. fac. of philos. and theol. 1654–1773), Prague. (Summary in German).

Egglmaier, H. B.: Jan Kvíčala, česká škola klasické filol. a předpoklady jejího rozvoje z hlediska rakouské školské pol. (Prof. J.K.: the Czech schl of classical philol. and the presumption of its devel.), *AUC: HUCP*, 26, Fasc. 1: 37–49. (Summary in German).

Havránek, J.: Karolinum v revoluci 1848 (The Carolinum in the revoln of 1848), *AUC: HUCP*, 26, Fasc. 2: 35–75. (Summary in German).

——, Petráň, J. and Skýbová, A.: *Universitas Carolina 1348–1984*, Prague. (Text also in English, French and Russian).

Kejř, J.: Díla pražských mistrů v rukopisech knihovny Corpus Christi Coll.,
   Cambridge (The works of Prague masters in the MSS of the Library of
   Corpus Christi Coll., Cambridge), *AUC: HUCP*, 26, Fasc. 2: 109–48.
   (Summary in English).
Litsch, K.: Intabulace budovy Karolina podle nových knihovnách zákonů v
   19. a 20. stoleti (The changes in the legal status of the Carolinum
   building in the 19th and 20th cents), *AUC: HUCP*, 26, Fasc. 2: 77–84.
   (Summary in German).
Petráň, J.: Svědectví ikonografických pramenů o podobě Karolina do
   počátku 18. století (The witness of the iconographical sources to the
   appearance of the Carolinum to the beginning of the 18th cent.), *AUC:
   HUCP*, 26, Fasc. 2: 9–22. (Summary in German).
Ransdorf, M.: *Kapitoly z geneze husitské ideologie* (Chapters on the genesis
   of the Hussite ideology), Prague. (Summary in German).
Svatoš, M.: *Graduale Magistri Wenceslai*, Prague. (Text also in English,
   French, German and Russian).
———— Hospodářství Karlovy kol.: srovnání předhusitského a předbělo-
   horského stavu (The econ. of Charles Coll. A comparative study of the
   14th and 16th cents), *AUC: HUCP*, 26, Fasc. 2: 23–33. (Summary in
   German).
Svobodný, P.: Soc. a regionální Struktura literárně činných absolventů
   pražské univ. v letech 1500–1620 (The soc. and regional background of
   the graduates of Prague Univ. 1500–1620), *AUC: HUCP*, 26, Fasc. 1:
   7–36. (Summary in German).
Tříška, J.: Autoři užívající starší pražské univ. terminologie (The oldest
   acad. terminology in the works of Prague authors), *AUC: HUCP*, 26,
   Fasc. 1: 65–93. (Summary in German).

Publications 1987

Bílek, K.: Písemná pozůstalost Jana Evangelisty Purkyně a další purky-
   ňovské písemnosti v literárním archivu Památníku národního písem-
   nictví (The lit. estate of prof. J.E.P. in the Lit. Archives in Prague),
   AUC: HUCP, 27, Fasc. 1: 161–69. (Summary in German).
Brázda, O.: Příchod Jana Evangelisty Purkyné na pražskou univ. (The
   coming of prof. J.E.P. to Prague Univ.), *AUC: HUCP*, 27, Fasc. 1: 55–
   89. (Summary in German).
Duchoňová, J. and Zilynská, B, eds: *Jan Evangelista Purkyně v dokumentech
   Archivu Univerzity Karlovy* (Prof. J.E.P. in the docs of the Archives of
   Charles Univ. at Prague), Prague. (Summaries in English and Russian).
Halas, F. X. ed.: K podílu Jana Evangelisty Purkyně na českém národním
   obrození: cedice korespondence J. E. Purkyně s Václavem Hankou a
   Pavlem Josefem Šafaříkem (The correspondence of prof. J.E.P. with
   V.H. and P.J.S.), *AUC: HUCP*, 27, Fasc. 1: 171–231. (Summary in
   German).
Havránek, J. and Herber, O.: *Insignie, medaile a taláry Univerzity Karlovy*

(Sceptres, medals and gowns of the Charles Univ.), Prague. (Text also in German and Russian).

Heřman, S. and Syllaba, T.: *A. Teodorov-Balan na univerzitě v Praze* (A.T.-B. at Prague Univ.), Prague. (Summaries in German and Russian).

Hlaváčková, L., Nosáková, J. and Svobodný, P.: Přehled dějin výuky biolog. věd na pražské lékařské fak. (A survey of the hist. of instruction in biol. in the Prague fac. of Med.), *AUC: HUCP*, 27, Fasc. 2: 21–53. (Summary in German).

Lapteva, L. P.: Jan Evangelista Purkyně a Rusko (Prof. J.E.P. and Russia), *AUC: HUCP*, 27, Fasc. 1: 133–58. (Summaries in German and Russian).

Moškoř, M.: Skladba a uplatnění intelig. vychovávané pražskou filoz. fak. v letech 1654–1730 (The structure and careers of the intelligentsia educ. at the Prague fac. of philos. 1654–1730), *AUC: HUCP*, 27, Fasc. 2: 81–108. (Summary in German).

Niklíček, L.: Význam druhého pražského období Jana Evangelisty Purkyně pro dějiny české vědy (The importance of the second Prague period of prof. J.E.P. for a hist. of Czech science), *AUC: HUCP*, 27, Fasc. 1: 91–122. (Summary in German).

Novák, J. and Sopoušková, A.: *Filozofická fakulta Univerzity Komenského v Bratislave* (The fac. of philos. of the Komenský Univ. at Bratislava), Bratislava. (Summaries in English, French, German and Russian).

Rozsívalová, E.: Mladá léta Jana E. Purkyně (The schl yrs of prof. J.E.P.), *AUC: HUCP*, 27, Fasc. 1: 13–53. (Summary in German).

Svatoš, M.: Pražská lékařská fak. a zdravotnictví v pražských městech 14.–16. století (Prague fac. of Med. and health service in the Prague towns: the 14th–16th centuries), *Documenta Pragensia*, 7(1): 225–35. (Summary in German).

Szelińska, W.: Alexej z Třeboně—český student na krakovské univ. (A. of T.—a Czech student at the univ. of Cracow), *AUC: HUCP*, 27, Fasc. 2: 55–66. (Summaries in German and Polish).

Vencovský, E.: *Sto let české psychiatrické kliniky v Praze 1886–1986* (100 yrs of the Czech Psychiatric Clinic of the Charles Univ. at Prague 1886–1986), Prague. (Summaries in English, German and Russian).

Publications 1988

Beránek, K. ed.: *Bakaláři a mistři promovaní na filozofické fakultě Univerzity Karlovy v Praze v létech 1586–1620. Baccalaurei et magistri in facultate philosophica Universitatis Carolinae Pragensis ab anno 1586 usque ad annum 1620 determinati* (A list of masters and bachelors of the fac. of philos. of Prague Univ. 1586–1620), Prague. (Text also in Latin. Summary in German).

Čornejová, I.: Zrušení Tovaryšstva Ježíšova v r. 1773 a osudy jezuítů z pražské univ. (The abolition of the Jesuit Order in 1773 and the fate of the Jesuits of Prague Univ.), *AUC: HUCP*, 28, Fasc. 1: 65–75. (Summary in German).

Hlaváček, I.: K podílu Josefa Emlera na boji o českou univ. v roce 1872 (Prof. J.E. and the struggle for the Czech Univ. at Prague in 1872), *AUC: HUCP*, 28, Fasc. 1: 107–115. (Summary in German).

Hlaváčková, L. and Veselý, M.: *Fakultní nemocnice v Praze-Motole. Vznik-vývoj-perspektiva* (The origins, devel. and future of the Teaching Hospital in Prague-Motol), Prague.

Hůrský, J.: Vznik a počáteční období Akad. spolku ve Vídni 1866–75 (The origin and the first period of the Acad. Association at Vienna 1866–75), *AUC: HUCP*, 28, Fasc. 2: 9–30. (Summary in German).

Petráň, J.: *Karolinum* (The Carolinum), Prague. (Text also in English, German and Russian).

Polišenský, J. and Štemberková, M.: *Alma mater Carolina Pragensis. Výběr svědectví cizích návštěvníků* (Prague Univ. and foreign visitors), Prague. (Text also in English and Russian).

Šimeček, Z.: Slavistika na německé univ. v Praze a zápasy o její charakter (Slavonic studies at the German Univ. at Prague and their character 1909–1914), *AUC: HUCP*, 28, Fasc. 2: 31–58. (Summary in German).

Štemberková, M.: Alma mater v beletrii. Obraz pražské univ. v české próze od počátku 20. století do okupace (Prague Univ. in Czech prose between 1900 and 1939), *AUC: HUCP*, 28, Fasc. 1: 147–62. (Summary in German).

Stolet I. chirurgické kliniky fakulty všeobecného lékařství Karlovy univerzity (100 yrs of the first Surgery Clinic of the fac. of Med. of the Charles Univ. at Prague), Prague.

Svatoš, M.: Jan Kvíčala a zřízení mimořádné prof. filoz. na české univ. v Praze (Prof. J.K. and the constitution of the extraordinary prof. of philos. at the Czech Univ. at Prague), *AUC: HUCP*, 28, Fasc. 1: 117–32. (Summary in German).

Syllaba, T.: Ke kult. pol. činnosti prof. Augusta Schleichera v českých zemích (On the cult. and pol. activities of prof. A.S. in the Czech lands), *AUC: HUCP*, 28, Fasc. 1: 77–90. (Summary in German).

Tretera, I.: *E. Mach na pražské univerzitě* (Prof. E.M. at Prague Univ.), Prague. (Text also in English and German).

——— Spor kolem habilitace Petra Durdíka (A controversy concerning a *venia docendi* for P.D.), *AUC: HUCP*, 28, Fasc. 1: 133–46. (Summary in German).

Tuček, K.: *Přehled historie Mineralogického a petrografického ústavu přírodovědecké fakulty Univerzity Karlovy. Příspěvek k dějinám obou dnešních kateder* (Hist. of the Minerology and Petrology depts of the Charles Univ. at Prague), Prague. (Summary in English).

Veselá, M.: Československý akad. spolek Právník: k dějinám brněnské univ. (The Czechoslovak. Acad. Association Právník and a hist. of the univ. at Brno), *AUC: HUCP*, 28, Fasc. 2: 59–76. (Summary in German).

Zilynská, B.: 'Epilogatio' sporu pražských mistrů a táborských kněží (*Epilogatio* and the controversy between Prague masters and priests of Tábor), *AUC: HUCP*, 28, Fasc. 1: 31–40. (Summary in German).

Bibliography 319

Publications 1989
Dvě století ve službách zdraví 1786–1986. Fakultní nemocnice s poliklinikou v Brně, Na pekařské (200 yrs in the service of health 1786–1986. The teaching hospital in Brno), Brno. (Summaries in English, German and Russian).
Hanzal, J.: Bolzanovy univ. promluvy (The univ. speeches of prof. B. Bolzano), *Zprávy AUK*, 8: 23–51.
Kejř, J.: Sbírka projevů z doby rozkvětu pražské právnické univ. (A collection of speeches from the time when Prague's Law Univ. flourished), *AUC: HUCP*, 29, Fasc. 2: 15–69. (Summary in English).
Kuděla, J.: Dědictví po Janu Evangelistovi Purkyně, prof. fyziol. lékařské fak. Univ. Karlovy: k 200. výročí jeho narození (The inheritance from J.E.P. prof. of physiol. in the fac. of Med. of Prague Univ.), *Zprávy AUK*, 8: 52–83.
Lapteva, L. P.: Ruský hist. N. V. Jastrebov 1869–1923 a jeho styky s Čechami a pražskou univ. (A Russian hist. N.V.J. 1869–1923 and his relations with Bohemia and Prague Univ.), *AUC: HUCP*, 29, Fasc. 1: 13–52. (Summaries in German and Russian).
Litsch, K.: *Die Karlsuniversität Prag. Geschichte und Gegenwart*, Prague.
——— K výročí 17. listopadu 1939 (On the anniversary of 17th Nov. 1939), *AUC: HUCP*, 29, Fasc. 2: 9–13.
Mates, P.: K situaci na vysokých školách v období tzv. II. republiky (On the situation at the Czechoslovak univs in the period of the Second Republic 1938–39), *AUC: HUCP*, 29, Fasc. 1: 101–112. (Summary in German).
Šimeček, Z.: Slavistika na německé univ. a zápasy o její charakter (Slavonic studies at the German Univ. at Prague and their character 1914–1918), *AUC: HUCP*, 29, Fasc. 1: 53–78. (Summary in German).
Svatoš, M.: Diplomatický rozbor listin k dějinám pražské univ. (An analysis of the papers concerning the medieval hist. of Prague Univ.), *AUC: HUCP*, 29, Fasc. 2: 72–95. (Summary in German).
Svatoš, M.: *Výbor z korespondence filologa Josefa Krále* (Selected letters of the philologist J.K.), Prague. (Summary in German).
Sousedík, S.: *Jan Duns Scotus. Doctor subtilis a jeho čeští žáci* (J.D.S. Doctor subtilis and his Bohemian scholars), Prague.
Tretera, I.: Čeští herbartisté na pražské univerzitě (The Bohemian Herbartists at Prague Univ.), Prague. (Summary in German).

Egypt

Publication 1987
Murphy, L. R.: *The American University in Cairo 1919–87*, Cairo.

France

Additions to Earlier Lists

For 1977

Baldwin, J. W.: *Studium et regnum*. The penetration of univ. personnel into Fr. and Eng. admin. at the turn of the 12th and 13th cents, in G. Makdisi, D. Sourdel, and J. Sourdel-Thomine eds: *L'enseignement en Islam et en Occident au moyen âge*, Paris: 199–215.

Beauvois, D.: *Lumières et société en l'Europe de l'Est: L'université de Vilna et les écoles polonaises de l'Empire Russe 1803–32*, 2 vols, Paris.

For 1978

Meyer, K.: L'hist. de la question univ. au 19e s., *Cahiers du monde russe et soviétique*, 19: 301–303.

For 1980

Freudenthal, G.: Litt. et sc. de la nature au début du 18e s.: Pierre Polinière, l'introd. de la physique expérimentale à l'univ. de Paris et *L'arrêt burlesque* de Boileau, *Rev. de synthèse*, 99–100: 167–95.

For 1984

Giard, L.: Hist. de l'univ. et hist. du savoir: Padoue 14e–16e s. (2), *Rev. de synthèse*, 105: 259–98.

Gouron, A.: Deux univs pour une ville, in G. Cholvy ed.: *Histoire de Montpellier*, Toulouse: 103–25.

For 1985

Barbey, J.: Organ. générale des études et méthodes d'enseignement du droit au moyen âge, *Annales d'hist. des facs de droit*, 2: 13–20.

Billoux, C. and Bayle, N.: Les archives de l'Ec. Polytech., *Rev. d'hist. des scs*, 38: 73–82.

Karady, V.: Le coll. Eötvös et l'Ec. Normale Sup. vers 1900, in J. le Goff and B. Köpeczi eds: *Intellectuels français, intellectuels hongrois, 13e–20e siècles*, Paris/Budapest (henceforth noted as *Intellectuels*): 235–54.

Székely, G.: Le rôle des univs hongroises du Moyen Age et des études univ. à l'étranger dans la formation des intellectuels de Hongrie, in *Intellectuels*: 53–64.

Verger, J.: Les profs des univs fr. à la fin du Moyen Age, in *Intellectuels*: 23–40.

For 1987

Damamme, D.: Genèse soc. d'une instit. scolaire: l'Ec. libre des scs pol., *Actes de la recherche en scs soc.*, 70: 31–47.

L'enseignement de la Musique au Moyen Age et à la Renaissance, Royaumont. (Notes of univ. teaching of music).

Martin, D.: Les univs belges pendant la deuxième guerre mondiale, in E. Dejonghe ed.: *L'occupation en France et en Belgique 1940–44. Actes du colloque de Lille 26–28 avril 1985*, Lille (henceforth noted as *L'occupation*): 315–36.

Ory, P.: Les univs belges et fr. face à l'occupation allemande, in *L'occupation*: 51–59.

Woitrin, M.: *Louvain-la-Neuve et Louvain-en-Woluwe. Le grand dessein*, Paris/Gembloux.

For 1988

Burney, J. M.: *Toulouse et son université: Facultés et étudiants dans la France méridionale du 19e siècle*, Toulouse/Paris. (Trans by P. Wolff of the New York pub. noted in *Hist. of univs*, 8: 314).

Cahiers pour l'histoire du CNRS 1939–89, 2 vols, Paris.

Dulieu, L.: L'éc. de médecine de Montpellier a-t-elle été fondée par des médecins juifs? in C. Iancu ed.: *Les juifs à Montpellier et dans le Languedoc du Moyen Age à nos jours*, Montpellier (henceforth noted as *Les juifs à Montpellier*): 93–98.

Duvernois, P.: La vie univ. à Toulouse au cours des âges, *Les dossiers de l'éduc.*, 14/15: 101–107.

Gabriel, A. L.: Franciscus Ossmanus, a popular officer of the Eng.-Germ. nat. in great demand at the univ. of Paris 1515–24, in *Mélanges de la Bibliothèque de la Sorbonne offerts à André Tuilier*, Paris (henceforth noted as *André Tuilier*): 142–57.

Gatti-Montain, J.: *Le système d'enseignement du droit en France*, Lyons. (Considers teaching of law in univs since 19th century).

Gillon, L.: *Servir en actes et en vérité*, Paris/Gembloux. (Inform. about early yrs of univ. of Kinshasa, Zaire).

Guenée, S.: Nicolas Psaume a-t-il fondé une univ. à Verdun au 16e s.? in *André Tuilier*: 158–82.

Iancu, C.: Les étudiants juifs à Montpellier et les débuts du sionisme pol., in *Les juifs à Montpellier*: 321–36.

Karady, V.: Durkheim et les débuts de l'ethnologie univ., *Actes de la recherche en scs soc.*, 74: 23–32.

Les Universités du Rhin supérieur de la fin du Moyen Age à nos jours. Actes du colloque organisé à l'occasion du 450e anniversaire des enseignements supérieurs à Strasbourg, Strasbourg. (Inform. about the univs of Basle, Freiburg i. Br. and Strasbourg).

Mazon, B.: *Aux origines de l'EHSS, l'Ecole des Hautes Etudes en Sciences Sociales. Le rôle du mécénat américain*, Paris. (The role of the Rockefeller fndation in 1948).

Ventre-Denis, M.: Victor Hugo, étudiant en droit, in *André Tuilier*: 252–63.

Verger, J.: *Ad studium augmentandum*: l'utopie éduc. de Pierre Dubois dans son *De recuperatione Terre Sancte (v. 1306)*, in *André Tuilier*: 106–22.

Publications 1989

Belhoste, B.: Les origines de l'Ec. polytech. Des anciennes écs d'ingénieurs à l'Ec. centrale des travaux publics, *Hist. de l'éduc.*, 42: 13–53.

Bourdieu, P.: *La noblesse d'Etat. Grandes Ecoles et esprit de corps*, Paris.

Brockliss, L. W. B.: L'enseignement médical et la Revn. Essai de réévaluation, *Hist. de l'éduc.*, 42: 79–110.

——— Patterns of attendance at the univ. of Paris 1400–1800, in D. Julia and J. Revel eds: *Les universités européennes du 16e au 18e siècle. Histoire sociale des populations étudiantes. 2. La France*, Paris (henceforth noted as *Univs européennes*): 487–526.

——— The univ. of Paris and the maintenance of Catholicism in the British Isles 1426–1789. A study in clerical recruitment, in *Univs européennes*: 577–616.

Farge, J. K. ed.: *Registre des procès-verbaux de la faculté de théologie de Paris. 2. 1524–nov. 1533*, Paris.

Favre, P.: *Naissance de la science politique en France*, Paris. (Origins of the Ec. libre des sc. pol. 1872).

Ferte, P.: la population étudiante du Rouergue au 18e s., in *Univs européennes*: 527–75.

Gispert, H.: L'enseignement scientif. sup. et ses enseignants 1860–1900: les mathématiques, *Hist. de l'éduc.*, 41: 47–78.

Julia, D. and Revel, J. eds: *Les universités européennes du 16e au 18e siècle. Histoire sociale des populations étudiantes. 2. La France*, Paris. (All items noted separately).

——— Les étudiants et leurs études dans la France mod., in *Univs européennes*: 25–486.

Nouschi, M.: *Histoire et pouvoir d'une Grande Ecole. H.E.C.*, Paris. (Considers especially last 3 decades of the Ec. des Hautes Etudes Commerciales).

Vernet, A., ed.: *Histoire des bibliothèques françaises. 1. Les bibliotheques médiévales. Du 6e siècle à 1530*, Paris. (Ch. on univ. and coll. libraries).

Verger, J.: Les chanoines et les univs, *Cahiers de Fanjeaux* (Toulouse), 24: 285–307.

——— Les univs médiévales: intérêt et limites d'une hist. quantitative. Notes à propos d'une enquête sur les univs du Midi de la France à la fin du Moyen Age, in *Univs européennes*: 9–24.

German Federal Republic

Additions to Earlier Lists

For 1977

Ditsche, M.: Zur Studienförderung im Mittelalter, *Rheinische Vierteljahrblätter*, 41: 51–62.

Illmer, D.: Die Statuten d. deutschen Nat. an d. alten Univ. Orléans von 1378 bis 1526, *Ius commune*, 6: 10–107.

Locke, R. R.: Industrialisierung u. Erziehungssystem in Frankreich u. Deutschland vor d. 1. Weltkrieg, *Hist. Z.*, 225/2: 265–96.

For 1978

Meinel, C.: *Die Chemie an der Universität Marburg seit Beginn des 19. Jahrhunderts. Ein Beitrag zu ihrer Entwicklung als Hochschulfach*, Marburg.

Meyer, K.: Die Entstehung d. Universitätsfrage in Russland. Zum Verhältnis von Univ., Staat u. Gesellschaft zu Beginn d. 19. Jh., *Forschungen zur osteurop. Gesch.*, 25: 229–38.

Mommsen, K.: *Katalog der Basler Juristischen Disputationen, 1558–1818. Aus dem Nachlass herausgegeben von Werner Kundert. (= Ius Commune Sonderheft 9)*, Frankfurt a. Main.

For 1979

Markowski, M.: Soz. Grundlagen d. Praktizismus u. Naturalismus an d. Krakauer Univ. im 15. Jh., in A. Zimmerman ed.: *Miscellanea Medievalia*, 12(1), *Soziale Ordnungen im Selbstverständnis des Mittelalters*, Berlin/New York: 314–22.

For 1980

Beer, G.: Der Versuch Johann Christoph Cron's zur Errichtung eines ersten chem. Lab. an d. Univ. Göttingen im Jahre 1735, *Göttinger Jb.*, 28: 97–108.

Lange, H.: Vom Adel d. Doktor, in K. Luig and P. Liebs eds: *Das Profil des Juristen in europäischer Tradition*, Ebelsbach: 279–94.

Paul, M.: *Gaspard Monges Géométrie Descriptive und die Ecole Polytechnique*, Bielefeld.

Volkmann, R.: Die gesch. Entwicklung d. Univ. Helmstedt. Ein Überblick, *Braunschweigische Heimat*, 1976–77. Special edition.

For 1981

Bleker, J.: *Die Naturhistorische Schule 1825–45. Ein Beitrag zur Geschichte der klinischen Medizin in Deutschland*, Stuttgart/New York.

Herberger, P. and Stolleis, M.: *Hermann Conring 1606–81: Ein Gelehter der Universität Helmstedt. Austellungs Kataloge*, Wolfenbüttel.

Keussen, H. etc. eds: *Die Matrikel der Universität Köln, 4–7, 1559–1797*, Düsseldorf.

Kiene, M.: Die englischen und französischen Kollegientypen. Universitätsarchitektur zwischen Sakralisierung und Säkularisierung. Thesis. Münster.

Pölnitz, G. Frhr von and Boehm, L. eds: *Die Matrikel des Ludwig-Maximilians Universität Ingolstadt-Landshut-München. 4. Personenregister*, Munich.

For 1983

Boehm, L. and Müller, R. A., eds: *Universitäten und Hochschulen in Deutschland, Österreich und der Schweiz. Eine Universitätsgeschichte in Einzeldarstellungen*, Düsseldorf.

Classen, P. and Wolgast, E.: *Kleine Geschichte der Universität Heidelberg*, Berlin/Heidelberg/New York.

Grössing, H.: *Humanistische Naturwissenschaft. Zur Geschichte der Wiener mathematischen Schulen des 15. und 16. Jahrhunderts*, Baden-Baden.

Jacob, M.: Etude comparative des systèmes univ. et place des études classiques au 19e s. en Allemagne, en Belgique et en France, in T. Lindkern ed.: *Philologie und Hermeneutik im 19. Jahrhundert*, Göttingen, 2: 108–42.

Phillips, D.: *Zur Universitätsreform in der britischen Besatzungszone 1945–48*, Cologne.

Scheible, H.: Die Univ. Heidelberg u. Luthers Disputation, *Z. f. Gesch. d. Oberrheins*, 131: 309–29.

Schöne, A.: *Göttinger Bücherverbrennung 1933*, Göttingen.

Weisert, H.: *Geschichte der Universität Heidelberg*, Heidelberg.

For 1984

Baier, J. J.: *Ausfürliche Nachricht von der Nürnbergischer Universitäts-Stadt Altdorf*, New ed., Neustadt an der Aisch.

Baumgart, P.: Humanistische Bildungsreform an d. deutschen Univ. d. 16 Jh., in W. Reinhard ed.: *Humanismus im Bildungswesen des 15. und 16. Jahrhunderts*, Weinheim (henceforth noted as *Humanismus im Bildungswesen*): 171–97.

Buzas, L.: *Bibliographie zur Geschichte der Universität Ingolstadt-Landshut-München 1472–1982*, Munich.

Ewert, P. and Lullies, S.: *Das Hochschulwesen in Frankreich. Geschichte, Strukturen und gegenwärtige Probleme im Vergleich*, Munich.

Komorowski, M.: *Bibliographie der Duisburger Universitätsschriften 1652–1817*, Richarz.

Liess, L.: *Geschichte der medizinischen Fakultät in Ingolstadt von 1472 bis 1600*, Munich.

Reinhard, W. ed.: *Humanismus im Bildungswesen des 15. und 16. Jahrhunderts*, Weinheim.

Seibt, F.: *Die Teilung der Prager Universität 1882 und die intellektuelle Desintegration in den böhmischen Ländern*, Munich.

Seifert, A.: Der Humanismus an d. Artistenfak. d. kath. Deutschlands, in *Humanismus im Bildungswesen*: 135–54.

Sottili, A.: 'Tunc floruit Alamannorum natio': Doktorate deutscher Studenten in Pavia in d. zweiten Hälfte d. 15. Jh., in R. Schmitz and G. Keil eds: *Bildungswesen des 15. Jahrhunderts*, Weinheim: 25–44.

Zierold, K.: *Forschung, Lehre und Erziehung. Aufsätze aus der Zeit des Wiederaufbaus und der Neugründung deutscher Hochschulen*, Weinheim.

For 1985
Aschermann, H. and Schneider, W.: *Studium im Auftrag der Kirche. Die Anfänge der Kirchlichen Hochschule Wuppertal 1935 bis 1945*, Cologne.
Belloni, A.: Neue Erkenntnisse über d. Rechtsunterricht in Padua im fünfzehnten Jh., *Ius commune*, 13: 1–12.
Festschrift. Semper Apertus. Sechshundert Jahre Ruprecht-Karls-Universität Heidelberg 1386–1986. 1. Mittelalter und Frühe Neuzeit 1386–1803, Berlin/Heidelberg/New York/Tokyo.
Gabriel, A. L.: German receptors, 'reformators' and proctors at the univ. of Paris 1495–1525, in *Rapports 2. XVI Congrès International des Sciences Historiques*, Stuttgart: 761–67.
Hammerstein, N.: Univ. u. gelehrte Inst. von d. Aufklärung zum Neuhumanismus u. Idealismus, in G. Mann ed.: *Samual Thomas Soemmerring und die Gelehrten der Goethe-Zeit*, Stuttgart/New York: 309–29.
Kamp, N., Wellenreuther, H. and Hund, F.: *250 Jahre Vorlesungen an der Georgia Augusta 1734–1984*, Göttingen.
Mielescu, M.: *Die spanische Universität in Geschichte und Gegenwart. Eine Untersuchung des Autonomieproblems*, Cologne/Vienna.
Schwarzbach, M.: *Naturwissenschaften und Naturwissenschaftler in Köln zwischen der alten und der neuen Universität 1798–1919*, Cologne/Vienna.
Stieler, F.: *Satzungsgebung der Universitäten. Staatliche Aufsicht und Mitwirkung*, Frankfurt a. M.
Wawrykowa, M.: *'Für eure und unsere Freiheit'. Studentenschaft und junge Intelligenz in Ost- und Mitteleuropa in der ersten Hälfte des 19. Jahrhunderts*, Stuttgart.
Wildermuth, R.: *Die Tübinger Universitätsbibliothek von Paul Bonatz und Karl Geiger*, Tübingen.

For 1986
Baumgärtner, I.: 'De privilegiis doctorum'. Über Gelehrtenstand u. Doktorwürde im Späten Mittelalter, *Hist. Jb.*, 106: 298–332.
Bruch, R. vom: *Deutsche Universitäten 1734–1980*, Düsseldorf.
Burger, C.: *Aedificatio, fructus, utilitas; Johannes Gerson als Professor der Theologie und Kanzler der Universität Paris*, Tübingen.
Graf, H.: *Das Promotionsrecht der Katholisch-Theologischen Fakultät der Universität Breslau. Ein Gutachten der Münchener Juristischen Fakultät aus dem Jahre 1859*. Special issue from *Archiv f. schlesische Kirchengesch.*, 44: 165–90, Sigmaringen.
Hardtwig, W.: Studentische Mentalität—Pol. Jugendbewegung—Nationalismus. Die Anfänge d. deutschen Burschenschaft, *Hist. Z.*, 242: 581–628.
Kellermann, P. ed.: *Universität und Hochschulpolitik*, Vienna/Cologne.
Lundgreen, P. etc.: *Staatliche Forschung in Deutschland 1870–1980*, Frankfurt a. M.

Miethke, J. ed.: *Acta universitatis Heidelbergensis. 1. 1386–1410. Fasc. 1*, Heidelberg.

Mittler, E. ed.: *Bibliotheca Palatina. Katalog zur Ausstellung vom 8.7.– 2.11.1986 in der Heiliggeistkirche Heidelberg*, Heidelberg.

Ranieri, F. ed.: Juristische Dissertationen deutscher Univ. 17.–18. Jh., 2 vols, *Ius commune*, Sonderheft 27.

Rummel, P.: *P. Julius Priscianesis S.J. 1542–1607. Ein Beitrag zur Geschichte der Katholischen Restauration der Kloster im Einflußbereich der ehemaligen Universität Dillingen*, Augsburg.

Ruprecht-Karls Univ. Heidelberg ed.: *Die Geschichte der Universität Heidelberg. Vorträge im Wintersemester 1985–86*, Heidelberg.

Vierhaus, R. and Brocke, B. eds: *Forschung im Spannungsfeld vor Politik und Gesellschaft. Zum 75jährigen Bestehen der Kaiser-Wilhelm-/Max-Planck-Gesellschaft 1911–86*, Stuttgart.

Publications 1987

Becker, H., Dahms, H.-J. and Wegeler, C. eds: *Die Universität Göttingen unter dem Nationalsozialismus. Das verdrängte Kapitel ihrer 250jährigen Geschichte*, Munich.

Becker, H.-J.: Die Entwicklung d. jurist. Fak. in Köln bis zum Jahre 1600, in G. Keil, B. Moeller and W. Trusen eds: *Der Humanismus und die oberen Fakultäten*, Weinheim (henceforth noted as *Oberen Fakultäten*): 43–64.

Bekemeier, B.: *Martin Ohm 1792–1872: Universitäts- und Schulmathematik in der neuhumanistischen Bildungsreform*, Göttingen.

Beuermann, G. etc. eds: *250 Jahre Georg-August-Universität Göttingen. Katalog zur Ausstellung im Auditorium*, Göttingen.

Bolten, J.: *Hochschulstudium für kommunale und soziale Verwaltung in Köln 1912–29. Eine Studie zur Wiedererrichtung der Universität zu Köln*, Cologne/Vienna.

Boockmann, H. and Wellenreuther, H. eds: *Geschichtswissenschaft in Göttingen. Eine Vorlesungsreihe*, Göttingen.

Buck, A.: Die Rezeption d. Humanismus in d. jurist. u. medizin. Fak. d. it. Univ., in *Oberen Fakultäten*: 267–84.

Burmeister, K. H.: Einflüsse d. Humanismus auf d. Rechtsstudium am Beispiel d. Wiener Juristenfak., in *Oberen Fakultäten*: 159–72.

Cheval, R.: Die Univ. Tübingen zwischen Vergangenheit u. Zukunft in d. Nachkriegsjahren, in F. Knipping and J. Le Rider eds: *Frankreichs Kulturpolitik in Deutschland 1945–50*, Tübingen (henceforth noted as *Frankreichs Kulturpolitik*): 247–60.

Derecke, D. and Kühn, H.-M.: *Göttingen. Geschichte einer Universitätsstadt. 1: Von den Anfängen bis zum Ende des Dreißigjährigen Krieges*, Göttingen.

Fleckenstein, J.: *Die sozial- und geistesgeschichtlichen Voraussetzungen der Universität. Marginalien zur Entstehungsgeschichte der Georgia Augusta*, Göttingen.

Franz-Willing, G.: *'Bin ich schuldig?' Leben und Wirken des Reichsstudenten-führers und Gauleiters Dr Gustav Adolf Schee, 1907–79. Eine Biographie*, Landsberg am Lech.

Gierloff-Emden, H.-G. and Wilhelm, F. eds: *Entwicklung des Institutes für Geographie an der Ludwig-Maximilians-Universität München. Beiträge zur Hydrogeographie und Fernerkundung—Ehrenpromotionen der Fakultät für Geowissenschaften*, Munich.

Grane, L.: Studia humanitatis u. Theol. an d. Univ. Wittenberg u. Kopenhagen im 16. Jh.: komparative Überlegungen, in *Oberen Fakultäten*: 65–114.

Grothusen, K.-D. etc. eds: *Der Scurla-Bericht; Bericht des Oberregierungsrates Dr rer. pol. Herbert Scurla von der Auslandsabteilung des Reichserziehungsministeriums in Berlin über seine Dienstreise nach Ankara und Istanbul vom 11.–25. Mai 1939: Die Tätigkeit deutscher Hochschullehrer an turkischen wissenschaftlichen Hochschulen*, Frankfurt a. M.

Hammerstein, N.: Universitäten—Territorialstaaten—Gelehrte Räte, in R. Schnur ed.: *Die Rolle der Juristen bei der Entstehung des modernen Staates*, Berlin: 687–735.

———— Universitätsgesch. im Heiligen Römischen Reich am Ende d. Renaissance, in A. Buck and T. Klaniczay eds: *Das Ende der Renaissance: Europäische Kultur um 1600*, Wiesbaden: 109–23.

Herrlitz, H. G. and Kern, H. eds: *Anfänge Göttinger Sozialwissenschaft. Methoden, Inhalte und soziale Prozesse im 18. und 19. Jahrhundert*, Göttingen.

Himme, H.-H.: *Stich-haltige Beiträge zur Geschichte der Georgia Augusta in Göttingen. 200 Stiche aus den ersten 150 Jahren der Göttinger Universität zusammengetragen und mit Texten versehen anläßlich ihres 250jährigen Jubiläums*, Göttingen.

Hoffmann, D. ed.: *Pädagogik an der Georg-August-Universität Göttingen. Eine Vorlesungsreihe*, Göttingen.

Huber, U.: *Universität und Ministerialverwaltung. Die hochschulpolitische Situation der Ludwig-Maximilians-Universität München während der Ministerien Oettingen-Wallerstein und Abel 1832–47*, Berlin.

Jeismann, K. E. and Lundgreen, P. eds: *Handbuch der deutschen Bildungsgeschichte. 3. 1800–70. Von der Neuordnung Deutschlands bis zur Gründung des Deutschen Reiches*, Munich.

Kamp, N.: *Das Göttinger Jubiläum von 1937: Glanz und Elend einer Universität*, Göttingen.

Keil, G., Moeller, B. and Trusen, W. eds: *Der Humanismus und die oberen Fakultäten*, Weinheim. (Relevant items noted separately).

Keil, G. and Peitz, R.: 'Decem quaestiones de medicorum statu'. Beobachtungen zum Fakultätenstreit u. zum mittelalter. Unterrichtsplan Ingolstadts, in *Oberen Fakultäten*: 215–38.

Knipping, F.: Umerziehung oder Verwaltung? Zur Gründungsgesch. d. Hochschule f. Verwaltungswiss. in Speyer, in *Frankreichs Kulturpolitik*: 91–110.

Knipping, F. and Le Rider, J. eds: *Frankreichs Kulturpolitik in Deutschland 1945 bis 1950*, Tübingen. (Relevant items noted separately).

Kristeller, P. O.: Scholastik u. Humanismus an d. Univ. Heidelberg, in *Oberen Fakultäten*: 1–20.

Kuhn, W. and Tröhler, U. eds: *Armamentarium obstetricium Gottingense. Eine historische Sammlung zur Geburtsmedizin*, Göttingen.

Loos, F. ed.: *Rechtswissenschaft in Göttingen. Göttinger Juristen aus 250 Jahren*, Göttingen.

Mallmann, L.: *Französische Juristenausbildung im Rheinland, 1794–1814. Die Rechtsschule von Koblenz*, Cologne/Vienna.

Marten, H.-G.: *Der niedersächsische Ministersturz. Protest und Wiederstand der Georg-August-Universität Göttingen gegen den Kultusminister Schlüter im Jahre 1955*, Göttingen.

Meinel, C.: Zur Sozialgesch. d. chem. Hochschulfaches im 18. Jh., *Ber. zur Wissenschaftsgesch.*, 10: 147–68.

Moeller, B. ed.: *Theologie in Göttingen. Eine Vorlesungsreihe*, Göttingen.

Müller, D. K. and Zymek, B.: *Datenhandbuch zur deutscher Bildungsgeschichte. Sozialgeschichte und Statistik des Schulsystems in den Staaten des Deutschen Reiches 1800–1945*, Göttingen.

Neumeister, S. and Wiedemann, C. eds: *Res Publica Litteraria. Die Institutionen der Gelehrsamkeit in der frühen Neuzeit*, 2 vols, Wiesbaden.

Nutton, V.: 'Qui magni Galeni doctrinam in re medica revocavit'. Matteo Corti u. d. Galenismus in medizin. Unterricht d. Renaissance, in *Oberen Fakultäten*: 173–84.

Pistohlkors, G. von, Raun, T. U. and Kaegbein, P. eds: *The Universities in Dorpat/Tartu, Riga and Wilna/Vilnius 1579–1979. Papers on their History and Impact on the Borderland between West and East*, Cologne/Vienna.

Rauscher, A. ed.: *Katholizismus, Bildung und Wissenschaft im 19. und 20. Jahrhundert*, Paderborn/Munich.

Ridder-Symoens, H. de: Internationalismus versus Nationalismus an Univ. um 1500 nach zumeist südniederländ. Quellen, in F. Seibt and W. Eberhardt eds: *Europa 1500. Integrationsprozesse im Widerstreit: Staaten, Regionen, Personenverbande, Christenheit*, Stuttgart: 397–414.

Röhrs, H. and Hess, G. eds: *Tradition und Reform der Universität unter internationalem Aspekt*, Frankfurt a. M.

Sachse, W.: *Göttingen im 18. und 19. Jahrhundert. Zur Bevölkerungs- und Sozialstruktur einer deutschen Universitätsstadt*, Göttingen.

Schmitt, C. B.: Aristoteles bei d. Arzten, in *Oberen Fakultäten*: 239–66.

Schoßig, B. ed.: *Die studentischen Arbeiterunterrichtskurse in Deutschland*, Bad Heilbrunn.

Smolinsky, H.: Der Humanismus an Theol. Fak. d. kath. Deutschland, in *Oberen Fakultäten*: 21–42.

Staehelin, M. ed.: *Musikwissenschaft und Musikpflege an der Georg-August-Universität Göttingen. Beiträge zu ihrer Geschichte*, Göttingen.

Titze, H. etc. eds: *Das Hochschulstudium in Preußen und Deutschland, 1820–1944*, Göttingen.

Trusen, W.: Johannes Reuchlin u. d. Fak. Voraussetzungen u. Hintergründe d. Prozesses gegen d. 'Augenspiegel', in *Oberen Fakultäten:* 115–58.

Volkov, S.: Soz. Ursachen d. Erfolgs in d. Wiss. Juden im Kaiserreich, *Hist. Z.*, 245: 315–42.

Publications 1988

Ausstellung d. Hist. Archivs d. Stadt Köln: *Alteste Stadtuniversität Nordwesteuropas. 600 Jahre Kölner Universität*, Cologne.

Baumgarten, M.: *Vom Gelehrten zum Wissenschaftler. Studien zum Lehrkörper einer kleinen Universität am Beispiel der Ludoviciana Giessen 1815–1914*, Giessen.

Blanke, E. etc. eds: *Die Göttinger Sieben. Ansprachen und Reden anläßlich der 150. Wiederkehr ihrer Protestation*, Göttingen.

Blaschke, W. etc.: *Nachhilfe zur Erinnerung. 600 Jahre Universität Köln*, Cologne.

Courtenay, W. J.: Marsilius von Inghen (†1396) als Heidelberger Theol., *Heidelberger Jb.*, 32: 25–42.

———— The Franciscan *Studia* in south. Germany in the 14th cent., in F. Seibt ed.: *Gesellschaftsgeschichte Festschrift für Karl Bosl zum 80. Geburtstag*, Munich (henceforth noted as *Gesellschaftsgeschichte*): 81–90.

Eisenmann, P. and Schmirber, G. eds: *Die Hochschule im Spannungsfeld von Qualität und Quantität: Die veränderten Rahmenbedingungen der 90er Jahre*, Regensburg.

Fleckenstein, J.: *Die sozial- und geistesgeschichtlichen Voraussetzungen der Universität*, Göttingen.

Folkerts, M. ed.: *Gemeinschaft der Forschungsinstitute für Naturwissenschafts- und Technikgeschichte am Deutscher Museum 1963–68*, Munich.

Frank, I. W.: *Die Bettelordenstudia im Gefüge des spätmittelalterlichen Universitätswesens*, Stuttgart.

Füßl, W.: *Professor in der Politik: Friedrich Julius Stahl 1802–61*, Göttingen.

Gabriel, A. L.: Georgius Wolff (†1499), printer and officer of the Eng.-Germ. nat. at the univ. of Paris, in *Gesellschaftsgeschichte*: 91–114.

———— Translatio Studii. Spurious dates of fndation of some early univs, in *Fälschungen im Mittelalter*, 1, Hanover: 601–26.

Golczewski, F.: *Kölner Universitätslehrer und der Nationalsozialismus*, Cologne/Vienna.

Häkli, E. ed.: *Gelehrte Kontakte zwischen Finnland und Göttingen zur Zeit der Aufklärung, Ausstellung aus Anlaß der 500jährigen Jubiläums des finnischen Buches*, Göttingen.

Heimbüchel, B. and Pabst, K.: *Kölner Universitätsgeschichte. 2. Das 19. und 20. Jahrhundert*, Cologne/Vienna.

Henning, F.-W. ed.: *Betriebswirte in Köln. Über den Beitrag Kölner Betriebswirte zur Entwicklung der Betriebswirtschaftslehre*, Cologne/Vienna.

330   *History of Universities*

Henning, F.-W. ed.: *Kölner Volkswirte und Sozialwissenschaftler. Über den Beitrag Kölner Volkswirte und Sozialwissenschaftler zur Entwicklung der wirtschafts- und Sozialwissenschaften*, Cologne/Vienna.

Kamp, N.: *Studenten und 'Judenfrage' im Deutschen Kaiserreich*, Göttingen.

Komorowski, M.: *Promotionen an der Universität Königsberg 1548–1799. Bibliographie der pro-gradu-Dissertationen in der oberen Fakultäten und Verzeichnis der Magisterpromotionen in der philosophischen Fakultät*, Munich/London.

Koza, I.: *Deutsch-britische Begegnungen in Unterricht, Wissenschaft und Kunst 1949–55*, Cologne/Vienna.

Lohse, G.: *Die Bibliotheksdirektoren der ehemals preußischer Universitäten und Technischen Hochschulen 1900–45. Mit einem Exkurs: Die Direktoren der Preußischen Staatsbibliothek 1900–45*, Cologne/Vienna.

Lönnendonker, S.: *Freie Universität Berlin. Gründung einer politischen Universität*, Berlin.

Lüdemann, G. and Schröder, M.: *Die Religionsgeschichtliche Schule in Göttingen. Eine Dokumentation*, Göttingen/Zurich.

Meuthen, E.: *Kölner Universitätsgeschichte. 1. Die alte Universität*, Cologne/Vienna.

—— ed.: *Kölner Universitätsgeschichte. 3. Die neue Universität. Daten und Fakten*, Cologne/Vienna.

Missiroli, A.: *Die Deutsche Hochschule für Politik*, Bonn/St Augustin.

Moeller, B. ed.: *Stationen der Göttinger Universitätsgeschichte 1737–1787–1837–1887–1937. Eine Vortragsreihe*, Göttingen.

Mussgnug, D.: *Die vertriebenen Dozenten der Universität Heidelberg. Zur Geschichte der Universität nach 1933*, Heidelberg.

Portmann-Tinguely, A.: *Kirche, Staat und katholische Wissenschaft in der Neuzeit. Festschrift für Heribert Raab zum 65. Geburtstag am 16. März 1988*, Paderborn.

Rabehl, B.: *Am Ende der Utopie. Die politische Geschichte der Freien Universität Berlin*, Berlin.

Sauthoff, S.: *Adliges Studentenleben und Universitätsstudium zu Beginn des 16. Jahrhunderts. Darstellung anhand des Ausgabenbüchleins von Conrad zu Castell*, Frankfurt a. M. etc.

Schivelbusch, W.: *Die Bibliothek von Löwen. Eine Episode aus der Zeit der Weltkriege*, Munich/Wenen.

Schwabe, K. ed.: *Deutsche Hochschullehrer als Elite 1815–1945*, Boppard a. Rhein.

Schwinges, R. C.: Migration u. Austausch: Studentenwanderungen im Deutschen Reich d. späten Mittelalters, in G. Jaritz and A. Müller eds: *Migration in der Feudalgesellschaft*, Frankfurt/New York: 141–55.

Sieg, U.: *Die Geschichte der Philosophie an der Universität Marburg von 1527 bis 1970*, Marburg.

Siegrist, H. ed.: *Bürgerliche Berufe. Zur Sozialgeschichte der freien und akademischen Berufe im internationalen Vergleich*, Göttingen.

Siemann, W.: Chancen u. Schranken von Wissenschaftsfreiheit im deutschen Konstitutionalismus 1815–1918, *Hist. Jb.*, 107: 315–48.

Simon, C.: *Staat und Geschichtswissenschaft in Deutschland und Frankreich 1871–1914. Situation und Werk von Geschichtsprofessoren an den Universitäten Berlin, München, Paris*, 2 vols, Frankfurt a. M.

Stackelberg, J. von ed.: *Zur geistigen Situation der Zeit der Göttinger Universitätsgründung 1737. Eine Vortragsreihe*, Göttingen.

Tent, J. F.: *Freie Universität Berlin 1948–88. Eine deutsche Hochschule im Zeitgeschehen*, Berlin.

Voigt, H.-H. ed.: *Naturwissenschaften in Göttingen. Eine Vortragsreihe*, Göttingen.

Wagenitz, G.: *Göttinger Biologen 1737–1945. Eine biographisch-bibliographische Liste*, Göttingen.

Weigel, H.: *Adelobert Keller und Johannes Fallati als Leiter der Tübinger Universitätsbibliothek 1844–55*, Tübingen.

Weiss, W.: *Der anglo-amerikanische Universitätsroman*, Darmstadt.

Wellenreuther, H. ed.: *Göttingen 1690–1755. Studien zur Sozialgeschichte einer Stadt*, Göttingen.

Wieacker, F. etc.: *250 Jahre Georgia Augusta. Akademische Feier zur 250. Wiederkehr des Inaugurationstages der Universität Göttingen*, Göttingen/Stuttgart.

Publications 1989

Bethge, K. and Klein, H. eds: *Physiker und Astronomen in Frankfurt*, Frankfurt a. M

Blanke, H. W.: Historiker als Beruf. Die Herausbildung d. Karrieremusters 'Geschichtswissenschaftler' an d. deutschen Univ. von d. Aufklärung bis zum klassischen Historismus, in K. E. Jeismann ed.: *Bildung, Staat und Gesellschaft im 19. Jahrhundert. Mobilisierung und Disziplinierung*, Stuttgart (henceforth noted as *Bildung, Staat und Gesellschaft*): 343–60.

Bruch, R. vom: Die Professionalisierung d. akad. gebildeten Volkswirte in Deutschland zu Beginn d. 20. Jh., in *Bildung, Staat und Gesellschaft*: 361–86.

Brüdermann, S.: *Göttinger Studenten und akademische Gerichtsbarkeit im 19. Jahrhundert*, Göttingen.

Brünner, C. and Konrad, H. eds: *Die Universität und 1938*, Cologne/Vienna.

Classen, C. J. ed.: *Die Klassische Altertumswissenschaft an der Georg-August-Universität Göttingen. Eine Ringvorlesung zu ihrer Geschichte*, Göttingen.

Diestelkamp, B. and Stolleis, M. eds: *Juristen an der Universität Frankfurt am Main*, Baden-Baden.

Führ, C.: *Schulen und Hochschulen in der Bundesrepublik Deutschland*, Cologne/Vienna.

Gestrich, C.: Das Erbe Hegels in d. Systemat. Theol. an d. Berliner Univ. im 19. Jh., in G. Besier and C. Gestrich eds: *450 Jahre Evangelische*

Theologie in Berlin, Göttingen (henceforth noted as *Evangelische Theologie*): 183–206.

Hahn, P. M.: *Die Gerichtspraxis der altständischen gesellschaft im Zeitalter der 'Absolutismus'.* *Die Gutachtertätigkeit der Helmstadter Juristenfakultät für die brandenburgisch-preußischen Territorien 1675–1710*, Berlin.

Hammerstein, N.: Der Wandel d. Wissenschafts-Hierarchie u. d. bürgerliche Selbstbewußtsein. Anmerkungen zur aufgeklärten Universitätslandschaft, in W. Barner ed.: *Tradition, Norm, Innovation*, Munich: 277–95.

————— *Die Johann Wolfgang Goethe-Universität Frankfurt a. M. Von der Stiftungsuniversität zur staatlicher Hochschule, 1, 1914–50*, Frankfurt a. M.

Hinske, N. ed.: *Halle. Aufklärung und Pietismus*, Heidelberg.

Kath. Hochschulgemeinde Düsseldorf ed.: *Die Auseinandersetzungen um die theologische Fakultät der napoleonischen Universität Düsseldorf 1811–1813*, Düsseldorf.

Kuhn, A. etc. eds: *Revolutionsbegeisterung an der Hohen Carlsschule*, Stuttgart.

Langewiesche, D. and Tenorth, H.-E. eds: *Handbuch der deutschen Bildungsgeschichte 5: 1918–45. Die Weimarer Republik und die nationalsozialistische Diktatur*, Munich.

Liwak, R.: Das Alte Testament u. d. Theol. Fak. in d. Gründungzeit d. Friedrich-Wilhelms-Univ. Berlin, in *Evangelische Theologie*: 163–82.

Machinek, A. ed.: *'Dann wird Gehorsam zum Verbrechen'. Ein Konflikt um Obrigkeitswillkür und Zivilcourage. Die Göttinger Sieben*, Göttingen.

Meschkowskiy, H.: *Von Humboldt bis Einstein. Berlin als Weltzentrum der exakten Wissenschaften*, Munich.

Müller, R. A.: Die deutschen Univ. als Freiheitsraum—Verfassungen u. Parteiprogramme 1848 bis 1949, in B. Rill, ed.: *Freiheitliche Tendenzen der Deutschen Geschichte*, Regensburg: 62–84.

Müller-Luckner, E. and Müller, R. A.: Hochschulpläne u. Hochschulwesen in d. Oberpfalz von Spätmittelalter bis zur frühen Neuzeit, in K. Ackermann and G. Girisch eds: *Gustl Lang. Leben für die Heimat*, Weiden: 368–83.

Polster, G.: *Politische Studentenbewegung und bürgerliche Gesellschaft. Die Würzburger Burschenschaft im Kraftefeld von Staat, Universität und Stadt 1814–50*, Heidelberg.

Prel, U. and Wilker, L. eds: *Die Freie Universität Berlin. 1948–1968–1988. Ansichten und Einsichten*, Berlin.

Schefold, B.: *Wirtschafts- und Sozialwissenschaftler in Frankfurt a. M.*, Marburg.

Selge, K.-V.: August Neander—ein getaufter Hamburger Jude d. Emanzipations- u. Restaurationszeit als erster Berliner Kirchenhist. 1813–50, in *Evangelische Theologie*: 233–76.

Swinne, E.: *Friedrich Paschen als Hochschullehrer*, Berlin.

Zimmerman, A. ed.: *Die Kölner Universität im Mittelalter. Vorgeschichte—Gründungsphase—Folgezeit*, Berlin.

Hungary

Additions to Earlier Lists

For 1988

Balogh, J.: A román kormányzat iskolapolitikája Erdélyben 1918–48 (The educ. pol. of the Romanian govt in Transylvania 1918–48), *Történelmi Szemle*, 3 (1987–88): 267–94.

Barcza, J. ed.: *A debreceni református kollégium története 1538–1988* (Hist. of the D. calvinist coll. 1538–1988), Budapest.

Duka, Z. N.: Die Physiol. an d. medizin. Fak. in Tyrnau u. ihre ungarländischen Präzedenzen, *Comm. de hist. artis med.*, 115–116 (1986): 83–88.

Köblös, J.: A Jagelló-kori egyházi középréteg egyetemjárása (The univ. studies of the clergy in the Jagellonian period), in *Az értelmiség Magyarországon a 16–17. században*, Szeged: 23–48.

Nárai, I.: A katonai főiskolák a magyar felsőoktatás rendszerében (Military Instits of higher educ. in the Hungarian educ. system), *Felsőoktatási Szemle*, 9: 513–519.

Némedi, L.: *A debreceni Kossuth Lajos Tudományegyetem 75 éve* (75 yrs of the L.K. univ. of D.), Debrecen.

Székely, G.: A reneszánsz és a reformáció hatása az egyetemek szellemi életére Közép-Európában (The influence of the Renaiss. and Refn on the intellect. life of univs in central Europe), *Comm. de hist. artis med.*, 109–112 (1985): 19–24.

Szögi, L.: *A Marx Károly Közgazdaságtudományi Egyetem Levéltára 1891–1978* (The archives of the Karl Marx univ. of econs 1891–1978), Budapest.

——— A nők egyetemi tanulmányainak kérdése a budapesti Orvostudományi Karon (Women in the med. fac. at Budapest 1896–1926), *Comm. de hist. artis med.*, 115–116 (1986): 139–42.

Völker, A.: Zum präakad. Ausbildungsgang ungarischer Absolventen d. Univ. Halle, *Comm. de hist. artis med.*, 115–116 (1986): 67–82.

Publications 1989

Csáki, C.: A Marx Károly Közgazdaságtudományi Egyetem 40 éve (40 yrs of the Karl Marx univ. of econs), *Felsőoktatási Szemle*, 2: 65–71.

Csiki, L.: *A keszthelyi agrárfelsőoktatás története* (Hist. of agricult. higher educ. in K.), Keszthely.

Diószegi, I. ed.: *Az ELTE Bölcsészettudományi Karának története* (Hist. of the philos. fac. of the Loránd Eötvös univ.), Budapest.

Horváth, P.: *A tanszabadság Magyarországon* (Freedom of teaching in Hungary), Budapest.

Karády, V.: Assimilation and schooling: nat. and denominational minorities in the univs of Budapest around 1900, in G. Ránki ed.: *Hungary and European civilization*, Budapest: 285–319.

Kiss, J. M.: A hagyományok kérdése a budapesti egyetemen 1949–50-ben (The question of tradits at the univ. of B. 1949–50), *Levéltári Szemle*, 3: 67–71.

László, T.: A felsőoktatás minisztériumi irányításának történetéböl 1945–85 (From the hist. of minist. directives concerning higher educ. 1945–85), *Felsőoktatási Szemle*, 5: 261–71.

Pokol, B.: Az egyetemi tudományos szféra (The scientif. aspect of the univ.), in B. Pokol ed.: *Politikai reform és modernizáció*, Budapest: 97–209.

Italy

Additions to Earlier Lists

For 1977

Bolletti, G. G.: *Dell'origine e dei progressi dell' Istituto delle Scienze 1751*, Bologna.

Carranza , N.: Lo studio pisano e una provvisione degli Anziani di Pisa in materia univ. del 20 dicembre 1382, in *Studi filologici letterari e storici in memoria di Guido Favati*, Padua: 177–203.

Rijk, L. M. de: Logica Oxonienis, *Medioevo*, 3: 121–64.

For 1978

Verger, J.: Studia et univ., in *Le scuole degli ordini mendicanti (secoli 13– 14)*, Todi: 175–203.

For 1979

Augliera, L. and Soppelsa, M. L.: 'Mathesis universalis' e 'clavis universalis': un dibattito metodologico nella scl. fil. di Padova tra la fine del 17 e gli inizi del 18 sec., in U. Margiotta ed.: *Razionalità e condotta. Studi sulla genesi dello spazio educativo*, Treviso: 151–92.

I materiali dell'Istituto delle Scienze. Catalogo della mostra, Bologna.

Semenzato, C.: *L'Università di Padova. Il Palazzo del Bo: arte e storia*, Padua.

For 1980

Amelio, G. d' etc.: *Studi sulle 'Quaestiones' civilistiche disputate nelle università medievali*, Catania.

Arnaldi, G.: Sul concetto di 'Studium generale', *La cultura*, 18(4): 411–415.

Plessi, G.: *Araldica ultramontana a Bologna 1393–1660*, Bologna.

Villari, L.: L'univ. degli studi di Piazza Armerina, *Studi meridionali*, 12: 91–110.

For 1981

Atti legali per la fondazione dell'Istituto delle Scienze 1728, Bologna.

Cavazza, M.: Accad. scientif. a Bologna dal 'Coro Anatomico' agli Inquieti 1650–1714, *Quad. storici*, 48: 884–921.

Il ferro chirurgico nella raccolta Vittorio Putti di Bologna. Catalogo della mostra, Bologna.

Le cere anatomiche bolognesi del Settecento. Catalogo della mostra, Bologna.

Libri di medicina e di biologia a Bologna nei secoli 16.–18. Catalogo della mostra, Bologna.

Turtas, R.: La questione linguistica nei coll. gesuitici sardi nella seconda metà del Cinquecento, *Quad. sardi di storia*, 2: 57–87.

Zampieri, L.: *Un illustre medico umanista dello Studio pisano: Giulio Angeli*, Pisa.

—— Lettori di med. a Pisa: MS della Bibl. Univ., in *Catalogo della mostra di storia della medicina*, Pisa: 267–86.

For 1982

Campagnola, S. da: La 'cult.' umanistica nell' univ. di Perugia dell' Ottocento, *Annali della fac. di lettere e fil. univ. di Perugia. 2. Studii storico-antropol.*, 19 (1981–82): 5–37.

Ciardi, R. P.: La pubb. utilità delle arti: una giustificazione per l'esistenza delle accad. tra Sette- e Ottocento, in *Scritti in onore di Ottavio Morisani*, Catania: 427–53.

Iggers, G. C.: The univ. of Göttingen 1760–1800 and the transform. of hist. scholarship, *Storia della storiografia*, 2: 11–37.

Moscheo, R.: Melchior Inchofer 1585–1648 ed un suo ined. corso messinese di logica dell' anno 1617, *Quad. dell' Istit. Galvano della Volpe*, 3: 181–94.

Sottili, A.: L'Univ. di Pavia nella pol. cult. sforzesca, in *Gli Sforza a Milano e in Lombardia e i loro rapporti con gli stati italiani ed europei 1450–1530*, Milan: 519–80.

For 1983

Bernardinello, S.: Le orazioni per l'annuale apertura degli studi nell' univ. di Padova (dal 1405 al 1796): Saggio bibliog., *Atti e memorie dell' accad. Patavina*, 95 (1982–83): 320–423.

Dooley, B.: Giornalismo, univ. e organ. della scienza: tentativi di formare una accad. scientif. veneta all'inizio del Settecento, *Arch. veneto*, 120: 5–39.

Gratta, R. del and Gionta, M.: *Libri matricularum Studii Pisani 1543–1634*, Pisa.

Mantovani, G.: *Acta nationis Germanicae iuristorum 1650–1709*, Padua.

Moschetti, G.: Il volto econ. e giuridico de Padova dei primi decenni del sec. 13 nella vita della scl. notarile del magister Carradinus, in *Studi in onore de Gino Barbieri: Problemi e metodi de storia ed economia*, Salerno (henceforth noted as *Gino Barbieri*), 3: 1149–69.

Zanetti, D.: Dalle note di viaggio di Fynes Moryson: Le attività accad. e la vita materiale all' univ. di Padova alla fine del Cinquecento, in *Gino Barbieri*, 3: 1451–75.

Publications 1984

Albiñana, S.: La Univ. de València i els Jesuïtes. El conflicte de les Aules de Gràmatica 1720–33, in *Studia historica et philologica in honorem M. Batllori*, Rome: 11–31.

Arnaldi, G.: Alle origini dello studio di Bologna, in O. Capitani etc. eds: *Le sedi della cultura nell' Emilia Romagna: L'età communale*, Milan: 99–115.

Brizzi, G. P.: *I collegi per borsisti e lo Studio bolognese. Caratteri ed evoluzione di un'istituzione educativo-assistenziale fra 13. e 18 secolo*, Bologna.

Duranti, M.: Sull' insegnamento della 'storia eccles.' nell' univ. di Perugia 1844, *Annali della fac. di lettere e fil.—univ. di Perugia. 2. Studi storico—antropol.*, 20–21 (1982–84): 5–25.

Gambasin, A.: *Theses in sacra teologia nell'università di Padova dal 1815 al 1873*, Padua.

Gasnault, F.: La Congrégation des Etudes de 1824 à 1870, *Arch. hist. pontificiae*, 22: 153–225.

Giormani, V.: L'insegnamento della chimica all'Univ. di Padova dal 1749 al 1808, *Quad. per la storia dell' Univ. di Padova*, 17: 91–133.

Giovinazzo, E. and Tavilla, C. E.: L'origine dell' univ. e l'organ. del sapere, *Quad. catanesi di studi classici e medievale*, 6: 616–618.

Hervada, J.: Sobre el estatuto de las univs católicas y ecles., in *Diritto, persona e vita sociale. Scritti in onore di Orio Giacchi. I*, Milan (henceforth noted as *Orio Giacchi*): 491–511.

Kiene, M.: Zum architekt. Selbstverständnis d. univ. Gelehrtenstandes im Sei-Settecento am Beispiel d. Coll. Jacobs in Bologna, *Bull. de l'instit. hist. Belge de Rome*, 53–54: 177–91.

Luca, L. de: Profili attuali dell'insegnamento del diritto canonico nelle univ. italiana, in *Orio Giacchi*: 285–90.

Martels Dankern, Z. R. W. M. von: Het leven en werk van Petrus Adrianus van de Broecke 1619–75, publicus prof. eloquentiae te Pisa (The life and work of P. A. van de B. pub. prof. of eloquence at P.), *Bull. de l'instit. hist. Belge de Rome*: 53–54: 201–34.

Migliorino, F.: Alle origini dell' univ. di Catania: Progetto per un 'Chartularium', *Quad. catanesi di studi classici e medievali*, 6: 611–615.

Minnucci, G.: *Le lauree dello Studio Senese all'inizio del secolo 16. 1. 1501–1506*, Milan .

——— San Bernardino patrono dell' univ. di Siena, *L'Osservatore Romano*, 148: 7.

Pesenti, T.: *Professori e promotori di medicina nello Studio di Padova dal 1405 al 1509*, Padua.

Piana, C.: *Il 'Liber Secretus Iuris Caesarei' dell' Università di Bologna 1451–1500*, 1, Milan.

Rossetti, L.: I coll. per i dottorati 'auctoritate veneta', in *Viridarium floridum: studi di storia veneta offerti dagli allievi a Paolo Sambin*, Padua: 365–86.

Simoni, C. A.: Lo studio pisano nei seicento: Aspetti ammin. e vicende accad. da un codice ined. dell' Archivio di Stato di Pisa, *Boll. storico pisano*, 53: 187–209.

Turtas, R.: Appunti sull' attività teatrale nei coll. gesuitici sardi nei s. 16 e 17, in T. K. Kirova ed.: *Arte e cultura del' 600 e del' 700 in Sardegna*, Naples: 157–63.

Università di Bologna ed: *Scienza e storia. I musei della facoltà di scienze*, Bologna.

Volpi, G.: Lineamenti per uno studio sull univ. di Pisa nel 17 s., in *Scritti in onore di Dante Gaeta*, Milan: 640–783.

Publications 1985

Bellomo, M.: Intorno a Roffredo Beneventano: Prof. a Roma ? in M. Bellomo ed.: *Scuole, diritto e società nel mezzogiorno medievale d'Italia*, 1, Catania: 135–81.

Belloni, A.: Signorolo Omodei e gli inizi della scl. giuridica pavese, *Boll. della soc. pavese di storia patria*, 85: 29–39.

Bitskey, I.: Il Coll. Germanico-Ungarico di Roma e la formazione della Controriforma ungherese, in *Roma e l'Italia nel contesto della storia delle università ungheresi*, Rome (henceforth noted as *Roma e l'Italia*): 115–26.

Borzsák, I.: Storia degli studi di filologia classica e ricerche sulla storia delle univ. ungheresi, in *Roma e l'Italia*: 73–83.

Conte, E.: *Accademie studentesche a Roma nel Cinquecento: De modis docendi et discendi in iure*, Rome.

———Univ. e formazione giuridica a Roma nel Cinquecento, *La cultura*, 2: 328–46.

Cropera, C.: La 'fac. med.' parmense nel '700 dalla riforma del protomed. alla caduta del Du Tillot 1749–71, *Arch. storico per le prov. parmensi*, 37: 139–60.

Erdélyi, T. I.: Viaggi di studio di 'studenti inconsueti' ungheresi in Italia nella prima metà dell'Ottocento, in *Roma e l'Italia*: 167–79.

Forti Messina, A.: Studenti e laureati in med. a Pavia nell' Ottocento

338   *History of Universities*

preunitario, *Mél. de l'Ec. fr. de Rome. Moyen Age, Temps modernes*, 97: 489–530.
Giormani, V.: Le vicende della cattedra di chim. a Padova dal 1726 al 1749, in P. Antoniotti and L. Cerrati eds: *Atti del 10 convegno di storia della Chimica*, Turin: 99–106.
Klaniczay, T.: Lovanio, Roma, Padova, Ungheria: gli studi dell'umanista fiammingo Nicasio Ellebodio, in *Roma e l'Italia*: 97–113.
Matsen, H. S.: Selected extant Latin docs pertaining to the studio of Bologna around 1500, in R. J. Schoeck ed.: *Acta Conventus Neo-Latini Bononensis*, Bologna: 292–302.
Minnucci, G.: *Le Lauree dello Studio Senese all'inizio del secolo 16. 2. 1507–1514*, Milan.
Pesenti, T.: Studenti ungheresi nello studio padovano prima del 1241, in *Roma e l'Italia*: 35–38.
Sárközy, P.: Il Coll. Protestante di Debrecen a la formazione 'all'italiana' della poesia di Mihály Csokonai Vitéz, in *Roma e l'Italia*: 127–54.
Siegel, M.: Clio at the Ec. Normale Sup.: Hist. studies at an elite instit. in Fr. 1870–1904, *Storia della Storiografia*, 8: 37–49.
Sinkovics, I.: Le ricerche ungheresi sulla storia delle univ. e alcuni problemi metodologici, in *Roma e l'Italia*: 21–33.
Storia della cultura veneta. 5. Il Settecento, Vicenza.
Szalay-Ritoók, A.: Perché un gruppo di studenti ungheresi scelsero come meta dei loro studi l'Archiginnasio di Roma, in *Roma e l'Italia*: 85–96.
Székely, G.: Il ruolo delle univ. ungheresi medioevali e degli studi univ. all'estero nella formazione degli intell. ungheresi, in *Roma e l'Italia*: 53–72.
Verde, A. F.: *Lo studio Fiorentino 1473–1503. Ricerche e documenti. 4. La vita universitaria*, 3 vols, Florence.
Vernacchia-Galli, J.: *Le lauree ad honorem nel periodo fascista 23–10–1919–16–11–1943*, Rome.

Publications 1986
Ascheri, M.: Diritto e istituzioni: la cattedra di istituzioni medievali a Siena, *Critica storica*, 23: 295–97.
Bellone, E.: *Il primo secolo di vita della Universtà di Torino*, Turin.
Black, R.: Arezzo e la sua univ. sconosciuta del Rinascimento, *Atti e memorie della accad. Petrarca di lettere, arti e scienze*, 48: 119–51.
Ceyssens, L.: Lettres de Jean Opstraet, prof. à Louvain, à son collègue Jean Libert Hennebel en mission à Rome 1694, *Bull. de l'instit. hist. Belge de Rome*, 55–56: 109–22. (Concerns a recent papal condemnation).
Collin, L.: Maurice de Baets et l'Inst. Sup. de phil. de Louvain, *Bull. de l'instit. hist. Belge de Rome*, 55–56: 253–85. (A dispute of 1896–98).
Ferraresi, A., Grassano, A. M. and Testa, A. P.: *Cultura e vita universitaria nelle miscellanee Beloredi, Giardini, Ticinensia*, Pavia. (Collection especially valuable for hist. of univ. of Pavia in 17th and 18th centuries).

Giannatale, G. di: La cattedra di giurisprud. nel Real Coll. San Matteo di Teramo, *Aprutium*, 4: 33–52. (Coll. suppressed in 1861).

Guarnieri, R.: Ricordo di Romano Guarnieri, *Incontri*, 1(2): 58–67. (R.G. 1883–1955 prof. of Ital. lang. and lit. at several Dutch universities).

Molinari, F.: La figura di P. Gemelli 1878–1959 fondatore dell' Univ. Cattolica di Milano, attraverso i rapporti della polizia fascista, *La scl. cattolica*, 114: 459–93.

Simone, M. R. di: Per una storia delle univ. europ.: consistenza e composizione del corpo student. dal Cinquecento al Settecento, *Clio*, 22: 348–88.

Sorgia, G.: *Lo Studio generale cagliaritano*, Cagliari.

Turtas, R.: *La Casa dell' Università*, Sassari. (Bldg pol. of Jesuits at Sassari 1562–1632).

Zorzoli, M. C.: *Università, dottori, giureconsulti—L'organizzazione della 'facoltà legale' di Pavia nell' età spagnola*, Padua.

Publications 1987
Betti, G. L.: Un teol. dello studio bolognese contro fra Paolo Sarpi nel 1606, *Studi storici dell'Ordine dei Servi di Maria*, 37: 211–218.

Bologna 1088–1988: Alma mater studiorum saecularia nona, Milan.

Breve guida alla storia dell' Università di Bologna, Bologna.

Camporeale, S. I.: Lo studio Fiorentino e la vita univ. 1473–1503. Cronache di cult. a Firenze nel' 400, *Memorie domenicane*, 18: 347–67. (Discusses 3 vols (1985) by A. F. Verde).

Capitani, O.: *L'Università a Bologna. Personaggi, momenti e luoghi dalle origini al 16. secolo*, Bologna.

Cavazza, M. ed.: *Rapporti di scienziati europei con lo studio bolognese fra '600 e '700*, Bologna.

Decleva, E.: Alle origini del sistema univ. milanese, *Acme*, 40(2): 5–15.

I musei dell' Università, Bologna.

La città del sapere. I laboratori storici e i musei dell' Università di Bologna, Bologna.

Maffioli, C. S.: Domenico Guglielmini, Geminiano Rondelli e la nuova cattedra d'idrometria nello studio di Bologna 1694, *Studi e memorie per la storia dell' univ. di Bologna*, 6: 81–124.

Minelli, G.: *All' origine della biologia moderna. La vita di un testimone e protagonista: Marcello Malpighi nell' Università di Bologna*, Milan.

Missiroli, A.: Scienze della pol., stato, democrazia. La 'Deutsche Hochschule f. Pol.' di Berlino, *Annali dell' Istit. storico italogermanico in Trento*, 12: 411–76.

Roggero, M.: *Il Sapere e la Virtù: Stato, Università e Professioni nel Piemonte tra Settecento ed Ottocento*, Turin.

Szczucki, L.: Tra scolastica e umanesimo. La fil. all' univ. di Cracovia nel sec. 16, *Giornale critico della fil. ital.*, 66: 220–34.

Università di Bologna. Luoghi e musei, Bologna.

Vanysacker, D.: Mgr Giuseppe Garampi aux Pays-Bas autrichiens et dans la principauté de Liège en 1764, *Bull. de l'instit. hist. Belge de Rome*, 57: 165–97. (Information about the conflicts between the univ. of Louvain and the Holy See concerning eccles. benefices).

Verde, A. F.: Libri tra le pareti domestiche. Una necessaria appendice a *Lo Studio Fiorentino 1473–1503, Memorie domenicane*, 18: 1–225.

Weijers, O.: *Terminologie des universités au 13e siècle*, Rome.

Publications 1988

Angelozzi, G.: 'Insegnarli la vita christiana insieme con bone lettere'. Il convitto gesuitico e la formazione delle classi dirigenti, in G. P. Brizzi and A. I. Pini eds: *Studenti e università degli studenti dal 12 al 19 secolo*, Bologna (henceforth noted as *Studenti e univ.*): 261–82.

Arnaldi, G.: Il natale dell' Univ. di Bologna, *Nuova antologia* (Florence), 2165: 224–40.

Bastianoni, C. and Catoni, G.: *Impressum Senis. Storie di tipografi, incunaboli e librai*, Siena. (Many refs to univ. and details of its teachers).

Benedictis, A. de: La fine dell' autonomia student. tra autorità e disciplin., in *Studenti e univ.*: 193–223.

Bosna, E.: L'univ. degli studi di Altamura, *Altamura*, 29–30 (1987–88): 191–214.

Brizzi, G. P.: Matricole ed effettivi. Aspetto della presenza student. a Bologna fra Cinque e Seicento, in *Studenti e univ.*: 225–59.

———— and Pini, A. I. eds: *Studenti e università degli studenti dal 12 al 19 secolo*, Bologna. (All items noted separately).

Charle, C.: Une enquête en cours: Le dictionnaire biograph. des univs fr. aux 19e et 20e s., *Mél. de l'Ec. fr. de Rome. Moyen âge. Temps modernes* (= *ME fr. R*), 100: 63–68.

Clercq, P. de: The 's Gravesande collection in the Museum Boerhaave, Leiden, *Nuncius. Annali di storia della scienza*, 3(1): 127–37.

Continelli, L.: *L'archivio dell' ufficio dei Memoriali. Inventario. 1. Memoriali 1265–1436. 1. 1265–1333*, Bologna.

Dolcini, C. ed.: *Università e studenti a Bologna nei secoli 13. e 14.*, Turin.

Gasnault, F.: Anticlericalismo e agitazioni student. a Bologna nell' Ottocento preunitario, in *Studenti e univ.*: 319–51.

———— Le milieu univ. à Bologne au 19e s. Les aléas de l'enquête documentaire prosop., *ME fr. R*, 100: 155–73.

Greci, R.: L'associazionismo degli studenti dalle origini alla fini del 14 sec., in *Studenti e univ.*: 13–44.

Kaluza, Z.: *Les querelles doctrinales à Paris. Nominalistes et réalistes aux confins du 14e et du 15e siècles*, Bergamo.

Kiene, M.: Der Palazzo della Sapienza — zur Ital. Universitätsarchitektur d. 15. u. 16 Jh., *Römisches Jb. f. Kunstgesch.*, 23–24: 219–71. (Plans for bldg at Siena).

L'Aula Carducci, Bologna.

Marchesini, D.: Lo studente di coll. a Bologna. Aspetti della vita quotidiana, in *Studenti e univ.*: 283–317. (Students of 18th century).

Minnucci, G. ed.: *I tedeschi nella storia dell' università di Siena*, Siena. (Trans. into Ital. of German studies with bibliog. for hist. of univ. to end of 16th century).

Montanari, V. and Roversi, G. eds: *L'Italia a Bologna. Lettere di Matilde Serao per le feste del 1888*, Bologna.

Nardi, P.: La carriera accad. di Lodovico Zdekauer storico del diritto nell' univ. di Siena 1888–96, *Studi senesi*, 100: 751–81.

Nicolosi Grassi, G.: Per rinnovare lo studium di Catania: le 'riforme' del Monteleone 1522, in *Studi in memoria M. Condorelli*, 3, Milan: 217–45.

Paolini, L.: L'evoluzione di una funzione eccles.: l'arcidiacono e lo studio a Bologna nel 13 sec., *Studi medievali*, 29: 129–72.

Piana, C.: Lo studio dell' Osservanza nel '400 e l'univ. di Bologna, in *'Osservanza' francescana e università di Bologna: cultura laica e religiosa tra umanesimo e rinascimento*, Bologna/Ravenna (henceforth noted as *'Osservanza' francescana*): 35–43.

Pini, A. I.: 'Discere turba volens.' Studenti e vita student. a Bologna dalle origine dello studio alla metà del Trecento, in *Studenti e univ.*: 45–136.

Schmitt, C.: L'osservanza francescana in Toscana secondo il Regesto dei Vicari generali dal 1464 al 1488, *Studi francescani*, 85: 57–79. (Inform. about lecturers of the order).

Stirpe, M.: Diploma di laurea e stemma gentilizio di Mons. Vittorio Giovardi, *Latium*, 5: 297–304. (18th century).

Toschi, T.: I francescani e l'univ. di Bologna, in *'Osservanza' francescana*: 29–33.

Trombetti Budriesi, A. L.: L'esame di laurea presso lo studio bolognese. Laureati in diritto civile nel sec. 15, in *Studenti e univ.*: 137–91.

—— and Foresti, F.: Lo studio e la città. 9 centenario dell' univ. di Bologna 1088–1988. Preface to new ed. of S. Mazzetti: *Repertorio di tutti e professori antichi e moderni della ... università di Bologna*.

Turtas, R.: *La nascita dell' università in Sardegna*, Sassari.

Vallone, G.: Nota sul giurista napoletano Cicco Loffredo e il suo insegnamento a Padova, *Studi senesi*, 100: 535–38.

Verger, J.: Peut-on faire une prosop. des profs des univs fr. à la fin du Moyen Age? *ME fr. R*, 100: 55–62.

Publications 1989.

Citruni, T.: I venti anni della fac. teol. dell' Italia settentrionale, *La scl. cattolica*, 117: 104–111.

Ferrara, F., Orlandelli, G. and Vasina, A. eds: *G. Cencetti: Lo studio di Bologna. Aspetti momenti e problemi 1935–70*, Bologna. (Collection of previously pub. pieces).

Minnucci, G. and Kosuta, L.: *Lo studio di Siena nei secoli 14–16. Documenti e notizie biografiche*, Milan.

Morpurgo, P.: La scl. med. salernitana: storia, immagini e problemi. Note critiche in margine a recenti congressi ... nell' attesa di incontri annunciati, *Clio*, 25: 99–104.

Piana, C.: *Il 'Liber secretus iuris pontificii' dell' università di Bologna 1451–1500*, 2, Milan.

Zampieri, A., Mazzoncini, V. and Angelotti, N.: Lettori di med. dell' univ. di Pisa e cavalieri di S. Stefano. Documenti e testimonianze dei sec. 16–18, in *Le imprese e i simboli*, Pisa: 179–201. (Cat. of exhib. of May 1989).

Japan

Publication 1981
Hayashima, A.: Zur Gesch. d. Kölner Handelshochschule, *Kwansei Gakuin Univ. annual studies*, 30: 181–218.

Publication 1984
Hayashima, A.: Die Frequenz d. deutschen Handelshochschulen 1898–1920, *Kwansei Gakuin Univ. annual studies*, 33: 121–52.

Publications 1985
Ishida, S. and Beukers, H.: The influence of the Training Coll. for Military Surgeons in Utrecht on the med. schls in Japan, *Nihon Ishigaku Zasshi*, 31: 33–34.
Luyendijk-Elshout, A. M.: The beginning of the univ. of Leiden, *Koroth*, 33: 101–111.

Publication 1986
Hayashima, A.: Max Weber u.d. deutschen Handelshochschulen, *Kwansei Gakuin Univ. annual studies*, 35: 143–76.

Publication 1987
Hayashima, A.: Die Absolventen d. Leipziger Handelshochschule 1900–20, *Kwansei Gakuin Univ. annual studies*, 36: 113–94.

Publication 1988
Hayashima, A.: Die Absolventen d. preussischen Handelshochschule. Erster teil, *Kwansei Gakuin Univ. annual studies*, 37: 23–96.

Philippines

Publication 1988
Villarroel, F.: The univ. of Santo Tomás of Manila 1611–1987, *Philippiniana sacra*, 23: 81–119.

Poland

Additions to Earlier Lists

For 1978

Nędza, M.: *Polityka stypendialna Akademii Umiejetnósci w latach 1878–1920* (The pol. of the Acad. of Sciences towards scholarships 1878–1920), Wrocław.

Schmitt, C. B.: Filippo Fantoni Galileo Galilei's predecessor as maths lecturer at Pisa, *Studia Copernicana*, 16: 53–62.

Kalicki, W.: Dziesięć lat Instyt. Nauk Politycznych Uniw. Wrockławskiego (10 yrs of the Inst. of Pol. Studies of the univ. of W.), *Sobótka*, 34(4): 541–50. (Summary in German).

For 1980

Biedroń, T.: Udział młodzieży studenckiej w życiu kult. i artystycznym Krakowa w latach 1945–50 (Students' participation in cult. and artistic life in C. in the yrs 1945–50), *Studia hist.*, 23(3): 431–54. (Summary in English).

For 1981

Buszko, J.: Akcja solidarnościowa na rzecz prof. krakowskich arestowanych w ramach tzw. *Sonderaktion* (The solidarity action on behalf of the profs of C. arrested in the so-called *Sonderaktion*), *Studia hist.*, 24(3): 441–70. (Summary in English).

Mycielska, D.: Drogi życiowe prof. przed objęciem katedr akad. w niedpodległej Polsce (Careers of profs before their appoint. to univ. chairs in independent Poland), *Intelig. polska 19 i 20 w.*, 2: 243–90. (Summaries in Russian and French).

Ossowska, I.: Pokolenie Szkoły Głównej (The generation produced by the Main School), *Intelig. Polska 19 i 20 w.*, 2: 169–208. (Summaries in Russian and French).

For 1982

Ergetowski, R.: *Studenckie organizacje Polaków w Uniwersytecie Lipskim w latach 1872–1919* (Pol. student organis at the univ. of Leipzig 1872–1919), Wrocław.

For 1983

Ożóg, K.: Studia nad wykształceriem uniw. krakowskiego duchowieństwa świeckiego w 14 w. (On the univ. educ. of the secular clergy in C. during the 14th cent.), *Studia hist.*, 26(4): 551–71. (Summary in English).

Publications 1984
Kurás, S.: Amboldus syn Jana z Kępina, pierwszy znany prof. Uniw. Krakowskiego (ok. 1355–75) (A. the son of J. of K. the first known prof. of the univ. of C. (*c.* 1355–75)), *Studia hist.*, 27(3): 491–93.
Lück, H.: Die Spruchtätigkeit d. Juristenfak. u. d. Schöffenstuhls zu Wittenberg, *Czasopismo Prawno-hist.*, 36(2) (Poznan): 117–43.
Michalewska, K.: Sprawa uniw. ukraińskiego w latach 1848–1914 (On the question of the Ukrainian univ. at Lvov in the yrs 1848–1914), *Studia hist.*, 27 (1): 35–60. (Summary in English).

Publications 1985
Albin, J. ed.: Przemówienie sprawozdawcze za rok akad. 1947–48 i 1948–49 prorekt. Uniw. Wrocławskiego prof. dra Seweryna Wysłoucha w dniu 3 X 1949 (The reporting speech of the prorect. of the univ. of W. prof. dr S. W. covering the acad. yrs 1947–48 and 1948–49 presented on 3 Oct. 1949), *Sobótka*, 40(3): 417–39.
Barcik, M.: Udział Uniw. Jagiellońskiego w akcji społecznofilantropijnej w latach 1914–21 (The share of the Jagiellonian univ. in soc. and philanthropic actions in the yrs 1914–21), *Studia hist.*, 28(4): 577–95. (Summary in English).
Biedroń, T.: Organizacje studenckie młodzieży wiejskiej w Krakowie w latach 1945–49 (Organis. of students of peasant origin in C. in the yrs 1945–49), *Studia hist.*, 28 (4): 607–25. (Summary in English).
Buszko, J.: Nieznane aspekty akcji na rzecz prof. Krakowskich uwięzionych 6 listopada 1939 (Some unknown aspects of the action on behalf of the profs of C. imprisoned on 6 Nov. 1939), *Studia hist.*, 28(4): 597–606. (Summary in English).
Chamiec, M.: La grande réforme de Kołłataj, in M. Kulczykowski ed.: *Les grandes réformes des universités européennes du 16e au 20e siècles*, Cracow (henceforth noted as *Les grandes réformes*): 13–14.
Fletcher, J. M.: Proposals for the reform of higher educ. in 16th-cent. Eng., in *Les grandes réformes*: 15–25.
Kulczykowski, M. ed.: *Les grandes réformes des universités européennes du 16e au 20e siècles*, Cracow. (All items noted separately).
Luyendijk-Elshout, A. M.: The beginning of Leiden univ., an 'asylum for the muses' in a country in revolt, in *Les grandes réformes*: 27–36.
Mycielska, D.: Postawy pol. prof. wyższych uczeini w dwudziestoleciu międzywojennym (The pol. attitudes of univ. profs in the 20 inter-war yrs), *Intelig. polska 19 i 20 w.*, 4: 293–335. (Summaries in Russian and French).
Nowak, K.: Krakowskie Towarzystwo Uniw. Robotniczego (The Workers' Univ. Soc. in C.), *Studia hist.*, 28(1): 93–107. (Summary in English).
Perkowska, U.: La genèse et la caractéristique de la loi sur les écs sup. du 13 juillet 1920, in *Les grandes réformes*: 95–107.
Rakovà, I.: Les essais de réforme à l'univ. de Prague dans la première moitié du 18e s., in *Les grandes réformes*: 75–82.

Ridder-Symoens, H. de: L'aristocratisation des univs au 16e s., in *Les grandes réformes*: 37–47.

Schmidt, S.: Revol. u. Universitätsreform. Reformbestrebungen d. Hochschullehrer in d. deutschen bürgerlich-demokrat. Revol. von 1448–49, in *Les grandes réformes*: 83–94.

Suchodolski, B.: Liberté ou soumission. Expériences des univs polonaises dans la période d'entre-deux-guerres, in *Les grandes réformes*: 121–28.

Urfus, V.: L'univ. de Prague et sa fac. de droit à l'époque des changements du s. des lumières et de l'absolutisme policier, in *Les grandes réformes*: 67–74.

Wrzesiński, W. ed.: Pierwszy rok Senatu akad. Uniw. i Politech. Wrocławskiej (The first yr of the acad. Senate of the univ. of W. and the Polytech.), *Sobótka*, 40(3): 339–87.

Publication 1986
Kiryk, F.: *Nauk przemożnych perła* (The pearl of overwhelming sciences), Cracow.

Publications 1987
Molik, W.: Z dziejów kształcenia polskiej intelig. na obczyżnie. Polscy studenci w uniw. niemieckich w latach 1871–1914 (From the hist. of educ. of Polish intellects abroad. Polish students at Germ. univs 1871–1914), *Intelig. polska 19 i 20 w.*, 5: 243–68.

Oraczewski, Z.: Ruch młodzieżowy w krakowskich uczelniach wyższych w latach 1948–56 (Youth organis. at the univ. and other instits of higher educ. in C. 1848–56), *Studia hist.*, 30(3): 433–47. (Summary in English).

Szarras, H.: *Francuskie szkolnictwo wyzsze w polowie lat osiemdziesiatych* (The Fr. higher educ. system in the middle of the 80s), Warsaw.

Publication 1988
Pawlak, M.: *Studia uniwersyteckie młodzieży z Prus Królewskich w 16–18 w.* (The univ. studies of youth from Royal Prussia from the 16th to the 18th cents), Toruń. (Summary in German).

Publications 1989
Bartnicka, K. and Szybiak, I.: 'Natives and strangers' in the Polish univ. staff in the yrs 1780–1830. An attempt of statistical approach, in M. Kulczykowski ed.: *Pérégrinations académiques*, Cracow (henceforth noted as *Pérégrinations*): 275–81.

Beauvois, D.: Les voyages d'étude à l'univ. de Vilna 1803–32, in *Pérégrinations*: 259–74.

Bois, H. and Frijhoff, W.: Pérégrination acad. ou voyage éducatif? Remarques à propos des voyageurs du Brabant septentrional: Nature, fréquence et circuits de leurs voyages sous l'Ancien Régime, in *Pérégrinations*: 117–29.

Brzozowski, S.: Les problèmes d'études polonaises en Allemagne 1860–1918, in *Pérégrinations*: 215–28.

Dutkowa, R.: Les études de jeunes polonais dans les univs étrangères au 19e s. Une esquisse du problème, in *Pérégrinations*: 131–60.

Dybiec, J.: Polonais en voyages d'études et d'éduc. en Grande Bretagne de 1795 à 1918, in *Pérégrinations*: 313–27.

Ergetowski, R.: L'adresse de remerciements des étudiants polonais de Berlin au syndic de Rome, in *Pérégrinations*: 283–94.

Hajdukiewicz, L.: Réflexions sur les pérégrinations acad. de Polonais au 17e s., in *Pérégrinations*: 13–25.

Hojda, Z.: 'Voyages de chevaliers' de Bohème au 17e s., in *Pérégrinations*: 99–105.

Julia, D.: La pérégrination acad. en Fr. à l'époque mod., in *Pérégrinations*: 27–50.

Konarska, B.: Les étudiants d'univs polonaises dans les univs de Fr. après l'insurrection de nov. 1832–48, in *Pérégrinations*: 161–79.

Kubik, K.: Habitants de Gdańsk en voyage d'études univ. à l'étranger au 17e s., in *Pérégrinations*: 55–69.

Kulczykowski, M. ed.: *Pérégrinations académiques*, Cracow. (All items noted separately).

―――― Les Polonais étudiant en Fr. après l'insurrection de jan., in *Pérégrinations*: 181–96.

Libiszowska, Z.: Les voyages scientif. aux temps des Lumières, in *Pérégrinations*: 107–16.

Lukawski, Z.: Les étudiants polonais dans les univs de l'empire Russe dans la première moitié du 19e s., in *Pérégrinations*: 229–46.

Molik, W.: *Polskie peregrynacje uniwersyteckie do Niemiec 1871–1914* (Pol. univ. peregrinations to Germ. 1871–1914), Poznań. (Summary in German).

Mrozowska, K.: Les étudiants polonais à Gand 1856–1913, in *Pérégrinations*: 197–214.

Perkowska, U.: Etudes scientif. des univs de Cracovie à Vienne dans les années 1800–1918, in *Pérégrinations*: 295–312.

Pešek, J. and Svatoš, M.: Die soz. Folgen d. akad. Peregrination in d. böhmischen Ländern in d. zweiten Hälfte d. 16. Jh., in *Pérégrinations*: 51–54.

Ridder-Symoens, H. de: L'évol. quantitative et qualitative de la pérégrination acad. des étudiants Néerland. méridionaux de la Renaissance à l'époque des Lumières, in *Pérégrinations*: 87–97.

Scandinavia

Additions to Earlier Lists

For 1977
Uppsala Universitet 500 år, Uppsala. (Cat. of an exhib. 20 Jan.–31 Dec.
1977).

Publication 1980
Heininen, S.: *Die finnischen Studenten in Wittenberg 1531–52*, Helsinki.

Publication 1981
Pinborg, J.: Danish students 1450–1535 and the univ. of Copenhagen,
Cahiers de l'Instit. du Moyen-Age grec et latin, 37: 70–122.

Publication 1988
Klinge, M. etc.: *Kungliga akademien i Abo 1640–1808* (The ryl acad. in Abo
1640–1808), Helsinki.

Spain and Portugal

Additions to Earlier Lists

For 1982
Garcia Ballester, L.: Arnau de Vilanova (*c.*1240–1311) y la ref. de los
estudios médicos en Montpellier 1309: El Hipócrates latino y la introd.
del nuevo Galeno, *Dynamis*, 2: 97–158.

For 1984
Mateu Ibars, J.: Scholares, bacalarii, doctores y magistri del Estudio
General de Lérida. Contrib. a su nómina en los s. 14 y 15, *Ilerda*, 15:
175–207.
Ten, A. ed.: *Plan de estudios aprobado per S.M. y mandado observar en la
Universidad de Valencia*, Valencia. (A scheme of 1787).

For 1985
Alvarez de Morales, A.: *La ilustración y la reforma de la universidad en la
España del siglo 18*, 3, Madrid.
Giles, G. J.: The soc. profile of the Germ. student body in the Third Reich,
in *Higher Education and Society. Historical Perspectives/Educación
superior y sociedad. Perspectivas históricas*, Salamanca, 1: 162–70.
Lértora Mendoza, C. A.: Las ciencias modernas en la univ. y cols riopla-
tenses (s. 18), in J. L. Peset ed.: *La ciencia moderna y el Nuevo Mundo*,
Madrid (henceforth noted as *Ciencia moderna*): 271–96.

Miralles Vives, F.: Nuevos docs para la hist. de la univ. Los desórdenes de 1580–90, *Saitabi*, 35: 111–27.

Peset, M.: Poderes y univ. de México durante la época colonial, in *Ciencia moderna*: 57–84.

Rodríguez-San Pedro Bezares, L. E.: Declive y regionalización de la matricula salmantina de los s. 17 y 18. Aproximación descriptiva, *Studia hist. Hist. moderna*, 3: 143–62.

For 1986

Baldó, M.: *La universitat de Valéncia*, Valencia.

Carnes García, E.: Bases del mantenemíento econ. del Col. de Sancti Spiritus, *Cuadernos des estudios Gallegos*, 36: 89–115.

Frijhoff, W.: La univ. como espacio de mediación cult., *Hist. de la educ. Rev. interuniv.*, 5: 41–60.

Martínez Gomis, M.: La actitud regalista de Campomanes en la ref. univ.: ed proyecto de transformación de la univ. de Orihuela en col. de lenguas, artes y teol., in *La Ilustración española*, Alicante: 299–332.

For 1987

Albiñana, S.: Cátedras y catedráticos en la Univ. de Valencia 1734–1807, in *Universidades Españolas y Americanas. Epoca colonial*, Valencia (henceforth noted as *U.E. y A.*): 15–33.

———— and Hernández, T. M.: Comentario en torno a la biog. de Tomás Vincente Tosca, in *U.E. y A.*: 35–55.

Aloy Ruíz, M. de las M.: *Historia de la formación profesional en el s. 20 en Alava*, Lejona.

———— *Historia de la formación profesional en el s. 20 en Guipúzcoa*, Lejona.

———— *Historia de la formación profesional en el s. 20 en Vizcaya*, Lejona.

———— *Historia de la formación profesional en la Comunidad Autónoma Vasca en el s. 20*, Lejona.

Alvarez de Morales, A.: La univ. y sus denominaciones, in *U.E. y A.*: 57–65.

Alvarez, F. M.: *Educación y analfabetismo en la Extremadura meridional (Siglo 17)*, Cáceres.

Baldo Lacomba, M.: La Univ. de Córdoba ante la Ilustración 1767–1810, in *U.E. y A.*: 57–65.

Beuchot, M.: Algunos profs dominicos de la Univ. de México durante el s. 17, in *U.E. y A.*: 101–108.

Botello de Morales y Vasconcelos, F.: *Historia de las Cuevas de Salamanca*, Madrid.

Cuellas Casado, J. I. etc.: *Cien años de la Escuela de Comercio y de Estudios Empresariales de Valladolid*, Valladolid.

Domínguez Rodríguez, E.: *La Universidad de Extremadura: sus antecedentes*, Cáceres.

Esteban, L.: Textos, impresores, correctores y libreros en la Univ. de Valencia de finales del s. 18 (1778–1802), in *U.E. y A.*: 109–25.

Felipo, A.: Los estudios de Latinidad en la Univ. de Valencia entre 1611 y 1651, in *U.E. y A.*: 127–40.

Ferrero Micó, R.: Capítulos de 1517. Acerca de una reforma de la Univ. de Valencia, in *U.E. y A.*: 141–48.

Gallego Barnés, A. and Pérez de Clarenc, N.: El libro del priorato de cánones y leyes 1638–1701. Contrib. a la hist. del Studi General de Valencia, in *U.E. y A.*: 149–74.

García Trobat, P.: Los grados de la Univ. de Gandía 1630–1772, in *U.E. y A.*: 175–86.

González González, E.: Los primitivos estatutos y ordenanzas de la real Univ. de México, in *U.E. y A.*: 207–24.

Grande Juesas, J.: Escolares médicos asturianos en Valladolid 1546–1936, *Bol. del inst. de estudios asturianos*, 41: 1185–94.

Graullera Sanz, V.: La cátedra de arte de la notaría en la Univ. de Valencia del s. 16, in *U.E. y A.*: 225–35.

Gutiérrez Cuadrado, J.: La sustitución del Latin por el romance en la univ. españ. del s. 18, in *U.E. y A.*: 237–52.

Harding, I.: Instit. de la enseñanza de la matemática en Chile entre la segunda mitad del s. 16 y el s. 17, in *U.E. y A.*: 253–76.

Hernández Díaz, J. M.: Un discurso sobre la univ. en la Acad. Estudiantil 'Santo Tomás de Aquino' de Salamanca, *Salamanca. Rev. prov. de estudios*, 24–25: 147–54.

Lario, D. de: Mecenazgo de los cols mayores en la formación de la burocracia españ. (s. 14–18), in *U.E. y A.*: 277–309.

Lértora Mendoza, C. A.: El rol de las univs en el avance científico argentino, in *U.E. y A.*: 311–28.

Lluch, M. A.: Grados de la Univ. de Valencia durante el s. 18, in *U.E. y A.*: 351–60.

Luna Díaz, L. and Pavón Romero, A.: El claustro de consiliarios de la real Univ. de México de 1553 al segundo rectorado de Farfán, in *U.E. y A.*: 329–50.

Martínez Gomis, M.: La función soc. de una univ. menor durante los s. 17 y 18. El caso de Estudio General de Orihuela, in *U.E. y A.*: 361–94.

Mestre, A.: Ilustrados y reforma univ.: Las 'escuelas', in *U.E. y A.*: 395–402.

Muñoz Delgado, V.: Jacinto Angueira, comendador de la Orden de la Merced de Conjo y prof. de la univ. Compostelana, *Analecta mercedaria*, 6: 285–98.

Muñoz Ferrer, F.: Jovellanos. La enseñanza y las acads, *Bol. del inst. de estudios asturianos*, 41: 1055–61.

Osorio Pérez, M. J.: *Historia del Real Colegio de San Bartolomé y Santiago*, Granada.

Peset, J. L.: Los origenes de la enseñanza téc. en América: el col. de minería de México, in *U.E. y A.*: 415–31.

Peset, M.: La Ilustración y la Univ. de México, in *La real expedición botánica a Nueva España 1787–1803*, Madrid: 131–47.

Peset, M., Mancebo, M. F. and Peset, M. F.: El recuento de los libros de matrícula de la Univ. de México, in *U.E. y A.*: 433–43.

Rodríguez Cruz, A. M.: La univ. más antigua de América, in *U.E. y A.*: 445–56.

Rodríguez-San Pedro Bezares, L. E.: Univ. moderna y promoción jurídica. El Diario salmantino de Gaspar Ramos Ortiz 1568–69, in *U.E. y A.*: 457–77.

────── *Vida, aspiraciones y fracasos de un estudiante de Salamanca: El diario de Gaspar Ramos Ortiz 1568–69*, Salamanca.

Rustán, V.: La real Univ. de San Carlos y Nuestra Señora de Monserrat. Su fundación, in *U.E. y A.*: 479–504.

Sala Catalá, J.: Enseñanza e investigación biol. en la univ. de la Restauración 1875–1923, in *U.E. y A.*: 505–518.

Sobaler, M. de los A.: *Los colegiales de Santa Cruz, una élite de poder*, Valladolid.

Ten, A. E.: El convictorio carolino de Lima y la introd. de la ciencia moderna en el Perú virreinal, in *U.E. y A.*: 519–33.

Universidades Españolas y Americanas. Epoca colonial, Valencia. (Relevant items noted separately).

Varela González, L.: La población univ. de Santiago durante el s. 18, in *U.E. y A.*: 535–51.

Vega Perrín, M. C. de etc.: El col. de Santo Tomás de Salamanca, *Salamanca. Rev. prov. de estudios*, 24–25: 65–82.

Velázquez Zambrano, A. M.: La Univ. de Córdoba del Tucamán en la etapa franciscana 1767–1800, in *Actas del I Congreso Internacional sobre los franciscanos y el Nuevo Mundo*, Madrid: 901–24.

Vera de Flachs, M. C.: El comportamiento de los claustros de la Univ. de Córdoba 1664–1800, in *U.E. y A.*: 553–67.

Publications 1988

Baeza, F. J.: Proyección iberoamericana de la Univ. Pontificia de Comillas, *Miscelánea Comillas*, 46: 471–87.

Barrientos García, J.: La Univ. de Salamanca ante el proceso de Fray Luis de León, *La Ciudad de Dios*, 201: 151–70.

Claramunt, S.: Origen de los univs Catalanas medievales, in *Estudios sobre los orígenes de las universidades españolas. Homenaje de la Universidad de Valladolid a la de Bolonia en su 9 centenario*, Valladolid (henceforth noted as *Orígenes*): 97–111.

Estudios de geografía e historia: 25 años de la facultad de filosofía y letras, Bilbao. (Concerns univ. of Deusto).

Falcón, M. I. etc.: Las univs de Reino de Aragón (Huesca y Zaragoza) y de Lérida en la edad media, in *Orígenes*: 85–95.

Gallego Salvadores, J.: Grados acad. concedidos por la Univ. de Valencia entre 1562 y 1580, *Analecta sacra Tarraconensia*, 60: 5–155.

García Oro, J.: Compostela, acad. de Galicia medieval, in *Orígenes*: 69–84.

García Sánchez, J.: Notas referentes a la aplicación de los 'Estatutos viejos' de la Univ. de Oviedo de 1609: Primeros problemas surgidos por la ejecución de algunas prescripciones estatutarias al cumplirse el primer cuatrienio de su vigencia, in *Liber Amicorum. Colección de estudios jurídicos en Homenaje al Prof. Dr D. José Pérez Montero*, Oviedo: 595–624.

García y García, A.: Escolares ibéricos en Bolonia 1300–30, in *Orígenes*: 113–34.

González Díaz, V.: *Reflexiones sobre la investigación en la universidad*, Alcalá de Henares.

Gutiérrez Torrecilla, L. M.: *El Colegio de San Ciriaco y Santa Paula o 'De Málaga' de la Universidad de Alcalá de Henares 1611–1843*, Alcalá de Henares.

Jarque Martínez, E. and Salas Ausens, J. A.: El *cursus honorum* de los letrados aragoneses en los s. 16 y 17, *Studia hist. Hist. moderna*, 6: 411–22.

Julia Irigoyen de la Rasilla, M. and Peláez, A.: *Patrimonio artístico de la Universidad Complutense*, Madrid.

Mancebo, M. F.: *La Universidad de Valencia en guerra. La FUE 1936–39*, Valencia.

Martin Rodríguez, E.: Juan Torobo, prof. de cirugía en la Univ. de Santiago, *Compostellanum*, 33: 509–514.

Núñez González, J. M.: Bolonia y el ciceronianismo en España: Juan Ginés de Sepúlveda y Antonio Agustín, in *Orígenes*: 205–20.

Riobó González, M.: La controversia sobre la fisica experimental a finales del s. 18 en la Univ. de Santiago de Compostela, *Compostellanum*, 33: 515–30.

Rodríguez Cruz, A. M.: Mateo Arévalo Sedeño, canonista salmantino, prof. del primer claustro de la Univ. de Méjico, in *5 Coloquio Nacional de Historia de la Educación. Historia de las relaciones educativas entre España y América*, Seville: 43–49.

———— La Univ. de Salamanca en el alba de su hist., in *Orígenes*: 31–42.

Rodríguez-San Pedro Bezares, L. E.: *La nación de Vizcaya en la Universidad Castellana de la Edad Moderna*, San Sebastián.

Ruiz Asencio, J. M. and Montero Cartelle, E.: *Capitulaciones entre el Colegio de Santa Cruz y la Universidad de Valladolid 1483*, Valladolid.

Sánchez Herrero, J. and Romero-Camacho, M.: Los cols sevillanos del Col. Españ. de San Clemente de Bolonia 1368–1600, in *Orígenes*: 135–204.

Sánchez Movellán, E.: Los inciertos orígenes de la Univ. de Valladolid (s. 13), in *Orígenes*: 11–30.

———— etc.: *Estudios sobre los orígenes de las universidades españolas. Homenaje de la Universidad de Valladolid a la de Bolonia en su 9 centenario*, Valladolid. (All items noted separately).

Valero García, P.: *La Universidad de Salamanca en la época de Carlos V*, Salamanca.

352 *History of Universities*

Publications 1989

Ares Queija, B.: El oidor Tomás López Medel: Una visión 'letrada' del indio americano, in *El poder civil de los colegiales en la Administración Civil y Eclesiástica* (= *Estudios de hist. soc. y econ. de América*, 5), Alcalá (henceforth noted as *El poder civil*): 113–21.

Carabias Torres, A. M.: Notas sobre las relaciones entre el Estado y la Univ. en la España Moderna, *Studia hist. Hist. moderna*, 7: 707–21.

Casado Arbonies, F. J., Gil Blanco, E. and Casado Arbonies, M.: Estudiantes de Alcalá: Obispos y Arzobispos virreyes en Nueva España, in *El poder civil*: 43–72.

Cuart Moner, B.: Algunas notas sobre los cols de San Clemente en la admin. americana: s. 16–17, *Studia hist. Hist. moderna*, 7: 799–823.

Fernández Alvarez, M., Robles Carcedo, L. and Rodríguez-San Pedro Bezares eds: *La Universidad de Salamanca. 1. Trayectoria histórica y proyecciones*, Salamanca. (Short sections consider hist. of univ., of Pontifical Univ., of the colleges and aspects of the impact of the univ. on America and the Philippines).

Fernandez Ugarte, M.: Estatutos de la Univ. de Salamanca: La reforma de 1550–51, *Studia hist. Hist. moderna*, 7: 687–705.

García y García, A. ed.: *La Universidad Pontificia de Salamanca. Sus raices. Su pasado. Su futuro*, Salamanca.

González González, E.: Dos reformadores antagónicos de la Real Univ. de México: Pedro Farfán y Moya de Contreras, in *El poder civil*: 73–89.

Hernández Montes, B.: El Col. de la Compañía y la Univ. de Salamanca en el s. 16. Desde los orígenes hasta la incorp. a la univ., *Studia hist. Hist. moderna*, 7: 723–44.

Martin Hernández, F.: Presencia univ. salmantina en las primeras univs americanas, in *El poder civil*: 9–42.

Martin Martin, T.: Resistencias al cambio en la Univ. de Salamanca en tiempos de Felipe IV, *Studia hist. Hist. moderna*, 7: 745–52.

Martínez Martínez, M. del C.: Los cols de Santa Cruz de Valladolid y su proyección en América, in *El poder civil*: 90–104.

Porro Gutiérrez, M. J.: La Univ., la Chancillería y el Col. de Santa Cruz. Algunos juristas señalados del Valladolid del s. 16, in *El poder civil*: 105–112.

Rodríguez-San Pedro Bezares, L. E.: *Discursos medicinales del licenciado Juan Mendez Nieto, 1607*, Salamanca.

—— *Peripecia universitaria de San Juan de la Cruz en Salamanca 1564–68*, Avila.

—— San Juan de la Cruz en la Univ. de Salamanca, 1564–68, *Salmanticensis*, 36(2): 157–92.

—— Hacienda univ. salmantina del s. 17: Gastos y alcances, *Studia hist. Hist. moderna*, 7: 753–83.

Valero García, P.: Nuevo criterio sancionador de los Estatutos de 1538 de la Univ. de Salamanca, *Studia hist. Hist. moderna*, 7: 667–86.

The United States

Additions to Earlier Lists

For 1977

Findlay, J.: The SPCTEW and Western Colls: Religion and higher educ. in mid-19th-cent. America, *Hist. of educ. quarterly*, 17: 31–62.

Novak, S. J.: *The rights of youth: American colleges and student revolt 1798–1815*, Cambridge, Mass.

Potts, D. B.: 'Coll. enthusiasm!' As public response 1800–60, *Harvard educ. rev.*, 47: 28–42.

Rockefeller University: *Institute to university. A 75th anniversary colloquium June 8 1976*, New York.

Rudolph, F.: Curriculum: *A history of the undergraduate course of study since 1636*, San Francisco, Calif.

For 1978

Barnes, T. G.: *Hastings College of the law. The first century*, Berkeley, Calif.

Bernstein, A. E.: Magisterium and License: Corporate autonomy against papal authority in the medieval univ. of Paris, *Viator*, 9: 291–307.

McLachlan, J.: The American coll. in the 19th cent. Towards a reappraisal, *Teachers coll. record*, 80: 287–306.

Murdoch, J. E.: *Subtilitates Anglicanae* in 14th-cent. Paris: John of Mirecourt and Peter Ceffons, in M. P. Cosman ed.: *Machaut's World*, New York: 51–86.

For 1979

McClelland, J. C.: *Aristocrats and academics: Education, culture and society in Tsarist Russia*, Chicago, Ill.

For 1980

Cheslik, H. E.: The effect of World War 2 military educational training on black colleges. Thesis. Wayne State University.

Dooher, P. M.: Higher education and the veterans. An historical study of change in a select number of Massachusetts' colleges and universities 1944–49. Thesis. Boston College.

For 1981

Fiering, N.: *Moral Philosophy at 17th-century Harvard. A discipline in transition*, Chapel Hill, Carol.

Findlay, J.: Agency denominations and the Western Colls 1830–60: Some connections between evangelicalism and American higher educ., *Church hist*, 50: 64–80.

Potts, D. B.: Curriculum and enrollments: Some thoughts on assessing the popularity of antebellum colls, *Hist. of higher educ. annual*, 1: 88–109.

For 1982

Burke, C. B.: *American collegiate populations: A test of the traditional view*, New York.

Findlay, J.: 'Western' Colls 1830–70: Educ. instits in transition, *Hist. of higher educ. annual*, 2: 35–64.

Herbst, J.: *From crisis to crisis: American college government 1636–1819*, Cambridge, Mass.

Underwood, M.: The Lady Margaret and her Cambridge connection, *The 16th-cent. jnl*, 13: 67–82.

For 1983

Leader, D. R.: Professorships and acad. reform in Cambridge 1488–1520, *The 16th-cent. jnl*, 14: 215–27.

Swarz, I. P.: A historical investigation of the impact of World War 2 on Harvard medical school 1938–48. Thesis. Univ. of Connecticut.

For 1984

Courtenay, W. J.: Recent work on 14th-cent. Oxford thought, *Hist. of educ. quarterly*, 25: 229–33.

Horowitz, H. L.: *Alma Mater. Design and experience in the women's colleges from their 19th-century beginnings to the 1930s*, New York.

Locke, R. R.: *The end of the practical man: Entrepreneurship and higher education in Germany, France and Great Britain 1880 to 1940*, Greenwich, Conn.

For 1985

Heitzenrater, R. P. ed.: *Diary of an Oxford methodist. Benjamin Ingham 1733–34*, Durham, N.C.

For 1986

Alberts, R. C.: *Pitt: The story of the university of Pittsburg 1787–1987*, Pittsburg, Ka.

Beasley, J. H.: The university of Denver defines its purpose: a history of the junior college and the community college 1940 to 1961. Thesis. Univ. of Denver.

Cohen, J.: Scholarship and intolerance in the medieval acad. The study and evaluation of Judaism in Europ. Christendom, *American hist. rev.*, 91: 592–613.

Geiger, R. L.: *To advance knowledge: the growth of American research universities 1900–40*, New York/Oxford.

Levine, D. O.: *The American college and the culture of aspiration 1915–40*, Ithaca/London.

Parks, S.: *The Elizabethan Club of Yale University and its library*, New Haven/London.

For 1987

Barblan, A., Puymège-Browning, A. de and Rüegg, W.: The hist. of the Europ. univ. in soc. A joint univ. research project, *Hist. of europ. ideas*, 8(2): 127–38.

Benson, A. G. and Adams, F.: *To know for real. Royce S. Pitkin and Goddard College*, Adamant, Vt.

Bogue, L.: *Miracle on a mountain: The story of a college*, San Francisco, Calif.

Eyerman, R., Svensson, L. G. and Soderqvist, T. eds: *Intellectuals, universities and the state in western modern societies*, Berkeley, Calif.

Hammerstein, N.: Hist. of Germ. univs, *Hist. of europ. ideas*, 8(2): 139–45.

Kincaid, W. M. and Carlson, A. eds: *A history of the Oklahoma State University College of Business Administration*, Stillwater, Okla.

Lane, J. C.: The Yale Report of 1828 and liberal educ. A neorepub. manifesto, *Hist. of educ. quarterly*, 27: 325–38.

Lester, J.: *The people's college: Little Rock Junior College and Little Rock University 1927–69*, Little Rock, Ark.

Morgan, C. M.: *Dearly bought, deeply treasured. The university of Southern Mississippi 1912–87*, Lafayette, Miss.

Mullaly, C.: *Trinity College, Washington, DC: The first eighty years 1897–1977*, Westminster, Md.

Shank, M. H.: A female univ. student in late medieval Kraków, *Signs: A jnl of women and cult.*, 12: 373–80.

For 1988

Courtenay, W. J.: The 14th-cent. booklist of the Oriel Coll. Library, *Viator*, 19: 283–90.

Dippel, S. A.: *A study in religious thought at Oxford and Cambridge 1590–1640*, Lanham, Md.

Elliott, J. R.: Queen Elizabeth at Oxford: New light on the royal plays of 1566, *Eng. lit. renaissance*, 18: 218–29.

Field, A.: *The origins of the Platonic Academy of Florence*, Princeton, N.J.

Gabriel, A. L.: Marcus Mark de Kémes: Hungarian master at the univ. of Paris c.1521–23, in S. B. and A. H. Várdy: *Triumph in Adversity. Studies in honor of Professor F. Somogyi*, Boulder/New York: 113–24.

Goggins, L.: *Central State University: the first 100 years 1887–1987*, Kent, Ohio.

Harney, T. E.: *A history of Canisius College*, 3, New York.

Hunt, T. C. and Carper, J. C.: *Religious colleges and universities in America: a selected bibliography*, New York.

Miller, L.: The burning of Milton's books in 1660. Two mysteries, *Eng. lit. renaissance*, 18: 424–37. (Concerns order to burn M's books at Oxford).

Parcher, J. V. and Carlson, A. eds: *A history of the Oklahoma State University College of Engineering, Architecture and Technology*, Stillwater, Okla.

Pierson, G. W.: *The founding of Yale. The legend of the 40 folios*, Yale.
Wiggins, D.: *An Iowa tragedy: the fall of Old Des Moines U.*, Mount Horeb, Ill.

For 1989

Allen, P.: A Victorian intellect. elite: records of the Cambridge Apostles 1820–77, *Victorian studies*, 33(1): 99–123.
Berrol, S. C.: *Getting down to business: Baruch College in the City of New York 1847–1987*, New York.
Courtenay, W. J.: Inquiry and inquisition. Acad. freedom in medieval univs, *Church hist.*, 58: 168–81.
——— *Teaching careers at the university of Paris in the 13th and 14th centuries*, Notre Dame, Ind.
Holmes, D. R.: *Stalking the academic community. Intellectual freedom and the firing of Alex Noviko*, Hanover, N.H.
McCormick, C. H.: *This nest of vipers: McCarthyism and higher education in the Mundel Affair 1951–52*, Urbana/Chicago, Ill.

Index of Continents, Towns and Institutions